The Practice of Research in Criminology and Criminal Justice

Sixth Edition

The Practice of
Research in Criminology
and Criminal Justice

Sixth Edition

Ronet D. Bachman

University of Delaware

Russell K. Schutt

University of Massachusetts Boston

Los Angeles | London | New Delhi
Singapore | Washington DC

Los Angeles | London | New Delhi
Singapore | Washington DC

FOR INFORMATION:

SAGE Publications, Inc.
2455 Teller Road
Thousand Oaks, California 91320
E-mail: order@sagepub.com

SAGE Publications Ltd.
1 Oliver's Yard
55 City Road
London EC1Y 1SP
United Kingdom

SAGE Publications India Pvt. Ltd.
B 1/I 1 Mohan Cooperative Industrial Area
Mathura Road, New Delhi 110 044
India

SAGE Publications Asia-Pacific Pte. Ltd.
3 Church Street
#10-04 Samsung Hub
Singapore 049483

Acquisitions Editor: Jerry Westby
Associate Editor: Jessica Miller
Editorial Assistant: Laura Kirkhuff
eLearning Editor: Nicole Mangona
Production Editor: Kelly DeRosa
Copy Editor: Cate Huisman
Typesetter: C&M Digitals (P) Ltd.
Proofreader: Alison Syring
Indexer: Mary Harper
Cover Designer: Anupama Krishnan
Marketing Manager: Amy Lammers

Printed in the United States of America

Library of Congress Cataloging-in-Publication Data

Bachman, Ronet.

The practice of research in criminology and criminal justice / Ronet D. Bachman, University of Delaware, Russell K. Schutt, University of Massachusetts Boston.—Sixth Edition.

pages cm

Includes bibliographical references and index.

Revised edition of the authors' The practice of research in criminology and criminal justice, 2014.

ISBN 978-1-5063-0681-0 (pbk. : alk. paper)

1. Criminology—Research. 2. Criminal justice, Administration of—Research. I. Schutt, Russell K. II. Title.

HV6024.5.B33 2016

364.072—dc23   2015029095

This book is printed on acid-free paper.

16 17 18 19 20 10 9 8 7 6 5 4 3 2 1

Brief Contents

On Student Study Site: edge.sagepub.com/bachmanprccj6e

Appendix C: How to Use a Statistical Package: IBM SPSS Statistics

Appendix D: How to Use a Data Spreadsheet: Excel

Appendix E: Datasets

Detailed Contents

On Student Study Site: edge.sagepub.com/bachmanprccj6e

Preface

O ne of the most important aspects of teaching a research methods course is conveying to students the vital role that research plays in our discipline. After years of teaching courses in research methods, we have found that the best avenue of achieving this goal has been to link the teaching of key topics to contemporary research in the discipline. By combining discussions of research techniques with practical research examples from the field, students learn not only how to conduct research but also why it is important to do so. In the sixth edition of *The Practice of Research in Criminology and Criminal Justice*, we have drawn on comments by students in the classroom, insightful reviews by those who teach research methods, and our own continuing learning experience as scholars and teachers; we think the resulting innovations will add a great deal to your learning experience.

The purpose of this book is to introduce you to the scientific methods of research in criminology and criminal justice and show how they are actually used. Each chapter combines instructions in research methods with investigations of key research questions in our field: How do we measure offending and victimization? What are the causes of violent crime? What is the best police response to intimate partner violence? How do gang members perceive their world? Are violence prevention programs effective in reducing violence in schools? What is the impact of having a criminal record on finding a job? These are just a sample of the many research examples used to demonstrate particular research methods.

You will learn not only the skills necessary for conducting research, but also the skills necessary to evaluate research done by others. You will learn to ask many questions as you consider whether research-based conclusions are appropriate and valid. What did the researchers set out to investigate? How were people or places selected for the study? What were the phenomena being studied, and how were they defined and measured? How was information analyzed? Throughout this book, you will learn what questions to ask when critiquing a research study and how to evaluate the answers.

Another goal of this book is to train you to actually do research. Substantive research examples will help you see how methods are used in practice. Exercises at the end of each chapter give you ways to try different methods alone or in a group. But research methods cannot be learned by rote and applied mechanically. It is our hope that you will realize that all research methods come with their own strengths and limitations. In fact, the underlying theme of our book is that employing a combination of methods together to answer the same research question is often preferable. You will come to appreciate why the results of particular research studies must always be interpreted within the context of prior research and through the lens of social and criminological theory.

🗐 Organization of the Book

The way this book is organized reflects our beliefs in making research methods interesting, teaching students how to critique research, and viewing specific research techniques as parts of an integrated research strategy. Our concern with ethical issues in all types of research is underscored by the fact that we have an entire chapter devoted exclusively to research ethics in addition to sections on ethics in every methodology chapter.

This new edition is organized into four sections. The first, Foundations for Social Research, includes the first three chapters and introduces the why and how of research in general. Chapter 1 shows how research has helped us understand the magnitude of and the factors related to youth violence. It introduces the different types of research questions along with the contrast between positivist and interpretivist philosophies and quantitative and qualitative methods. Chapter 2 illustrates the basic stages of research with a series of experiments on the police response to intimate partner violence. This chapter emphasizes the role of theory in guiding research and describes the

Science, Society, and Criminological Research

The population of the United States all too frequently mourns the deaths of young innocent lives taken in school shootings. The deadliest elementary school shooting to date took place on December 14, 2012, when a 20-year-old man named Adam Lanza walked into an elementary school in Newtown, Connecticut, armed with several semiautomatic weapons, and killed 20 children and 6 adults. On April 16, 2007, Cho Seung-Hui perpetrated the deadliest college mass shooting when he killed 32 students, faculty, and staff and left over 30 others injured on the campus of Virginia Tech in Blacksburg, Virginia. Cho was armed with two semiautomatic handguns that he had legally purchased and a vest filled with ammunition. As police were closing in on the scene, he killed himself. The deadliest high school shooting occurred on April 20, 1999, when Eric Harris and Dylan Klebold killed 12 students and a teacher before killing themselves at Columbine High School in suburban Colorado.

None of these mass murderers was a typical terrorist, and each of these incidents caused a media frenzy. Headlines such as "The School Violence Crisis" and "School Crime Epidemic" were plastered across national newspapers and weekly news journals. Unfortunately, the media play a large role in how we perceive both problems and solutions. In fact, 95% of

Americans say that mass media sources such as television and newspapers are their main source of information on crime and violence (Surrette 1998). What are your perceptions of violence committed by youth, and how did you acquire them? What do you believe are the causes of youth violence? Many factors have been blamed for youth violence in American society, including the easy availability of guns, the lack of guns in classrooms for protection, the use of weapons in movies and television, the moral decay of our nation, poor parenting, unaware teachers, school and class size, racial prejudice, teenage alienation, the Internet and the World Wide Web, anti-Semitism, and rap and rock music, and the list goes on.

You probably have your own ideas about the factors related to violence in general and youth violence in particular. However, these beliefs may not always be supported by empirical research. In fact, the factors often touted by politicians and the media to be related to violence are not always supported by empirical evidence. In the rest of this chapter, you will learn how the methods of social science research go beyond stories in the popular media to help us answer questions like "What are the causes of youth violence?" By the chapter's end, you should understand how scientific methods used in criminal justice and criminology can help us understand and answer research questions in this discipline.

回 Reasoning About the Social World

The story of just one murderous youth raises many questions. Take a few minutes to read each of the following questions about one of the Columbine High School shooters, and jot down your answers. Don't ruminate about the questions or worry about your responses. This is not a test; there are no wrong answers.

- How would you describe Eric Harris?
- Why do you think Eric Harris wanted to kill other students?
- Was Eric Harris typical of other murderers under 18 years of age?
- In general, why do people become murderers?
- How have you learned about youth violence?

Now let us consider the possible answers to some of these questions. The information about Eric Harris is somewhat inconsistent (Duggan, Shear, and Fisher 1999). He was the 18-year-old son of middle-class professionals. He had an older brother who attended the University of Colorado. Harris apparently thought of himself as a white supremacist, but he also loved music by antiracist rock bands. On his web page, he quoted KMFDM, a German rock band whose song "Waste" includes these lyrics: "What I don't say I don't do. What I don't do I don't like. What I don't like I waste." Online, Harris referred to himself as "Darkness."

Do you have enough information now to understand why he went on a shooting rampage in his school?

A year before the shootings at Columbine High School, Harris was arrested on a felony count of breaking into a car. A juvenile court put him on probation, required him to perform community service and take criminal justice classes, and sent him to a school counseling program. He was described by one of his probation officers as a "very bright young man who is likely to succeed in life."

Now can you construct an adequate description of Eric Harris? Can you explain the reason for his murderous rampage? Or do you feel you need to know more about Eric Harris, about his friends and the family he grew up in? How about his experiences in school and with the criminal justice system? We have attempted to investigate just one person's experiences, and already our investigation is spawning more questions than answers.

Questions and Answers

We cannot avoid asking questions about the actions and attitudes of others. We all try to make sense of the complexities of our social world and our position in it, in which we have quite a personal stake. In fact, the more you "think like a social scientist," the more questions will come to mind.

But why does each question have so many possible answers? Surely our individual perspectives play a role. One person may see a homicide offender as a victim of circumstance, while another person may see the same individual as inherently evil. Answers to questions we ask in the criminological sciences vary because individual life experiences and circumstances vary. When questions concern not just one person but many people or general social processes, the number of possible answers quickly multiplies. In fact, people have very different beliefs about the factors responsible for mass shootings. Exhibit 1.1 displays Gallup Poll results from the following question: "Thinking about mass shootings that have occurred in the U.S. in recent years, from what you know or have read, how much do you think each of the following factors is to blame for the shootings?" As you can see, a large percentage blame the mental health system; four out of ten blame easy access to guns as well, but nearly one out of five blame inflammatory language from political commentators.

Everyday Errors in Reasoning

People give different answers to research questions for yet another reason: It is simply too easy to make errors in logic, particularly when we are analyzing the social world in which we ourselves are conscious participants. We can call some of these "everyday errors," because they occur so frequently in the nonscientific, unreflective discourse about the social world that we hear on a daily basis.

For evidence of everyday errors, just listen to your conversations or the conversations of others for one day. At some point in the day, it is inevitable that you or someone you are talking with will say something like, "Well, I knew a person who did X, and Y happened." From this one piece of information, you draw a conclusion about the likelihood of Y. Four

Exhibit 1.1 Responses to the Question, "Thinking about mass shootings that have occurred in the U.S. in recent years, from what you know or have read, how much do you think each of the following factors is to blame for the shootings?"

	Great deal %	Fair amount %	Not much %	Not at all %
Failure of the mental health system to identify individuals who are a danger to others	48	32	11	8
Easy access to guns	40	21	16	20
Drug use	37	29	17	15
Violence in movies, video games, and music lyrics	32	24	23	20
The spread of extremist viewpoints on the Internet	29	28	22	15
Insufficient security at public buildings including businesses and schools	29	29	26	14
Inflammatory language from prominent political commentators	18	19	30	28

Source: Reprinted with permission from Gallup.

general errors in everyday reasoning can be made: overgeneralization, selective or inaccurate observation, illogical reasoning, and resistance to change.

Overgeneralization

Overgeneralization, an error in reasoning, occurs when we conclude that what we have observed or what we know to be true for some cases is true for all cases. We are always drawing conclusions about people and social processes from our own interactions with them, but sometimes we forget that our experiences are limited. The social (and natural) world is, after all, a complex place. We have the ability (and inclination) to interact with just a small fraction of the individuals who inhabit the social world, especially in a limited span of time.

> **Overgeneralization:** An error in reasoning that occurs when we conclude that what we have observed or know to be true for a subset of cases holds true for the entire set.

Selective or Inaccurate Observation

Selective observation is choosing to look only at things that are in accordance with our preferences or beliefs. When we are inclined to criticize individuals or institutions, it is all too easy to notice their every failing. For example, if we are convinced in advance that all kids who are violent are unlikely to be rehabilitated and will go on to commit violent offenses in adulthood, we will probably find many confirming instances. But what about other youths who have become productive and stable citizens after engaging in violence as adolescents? Or the child who was physically or sexually abused and joined a gang to satisfy the need for a family surrogate? If we acknowledge only the instances that confirm our predispositions, we are victims of our own selective observation. Exhibit 1.2 depicts the difference between selective observation and overgeneralization.

> **Selective observation:** Observations chosen because they are in accord with preferences or beliefs of the observer.

Exhibit 1.2	The Difference Between Overgeneralization and Selective Observation

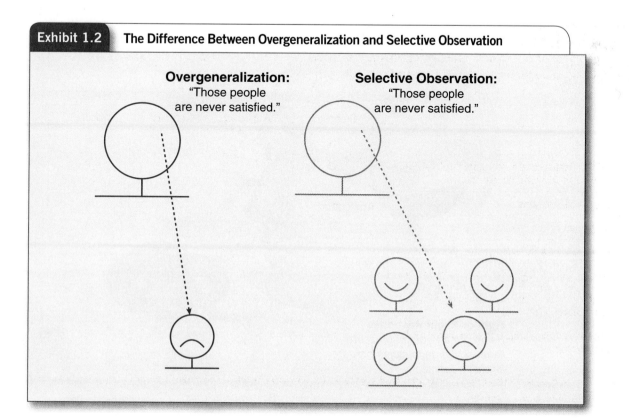

Recent research on cognitive functioning (how the brain works) helps explain why our feelings so readily shape our perceptions (Seidman 1997). Emotional responses to external stimuli travel a shorter circuit in the brain than do reasoned responses (see Exhibit 1.3). The result, according to some cognitive scientists, is "What something reminds us of can be far more important than what it is" (Goleman 1995, 294–95). Our emotions can influence us even before we begin to reason about what we have observed.

> **Inaccurate observation:** Observations based on faulty perceptions of empirical reality.

Our observations also can simply be inaccurate. If a woman says she is *hungry* and we think she said she is *hunted,* we have made an **inaccurate observation**. If we think five people are standing on a street corner when seven actually are, we have made an inaccurate observation. Such errors occur often in casual conversation and in everyday observation of the world around us. In fact, our perceptions do not provide a direct window onto the world around us, for what we think we have sensed is not necessarily what we have seen (or heard, smelled, felt, or tasted). Even when our senses are functioning fully, our minds have to interpret what we have sensed (Humphrey 1992). For example, when looking at the optical illusion in Exhibit 1.4, your visual system deceives you so that the monster in the background seems larger, even though the two monsters are exactly the same size.

Illogical Reasoning

> **Illogical reasoning:** Prematurely jumping to conclusions and arguing on the basis of invalid assumptions.

When we prematurely jump to conclusions or argue on the basis of invalid assumptions, we are using **illogical reasoning**. For example, it is not reasonable to propose that depictions of violence in media such as television and movies cause violence if evidence indicates that the majority of those who watch such programs do not become violent. However, it is also illogical to assume that media depictions of

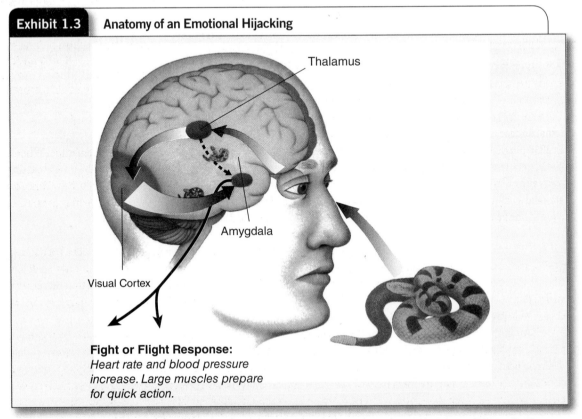

| Exhibit 1.3 | Anatomy of an Emotional Hijacking |

Thalamus

Amygdala

Visual Cortex

Fight or Flight Response:
Heart rate and blood pressure increase. Large muscles prepare for quick action.

gratuitous violence have no effect on individuals. Of course, logic that seems impeccable to one person can seem twisted to another; the problem usually is reasoning from different assumptions rather than failing to "think straight."

Resistance to Change

Resistance to change, the reluctance to change our ideas in light of new information, may occur for several reasons:

Ego-based commitments. We all learn to greet with some skepticism the claims by leaders of companies, schools, agencies, and so on that people in their organization are happy, that revenues are growing, that services are being delivered in the best possible way, and so forth. We know how tempting it is to make statements about the social world that conform to our own needs rather than to the observable facts. It also can be difficult to admit that we were wrong once we have staked out a position on an issue.

Excessive devotion to tradition. Some degree of devotion to tradition is necessary for the predictable functioning of society. Social life can be richer and more meaningful if it is allowed to flow along the paths charted by those who have preceded us. But too much devotion to tradition can stifle adaptation to changing circumstances. When we distort our observations or alter our reasoning so that we can maintain beliefs that "were good enough for my grandfather, so they're good enough for me," we hinder our ability to accept new findings and develop new knowledge. The consequences can be deadly, as residents of Hamburg, Germany, might have realized in 1892 (Freedman 1991). Until the last part of the 19th century, people believed that cholera, a potentially lethal disease, was due to minute, inanimate, airborne poison particles (miasmas). In 1850, English researcher John Snow demonstrated that cholera was, in fact, spread by contaminated water. When a cholera epidemic hit Hamburg in 1892, the authorities did what tradition deemed appropriate: digging up and carting away animal carcasses to prevent the generation of more miasmas. Despite their efforts, thousands died. New York City adopted a new approach based on Snow's discovery, which included boiling drinking water and disinfecting sewage. As a result, the death rate in New York City dropped to a tenth of what it had been in a previous epidemic.

Uncritical agreement with authority. If we do not have the courage to evaluate critically the ideas of those in positions of authority, we will have little basis for complaint if they exercise their authority over us in ways we do not like. And if we do not allow new discoveries to call our beliefs into question, our understanding of the social world will remain limited. As we will see in Chapter 3, an extreme example of this problem is obedience to authority figures that can harm and kill others, including acts of genocide.

Now take just a minute to reexamine the beliefs about youth violence that you recorded earlier. Did you grasp at a simple explanation even though reality was far more complex? Were your beliefs influenced by your own ego and feelings about your similarities to or differences from individuals prone to violence? Are your beliefs perhaps based on depictions of violence in the media or fiction? Did you weigh carefully the opinions of authority figures, including politicians, teachers, and even your parents, or just accept or reject those opinions out of hand? Could knowledge of research methods help improve your own understanding of the factors related to violent behavior? By now, we hope that you will see some of the challenges faced by social scientists studying issues related to crime and the criminal justice system.

Exhibit 1.4 An Optical Illusion

Resistance to change: Reluctance to change ideas in light of new information, due to ego-based commitments, excessive devotion to tradition, or uncritical agreement with authorities.

You do not have to be a scientist or use sophisticated research techniques to recognize and avoid these four errors in reasoning. If you recognize these errors for what they are and make a conscious effort to avoid them, you can improve your own reasoning. In the process, you will also be heeding the admonishments of your parents (or minister, teacher, or other adviser) to refrain from stereotyping people, to avoid jumping to conclusions, and to look at the big picture. These are the same errors that the methods of social science are designed to help criminologists avoid.

▣ The Social Science Approach

Social science: The use of scientific methods to investigate individuals, societies, and social processes, including questions related to criminology and criminal justice; the knowledge produced by these investigations.

Science: A set of logical, systematic, documented methods for investigating nature and natural processes; the knowledge produced by these investigations.

The **social science** approach to answering questions about the social world is designed to greatly reduce these potential sources of error in everyday reasoning. Science relies on logical and systematic methods to answer questions, and it does so in a way that allows others to inspect and evaluate its methods. In the realm of social research, these methods are not so unusual. After all, they involve asking questions, observing social groups, and counting people, which we often do in our everyday lives. However, social scientists develop, refine, apply, and report their understanding of the social world more systematically, or specifically, than Joanna Q. Public does:

- Social science research methods can reduce the likelihood of overgeneralization by using systematic procedures for selecting individuals or groups to study that are representative of the individuals or groups that we wish to generalize.

- Social science methods can reduce the risk of selective or inaccurate observation by requiring that we measure and sample phenomena systematically.

- To avoid illogical reasoning, social researchers use explicit criteria for identifying causes and for determining if these criteria are met in a particular instance.

- Because they require that we base our beliefs on evidence that can be examined and critiqued by others, scientific methods lessen the tendency to develop answers about the social world from ego-based commitments, excessive devotion to tradition, and/or unquestioning respect for authority.

Epistemology: A branch of philosophy that studies how knowledge is gained or acquired.

Science Versus Pseudoscience

Transparent: An important feature of the scientific method that requires procedures, methods, and data analyses of any study to be presented clearly for the purposes of replication.

In philosophical terms, the scientific method represents an **epistemology**, that is, a way of knowing that relies on objective, empirical investigation. Its techniques must be **transparent** so that the methods, procedures, and data analyses of any study can be replicated. This transparency allows other researchers to see if the same results can be reproduced. If findings can be replicated, we have greater confidence that the findings are real and not based on bias. Transparency also relies on **peer review**, the process by which other independent researchers evaluate the scientific merit of the study. (You will learn more about this in Chapter 14.)

Peer review: A process in which a journal editor sends a submitted article to two or three experts who judge whether the paper should be accepted, revised and resubmitted, or rejected; the experts also provide comments to explain their decision and guide any revisions.

In contrast, if we relied on findings based on intuition, gut reactions, or our own experience, we would be open to the errors we just covered above. If we based findings on these, it would not be science, but instead, it would fall under the classification of **pseudoscience**. Pseudoscientific beliefs are not based on the scientific method but rather on claims that may be touted as "scientifically proven," only bolstered by testimonials of believers who have experienced firsthand or who have claimed to have witnessed the phenomenon (Nester and Schutt 2012).

Of course, today's pseudoscience could be yesterday's science. In criminological research, phrenology is a good example. **Phrenology** is the belief that bumps and fissures of the skull determined the character and personality of a person. In the 19th century, doctors doing entry examinations at American prisons would examine a new inmate's head for bumps or cavities to develop a criminal profile. Advances in cognitive psychology and neurology have largely discredited phrenology and placed it within the domain of pseudoscience. It didn't take a genius to question phrenology, but just a group of researchers adhering to the scientific method. When inmates' heads were compared to individual heads in the general population, they were found to be essentially the same!

> **Pseudoscience:** Dubious but fascinating claims that are touted as "scientifically proven" and bolstered by fervent, public testimonials of believers who have experienced firsthand or have claimed to have witnessed the phenomenon; however, such evidence is not based on the principles of the scientific method.

> **Phrenology:** A now defunct field of study, once considered a science in the 19th century, that held that bumps and fissures of the skull determined the character and personality of a person.

Motives for Criminological Research

Like you, social scientists read stories about incidents of violence committed by youth, observe this violence occasionally in their lives, and try to make sense of what they see. For most, that is the end of it. But for some social scientists, the problem of youth violence has become a major research focus. The motivations for selecting this particular research focus, as with any social science topic, can be any one or some combination of the following:

Policy motivations. Many social service agencies and elected officials seek better assessments and descriptions of youth violence so they can identify needs and allocate responsibility among agencies that could meet these needs. For example, federal agencies such as the U.S. Department of Justice and the Centers for Disease Control and Prevention want to identify the magnitude of youth violence, and many state and local officials use social research to guide development of their social service budgets. Programs designed to rehabilitate young offenders often use research to learn more about the needs of their clientele. These policy guidance and program management needs have resulted in numerous research projects.

Academic motivations. Young offenders have been a logical focus for researchers interested in a number of questions ranging from how an individual's connection to parents and peers influences his or her behavior to how the social conditions under which an individual lives, such as poverty, affect his or her behavior. For example, social scientists have long been concerned with the impact that social disorganization has on individual behavior. Early in the 20th century, researchers at the University of Chicago were interested in the effects that residential mobility and immigration had on levels of crime and delinquency in urban neighborhoods. Today researchers are exploring similar questions concerning the impact of disintegrating economic bases in central cities and their relationship to crime and violence. Other researchers have focused on individual-level explanations such as neurological damage. Those who study social policy also have sought to determine whether correctional programs such as boot camps and other forms of shock incarceration serve to decrease the probability of juveniles reoffending in the future.

Personal motivations. Many who conduct research on youth violence feel that by doing so they can help prevent it and/or ameliorate the consequences of this violence when it occurs. Some social scientists first volunteered with at-risk youth in such organizations as Big Brothers Big Sisters and only later began to develop a research agenda based on their experiences.

Social Criminological Research in Practice

Of course, youth violence is not a new phenomenon in the United States. It has always been a popular topic of social science research. However, the sharp increase in this violence in the United States that began in the late 1980s was unprecedented. Predictably, whenever a phenomenon is perceived as an epidemic, numerous explanations emerge to explain it. Unfortunately, most of these explanations are based on the media and popular culture, not on empirical research. Unlike the mass media, which has floated anecdotal information, social scientists interested in this phenomenon have amassed a substantial body of findings that have refined knowledge about the factors related to the problem and shaped social policy (Tonry and Moore 1998). These studies fall into the four categories of purposes for social scientific research:

Descriptive research: Research in which phenomena are defined and described.

Descriptive research. Defining and describing social phenomena of interest is a part of almost any research investigation, but **descriptive research** is the primary focus of many studies of youth crime and violence. Some of the central questions used in these studies were "How many people are victims of youth violence?" "How many youth are offenders?" "What are the most common crimes committed by youthful offenders?" and "How many youth are arrested and incarcerated each year for crime?" Measurement (see Chapter 4) and sampling (see Chapter 5) are central concerns in descriptive research.

Exploratory research: Research in which social phenomena are investigated without a priori expectations, in order to develop explanations of them.

Exploratory research. **Exploratory research** seeks to find out how people get along in the setting under question, what meanings they give to their actions, and what issues concern them. The goal is to answer the question "What is going on here?" and to investigate social phenomena without expectations. This purpose is associated with the use of methods that capture large amounts of relatively unstructured information. For example, researchers investigating the emergence of youth gangs in the 1980s were encountering a phenomenon with which they had no direct experience. Thus, an early goal was to find out what it was like to be a gang member and how gang members made sense of their situation. Exploratory research like this frequently involves qualitative methods (see Chapter 9).

Explanatory research: Research that seeks to identify causes and/or effects of social phenomena.

Explanatory research. Many people consider explanation to be the premier goal of any science. **Explanatory research** seeks to identify causes and effects of social phenomena, to predict how one phenomenon will change or vary in response to variation in some other phenomenon. Researchers adopted explanation as a goal when they began to ask such questions as "Why do people become offenders?" and "Does the unemployment rate influence the frequency of youth crime?" Methods with which to identify causes and effects are the focus of Chapter 6.

Evaluation research: Research about social programs or interventions.

Evaluation research. **Evaluation research** seeks to determine the effects of a social program or other types of intervention. It is a type of explanatory research because it deals with cause and effect. However, evaluation research differs from other forms of explanatory research because evaluation research considers the implementation and effects of social policies and programs. These issues may not be relevant in other types of explanatory research. Research that examines cause and effect questions is reviewed in Chapter 7, which covers experimental design, and in Chapter 11, which covers evaluation research.

We will now summarize one study in each of these four areas to give you a feel for the projects motivated by those different concerns.

—————————— **Case Study of Description** ——————————

How Prevalent Is Youth Violence?

Police reports. One of the most enduring sources of information on lethal violence in the United States is the Federal Bureau of Investigation's (FBI) Supplementary Homicide Reports (SHR). Homicide victimization rates indicate that for those under the age of 24, vulnerability to murder increased dramatically from the mid-1980s through about 1994, when rates began a steady decline and have remained relatively stable since 2000 (Smith and Cooper 2013). Data measuring the prevalence of nonlethal forms of violence such as robbery and assaults are a bit more complicated. How do we know how many young people become victims of assault each year? People who report their victimizations to police represent one avenue for these calculations. The FBI compiles these numbers in its Uniform Crime Reporting (UCR) system, which is slowly being replaced by the National Incident-Based Reporting System (NIBRS). Both of these data sources rely on state, county, and city law enforcement agencies across the United States to voluntarily participate in the reporting program. Can you imagine why relying on these data sources may be problematic for estimating prevalence rates of violent victimizations? If victimizations are never reported to police, they are not counted. This is especially problematic for victimizations of intimate partners and for other offenses like rape, of which only a fraction are ever reported to police.

Surveys. Instead, most social scientists believe the best way to determine the magnitude of violent victimization is through random sample surveys. While we will discuss survey methodology in greater detail in Chapter 8, this basically means randomly selecting individuals in the population of interest and asking them about their victimization experiences. The only ongoing survey that does this on an annual basis is the National Crime Victimization Survey (NCVS), which is sponsored by the U.S. Department of Justice's Bureau of Justice Statistics. Among other questions, the NCVS asks questions like "Has anyone attacked or threatened you with a weapon, for instance, a gun or knife; by something thrown, such as a rock or bottle; include any grabbing, punching, or choking?" Estimates indicate that youth aged 12 to 24 have the highest rates of violent victimization of any age group, and these rates have been declining steadily since the highs witnessed in the early 1990s, although recent increases have been observed in homicide rates for this age group in some locations.

Another large research survey that estimates the magnitude of youth violence (as well as the prevalence of other risk-taking behavior, such as taking drugs and smoking) is called the Youth Risk Behavior Survey (YRBS), which has been conducted every two years in the United States since 1990. Respondents to this survey are a national sample of approximately 16,000 high school students in grades 9 through 12. To measure the extent of youth violence, students are asked the following questions: "During the past 30 days, on how many days did you carry a weapon such as a gun, knife, or club?" "During the past 12 months, how many times were you in a physical fight?" "During the past 12 months, how many times were you in a physical fight in which you were injured and had to be seen by a doctor or nurse?" "During the past 30 days, how many times did you carry a weapon such as a gun, knife, or club on school property?" "During the past 12 months, how many times were you in a physical fight on school property?" and "During the past 12 months, how many times did someone threaten or injure you with a gun, knife, or club on school property?"

Of course, another way to measure violence would be to ask respondents about their offending behaviors. Some surveys do this, including the National Youth Survey (NYS) and the Rochester Youth Development Study (RYDS). The RYDS sample consists of 1,000 students who were in the seventh and eighth grades of the Rochester, New York, public schools during the spring semester of the 1988 school year. Staff with this project have interviewed the original respondents at 12 different times (we will discuss longitudinal research of this kind in Chapter 6); the last interview took place in 1997, when respondents were in their early 20s (Thornberry et al. 2008). As you can imagine, respondents are typically more reluctant to reveal their offending behavior than they are to reveal their victimization experiences. However, these surveys have been a useful tool for examining the factors related to violent offending and other delinquency. We should also point out that although this discussion has been specific to violence, the measures we have discussed in this section, along with their strengths and weaknesses, apply to measuring all crime in general.

Case Study of Exploration

How Did Schools Avert a Shooting Rampage?

Research that is exploratory in nature is generally concerned with uncovering detailed information about a given phenomenon, learning as much as possible about particular people and/or events. While there have been far too many school shootings in the United States during the past decade, there have also been numerous incidents in which students were plotting to kill their peers or faculty members, but these plans came to the attention of authorities before they could be carried out. To examine how these incidents were stopped, Eric Madfis (2014) selected 11 schools where a mass shooting had been diverted between 2000 and 2009 and conducted intensive interviews with people who were involved, including 11 principals and 21 other administrators, teachers, and police officers. He also corroborated the interview data with newspaper reports and, where possible, court transcripts and police incident reports.

Madfis's (2014) research was truly exploratory. You will learn much more about qualitative research in Chapter 8, but for now, we simply want to highlight how this study is different from the other research types above. He let the people he interviewed speak for themselves; he didn't come with questions that were designed before the interviews to measure concepts such as violence or delinquency. After examining all of the interview transcripts, Madfis developed themes that emerged among them all. This is what made the research exploratory instead of explanatory.

Five out of the 11 school shootings were thwarted by other students who were not directly involved or entrusted by the accused students, but who came about the information indirectly. For example, one student reported the existence of disturbing posts and images on another student's network website. The second most common category of intervention involved people who had been told directly about the planned attacks by the students accused of plotting them. For example, after one student was sent threatening messages, she told her mother, who then called the police. When the accused student was questioned, he confessed, and weapons were discovered in his bedroom.

School administrators believed that students were more likely to come forward with information about their peers since the Columbine High School shootings than they had been before this catalyzing mass shooting. One school principal stated, "Columbine absolutely made kids much more vigilant about things going on around them…I think it made kids less afraid to speak up if something wasn't sitting right with them" (Madfis 2014, 235). Another theme that was clear from the interviews was that if school environments were going to break the "student code of silence," they must be supporting, cohesive, and trusting. For example, another principal stated, "The best mechanism we have as a deterrent for these sorts of violent acts is good relationships between kids and adults, because kids will tell you" (2014, 235).

As you can see from this discussion of Madfis's results, the goal of his research was to explore the factors related to instances where a school shooting had been successfully thwarted. He did not go into the school with a survey filled with questions, because the existing literature reveals that little is known about these factors. For this reason, the investigation was explorative in nature. It is different from a descriptive investigation, because an estimate of the prevalence of some phenomenon is not the goal. Rather, a deeper understanding of the processes and perceptions of study participants is the desired outcome in exploratory research.

Case Study of Explanation

What Factors Are Related to Youth Delinquency and Violence?

When we move from description to exploration and finally to explanation, we want to understand the direct relationship between two or more things. Does x explain y? Or if x happens, is y also likely to occur? What are some of the factors related to youth violence? Using the South Carolina YRBS (described above), MacDonald et al. (2005) examined whether constructs from general strain theory (GST) (Agnew 1992) and Gottfredson and Hirschi's general theory of crime (1990) could predict youth violence. GST generally contends that strain, such as disjunction between expectations and aspirations (e.g., wanting a good job but not being able to get one), increases the likelihood that individuals will experience negative emotions (e.g. anger, anxiety), which in turn increases the likelihood of antisocial or violent behavior. The general theory of crime claims that self-control, which is primarily formed by the relationship children have with their parents and/or guardians, is the motivating factor for all crime. Individuals with low self-control, the theory predicts, will be more likely to pursue immediate gratification, be impulsive, prefer simple tasks, engage in risky behavior, have volatile tempers, and so on.

To measure violent behavior, the YRBS asks respondents how many times in the past 30 days they carried a weapon and how many times they were in a physical fight. To measure life satisfaction, MacDonald et al. (2005) used six questions that asked respondents to report on general satisfaction or the degree to which they felt "terrible" or "delighted" about family life, friendships, school, self, residential location, and overall life. To measure self-control, the authors used the indicators of smoking and sexual behavior to represent risky behaviors that are not illegal, since they "reflect impulsivity and short-run hedonism" (p. 1502). When predicting violent behavior, they also controlled for a number of other factors such as employment, drug use, family structure, and religious participation, along with age, race, and gender.

Consistent with the general theory of crime, MacDonald et al. (2005) found that high school students who reported more impulsive behaviors—indicative of low self-control—also reported greater participation in violent behavior. In addition, results indicated that students who were more satisfied with life were significantly less likely to have engaged in violence compared to their less satisfied peers. In this way, MacDonald and his colleagues (2005) were conducting explanatory research.

Case Study of Evaluation

How Effective Are Violence Prevention Programs in Schools?

As many school administrators will tell you, there are direct mail, e-mail, and in-person direct sales efforts to sell them programs that reduce violence, increase empathy among students, promote a positive school environment, promote other forms of mental well-being, and on and on. Unfortunately, not many of these programs have been rigorously evaluated to ensure they actually do what they promise. One program that has been the target of rigorous evaluation is Gang Resistance Education and Training (GREAT), which is school-based gang and violence prevention program. Among other things, this program teaches students about crime and its effects on victims, gives them skills to resolve conflicts without violence, and helps them improve individual responsibility through goal setting. It addresses multiple risk factors for violent offending among three domains: school, peer, and individual. Because it is based in the school curriculum, it does not address risk factors in the family or neighborhood. It is a 13-week program taught in sixth or seventh grade and attempts to affect several risk factors, including school commitment and performance, association with conventional or delinquent peers, empathy, and self-control, among others.

Finn-Aage Esbensen and his colleagues (Esbensen et al. 2013) evaluated the long-term effects of the GREAT program in seven cities across the United States. Schools selected for the evaluation randomly assigned some seventh grade classrooms to participate in the program (experimental groups) while the other classrooms did not (control groups). As you will later learn, this is called a true experimental design. It is an extremely strong research method for determining the effects of programs or policies, because if groups are truly randomly assigned, there is a strong reason to believe that differences between the groups after program implementation, such as reduced violent offending, are a result of the program and not some other factor that existed before the introduction of the treatment.

Both experimental and control group students in the study (Esbensen et al. 2013) completed four follow-up surveys annually for four years. The researchers examined 33 outcome measures, including general delinquency, violent offending, gang affiliation, associations with delinquent peers, empathy, impulsivity, and problem-solving behavior, among others. The statistical methods employed by Esbensen and his colleagues are very complicated and beyond the scope of this text, so we will simply highlight the general findings. When the data for all seven sites were combined, no differences were revealed in violent offending between experimental and control group students over the four-year period. Those students who participated in the GREAT program, however, were less likely to become members of gangs, had higher levels of altruism, felt less anger, had fewer risk-taking behaviors, and had more favorable attitudes toward the police, among other differences.

With these results, would you deem the GREAT program a success? These are the important questions evaluation research must address. Esbensen et al. (2013) agree that the program did not reduce general delinquency or violent offending but note that it was effective in reducing gang membership, which is also a risk factor for violent offending.

Social Research Philosophies

What influences the choice of a research strategy? The motive for conducting research is critical: An explanatory or evaluative motive generally leads a researcher to use quantitative methods, whereas an exploratory motive often results in the use of qualitative methods. Of course, a descriptive motive means choosing a descriptive research strategy.

Positivism and Postpositivism

A researcher's philosophical perspective on reality and on the appropriate role of the researcher also will shape her methodological preferences. Researchers with a positivist philosophy believe that there is an objective reality that exists apart from the perceptions of those who observe it; the goal of science is to better understand this reality.

Positivism: The belief, shared by most scientists, that there is a reality that exists quite apart from our own perception of it, although our knowledge of this reality may never be complete.

Postpositivism: The belief that there is an empirical reality but that our understanding of it is limited by its complexity and by the biases and other limitations of researchers.

Whatever nature "really" is, we assume that it presents itself in precisely the same way to the same human observer standing at different points in time and space. . . . We assume that it also presents itself in precisely the same way across different human observers standing at the same point in time and space. (Wallace 1983, 461)

This philosophy is traditionally associated with science (Weber 1949), with the expectation that there are universal laws of human behavior, and with the belief that scientists must be objective and unbiased to see reality clearly.

Postpositivism is a philosophy of reality that is closely related to **positivism**. Postpositivists believe that there is an external, objective reality but are very sensitive to the complexity of this reality and the limitations of the scientists who study it—and, for social scientists, the biases they bring to the study of social beings like themselves (Guba and Lincoln 1994). As a result, they do not think scientists can ever be sure that their methods allow them to perceive objective reality; the goal of science can only be to achieve **intersubjective agreement** among scientists about the nature of reality (Wallace 1983). For example, postpositivists may worry that researchers' predispositions may bias them in favor of deterrence theory. Therefore, they will remain somewhat skeptical of results that support predictions based on deterrence until a number of researchers feel that they have found supportive evidence. The postpositivist retains much more confidence in the ability of the community of social researchers to develop an unbiased account of reality than in the ability of any individual social scientist to do so (Campbell and Russo 1999).

> **Intersubjective agreement:** Agreement between scientists about the nature of reality; often upheld as a more reasonable goal for science than certainty about an objective reality.

Positivist Research Guidelines

To achieve an accurate, or valid, understanding of the social world, a researcher operating within the positivist or postpositivist tradition must adhere to some basic guidelines about how to conduct research:

1. *Test ideas against empirical reality without becoming too personally invested in a particular outcome.* This guideline requires a commitment to "testing," as opposed to just reacting to events as they happen or looking for what we want to see (Kincaid 1996).

2. *Plan and carry out investigations systematically.* Social researchers have little hope of conducting a careful test of their ideas if they do not think through in advance how they should go about the test and then proceed accordingly.

3. *Document all procedures and disclose them publicly.* Social researchers should disclose the methods on which their conclusions are based so that others can evaluate for themselves the likely soundness of these conclusions. Such disclosure is a key feature of science. It is the community of researchers, reacting to each other's work that provides the best guarantee against purely self-interested conclusions (Kincaid 1996).

4. *Clarify assumptions.* No investigation is complete unto itself; whatever the researcher's method, the research rests on some background assumptions. For example, research to determine whether arrest has a deterrent effect assumes that potential law violators think rationally and that they calculate potential costs and benefits prior to committing crimes. By definition, research assumptions are not tested, so we do not know for sure whether they are correct. By taking the time to think about and disclose their assumptions, researchers provide important information for those who seek to evaluate the validity of research conclusions.

5. *Specify the meaning of all terms.* Words often have multiple or unclear meanings. "Recidivism," "self-control," "poverty," "overcrowded," and so on can mean different things to different people. In scientific research, all terms must be defined explicitly and used consistently.

6. *Maintain a skeptical stance toward current knowledge.* The results of any particular investigation must be examined critically, although confidence about interpretations of the social or natural world increases after repeated investigations yield similar results. A general skepticism about current knowledge stimulates researchers to improve the validity of current research results and expand the frontier of knowledge.

7. *Replicate research and build social theory.* No one study is definitive by itself. We cannot fully understand a single study's results apart from the larger body of knowledge to which it is related, and we cannot place much confidence in these results until the study has been replicated. Theories organize the knowledge accumulated by numerous investigations into a coherent whole and serve as a guide to future inquiries.

8. *Search for regularities or patterns.* Positivist and postpositivist scientists assume that the natural world has some underlying order of relationships so that unique events and individuals can be understood at least in part in terms of general principles (Grinnell 1992).

Real investigations by social scientists do not always include much attention to theory, specific definitions of all terms, and so forth. But it behooves any social researcher to study these guidelines and to consider the consequences of not following any with which he or she does not agree.

A Positivist Research Goal: Advancing Knowledge

The goal of the traditional positivist scientific approach is to advance scientific knowledge. This goal is achieved when research results are published in academic journals or presented at academic conferences.

The positivist approach regards value considerations to be beyond the scope of science: "An empirical science cannot tell anyone what he should do—but rather what he can do—and under certain circumstances—what he wishes to do" (Weber 1949, 54). The idea is that developing valid knowledge about how society is organized, or how we live our lives, does not tell us how society should be organized or how we should live our lives. The determination of empirical facts should be a separate process from the evaluation of these facts as satisfactory or unsatisfactory (Weber 1949).

The idea is not to ignore value considerations, because they are viewed as a legitimate basis for selecting a research problem to investigate. In addition, many scientists also consider it acceptable to encourage government officials or private organizations to act on the basis of a study's findings after the research is over. During a research project, however, value considerations are to be held in abeyance.

Interpretivism and Constructivism

Interpretivism (interpretivist philosophy): The belief that reality is socially constructed and that the goal of social scientists is to understand what meanings people give to that reality.

Verstehen: German term for "understanding."

Constructivist paradigm: Methodology based on rejection of belief in an external reality; it emphasizes the importance of exploring the way in which different stakeholders in a social setting construct their beliefs.

Scientists with an **interpretivist philosophy** believe that social reality is socially constructed and that the goal of social scientists is to understand what meanings people give to reality, not to determine how reality works apart from these interpretations. This philosophy rejects the positivist belief that there is a concrete, objective reality that scientific methods help us understand (Lynch and Bogen 1997). Instead, interpretivists believe that scientists construct an image of reality based on their own preferences and prejudices and their interactions with others. Max Weber termed the goal of interpretivist research *verstehen*, or "understanding."

Here is the basic argument: All the empirical data we collect come to us through our own senses and must be interpreted with our own minds. This suggests that we can never be sure that we have understood reality properly—or that we ever can—or that our own understandings can really be judged more valid than someone else's. Concerns like this have begun to appear in many areas of social science and have begun to shape some research methods. From this standpoint, the goal of validity becomes misleading: "Truth is a matter of the best-informed and most sophisticated construction on which there is consensus at a given time" (Schwandt 1994, 128).

The **constructivist paradigm** extends interpretivist philosophy by emphasizing the importance of exploring how different stakeholders in a social setting construct their beliefs (Guba and Lincoln 1989). It gives particular attention to the different goals of researchers and other participants in a research setting and seeks to develop a consensus among participants about how to understand the focus of inquiry. The constructivist research report will highlight different views of the social program or other issue and explain how a consensus can be reached among participants.

Constructivist inquiry uses an interactive research process, in which a researcher begins an evaluation in some social setting by identifying the different interest groups in that setting. The researcher goes on to learn what each group thinks and then gradually tries to develop a shared perspective on the problem being evaluated (Guba and Lincoln 1989).

These steps are diagrammed as a circular process in Exhibit 1.5. In this process, called a **hermeneutic circle**,

> the constructions of a variety of individuals—deliberately chosen so as to uncover widely variable viewpoints—are elicited, challenged, and exposed to new information and new, more sophisticated ways of interpretation, until some level of consensus is reached (although there may be more than one focus for consensus). (Guba and Lincoln 1989, 180–81)

Hermeneutic circle: Represents the dialectical process in which the researcher obtains information from multiple stakeholders in a setting, refines his or her understanding of the setting, and then tests that understanding with successive respondents.

The researcher conducts an open-ended interview with the first respondent (R1) to learn about her thoughts and feelings on the subject of inquiry, her "construction" (C1). The researcher then asks this respondent to nominate a second respondent (R2), who feels very differently. The second respondent is then interviewed in the same way but also asked to comment on the themes raised by the previous respondent. The process continues until all major perspectives are represented, and it may be repeated with the same set of respondents.

The final product is a **case report**. A case report is very unlike the technical reports we are accustomed to seeing in positivist inquiries. It is not a depiction of a "true" or "real" state of affairs. . . . It does not culminate in judgments, conclusions, or recommendations except insofar as these are concurred on by relevant respondents.

Case report: A report that helps the reader realize (in the sense of making real) not only the states of affairs that are believed by constructors [research respondents] to exist but also of the underlying motives, feelings, and rationales leading to those beliefs.

The case report helps the reader come to a realization (in the sense of making real) not only of the states of affairs that are believed by constructors [research respondents] to exist but also of the underlying motives, feelings, and rationales

---

Exhibit 1.5 **The Hermeneutic Circle**

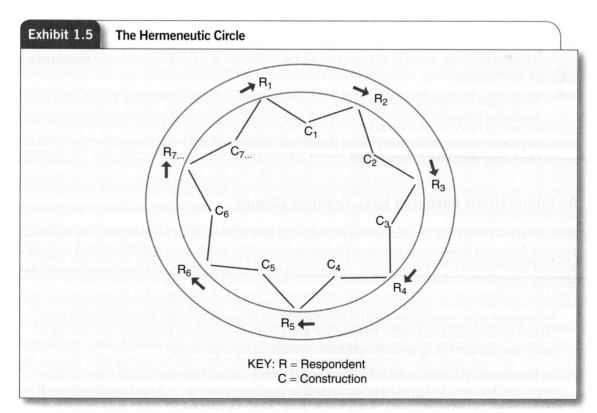

KEY: R = Respondent
C = Construction

Source: Adapted from Guba and Lincoln 1989, 152.

But even in areas of research that are fraught with controversy, where social scientists differ in their interpretations of the evidence, the quest for new and more sophisticated research has value. What is most important for improving understanding of the social world and issues in criminology is not the result of any particular study but the accumulation of evidence from different studies of related issues. By designing new studies that focus on the weak points or controversial conclusions of prior research, social scientists contribute to a body of findings that gradually expands our knowledge about the social world and resolves some of the disagreements about it.

Research in the News

A SCHOOL SHOOTING EVERY WEEK?

This article investigates a quote by Senator Chris Murphy (D-CT) who said, "Since Sandy Hook there has been a school shooting, on average, every week." He made this statement on the Senate floor after the killing of nine people at a prayer meeting in Charleston, South Carolina. This is not the first time this statistic has been used, but where did it come from? The article reports it was calculated by a group called "Everytown for Gun Safety" that has counted the tally of school shootings since the Sandy Hook Elementary School shooting as 126 as of June 8, 2015. How does the group define a school shooting? Any incident in which a firearm was discharged inside a school building or on school or campus grounds, as documented by the press or confirmed through further inquiries with law enforcement, was deemed a school shooting.

For Further Thought

1. Does this definition of school shootings capture what we typically mean by a school shooting? For example, it would include accidental shootings as well as suicides or attempted suicides.

2. What other types of incidents would be included in this definition that we don't typically associate with school shootings? What definition would you use if you were going to measure the incidence of school shootings?

Source: Lee, Michelle Y. H. 2015. "Has There Been One School Shooting Per Week Since Sandy Hook?" *Washington Post*, June 29. http://www.washingtonpost.com/blogs/fact-checker/wp/2015/06/29/has-there-been-one-school-shooting-per-week-since-sandy-hook/.

Social researchers investigating issues in criminal justice and criminology will always disagree somewhat because of their differing research opportunities, methodological approaches, and policy preferences. There are many heated debates in the criminological literature. For example, one issue that has recently received increased attention is how the availability of guns is related to overall levels of violence. Some researchers have found that greater gun availability is associated with more robberies, home burglaries, assaults, and homicides with guns. However, others have argued that gun ownership for self-defense can reduce robbery and home burglary completion rates, thus theoretically decreasing the rewards for these crimes and increasing the perceived risks to offenders. According to yet another view, someone who is planning an attack and fears that potential robbery and/or burglary victims are armed may simply decide to acquire superior firepower and carry out the attack regardless. (For review, see Reiss and Roth 1993.) As you can see, much more research is required using a variety of methods to resolve this debate.

Whether you plan to conduct your own research projects, read others' research reports, or just think about and act in the social world, knowing about research methods has many benefits. This knowledge will give you greater confidence in your own opinions, improve your ability to evaluate others' opinions, and encourage you to refine your questions, answers, and methods of inquiry about the social world.

Of course, the methods of social science, as careful as they may be, cannot answer all questions of interest to criminologists. Should we do unto others what we would have them do unto us? That is a very important question that has been asked throughout history, but we must turn to religion or philosophy to answer questions about values.

Social research on the consequences of forgiveness or the sources of interpersonal conflict may help us understand and implement our values, but even the best research cannot tell us which values should guide our lives.

▣ Conclusion

We hope this first chapter has given you an idea of what to expect in the rest of this book. Our aim is to introduce you to social research methods by describing what social scientists have learned about issues in criminology and criminal justice as well as how they learned it. The substance of social science inevitably is more interesting than its methods, but the methods also become more interesting when they are not taught as isolated techniques. We have focused attention on research on youth violence and delinquency in this chapter; in subsequent chapters, we will introduce research examples from other areas.

Chapter 2 continues to build the foundation for our study of social research by reviewing the types of problems that criminologists study, the role of theory, the major steps in the research process, and other sources of information that may be used in social research. We stress the importance of considering scientific standards in social research and review generally accepted ethical guidelines. Throughout the chapter, we use several studies of domestic violence to illustrate the research process.

Key Terms

➤ Review key terms with eFlashcards. **⑤SAGE** edge™

Case report   17
Constructivist paradigm   16
Content analysis   22
Crime mapping   23
Descriptive research   10
Epistemology   8
Evaluation research   10
Experimental approach   21
Explanatory research   10
Exploratory research   10
Feminist research   18
Hermeneutic circle   17
Historical events research   22
Illogical reasoning   6

Inaccurate observation   6
Intensive interviewing   21
Interpretivism
    (interpretivist philosophy)   16
Intersubjective agreement   15
Mixed methods   20
Overgeneralization   5
Participatory action research 19
Participant observation   21
Peer review   8
Phrenology   9
Positivism   14
Postpositivism   14
Pseudoscience   9

Qualitative methods   20
Quantitative methods   20
Questionnaire   21
Resistance to change   7
Science   8
Secondary data analysis   22
Selective observation   5
Social science   8
Surveys   21
Transparent   8
Triangulation   21
Verstehen   16

Highlights

- Criminological research cannot resolve value questions or provide answers that will convince everyone and remain settled for all time.

- All empirically based methods of investigation are based on either direct experience or others' statements.

- Four common errors in reasoning are overgeneralization, selective or inaccurate observation, illogical reasoning, and resistance to change. Illogical reasoning results from the complexity of the social world, self-interestedness, and human subjectivity. Resistance to change may be due to unquestioning acceptance of tradition or of those in positions of authority or to self-interested resistance to admitting the need to change one's beliefs.

- Social science is the use of logical, systematic, documented methods to investigate individuals, societies, and social processes, as well as the knowledge produced by these investigations.

- Pseudoscience is claims based on beliefs and/or public testimonials, not on the scientific method.
- Criminological research can be motivated by policy guidance and program management needs, academic concerns, and charitable impulses.
- Criminological research can be descriptive, exploratory, explanatory, evaluative, or some combination of these.
- Positivism is the belief that there is a reality that exists quite apart from one's own perception of it that is amenable to observation.
- Intersubjective agreement is an agreement by different observers on what is happening in the natural or social world.
- Postpositivism is the belief that there is an empirical reality but that our understanding of it is limited by its complexity and by the biases and other limitations of researchers.

- Interpretivism is the belief that reality is socially constructed and the goal of social science should be to understand what meanings people give to that reality.
- The constructivist paradigm emphasizes the importance of exploring and representing the ways in which different stakeholders in a social setting construct their beliefs. Constructivists interact with research subjects to gradually develop a shared perspective on the issue being studied.
- Quantitative methods record variation in social life in terms of categories that vary in amount. Qualitative methods are designed to capture social life as participants experience it, rather than in categories predetermined by the researcher.
- Triangulation is the use of multiple research methods to study a single research question.

Exercises

> Test your understanding of chapter content. Take the practice quiz. $SAGE edge™

1. What criminological topic or issue would you focus on if you could design a research project without any concern for costs? What are your motives for studying this topic? List at least four of your beliefs about this phenomenon. Try to identify the sources of each belief (e.g., television, newspaper, parental influence).

2. Develop four research questions related to your chosen topic or issue, one for each of the four types of research (descriptive, exploratory, explanatory, and evaluative). Be specific.

3. Read the abstracts of each article in a recent issue of a major criminological journal. Identify the type of research conducted for each study.

4. Find a report of social science research in an article in a daily newspaper. What are the motives for the research? How much

information is provided about the research design? What were the major findings? What additional evidence would you like to see in the article to increase your confidence in the research conclusions?

5. Continue the debate between positivism and interpretivism with an in-class discussion. Be sure to review the guidelines for these research philosophies and the associated goals. You might also consider whether an integrated philosophy is preferable.

6. Outline your own research philosophy. You can base your outline primarily on your reactions to the points you have read in this chapter, but try also to think seriously about which perspective seems more reasonable to you.

Developing a Research Proposal

Will you develop a research proposal in this course? If so, you should begin to consider your alternatives.

1. What topic would you focus on if you could design a social research project without any concern for costs? What are your motives for studying this topic?

2. Develop four questions that you might investigate about the topic you just selected. Each question should reflect a different

research motive: description, exploration, explanation, or evaluation. Be specific.

3. Which question most interests you? Would you prefer to attempt to answer that question with quantitative or qualitative methods? Why?

Web Exercises

1. You have been asked to prepare a brief presentation on a criminological topic or issue of interest to you. Go to the Bureau of Justice Statistics (BJS) website at www.ojp.usdoj.gov/bjs/. Browse the BJS publications for a topic that interests you. Write a short outline for a 5- to 10-minute presentation regarding your topic, including how the data were collected, statistics, and other relevant information.

2. Go to the Federal Bureau of Investigation (FBI) website at www.fbi.gov. Explore the types of programs and initiatives sponsored by the FBI. Discuss at least three of these programs or initiatives in terms of their purposes and goals. For each program or initiative examined, do you believe the program or initiative is effective?

What are the major weaknesses? What changes would you propose the FBI make to more effectively meet the goals of the program or initiative?

3. Go to the website of a major newspaper and find an article that talks about the causes of violence. What conclusions does the article draw, and what research methods does the author discuss to back up his or her claims?

4. There are many interesting websites that discuss philosophy of science issues. Read the summaries of positivism and interpretivism at www.misq.org/misq/downloads/download/editorial/25/. What do these summaries add to your understanding of these philosophical alternatives?

Ethics Exercises

Throughout the book, we will be discussing the ethical challenges that arise in research on crime and criminal justice. At the end of each chapter, we will ask you to consider some questions about ethical issues related to that chapter's focus. We introduce this critical topic formally in Chapter 3, but we will begin here with some questions for you to ponder.

1. You have now learned about the qualitative study by Eric Madfis (2014) that investigated schools that had averted mass shootings in school shooting incidents. We think it provided important information for policymakers about the social dynamics that may help prevent these tragedies. But what would you do if you were conducting a similar study in a high school, and you learned that a student was planning to bring a gun to school to

kill some other students? What if he was only thinking about it? Or just talking with his friends about how neat it would be? Can you suggest some guidelines for researchers?

2. Grossman et al. (1997) found that the Second Step program reduced aggressive behavior in schools and increased prosocial behavior. If you were David Grossman, would you announce your findings in a press conference and encourage schools to adopt this program? If you were a school principal who heard about this research, would you agree to let another researcher replicate (repeat) the Grossman et al. study in your school, with some classrooms assigned to receive the Second Step program randomly (on the basis of the toss of a coin) and others not allowed to receive the program for the duration of the study?

SPSS or Excel Exercises

Data for Exercise	
Dataset	**Description**
2013 YRBS.sav	The 2013 YRBS, short for Youth Risk Behavior Survey, is a national study of high school students. It focuses on gauging various behaviors and experiences of the adolescent population, including substance use and some victimization.
Monitoring the Future 2013 grade 10.sav	This dataset contains variables from the 2013 Monitoring the Future (MTF) study. This is data covers a national sample of 10th graders, with a focus on monitoring substance use and abuse.

Variables for Exercise	
Variable Name (Dataset)	**Description**
Q44 (YRBS)	This is a seven-category ordinal measure that asked how many times the respondent had drank five or more beverages in one sitting in the past 30 days.
V7108 (MTF)	This is a six-category ordinal measure that asked how many times the respondent had drank five or more drinks in a row in the past two weeks.

First, load the 2013 YRBS Subsample.sav file and complete the following:

1. Create a bar chart of variable Q44 by following the following menu options graphs->legacy dialogues->bar. Select the simple bar chart option, and click the arrow to add Q44 to the category axis text box. At a glance, what does this bar graph tell us about binge drinking among high school students? Are the data on the YRBS qualitative or quantitative? How do you know?

2. Write at least four research questions based on the bar chart you've created. Try to make one for each type of social research (descriptive, exploratory, explanatory, and evaluative). Think about the following: What stands out for you in this graph? What additional information do you need? Who should the research focus on?

3. Explain the possible reasons (policy, academic, or personal) we might want to research binge drinking or lack thereof. What organizations might be interested in this kind of research?

4. Triangulation refers to using multiple methods or measures to study a single research question. Let's see if we can triangulate the results from Part 1 using a different measure in the Grade10.2013.MTF.sav dataset.

    a. Create a bar chart of variable V7108.

    b. How do the estimates of binge drinking in the YRBS compare to these results?

    c. If there are any major differences, what do you think could explain them?

CHAPTER 2

The Process and Problems of Criminological Research

LEARNING OBJECTIVES

1. Describe the importance of theory to research.

2. Discuss the difference between deductive and inductive reasoning.

3. Describe the difference between a research question and a research hypothesis.

4. Explain how the research circle is really a research spiral.

5. Identify the difference between an independent variable and a dependent variable.

6. Define the different types of validity and generalizability.

When video of NFL player Ray Rice knocking his then-fiancée unconscious in an elevator hit the media, society got a firsthand image of intimate partner violence (IPV), which more often occurs behind closed doors than in public. Many celebrities have come forward with their stories and/or called the police for help after they have been assaulted by their partners, including Madonna, Halle Berry, Rihanna, and Evan Peters. While this media attention has increased society's awareness of IPV, it has always been a frequently committed and extremely costly crime, not only in terms of the physical and emotional injuries suffered by the parties involved, but also in terms of shattered families. What to do about this major social problem, then, is an important policy question. For over 30 years, the criminal justice system has attempted to effectively respond to intimate partner violence and other domestic assaults in a way that best protects victims and punishes offenders.

In 1981, a historic experiment was funded by the Police Foundation and the Minneapolis Police Department to determine whether immediately arresting accused spouse abusers on the spot would deter future offending incidents. For misdemeanor cases, the experimental course of action involved the random assignment of police to respond by either arresting the suspect or giving the suspect a simple warning. The experimental treatment, then, was whether the suspect was arrested, and the researchers wanted to know whether arresting the suspect was better than not arresting the suspect in reducing recidivism (subsequent assaults against the same victim). The study's results, which were widely publicized, indicated that arrest did have a deterrent effect. Partly as a result of these findings, the percentage of urban police departments that made arrest the preferred response to complaints of domestic violence rose from 10% in 1984 to 90% in 1988 (Sherman 1992). Six other cities later carried out studies like the Minneapolis experiment (collectively, this was called the Spouse Assault Replication Program [SARP]), but city to city, the results were mixed (Buzawa and Buzawa 1996; Hirschel, Hutchison, and Dean 1992; Pate and Hamilton 1992; Sherman 1992; Sherman and Berk 1984). In some cities (and for some people), arrest did seem to prevent future incidents of

Replication: The ability of an entire study or experiment to be duplicated.

domestic assault; in other cities, it seemed only to make matters worse, contributing to additional assault; and in still other cities, arrest seemed to have no discernible effect. After these **replications** of the original Minneapolis experiment, people still wondered, "Just what is the effect of arrest in reducing domestic violence cases, and how should the police respond to such cases?" The answer simply was not clear. The Minneapolis experiment, the studies modeled after it, and the related controversies provide many examples for a systematic overview of the social research process.

In this chapter, we shift from examining the *why* of social research to an overview of the *how*—the focus of the rest of the book. We will consider how to develop a question for social research and then how to review the existing literature about this question while connecting the question to social theory and, in many studies, formulating specific testable hypotheses. We will then discuss different social research strategies and standards for social research as a prelude to covering the details about these stages in subsequent chapters. You will find more details in appendixes A and B about reviewing the literature. We will use the Minneapolis experiment and the related research to illustrate the different research strategies and some of the related techniques. The chapter also expands on the role of social theories in developing research questions and guiding research decisions. By the chapter's end, you should be ready to formulate a research question, critique previous studies that addressed this question, and design a general strategy for answering the question.

▦ Criminological Research Questions

Criminological research question: A question about some aspect of crime, criminals, or the criminal justice system, the answer to which is sought through collection and analysis of the firsthand, verifiable, empirical data.

How does a researcher interested in criminology and criminal justice–related issues decide what to study and research? A **criminological research question** is a question about some aspect of crime or criminals that you seek to answer through the collection and analysis of firsthand, verifiable, empirical data. The types of questions that can be asked are virtually limitless. For example, "Are children who are violent more likely than nonviolent children to use violence as adults?" "Does the race of a victim who is killed influence whether someone is sentenced to death rather than life imprisonment?" "Why do some kinds of neighborhoods have more crime than others? Is it due to the kinds of people who live there or characteristics of the neighborhood itself?" "Does community policing reduce the crime rate?" "Has the U.S. government's war on drugs done anything to reduce the use of illegal drugs?" So many research questions are possible in criminology that it is more of a challenge to specify what does not qualify as a social research question than to specify what does.

But that does not mean it is easy to specify a research question. In fact, formulating a good research question can be surprisingly difficult. We can break the process into three stages: identifying one or more questions for study, refining the questions, and then evaluating the questions.

Identifying Criminological Research Questions

Formulating a research question is often an intensely personal process in addition to being a scientific or professional one. Curiosity about the social world may emerge from your "personal troubles," as Mills (1959) put it, or your personal experiences. Examples of these troubles or experiences could range from an awareness you may have that crime is not randomly distributed within a city but that there seem to be "good" or safe parts of town and "bad" or unsafe areas. Can you think of other possible research questions that flow from your own experiences in the world?

The experience of others is another fruitful source of research questions. Knowing a relative who was abused by a spouse, seeing a TV special about violence, or reading a gang member's autobiography can stimulate questions about general criminological processes. Can you draft a research question based on a relative's experiences, a TV show, or a book?

Other researchers may also pose interesting questions for you to study. Most research articles end with some suggestions for additional research that highlight unresolved issues. For example, Sherman et al. (1992) concluded an article on some of the replications of the Minneapolis experiment on police responses to spouse abuse by suggesting that "deterrence may be effective for a substantial segment of the offender population. . . . However, the underlying mechanisms remain obscure" (p. 706). A new study could focus on the mechanisms: Why or under what conditions does the arrest of offenders who are employed deter them from future criminal acts? Exactly what occurs when someone is arrested for domestic violence that may lead him or her not to be violent against a spouse in the future? Is it the brute fear of being arrested and having to go to jail? Is it the fear that one's employer may find out and fire him or her? Is it the fear that members of the community may learn about the arrest and the offender may lose his or her good standing in the neighborhood? Is it all these? Any issue of a journal in your field is likely to have comments that point toward unresolved issues.

The primary source of research questions for many researchers is theory. Many theoretical domains are used to inform research questions in our discipline, including sociological, psychological, and criminological theories. Some researchers spend much of their careers conducting research intended to refine an answer to one central question. For example, you may find rational choice theory to be a useful approach to understanding diverse forms of social behavior, like crime, because you think people do seem to make decisions on the basis of personal cost-benefit calculations. So you may ask whether rational choice theory can explain why some people commit crimes and others do not or why some people decide to quit committing crimes while others continue their criminal ways.

Finally, some research questions adopt a very pragmatic rationale concerning their research design. You may focus on a research question posed by someone else because doing so seems to be to your professional or financial advantage. For instance, some researchers conduct research on specific questions posed by a funding source in what is termed a request for proposals (RFP). (Sometimes the acronym RFA is used, meaning request for applications.) Or you may learn that the public defenders in your city are curious as to whether they are more successful in getting their clients acquitted of a criminal charge than private lawyers.

Refining Criminological Research Questions

As you may have guessed, coming up with interesting criminological questions for research is less problematic than focusing on a problem of manageable size. We are often interested in much more than we can reasonably investigate with our limited time and resources (or the limited resources of a funding agency). Researchers may worry about staking a research project (and thereby a grant) on a particular problem, so they commit to addressing several research questions at once, and often in a jumbled fashion. It may also seem risky to focus on a research question that may lead to results discrepant with our own cherished assumptions about the social world. In addition, the prospective commitment of time and effort for some research questions may seem overwhelming, resulting in a certain degree of paralysis (not that the authors have any experience with this!).

The best way to avoid these problems is to develop the research question one bit at a time with a step-by-step strategy. Do not keep hoping that the perfect research question will just spring forth from your pen. Instead, develop a list of possible research questions as you go along. At the appropriate time, you can look through this list for the research questions that appear more than once. Narrow your list to the most interesting, most workable candidates. Repeat this process as long as it helps improve your research questions. Keep in mind that the research you are currently working on will likely generate additional research questions for you to answer.

Evaluating Criminological Research Questions

In the third stage of selecting a criminological research question, you evaluate the best candidate against the criteria for good social research questions: feasibility, given the time and resources available, social importance, and scientific relevance (King, Keohane, and Verba 1994).

The research question in the Minneapolis Domestic Violence Experiment, "Does the formal sanction of police arrest versus nonarrest inhibit domestic violence?" certainly meets the criteria of social importance and scientific relevance, but it would not be a feasible question for a student project because it would require you to try to get the cooperation of a police department. You might instead ask the question "Do people (students) think that arrest will inhibit domestic violence?" This is a question that you could study with an on-campus survey. Or perhaps you could work out an arrangement with a local battered women's shelter to study the question "What leads some women to call the police when they are the victims of domestic violence, and why do they sometimes not call?" A review of the literature, however, might convince you that this and other questions may not be scientifically relevant because they have been studied enough.

Feasibility

You must be able to conduct any study within the time frame and with the resources you have. If time is limited, questions that involve long-term change may not be feasible—for example, "If a state has recently changed its law so that it now permits capital punishment for those convicted of murder, does it eventually see a reduction in the homicide rate over time?" This is an interesting and important question but one that requires years of data collection and research. Another issue is what people or groups you can expect to gain access to. Although well-experienced researchers may be granted access to police or correctional department files to do their research, less seasoned and lesser-known researchers or students may not be granted such access. It is also often difficult for even the most experienced of researchers to be given full access to the deliberations of a criminal jury. For someone interested in white-collar crime, recording the interactions that take place in corporate boardrooms may also be taboo.

The Minneapolis Domestic Violence Experiment shows how ambitious social research questions can be when a team of seasoned researchers secures the backing of influential groups. The project required hundreds of thousands of dollars, the collaboration of many social scientists and criminal justice personnel, and the volunteer efforts of 41 Minneapolis police officers. But don't worry; many worthwhile research questions can be investigated with much more limited resources. Of course, for this reason, the Sherman and Berk (1984) question would not be feasible for a student project. You might instead ask the question "Do students think punishment deters spouse abuse?" Or perhaps you could work out an arrangement with a local police department to study the question "How satisfied are police officers with their treatment of domestic violence cases?"

Social Importance

Criminological research is not a simple undertaking, so you must focus on a substantive area that you feel is important and that is important to the discipline and/or important for public policy. You also need to feel personally motivated to carry out the study; there is little point in trying to answer a question that does not interest you.

In addition, you should consider whether the research question is important to other people. Will an answer to the research question make a difference for society? Again, the Minneapolis Domestic Violence Experiment is an exemplary case. If that study had showed that a certain type of police response to domestic violence reduced the risk of subsequent victimization, a great deal of future violence could be prevented. But clearly, criminology and criminal justice are far from lacking important research questions.

CAREERS AND RESEARCH

Patrick J. Carr, PhD, Director, Program in Criminal Justice

Patrick J. Carr is the Program Director of the Program in Criminal Justice, as well as associate professor of sociology at Rutgers University; furthermore, he is an associate member of the MacArthur Foundation's Research Network on Transitions to Adulthood. He earned his PhD in sociology from the University of Chicago in 1998, and his master's degree in sociology from University College Dublin in 1990. His research interests include communities and crime, informal social control, youth violence, and the transition to adulthood.

Carr and his wife, Maria Kefalas (Saint Joseph's University), are founders of the Philadelphia Youth Solutions Project (www.pysp.org), which "offers a safe space for Philadelphia's young people to explain their views and emotions about the danger and violence that consumes so much of their daily lives, to ask questions of themselves and the people charged with running [Philadelphia], and to have a serious conversation with teachers, parents, city officials, community leaders, state legislators, reporters, politicians, and anyone else who wants to know what is going on in the city to move forward on solutions inspired by the youth perspective." The Philadelphia Youth Solutions Project is a venue for Philadelphia's young people to offer their own expert advice on how to transform the city based on their experiences and perspectives.

Carr and Kefalas are ethnographic researchers who seek to understand people's experiences through participating in their lives and interviewing them in depth. In another project, they investigated the experiences of young adults growing up in a small midwestern town by living in the town and sharing in community experiences. Their subsequent book was *Hollowing Out the Middle: The Rural Brain Drain and What It Means for America* (2009).

Scientific Relevance

Every research question in criminology should be grounded in the existing empirical literature. By *grounded* we mean the research we do must be informed by what others before us have done on the topic. Whether you formulate a research question because you have been stimulated by an academic article or are motivated by questions regarding your own personal experiences, you must turn to existing criminological literature to find out what has already been learned about this question. Even if your research topic has already been investigated by someone else, it would not necessarily be a bad idea for you to do research on the issue. It would be unreasonable to think of any criminological research question as being settled for all time. You can be sure that some prior study is relevant to almost any research question you can think of, and you can also think of better ways to do research than have been done in the past.

b. Is the research up to date? Be sure to include the most recent research, not just the "classic" studies.

c. Have you used direct quotes sparingly? To focus your literature review, you need to express the key points from prior research in your own words. Use direct quotes only when they are essential for making an important point (Pyrczak 2005).

2. *Critique prior research.* Evaluate the strengths and weaknesses of the prior research. In addition to all the points that you develop as you answer the article review questions in Appendix B, you should also select articles for review that reflect work published in peer-reviewed journals and written by credible authors who have been funded by reputable sources. Consider the following questions as you decide how much weight to give each article:

a. How was the report reviewed prior to its publication or release? Articles published in academic journals go through a rigorous review process, usually involving careful criticism and revision. Top refereed journals may accept only 10% of the submitted articles, so they can be very selective. Dissertations go through a lengthy process of criticism and revision by a few members of the dissertation writer's home institution. A report released directly by a research organization is likely to have had only a limited review, although some research organizations maintain a rigorous internal review process. Papers presented at professional meetings may have had little prior review. Needless to say, more confidence can be placed in research results that have been subject to a more rigorous review.

b. What is the author's reputation? Reports by an author or a team of authors who have published other work on the research question should be given somewhat greater credibility at the outset.

c. Who funded and sponsored the research? Major federal funding agencies and private foundations fund only research proposals that have been evaluated carefully and ranked highly by a panel of experts. They also often monitor closely the progress of the research. This does not guarantee that every such project report is good, but it goes a long way toward ensuring some worthwhile products. On the other hand, research that is funded by organizations that have a preference for a particular outcome should be given particularly close scrutiny (Locke, Silverman, and Spirduso 1998).

3. *Present pertinent conclusions.* Don't leave the reader guessing about the implications of the prior research for your own investigation. Present the conclusions you draw from the research you have reviewed. As you do so, follow several simple guidelines:

a. Distinguish clearly your own opinion of prior research from the conclusions of the authors of the articles you have reviewed.

b. Make it clear when your own approach is based on the theoretical framework that you use and not on the results of prior research.

c. Acknowledge the potential limitations of any empirical research project. Don't emphasize problems in prior research that you can't avoid (Pyrczak 2005).

d. Explain how the unanswered questions raised by prior research or the limitations of methods used in prior research make it important for you to conduct your own investigation (Fink 2005).

A good example of how to conclude an integrated literature review is provided by an article based on the replication in Milwaukee of the Minneapolis Domestic Violence Experiment. For this article, Paternoster et al. (1997) sought to determine whether police officers' use of fair procedures when arresting assault suspects would lessen the rate of subsequent domestic violence. For example, did suspects feel that their side of the story was heard? Did they feel that they were treated fairly? Paternoster et al. concluded that there was a major gap in the prior literature: "Even at the end of some seven experiments and millions of dollars, then, there is a great deal of ambiguity surrounding the question of how arrest impacts future spouse assault" (p. 164). Specifically, they noted that each of the seven experiments focused on the effect of arrest itself but ignored the possibility that "particular kinds of police procedure might inhibit the recurrence of spouse assault" (p. 165).

So Paternoster and his colleagues (1997) grounded their new analysis in additional literature on procedural justice and concluded that their new analysis would be "the first study to examine the effect of fairness judgments regarding a punitive criminal sanction (arrest) on serious criminal behavior (assaulting one's partner)" (p. 172).

The Role of Theory

We have already pointed out that criminological theory can be a rich source of research questions. What deserves more attention at this point is the larger role of **theory** in research. We have also noted that research investigating criminal justice and criminology related questions rely on many theories, including criminological, sociological, and psychological theories. These theories do many things:

> **Theory:** A logically interrelated set of propositions about empirical reality. Examples of criminological theories include social learning, routine activities, labeling, general strain, and social disorganization theory.

- They help us explain or understand things like why some people commit crimes or more crimes than others; why some people quit and others continue; and what the expected effect of good families, harsh punishment, or other factors on crime might be.

- They help us make predictions about the criminological world: "What would be the expected effect on the homicide rate if we employed capital punishment rather than life imprisonment?" "What would be the effect on the rate of property crimes if unemployment were to substantially increase?"

- They help us organize and make sense of empirical findings in a discipline.

- They help guide future research.

- They help guide public policy: "What should we do to reduce the level of domestic violence?"

Social scientists, such as criminologists, who connect their work to theories in their discipline, can generate better ideas about what to look for in a study and develop conclusions with more implications for other research. Building and evaluating theory is therefore one of the most important objectives of a social science like criminology.

Theories usually contain what are called **theoretical constructs**. These theoretical constructs describe what is important to look at to understand, explain, predict, and "do something about" crime. For example, an important theoretical construct in differential association theory is the notion of "definitions favorable and unfavorable to the violation of law." Theories usually link one or more theoretical constructs to others in what are called *relationship statements*. Differential association theory, for example, links the theoretical construct of favorable or unfavorable definitions to the theoretical construct of involvement in crime to argue as follows: "As one is exposed to more definitions favorable to the violation of law relative to definitions unfavorable to the violation of law, one is more at risk for criminal behavior." This is a relationship statement that links two theoretical constructs; it states that as exposure to definitions favorable to the violation of law increases, the risk of crime also increases. This is essentially a hypothesis that the theory of differential association entertains; if the theory is true, then the expected relationship should be true. The purpose of much criminological research is to examine the truth value, or empirical validity, of such theoretical relationship statements or hypotheses. Some criminological theories reflect a substantial body of research and the thinking of many social scientists; others are formulated in the course of one investigation. A few have been widely accepted, at least for a time; others are the subject of vigorous controversy, with frequent changes and refinements in response to criticism and new research.

> **Theoretical constructs:** Parts of a theory that describe what is important to look at to understand, explain, predict, and "do something about" the subject.

Most criminological research is guided by some theory, although the theory may be only partially developed in a particular study or may even be unrecognized by the researcher. When researchers are involved in conducting a research project or engrossed in writing a research report, they may easily lose sight of the larger picture. It is easy to focus on accumulating or clarifying particular findings rather than considering how the study's findings fit into a more general understanding of the social world. Furthermore, as we shall soon see, just as theory guides research, research findings also influence the development of theory.

We can use the studies of the police response to domestic assault to illustrate the value of theory for social research. Even in this very concrete and practical matter, we must draw on social theories to understand how people act and what should be done about those actions. Consider the three action options that police officers have when they confront a domestic assault suspect. Fellow officers might encourage separation to achieve short-term peace; police trainers might prefer mediation to resolve the underlying dispute; feminist groups may advocate arrest to protect the victim from further harm. None of these recommendations is really a theory, but each suggests a different perspective on crime and legal sanctions. You will encounter these different perspectives if you read much of the literature on domestic violence or even if you talk with your friends about it. In turn, these assumptions reflect different experiences with family conflict, police actions, and the legal system. What we believe about one crime and the appropriate response to it relates to a great many other ideas we have about the social world. Recognizing these relationships is a first step toward becoming a theoretically guided social researcher and a theoretically informed consumer of social research.

Remember that social theories do not provide the answers to research questions. Instead, social theories suggest the areas on which we should focus and the propositions that we should consider for a test. That is, theories suggest testable hypotheses about phenomena, and research verifies whether those hypotheses are true. In fact, one of the most important requirements of theory is that it be testable, or what philosophers of science call **falsifiable**; theoretical statements must be capable of being proven wrong. If a body of thought cannot be empirically tested, it is more likely philosophy than theory. For example, Sherman and Berk's (1984) domestic violence research was actually a test of predictions derived from two alternative theories of the impact of punishment on crime, deterrence theory and labeling theory.

> **Falsifiable:** When a theory can be tested and falsified or otherwise not supported by empirical evidence.

Deterrence theory presumes that human beings are at least marginally rational beings who are responsive to the expected costs and benefits of their actions. Committing a crime nets certain benefits for offenders; therefore, if we want to inhibit crime, there must be a compensating cost that outweighs the potential benefits associated with the offense. One cost is the criminal sanction (arrest, conviction, punishment). Deterrence theory expects punishment to inhibit crime in two ways. General deterrence occurs when people see that crime results in undesirable punishments for others, or that "crime doesn't pay." Those who are punished serve as examples for those who have not yet committed an offense but might be thinking of what awaits them should they engage in similarly punishable acts. Specific deterrence occurs when persons who are punished decide not to commit another offense so they can avoid further punishment (Lempert and Sanders 1986). Deterrence theory leads to the prediction that arresting spouse abusers will reduce the likelihood of their reoffending when compared with a less serious sanction (not being arrested but being warned or counseled).

Labeling theory distinguishes between primary deviance, the acts of individuals that lead to public sanctions, and secondary deviance, the deviance that occurs in response to public sanction (Hagan 1994). Arrest or some other public sanction for misdeeds labels the offender as deviant in the eyes of others. Once the offender is labeled, others will treat the offender as a deviant, and he or she is then more likely to act in a way that is consistent with the deviant label. Ironically, the act of punishment stimulates more of the very behavior that it was intended to eliminate (Tannenbaum 1938). This theory suggests that persons arrested for intimate partner violence are more likely to reoffend than those who are caught but not punished, because the formal sanction of arrest is more stigmatizing than being warned or counseled. This prediction about the effect of formal legal sanctions is the reverse of the deterrence theory prediction.

Theorizing about the logic behind formal legal punishment also can help us draw connections to more general theories about social processes. Deterrence theory reflects the assumptions of rational choice theory, which assumes behavior is shaped by practical calculations: People break the law if the benefits of doing so exceed the costs. If crime is a rational choice for some people, then increasing the certainty or severity of punishment for crime should shift the cost-benefit balance away from criminal behavior. Labeling theory is rooted in symbolic interactionism, which focuses on the symbolic meanings that people give to behavior (Hagan 1994). Instead of assuming that some forms of behavior are deviant in and of themselves (Scull 1988), symbolic interactionists view deviance as a consequence of the application of rules and sanctions to an offender (Becker 1963). Exhibit 2.2 summarizes how these general theories relate to the question of whether to arrest spouse abusers.

Does either deterrence theory or labeling theory make sense to you as an explanation for the impact of punishment? Do these theories seem consistent with your observations of social life? Over a decade after Sherman and Berk's (1984) study, Paternoster et al. (1997) decided to study punishment of domestic violence from a different perspective. They turned to a social psychological theory called procedural justice theory, which explains law-abiding behavior as resulting from a sense of duty or morality (Tyler 1990). People obey the law from a sense of obligation that flows from seeing legal authorities as moral and legitimate. From this perspective, individuals who are arrested seem less likely to reoffend if they are treated fairly, irrespective of the outcome of their case, because fair treatment will enhance their view of legal authorities as moral and legitimate. Procedural justice theory expands our view of the punishment process by focusing attention on how police act and how authorities treat subjects, rather than just on the legal decisions they make. Are you now less certain about the likely effect of arrest for intimate partner violence? Will arrest decrease recidivism because abusers do not wish to suffer from legal sanctions again? Will it increase recidivism because abusers feel stigmatized by being arrested and thus are more likely to act like criminals? Or will arrest reduce abuse only if the abusers feel they have been treated fairly by the legal authorities? By posing such questions, social theory makes us much more sensitive to the possibilities and so helps us design better research. Before, during, and after a research investigation, we need to keep thinking theoretically.

🔲 Social Research Strategies

With a research question formulated, a review of the pertinent literature taking shape, and a theoretical framework in mind, we are ready to consider the process of conducting our research. All research is an effort to connect theory and empirical data. As Exhibit 2.3 shows, theory and data have a two-way, mutually reinforcing relationship. Researchers may make this connection by starting with a social theory and then testing some of its implications with data. This is the process of **deductive reasoning**; it is most often the strategy used in quantitative methods. Alternatively, researchers may develop a connection between social theory and data by first collecting the data and then developing a theory that explains the patterns in the data. This is **inductive reasoning** and is more often the strategy used in qualitative methods. As you'll see, a research project can draw on both deductive and inductive strategies.

> **Deductive reasoning:** The type of reasoning that moves from the general to the specific.

> **Inductive reasoning:** The type of reasoning that moves from the specific to the general.

Exhibit 2.2	Two Social Theories and Their Predictions About the Effect of Arrest for Intimate Partner Assault		
	Rational Choice Theory		*Symbolic Interactionism*
Theoretical assumption	People's behavior is shaped by calculations of the costs and benefits of their actions.		People give symbolic meanings to objects, behaviors, and other people.
Criminological component	Deterrence theory: People break the law if the benefits of doing so outweigh the costs.		Labeling theory: People label offenders as deviant, promoting further deviance.
Prediction (effect of arrest for domestic assault)	Abusing spouse, having seen the costs of abuse (namely, arrest), decides not to abuse again.		Abusing spouse, having been labeled as "an abuser," abuses more often.

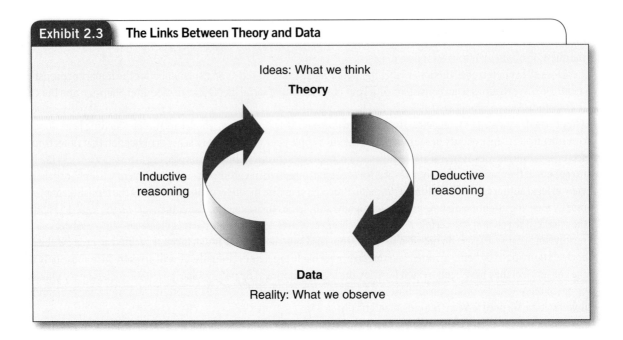

Exhibit 2.3   The Links Between Theory and Data

Ideas: What we think
Theory

Inductive
reasoning

Deductive
reasoning

Data
Reality: What we observe

Both deductive reasoning and inductive reasoning are essential to criminologists. We cannot test an idea fairly unless we use deductive reasoning, stating our expectations in advance and then designing a way to test the validity of our claims. A theory that has not survived these kinds of tests can be regarded only as very tentative. Yet theories, no matter how cherished, cannot always make useful predictions for every social situation or research problem that we seek to investigate. We may find unexpected patterns in the data we collect, called **serendipitous findings** or **anomalous findings**. In either situation, we should reason inductively, making whatever theoretical sense we can of our unanticipated findings. Then, if the new findings seem sufficiently important, we can return to deductive reasoning and plan a new study to formally test our new ideas.

> **Serendipitous findings (anomalous findings):** Unexpected patterns in data, which stimulate new ideas or theoretical approaches.

Explanatory Research

> **Research circle:** A diagram of the elements of the research process, including theories, hypotheses, data collection, and data analysis.

This process of conducting research, moving from theory to data and back again or from data to theory and back again, can be characterized as a **research circle**, as depicted in Exhibit 2.4. Note that it mirrors the relationship between theory and data shown in Exhibit 2.3 and that it comprises three main research strategies: deductive research, inductive research, and descriptive research.

> **Deductive research:** The type of research in which a specific expectation is deduced from a general premise and is then tested.

Deductive Research

As Exhibit 2.4 shows, **deductive research** proceeds from theorizing to data collection and then back to theorizing. In essence, a specific expectation is deduced from a general premise and then tested.

> **Hypothesis:** A tentative statement about empirical reality involving the relationship between two or more variables.

Notice that a theory leads first to a **hypothesis**, which is a specific implication deduced from the more general theory. Researchers actually test a hypothesis, not the complete theory itself, because theories usually contain many hypotheses. As we stated earlier, a hypothesis proposes a relationship between

Exhibit 2.4   The Research Circle

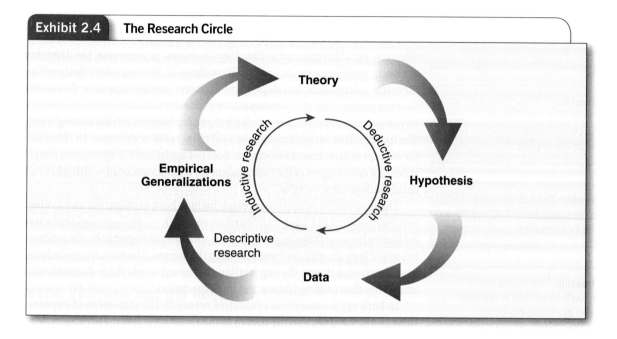

two or more theoretical constructs or variables. A **variable** is a characteristic or property that can vary. A **constant** is a characteristic or property that cannot vary. For example, if we were to conduct some research in a male adult penitentiary, the theoretical construct "type of crime committed" would be a variable, because persons will have been incarcerated for different offenses (one person is in for armed robbery, another for rape, etc.). However, the theoretical construct "gender" would be a constant, because every inmate in the penitentiary would be male; gender does not vary—it is constant. Would age be a variable or a constant in this group? Would "criminal status" (offender or nonoffender) be a variable or a constant?

Variables are of critical importance in research because in a hypothesis, variation in one variable is proposed to predict, influence, or cause variation in the other variable. The proposed influence is the **independent variable**; its effect or consequence is the **dependent variable**. Another way to think about this distinction is to say, "the dependent variable 'depends' on the independent variable." After the researchers formulate one or more hypotheses and develop research procedures, they collect data with which to test the hypothesis.

Hypotheses can be worded in several different ways, and identifying the independent and dependent variables is sometimes difficult. When in doubt, try to rephrase the hypothesis as an if-then statement: "If the independent variable increases (or decreases), then the dependent variable increases (or decreases)." Exhibit 2.5 presents several hypotheses with their independent and dependent variables and their if-then equivalents.

Exhibit 2.5 demonstrates another feature of hypotheses: **direction of association**. When researchers hypothesize that one variable increases as the other variable increases, the direction of the association is positive (Hypotheses 1 and 4 in the exhibit); when one variable decreases as the other variable decreases, the direction of association is also positive (Hypothesis 3). In a **positive relationship**,

Example of a hypothesis: The higher the level of poverty in a community, the higher its rate of crime.

Variable: Characteristics or properties that can vary (take on different values or attributes).

Constant: A variable that has a fixed value in a given situation; a characteristic or value that does not change.

Independent variable: A variable that is hypothesized to cause, or lead to, variation in another variable.

Example of an independent variable: Poverty level in a community (percent of population living below the poverty level).

Dependent variable: A variable that is hypothesized to change or vary depending on the variation in another variable.

CHAPTER 3

Research Ethics

1. Describe the design of the Milgram obedience experiments and some of the controversies surrounding their methods and results.

2. Identify three other research projects that helped to motivate the establishment of protections for human subjects.

3. Define the *Belmont Report's* three ethical standards for the protection of human subjects.

4. Explain how an institutional review board operates and how it classifies research.

5. List current standards for the protection of human subjects in research.

6. Describe the ethical issues related to conducting research with children and prisoners.

L et's begin with a thought experiment (or a trip down memory lane, depending on your earlier exposure to this example). One day as you are drinking coffee and reading the newspaper during your summer in California, you notice a small ad recruiting college students for a study at Stanford University. Feeling a bit bored with your part-time job waiting on tables and missing the campus environment you got used to in your previous year as a freshman, you go to the campus and complete an application.

Male college students needed for psychological study of prison life. $80 per day for 1–2 weeks beginning Aug. 14. For further information & applications, come to Room 248, Jordan Hall, Stanford U. (Zimbardo et al. 1973, 38)

After you arrive at the university, you are given an information form with more details about the research ("Prison Life Study").

Intrigued, you decide to continue. First you are asked to complete a long questionnaire about your family background, physical and mental health history, and prior criminal involvement; answer a researcher's questions in person; and sign a consent form. A few days later, you are informed that you and 20 other young men have been selected to participate in the experiment. You then return to the university to complete a battery of "psychological tests" and are told you will be picked up for the study the next day (Haney, Banks, and Zimbardo 1973).

The next morning, you hear a siren just before a squad car stops in front of your house. A police officer charges you with assault and battery, warns you of your constitutional rights, searches and handcuffs you, and drives you off to the police station. After fingerprinting and a short stay in a detention cell, you are blindfolded and driven to the "Stanford County Prison." Upon arrival, you are stripped naked, skin-searched, deloused, and issued a uniform (a loosely fitting smock with an ID number printed on it), bedding, soap, and a towel. You don't recognize anyone, but you notice that the other "prisoners" and the "guards" are college-age, apparently middle-class white men (and one Asian) like you (Haney et al. 1973; Zimbardo et al. 1973).

The prison warden welcomes you:

As you probably know, I'm your warden. All of you have shown that you are unable to function outside in the real world for one reason or another—that somehow you lack the responsibility of good citizens of this great country. We of this prison, your correctional staff, are going to help you learn what your responsibilities as citizens of this country are. . . . If you follow all of these rules and keep your hands clean, repent for your misdeeds and show a proper attitude of penitence, you and I will get along just fine. (Zimbardo et al. 1973, 38)

Prison Life Study: General Information

Purpose: A simulated prison will be established somewhere in the vicinity of Palo Alto, California, to study a number of problems of psychological and sociological relevance.

Paid volunteers will be randomly assigned to play the roles of either prisoners or guards for the duration of the study. This time period will vary somewhat from about 5 days to 2 weeks for any one volunteer—depending upon several factors, such as the "sentence" for the prisoner or the work effectiveness of the guards.

Payment will be $80 a day for performing various activities and work associated with the operation of our prison.

Each volunteer must enter a contractual arrangement with the principal investigator (Dr. P. G. Zimbardo) agreeing to participate for the full duration of the study. It is obviously essential that no prisoner can leave once jailed, except through established procedures. In addition, guards must report for their 8-hour work shifts promptly and regularly since surveillance by the guards will be around-the-clock—three work shifts will be rotated or guards will be assigned a regular shift—day, evening, or early morning. Failure to fulfill this contract will result in a partial loss of salary accumulated—according to a prearranged schedule to be agreed upon. Food and accommodations for the prisoners will be provided which will meet minimal standard nutrition, health and sanitation requirements.

A warden and several prison staff will be housed in adjacent cell blocks, meals and bedding also provided for them.

Medical and psychiatric facilities will be accessible should any of the participants desire or require such services.

All participants will agree to having their behavior observed and to be interviewed and perhaps also taking psychological tests. Films of parts of the study will be taken, participants agreeing to allow them to be shown, assuming their content has information of scientific value.

[The information form then summarizes two of the "problems to be studied" and provides a few more details.]

Thanks for your interest in this study. We hope it will be possible for you to participate and to share your experiences with us.

Philip G. Zimbardo, PhD
Professor of Social Psychology Stanford University

| Exhibit 3.1 | Prisoner in His Cell |

Source: From *The Lucifer Effect: Understanding How Good People Turn Evil* by Philip G. Zimbardo. Copyright © 2007 by Philip G. Zimbardo, Inc. Used by permission.

Among other behavioral restrictions, the rules stipulate that prisoners must remain silent during rest periods, during meals, and after lights out; that they must address each other only by their assigned ID numbers; that they must address guards as "Mr. Correctional Officer"; and that they may be punished for any infractions (Zimbardo et al. 1973)

You can tell that you are in the basement of a building. You are led down a corridor to a small cell (6' x 9') with three cots, where you are locked behind a steel-barred black door with two other prisoners (Exhibit 3.1). There is a small solitary confinement room across the hall for those who misbehave. There is little privacy, since you realize that the uniformed guards, behind their silver sunglasses, can always observe the prisoners. After you go to sleep, you are awakened by a whistle summoning you and the others for a roll call.

The next morning, you and the other eight prisoners must stand in line outside your cells and recite the rules until you remember all 17 of them. Prisoners must chant, "It's a wonderful day, Mr. Correctional Officer." Two prisoners who get out of line are put in solitary confinement. After a bit, the prisoners in Cell 1 decide to resist: They barricade their cell door and call on the prisoners in other cells to join in their resistance. As punishment, the guards pull the beds out from the other cells and spray some inmates with a fire extinguisher.

The guards succeed in enforcing control and become more authoritarian, while the prisoners become increasingly docile. Punishments are meted out for infractions of rules and sometimes for seemingly no reason at all; punishments include doing push-ups, being stripped naked, having legs chained, and being repeatedly wakened during the night. Would you join in the resistance? How would you react to this deprivation of your liberty by these authoritarian guards?

By the fifth day of the actual Stanford Prison Experiment, five student prisoners had to be released due to evident extreme stress (Zimbardo 2007). On the sixth day, Philip Zimbardo terminated the experiment. A prisoner subsequently reported,

The way we were made to degrade ourselves really brought us down and that's why we all sat docile towards the end of the experiment. (Haney et al. 1973, 88)

One guard later recounted his experience:

I was surprised at myself . . . I made them call each other names and clean the toilets out with their bare hands. I practically considered the prisoners cattle, and I kept thinking: "I have to watch out for them in case they try something." (Zimbardo et al. 1973, 174)

Exhibit 3.2 gives some idea of the difference in how the prisoners and guards behaved. What is most striking about this result is that all the guards and prisoners had been screened before the study began to ensure that they were physically and mentally healthy. The roles of guard and prisoner had been assigned randomly, by the toss of a coin, so the two groups were very similar when the study began. It seemed to be the "situation" that led to the deterioration of the mental state of the prisoners and the different behavior of the guards. Being a guard or a prisoner, with rules and physical arrangements reinforcing distinctive roles, changed their behavior.

Are you surprised by the outcome of the experiment? By the guard's report of his unexpected, abusive behavior? By the prisoners' ultimate submissiveness and the considerable psychic distress some felt? (We leave it to you to assess how you would have responded if you had been an actual research participant.)

Of course, our purpose in introducing this small "experiment" is not to focus attention on the prediction of behavior in prisons; instead, we want to introduce the topic of research ethics by encouraging you to think about research from the standpoint of the people who are the subjects of research. We will refer to **Philip Zimbardo's Stanford Prison Experiment** throughout this chapter, since it is fair to say that this research ultimately had a profound influence on the way that social scientists think about research ethics as well as on the way that criminologists understand behavior in prisons. We will also refer to **Stanley Milgram's** (1963) **experiments on obedience to authority**, since that research also pertains to criminal justice issues and has stimulated much debate about research ethics.

Every criminal justice researcher needs to consider how to practice his or her discipline ethically. Whenever we interact with other people as social scientists, we must give paramount importance to the rational concerns and emotional needs

Philip Zimbardo's Stanford Prison Experiment: A two-week experiment that simulated the prison life of both prisoners and guards that was ended in just six days because of what the simulation was doing to college students who participated.

Stanley Milgram's experiments on obedience to authority: Experiments by Stanley Milgram that sought to identify the conditions under which ordinary citizens would be obedient to authority figures' instructions to inflict pain on others.

Exhibit 3.2	Chart of Guard and Prisoner Behavior

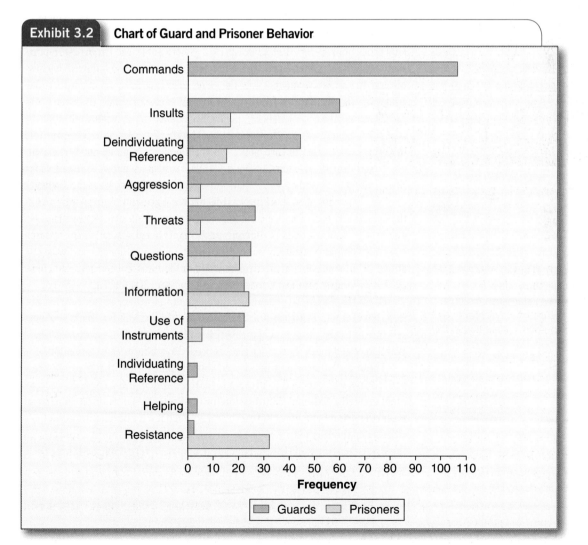

that shape their responses to our actions. It is here that ethical research practice begins, with the recognition that our research procedures involve people who deserve as much respect for their well-being as we do for ours.

Historical Background

Concern with ethical practice in relation to people who are in some respect dependent, whether as patients or research subjects, is not a new idea. Ethical guidelines for medicine trace back to Hippocrates in 5 BC Greece (Hippocratic Oath, n.d.), and the American Medical Association (AMA) adopted the world's first formal professional ethics code in medicine in 1847 (AMA 2011). Yet the history of medical practice makes it clear that having an ethics code is not sufficient to ensure ethical practice, at least when there are clear incentives to do otherwise.

Nuremberg War Crime Trials: The international military tribunal held by the victorious Allies after World War II in Nuremberg, Germany, that exposed the horrific medical experiments conducted by Nazi doctors and others in the name of "science".

Tuskegee Syphilis Experiment: U.S. Public Health Service study of the "natural" course of syphilis that followed 399 low-income African American men from the 1930s to 1972, without providing them with penicillin after it was discovered to be effective in treating the illness. The study was stopped after it was exposed in 1972, resulting in an out-of-court settlement and then, in 1997, an official public apology by President Bill Clinton.

Belmont Report: A 1979 National Commission for the Protection of Human Subjects of Biomedical and Behavioral Research report that established three basic ethical principles for the protection of human subjects, including respect for persons, beneficence, and justice.

Respect for persons: Treating persons as autonomous agents and protecting those with diminished autonomy.

Beneficence: Minimizing possible harms and maximizing benefits.

Justice (in research): Distributing benefits and risks of research fairly.

The formal procedures for the protection of participants in research we have today grew out of some widely publicized abuses. One defining event occurred in 1946, when the **Nuremberg War Crime Trials** exposed horrific medical experiments conducted by Nazi doctors and others in the name of "science." Almost 20 years later, Milgram's research on obedience also generated controversy about participant protections (Perry 2013). As late as 1972, Americans learned from news reports that researchers funded by the U.S. Public Health Service had followed 399 low-income African American men since the 1930s, collecting data to study the "natural" course of syphilis (Exhibit 3.3) (http://www.tuskegee.edu/about_us/centers_of_excellence/bioethics_center/about_the_usphs_syphilis_study.aspx). At the time the study began, there was no effective treatment for the disease, but the men were told they were being treated for "bad blood," whether they had syphilis or not. Participants received free medical exams, meals, and burial insurance but were not asked for their consent to be studied. What made this research study, known as the **Tuskegee Syphilis Experiment**, so shocking was that many participants were not informed of their illness and, even after penicillin was recognized as an effective treatment in 1945 and in large-scale use by 1947, the study participants were not treated. The research was ended only after the study was exposed. In 1973, congressional hearings began, and in 1974, an out-of-court settlement of $10 million was reached; it was not until 1997 that President Bill Clinton made an official apology (CDC 2009).

Of course, the United States is not the only country to have abused human subjects. For example, British military scientists exposed hundreds of Indian soldiers serving under the command of the British military to mustard gas during World War II to determine the how much gas was needed to produce death (Evans 2007).

These and other widely publicized abuses made it clear that formal review procedures were needed to protect research participants. The U.S. government created a National Commission for the Protection of Human Subjects of Biomedical and Behavioral Research and charged it with developing guidelines (Kitchener and Kitchener 2009). The commission's 1979 **Belmont Report** (from the U.S. Department of Health, Education, and Welfare) established three basic ethical principles for the protection of human subjects (Exhibit 3.4):

- **Respect for persons**: treating persons as autonomous agents and protecting those with diminished autonomy;
- **Beneficence**: minimizing possible harms and maximizing benefits; and
- **Justice**: distributing benefits and risks of research fairly.

Exhibit 3.3	Tuskegee Syphilis Experiment

Source: Tuskegee Syphilis Study Administrative Records. Records of the Centers for Disease Control and Prevention. National Archives—Southeast Region (Atlanta).

The Department of Health and Human Services and the Food and Drug Administration then translated these principles into specific regulations that were adopted in 1991 as the **Federal Policy for the Protection of Human Subjects**. This policy has shaped the course of social science research ever since, and you will have to take it into account as you design your own research investigations. Professional associations such as the Academy of Criminal Justice Sciences, university review boards, and ethics committees in other organizations also set standards for the treatment of human subjects by their members, employees, and students, although these standards are all designed to comply with the federal policy. This section introduces these regulations.

Federal regulations require that every institution that seeks federal funding for biomedical or behavioral research on human subjects have an **institutional review board** (IRB) that reviews research proposals. Other countries have similar entities, such as the United Kingdom's research ethics committees (RECs) (Calvey 2014). IRBs at universities and other agencies apply ethical standards that are set by federal regulations but can be expanded or specified by the IRB itself (Sieber 1992). To promote adequate review of ethical issues, the regulations require that IRBs include members with diverse backgrounds. The **Office for Protection From Research Risks in the National Institutes of Health** monitors IRBs, with the exception of research involving drugs (which is the responsibility of the federal Food and Drug Administration).

Federal Policy for the Protection of Human Subjects: Federal regulations established in 1991 that are based on the principles of the Belmont Report.

Institutional review board (IRB): Committee in all research organizations, including universities, that reviews research proposals to ensure the protection of human subjects.

Office for Protection From Research Risks in the National Institutes of Health : The organization within the federal government that monitors all IRBs, ensuring federal standards are followed.

Exhibit 3.4 **Belmont Report Principles**

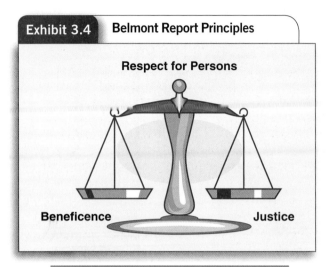

Respect for Persons

Beneficence   Justice

Academy of Criminal Justice Sciences (ACJS) Code of Ethics: The Code of Ethics of ACJS sets forth (1) General Principles and (2) Ethical Standards that underlie academy members' professional responsibilities and conduct, along with (3) the Policies and Procedures for enforcing those principles and standards. Membership in the Academy of Criminal Justice Sciences commits individual members to adhere to the ACJS Code of Ethics in determining ethical behavior in the context of their everyday professional activities..

The Academy of Criminal Justice Sciences (ACJS) and the American Society of Criminology (ASC), like most professional social science organizations, have adopted ethical guidelines for practicing criminologists that are more specific than the federal regulations. The **ACJS Code of Ethics** also establishes procedures for investigating and resolving complaints concerning the ethical conduct of the organization's members. The Code of Ethics of the ACJS (2000) is available on the ACJS website (www.acjs.org). The ASC follows the American Sociological Association's (ASA 1999) code of ethics, which is summarized on the ASA website(http://www .asanet.org/about/ethics.cfm).

🔲 Ethical Principles

Achieving Valid Results

Commitment to achieving valid results is the necessary starting point for ethical research practice. Simply put, we have no business asking people to answer questions, submit to observations, or participate in experimental procedures if we are simply seeking to verify our preexisting prejudices or convince others to take action on behalf of our personal interests. It is the pursuit of objective knowledge about human behavior—the goal of validity— that motivates and justifies our investigations and gives us some claim to the right to influence others to participate in our research. Knowledge is the foundation of human progress as well as the basis for our expectation that we, as social scientists, can help people achieve a brighter future. If we approach our research projects objectively, setting aside our personal predilections in the service of learning a bit more about human behavior, we can honestly represent our actions as potentially contributing to the advancement of knowledge.

The details in Zimbardo's articles and his recent book (2007) on the prison experiment make a compelling case for his commitment to achieving valid results—to learning how and why a prison-like situation influences behavior. In Zimbardo's (2009) own words,

> Social-psychological studies were showing that human nature was more pliable than previously imagined and more responsive to situational pressures than we cared to acknowledge. . . . Missing from the body of social-science research at the time was the direct confrontation . . . of good people pitted against the forces inherent in bad situations. . . . I decided that what was needed was to create a situation in a controlled experimental setting in which we could array on one side a host of variables, such as . . . coercive rules, power differentials, anonymity. . . . On the other side, we lined up a collection of the "best and brightest" of young college men . . . I wanted to know who wins—good people or an evil situation—when they were brought into direct confrontation.

Zimbardo (Haney et al. 1973) devised his experiment so the situation would seem realistic to the participants and still allow careful measurement of important variables and observation of behavior at all times. Questionnaires and rating scales, interviews with participants as the research proceeded and after it was over, ongoing video and audio recording, and logs maintained by the guards all ensured that very little would escape the researcher's gaze.

Zimbardo's (Haney et al. 1973) attention to validity is also apparent in his design of the physical conditions and organizational procedures for the experiment. The "prison" was constructed in a basement without any windows so that participants would not have a sense of where they were. Their isolation was reinforced by the practice of placing

Research in the News

SYPHILIS EXPERIMENTS IN GUATEMALA

Between 1946 and 1948, the United States experimented with over 1,000 residents of Guatemala to determine the efficacy of drugs like penicillin to treat and prevent syphilis, gonorrhea, and chancres. Unfortunately, the study not only treated infected individuals, but to increase their sample size, the researchers actually infected some individuals. In 2010, these victims sued the U.S. government over the experiment, but a U.S. district judge dismissed the lawsuit. The United States has apologized for the experiment, and President Obama has asked the Presidential Commission for the Study of Bioethical Issues to look into details of the research and to assure him that current rules protect people from unethical treatment.

For Further Thought

1. What current ethical standards and protections prevent this from happening today?

Source: Castillo, Mariana. 2012. "Guatemalans to File Appeal Over STD Experiments." CNN, Friday, June 15. http://www.cnn.com/2012/06/15/us/guatemala-std-experiments/index.html.

paper bags over their heads when they went with a guard to use the bathroom, which was in a corridor apart from the prison area. Meals were bland, and conditions were generally demeaning. This was a very different "situation" for the participants; it was no college dorm experience.

However, not all social scientists agree that Zimbardo's approach achieved valid results. British psychologists Stephen Reicher and S. Alexander Haslam (2006) argue that guard behavior was not so consistent and that it was determined by the instructions Zimbardo gave the guards at the start of the experiment, rather than by becoming a guard in itself. For example, in another experiment, when guards were trained to respect prisoners, their behavior was less extreme (Lovibond, Mithiran, and Adams 1979).

In response to such criticism, Zimbardo (2007) has pointed to several replications of his basic experiment that support his conclusions—as well as to the evidence of patterns of abuse in the real world of prisons, including the behavior of guards who tormented prisoners at Abu Ghraib.

Do you agree with Zimbardo's assumption that the effects of being a prisoner or guard could fruitfully be studied in a mock prison, with "pretend" prisoners? Do you find merit in the criticisms? Will your evaluation of the ethics of Zimbardo's experiment be influenced by your answers to these questions? Should our ethical judgments differ when we are confident a study's results provide valid information about important social processes?

We can't answer these questions for you, but before you dismiss them as inappropriate when we are dealing with ethical standards for the treatment of human subjects, bear in mind that both Zimbardo and his critics buttress their ethical arguments with assertions about the validity (or invalidity) of the experimental results. It is hard to justify *any* risk for human subjects, or *any* expenditure of time and resources, if our findings tell us nothing about the reality of crime and punishment.

Honesty and Openness

The scientific concern with validity requires in turn that scientists be open in disclosing their methods and honest in presenting their findings. In contrast, research distorted by political or personal pressures to find particular outcomes or to achieve the most marketable results is unlikely to be carried out in an honest and open fashion. To assess the validity of a researcher's conclusions and the ethics of his or her procedures, you need to know exactly how the research was conducted. This means that articles or other reports must include a detailed methodology section, perhaps supplemented by appendices containing the research instruments or websites or an address where more information can be obtained.

CAREERS AND RESEARCH

Kristen Kenny, Research Compliance Specialist

Kristen Kenny comes from a long line of musicians and artists and was the first in her family to graduate from college. Kenny majored in filmmaking and performance art at the Massachusetts College of Art and soon started working on small films and in theater doing everything from set design, hair, and makeup to costume design and acting. The arts have their fair share of interesting characters; this was the beginning of Kenny's training in dealing with a variety of difficult personalities and learning how to listen and how to react.

Source: Kristen Kenny

After years of working a variety of jobs in the entertainment field, Kenny found herself working as a receptionist in the music industry, a hotbed of difficult personalities, contracts, and negotiations. Within a year, Kenny had been promoted to assistant talent buyer for small clubs and festivals in the Boston area. This job helped Kenny develop the skill of reading dense contract documents and being able to identify what contractual clause language stays and what is deleted. Eventually the music industry started to wane and Kenny was laid off, but a friend at a local hospital who was in dire need of someone who could interpret volumes of documents and deal with bold personalities asked her to apply for a job as their IRB administrator. Kenny had no idea what an IRB was, but she attended trainings and conferences to learn the IRB trade. Three years later, Kenny was asked to join the Office of Research and Sponsored Programs at the University of Massachusetts, Boston, as the IRB administrator.

Now, as a research compliance specialist II, Kenny maintains the IRB and other regulatory units and has developed a training curriculum and program for the Office of Research and Sponsored Programs. And if you look hard enough you can find her clothing and fabric designs on eBay, Etsy, and her own website.

Philip Zimbardo's research reports seemed to present an honest and open account of his methods. His initial article (Haney et al. 1973) included a detailed description of study procedures, including the physical aspects of the prison, the instructions to participants, the uniforms used, the induction procedure, and the specific data collection methods and measures. Many more details, including forms and pictures, are available on Zimbardo's website (www.prisonexperiment.org) and in his recent book (Zimbardo 2007).

The act of publication itself is a vital element in maintaining openness and honesty. Others can review and question study procedures and so generate an open dialogue with the researcher. Although Zimbardo disagreed sharply with his critics about many aspects of his experiment, their mutual commitment to public discourse in widely available publications resulted in a more comprehensive presentation of study procedures and a more thoughtful discourse about research ethics (Savin 1973; Zimbardo 1973). Almost 40 years later, this commentary continues to inform debates about research ethics (Reicher and Haslam 2006; Zimbardo 2007).

Openness about research procedures and results goes hand in hand with honesty in research design. Openness is also essential if researchers are to learn from the work of others. In spite of this need for openness, some researchers may hesitate to disclose their procedures or results to prevent others from building on their ideas and taking some of the credit. You might have heard of the long legal battle between a U.S. researcher, Dr. Robert Gallo, and a French researcher, Dr. Luc Montagnier, about how credit for discovering the AIDS virus should be allocated. Although a public dispute such as this one is unusual—even more unusual than its resolution through an agreement announced by then-president Ronald Reagan and then–prime minister Jacques Chirac (Altman 1987)—concerns with priority of discovery are common. Scientists are like other people in their desire to be first. Enforcing standards of honesty and encouraging openness about research are the best solutions to these problems (as exemplified by the chronology of discovery that Gallo and Montagnier jointly developed as part of the agreement).

Protecting Research Participants

The ACJS code's standards concerning the treatment of human subjects include federal regulations and ethical guidelines emphasized by most professional social science organizations:

- Research should expose participants to no more than minimal risk of personal harm. (#16)

- Researchers should fully disclose the purposes of their research. (#13)

- Participation in research should be voluntary, and therefore subjects must give their informed consent to participate in the research. (#16)

- Confidentiality must be maintained for individual research participants unless it is voluntarily and explicitly waived. (#14, #18, #19)

Philip Zimbardo (2007) himself decided that his Stanford Prison Experiment was unethical because it violated the first two of these principles. Participants "did suffer considerable anguish . . . and [the experiment] resulted in such extreme stress and emotional turmoil that five of the sample of initially healthy young prisoners had to be released early" (pp. 233–34). The researchers did not disclose in advance the nature of the arrest or booking procedures at police headquarters, nor did they disclose to parents how bad the situation had become when the parents came to a visiting night. Nonetheless, Zimbardo (Zimbardo et al. 1973; Zimbardo 2007) argued that there was no long-lasting harm to participants and that there were some long-term social benefits from this research. In particular, debriefing participants—discussing their experiences and revealing the logic behind the experiment—and follow-up interviews enabled the participants to recover from the experience without lasting harm. Also, the experience led several participants in the experiment, including Zimbardo, to dedicate their careers to investigating and improving prison conditions. As a result, publicity about the experiment has also helped focus attention on problems in prison management.

Do you agree with Zimbardo's conclusion that his experiment was not ethical? Do you think it should have been prevented from being conducted in the first place? Are you relieved to learn that current standards in the United States for the protection of human subjects in research would not allow his experiment to be conducted?

In contrast to Zimbardo, Stanley Milgram (1963) believed that his experiments on obedience to authority were ethical, so debate about this has been long-lasting. His experiments on obedience to authority raise most of the relevant issues we want to highlight here.

Milgram had recruited community members to participate in his experiment at Yale University. His research was stimulated by the success of Germany's Nazi regime of the 1930s and 1940s in enlisting the participation of ordinary citizens in unconscionable acts of terror and genocide. Milgram set out to identify through laboratory experiments the conditions under which ordinary citizens will be obedient to authority figures' instructions to inflict pain on others. He operationalized this obedience by asking subjects to deliver electric shocks (fake, of course) to "students" supposedly learning a memory task; the students were actually members of the research team who had been trained to play specific roles. The experimental procedure had four simple steps: (1) The research subject read a series of word pairs aloud to the student, pairs such as *blue box, nice day, wild duck,* and so on. (2) The subject then read aloud one of the first words from those pairs, along with a set of four words, one of which was the original second word paired with the first. For example, "blue: sky ink box lamp" might be read. (3) The "student" was directed to state the word that he thought was paired with the first word the research subject had read ("blue"). If he gave a correct response, he was complimented and the game continued. If he made a mistake, a switch was flipped on the console. The research subject assumed that this caused the student to feel a shock on his wrist. (4) After each mistake, the next switch was flipped on a console, progressing from left to right. There was a label corresponding to every fifth switch on the console, with the first mark labeled *slight shock,* the fifth mark labeled *moderate shock,* the tenth *strong shock,* and so on through *very strong shock, intense shock, extreme intensity shock,* and *danger: severe shock.* Subjects were told to increase the shocks over time, and many did so, even after the supposed "students," behind a partition, began to cry out in (simulated)

| Exhibit 3.5 | **Diagram of Milgram Experiment** |

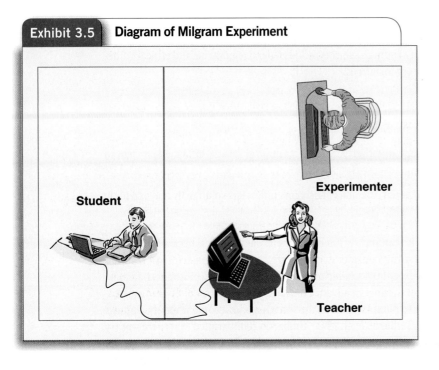

pain (Exhibit 3.5). The participants became very tense, and some resisted as the shocks increased to the (supposedly) lethal range, but many still complied with the authority in that situation and increased the shocks. Like Zimbardo, Milgram debriefed participants afterward and followed up later to check on their well-being. It seemed that none had suffered long-term harm.

As we discuss how the ACJS Code of Ethics standards apply to Milgram's experiments, you will begin to realize that there is no simple answer to the question "What *is* (or *isn't*) ethical research practice?" The issues are just too complicated and the relevant principles too subject to different interpretations. But we do promise that by the time you finish this chapter, you will be aware of the major issues in research ethics and be able to make informed, defensible decisions about the ethical conduct of social science research.

Avoid Harming Research Participants

Although this standard may seem straightforward, it can be difficult to interpret in specific cases and harder yet to define in a way that is agreeable to all social scientists. Does it mean that subjects should not at all be harmed psychologically or physically? That they should feel no anxiety or distress whatsoever during the study or even after their involvement ends? Should the possibility of any harm, no matter how remote, deter research?

Before we address these questions with respect to Milgram's experiments, consider this verbatim transcript of one Milgram's sessions, which will give you an idea of what participants experienced (Milgram 1965):

150 volts delivered.   You want me to keep going?

165 volts delivered.   That guy is hollering in there. There's a lot of them here. He's liable to have a heart condition. You want me to go on?

180 volts delivered.   He can't stand it! I'm not going to kill that man in there! You hear him hollering? He's hollering. He can't stand it. . . . I mean who is going to take responsibility if anything happens to that gentleman?

                         [The experimenter accepts responsibility.] All right.

195 volts delivered.   You see he's hollering. Hear that. Gee, I don't know. [The experimenter says: "The experiment requires that you go on."] I know it does, sir, but I mean—Hugh—he don't know what he's in for. He's up to 195 volts.

210 volts delivered.

225 volts delivered.

240 volts delivered. (p. 67)

This experimental manipulation generated "extraordinary tension" (Milgram 1963):

Subjects were observed to sweat, tremble, stutter, bite their lips, groan and dig their fingernails into their flesh. . . . Full-blown, uncontrollable seizures were observed for 3 subjects. [O]ne . . . seizure [was] so violently convulsive that it was necessary to call a halt to the experiment [for that individual]. (p. 375)

An observer (behind a one-way mirror) reported (Milgram 1963), "I observed a mature and initially poised businessman enter the laboratory smiling and confident. Within 20 minutes he was reduced to a twitching, stuttering wreck, who was rapidly approaching a point of nervous collapse" (p. 377).

Psychologist Diana Baumrind (1964) disagreed sharply with Milgram's approach, concluding that the emotional disturbance subjects experienced was "potentially harmful because it could easily affect an alteration in the subject's self-image or ability to trust adult authorities in the future" (p. 422). Stanley Milgram (1964) quickly countered,

As the experiment progressed there was no indication of injurious effects in the subjects; and as the subjects themselves strongly endorsed the experiment, the judgment I made was to continue the experiment. (p. 849)

When Milgram (1964) surveyed the subjects in a follow-up study, 83.7% endorsed the statement that they were "very glad" or "glad" "to have been in the experiment," 15.1% were "neither sorry nor glad," and just 1.3% were "sorry" or "very sorry" to have participated (p. 849). Interviews by a psychiatrist a year later found no evidence "of any traumatic reactions" (p. 197). Subsequently, Milgram (1974) argued that "the central moral justification for allowing my experiment is that it was judged acceptable by those who took part in it" (p. 21).

Milgram (1964) also attempted to minimize harm to subjects with postexperimental procedures "to assure that the subject would leave the laboratory in a state of well being" (p. 374). A friendly reconciliation was arranged between the subject and the victim, and an effort was made to reduce any tensions that arose as a result of the experiment.

In some cases, the "dehoaxing" (or "debriefing") discussion was extensive, and all subjects were promised (and later received) a comprehensive report (Milgram 1964).

In a later article, Baumrind (1985) dismissed the value of the self-reported "lack of harm" of subjects who had been willing to participate in the experiment—and noted that 16% did *not* endorse the statement that they were "glad" they had participated in the experiment (p. 168). Baumrind (1985) also argued that research indicates most students who have participated in a deception experiment report a decreased trust in authorities as a result—a tangible harm in itself.

Many social scientists, ethicists, and others concluded that Milgram's procedures had not harmed the subjects and so were justified for the knowledge they produced, but others sided with Baumrind's criticisms (Miller 1986). What is your opinion at this point? Does Milgram's debriefing process relieve your concerns? Are you as persuaded by the subjects' own endorsement of the procedures as was Milgram?

Would you ban such experiments because of the potential for harm to subjects? Does the fact that Zimbardo's and Milgram's experiments seemed to yield significant insights into the effect of a social situation on human behavior—insights that could be used to improve prisons or perhaps lessen the likelihood of another holocaust—make any difference (Reynolds 1979)? Do you believe that this benefit outweighs the foreseeable risks?

Obtain Informed Consent

The requirement of informed consent is also more difficult to define than it first appears. To be informed, consent must be given by the persons who are competent to consent, have consented voluntarily, are fully informed about the research, and have comprehended what they have been told (Reynolds 1979). Yet well-intentioned researchers may not foresee all the potential problems and so may not point them out in advance to potential participants (Baumrind 1985). Milgram (1974) reported that he and his colleagues were surprised by the subjects' willingness to carry out such severe shocks. In Zimbardo's prison simulation study, all the participants signed consent forms, but they were not "fully informed" in advance about potential risks. The researchers themselves did not realize that the study participants would experience so much stress so quickly, that some prisoners would have to be released for severe negative reactions within the first few days, or that even those who were not severely stressed would soon be begging to be released from the mock prison. But on the other hand, are you concerned that real harm "could result from *not doing* research on destructive obedience" and other troubling human behavior (Miller 1986, 138)?

Obtaining informed consent creates additional challenges for researchers. The researcher's actions and body language should help convey his verbal assurance that consent is voluntary. The language of the consent form must be clear and understandable to the research participants yet sufficiently long and detailed to explain what will actually happen in the research. Examples A (Exhibit 3.6) and B (Exhibit 3.7) illustrate two different approaches to these trade-offs.

Exhibit 3.6 | **Consent Form A**

INFORMED CONSENT

ROADS DIVERGE: LONG-TERM PATTERNS OF RELAPSE, RECIDIVISM AND DESISTANCE FOR A RE-ENTRY COHORT (National Institute of Justice, 2008-IJ-CX-0017)

PURPOSE: You are one of approximately 300 people being asked to participate in a research project conducted by the Center for Drug and Alcohol Studies at the University of Delaware. You were part of the original study of offenders in Delaware leaving prison in the 1990s, and we want to find out how things in your life have changed since that time. The overall purpose of this research is to help us understand what factors lead to changes in criminal activity and drug use over time.

PROCEDURES: If you agree to take part in this study, you will be asked to complete a survey, which will last approximately 60 to 90 minutes. We will ask you to provide us with some contact information so that we can locate you again if we are able to do another follow up study in the future. You will be asked about your employment, family history, criminal involvement, health history, drug use, and how these have changed over time. We will use this information, as well as information that you have previously provided or which is publicly available. We will not ask you for the names of anyone, or the specific dates or specific places of any of your activities. The interviews will be tape-recorded, but you will not be identified by name on the tape. The tapes will be stored in a locked cabinet until they can be transcribed to an electronic word processor. After the tapes have been transcribed and checked for accuracy they will be destroyed. Anonymous transcribed data will be kept indefinitely – no audio data will be kept.

RISKS: There are some risks to participating in this study. You may experience distress or discomfort when asked questions about your drug use, criminal history, and other experiences. Should this occur, you may choose not to answer such questions. If emotional distress occurs, our staff will make referrals to services you may need, including counseling, and drug abuse treatment and support services.

The risk that confidentiality could be broken is a concern, but it is very unlikely to occur. You will not be identified on the audiotape of the interview. We request that you not mention names of other people or places, but if this happens, those names will be deleted from the audiotape prior to transcription. All study materials are kept in locked file cabinets. Only three members of [the] research team will have access to study materials.

BENEFITS: You will have the opportunity to participate in an important research project, which may lead to the better understanding of what factors both help and prevent an individual's recovery from drug use and criminal activity.

COMPENSATION: You will receive $100 to compensate you for your time and travel costs for this interview.

CONFIDENTIALITY: Your records will be kept confidential. They will be kept under lock and key and will not be shared with anyone without your written permission. Your name will not appear on any data file or research report.

A Privacy Certificate has been approved by the U.S. Department of Justice. The data will be protected from being revealed to non-research interests by court subpoena in any federal, state, or local civil, criminal, administrative, legislative or other proceedings.

You should understand that a Privacy Certificate does not prevent you or a member of your family from voluntarily releasing information about yourself or your involvement in this research. If you give anyone written consent to receive research information, then we may not use the Certificate to withhold that information.

The Privacy Certificate does not prevent research staff from voluntary disclosures to authorities if we learn that you intend to harm yourself or someone else. These incidents would be reported as required by state and federal law. However, we will not ask you questions about these areas.

Because this research is paid for by the National Institute of Justice, staff of this research office may review copies of your records, but they also are required to keep that information confidential.

RIGHT TO QUIT THE STUDY: Participation in this research project is voluntary and you have the right to leave the study at any time. The researchers and their assistants have the right to remove you from this study if needed.

You may ask and will receive answers to any questions concerning this study. If you have any questions about this study, you may contact Ronet Bachman or Daniel O'Connell at (302) 831-6107. If you have any questions about your rights as a research participant you may contact the Chairperson of the University of Delaware's Human Subjects Review Board at (302) 831-2136.

CONSENT TO BE INTERVIEWED

I have read and understand this form (or it has been read to me), and I agree to participate in the in-depth interview portion of this research project.

_____
PARTICIPANT SIGNATURE   DATE

_____
SIGNATURE OF WITNESS/INTERVIEWER   DATE

CONSENT TO BE CONTACTED IN FUTURE

I have read and understand this form (or it has been read to me), and I agree to be recontacted in the future as part of this research project.

_____
PARTICIPANT SIGNATURE   DATE

_____
SIGNATURE OF WITNESS/INTERVIEWER   DATE

Ronet Bachman, PhD
Principal Investigator
University of Delaware
Telephone: (302) 831-6107

Consent form A was approved by the University of Delaware IRB for in-depth interviews with former inmates about their experiences after release from prison.

Consent form B is the one used by Philip Zimbardo. It is brief and to the point, leaving out many of the details that current standards for the protection of human subjects require. Zimbardo's consent form also released the researchers from any liability for problems arising out of the research. (Such a statement is no longer allowed.)

As in Milgram's (1963) study, experimental researchers whose research design requires some type of subject deception try to minimize disclosure of experimental details by withholding some information before the experiment begins but then **debriefing** subjects at the end. In the debriefing, the researcher explains to the subjects what happened in the experiment and why and responds to their questions. A carefully designed debriefing procedure can help the research participants learn from the experimental research and grapple constructively with feelings elicited by the realization that they were deceived (Sieber 1992). However, even though debriefing can be viewed as a substitute, in some cases, for securing fully informed consent prior to the experiment, debriefed subjects who disclose the nature of the experiment to other participants can contaminate subsequent

Debriefing: A researcher's informing subjects after an experiment about the experiment's purposes and methods and evaluating subjects' personal reactions to the experiment.

Exhibit 3.7 | **Consent Form B**

CONSENT

Prison Life Study

Dr. Zimbardo

August 1971

_____

(date) (name of volunteer)

I, _____, the undersigned, hereby consent to participate as a volunteer in a prison life study research project to be conducted by the Stanford University Psychology Department.

The nature of the research project has been fully explained to me, including, without limitation, the fact that paid volunteers will be randomly assigned to the roles of either "prisoners" or "guards" for the duration of the study. I understand that participation in the research project will involve a loss of privacy, that I will be expected to participate for the full duration of the study, that I will only be released from participation for reasons of health deemed adequate by the medical advisers to the research project or for other reasons deemed appropriate by Dr. Philip Zimbardo, Principal Investigator of the project, and that I will be expected to follow directions from staff members of the project or from other participants in the research project.

I am submitting myself for participation in this research project with full knowledge and understanding of the nature of the research project and of what will be expected of me. I specifically release the Principal Investigator and the staff members of the research project, Stanford University, its agents and employees, and the Federal Government, its agents and employees, from any liability to me arising in any way out of my participation in the project.

_____

(signature of volunteer)

Witness: _____

If volunteer is a minor:

_____

(signature of person authorized to consent for volunteer)

Witness: _____

_____

(relationship to volunteer)

---

results (Adair, Dushenko, and Lindsay 1985). Apparently for this reason, Milgram provided little information in his "debriefing" to participants in most of his experiments. It was only in the last two months of his study that he began to provide more information, while still asking participants not to reveal the true nature of the experimental procedures until after the study was completely over (Perry 2013). Unfortunately, if the debriefing process is delayed, the ability to lessen any harm resulting from the deception is also reduced.

If you were to serve on your university's IRB, would you allow this research to be conducted? Can students who are asked to participate in research by their professor be considered able to give informed consent? Do you consider informed consent to be meaningful if the true purpose or nature of an experimental manipulation is not revealed?

The process and even possibility of obtaining informed consent must take into account the capacity of prospective participants to give informed consent. Children cannot legally give consent to participate in research; instead, they must in most circumstances be given the opportunity to give or withhold their *assent* to participate in research, usually by a verbal response to an explanation of the research. In addition, a child's legal guardian must give written, informed consent to have the child participate in research (Sieber 1992). There are also special protections for other populations that are likely to be vulnerable to coercion—prisoners, pregnant women, mentally disabled persons, and educationally or economically disadvantaged persons. Would you allow research on prisoners, whose ability to give informed consent can be questioned? What special protections do you think would be appropriate?

Avoid Deception in Research, Except in Limited Circumstances

Deception occurs when subjects are misled about research procedures to determine how they would react to the treatment if they were not research subjects. Deception is a critical component of many social psychology experiments, in part because of the difficulty of simulating real-world stresses and dilemmas in a laboratory setting. The goal is to get subjects "to accept as true what is false or to give a false impression" (Korn 1997, 4). In Milgram's (1963) experiment, for example, deception seemed necessary because the subjects could not be permitted to administer real electric shocks to the "student," yet it would not have made sense to order the subjects to do something that they didn't find to be so troubling. Milgram (1992) insisted that the deception was absolutely essential. The results of many other social psychological experiments would be worthless if subjects understood what was really happening to them while the experiment was in progress. The real question: Is this sufficient justification to allow the use of deception?

> **Deception:** Used in social experiments to create more "realistic" treatments in which the true purpose of the research is not disclosed to participants, often within the confines of a laboratory.

Gary Marshall and Philip Zimbardo (1979) sought to determine the physiological basis of emotion by injecting student volunteers with adrenaline so that their heart rate and sweating would increase and then placing them in a room with a student "stooge" who acted silly. But the students were told that they were being injected with a vitamin supplement to test its effect on visual acuity (Korn 1997). Piliavin and Piliavin (1972) staged fake seizures on subway trains to study helpfulness (Korn 1997). Would you vote to allow such deceptive practices in research if you were a member of your university's IRB? What about less dramatic instances of deception in laboratory experiments with students like yourself? Do you react differently to the debriefing by Milgram compared to that by Zimbardo?

What scientific or educational or applied "value" would make deception justifiable, even if there is some potential for harm? Who determines whether a nondeceptive intervention is "equally effective" (Miller 1986, 103)? Diana Baumrind (1985) suggested that personal "introspection" would have been sufficient to test Milgram's hypothesis and has argued subsequently that intentional deception in research violates the ethical principles of self-determination, protection of others, and maintenance of trust between people and so can never be justified. How much risk, discomfort, or unpleasantness might be seen as affecting willingness to participate? When should a postexperimental "attempt to correct any misconception" due to deception be deemed sufficient?

Maintain Privacy and Confidentiality

Maintaining privacy and confidentiality is another key ethical standard for protecting research participants, and the researcher's commitment to that standard should be included in the informed consent agreement (Sieber 1992). Procedures to protect each subject's privacy, such as locking records and creating special identifying codes, must be created to minimize the risk of access by unauthorized persons. However, statements about confidentiality should be realistic: Laws allow research records to be subpoenaed and may require reporting child abuse; a researcher may feel compelled to release information if a health- or life-threatening situation arises and participants need to be alerted. Also, the standard of confidentiality does not apply to observation in public places and information available in public records.

> **Privacy Certificate:** NIJ document that protects researchers from being legally required to disclose confidential information.

There are two exceptions to some of these constraints: The National Institute of Justice can issue a **Privacy Certificate**, and the National Institutes of Health can issue a **Certificate of Confidentiality**. Both of these documents protect researchers from being legally required to disclose confidential information. Researchers who are focusing on high-risk populations or behaviors, such as crime, substance abuse, sexual activity, or genetic information, can request such

> **Certificate of Confidentiality:** NIH document that protects researchers from being legally required to disclose confidential information.

Social scientists who conduct research on behalf of specific organizations may face additional difficulties when the organization, instead of the researcher, controls the final report and the publicity it receives. If organizational leaders decide that particular research results are unwelcome, the researcher's desire to have findings used appropriately and reported fully can conflict with contractual obligations. Researchers can often anticipate such dilemmas in advance and resolve them when the contract for research is negotiated—or simply decline a particular research opportunity altogether. But often, such problems come up only after a report has been drafted, or the problems are ignored by a researcher who needs to have a job or needs to maintain particular personal relationships. These possibilities cannot be avoided entirely, but because of them, it is always important to acknowledge the source of research funding in reports and to consider carefully the sources of funding for research reports written by others.

The potential of withholding a beneficial treatment from some subjects also is a cause for ethical concern. The Sherman and Berk (1984) experiment required the random assignment of subjects to treatment conditions and thus had the potential of causing harm to the victims of domestic violence whose batterers were not arrested. The justification for the study design, however, is quite persuasive: The researchers didn't know prior to the experiment which response to a domestic violence complaint would be most likely to deter future incidents (Sherman 1992). The experiment provided clear evidence about the value of arrest, so it can be argued that the benefits outweighed the risks.

🔲 Research Involving Special Populations: Children and Prisoners

As you might imagine, there are special protections for certain segments of the population, including children and individuals under some form of correctional supervision. Regardless of the study being conducted, research relying on either children or prisoners usually requires a full review by an institutional IRB.

Research With Children: By regulatory definition, persons under 18 years old are considered to be children, and, as such, they have not attained the legal age for consent to treatments and procedures involved in research. Generally, IRBs analyze the same considerations for children as they would for other research participants, including whether the research benefits gained are worth the risks involved. The issue of "informed consent," however, must be handled differently, as children cannot legally provide their own consent to participate in a study. To conduct research on children, "active" parental consent usually is required before the child can be approached directly about the research. In active consent, parents or guardians of a child being asked to participate in a study must sign a consent form. As you might imagine, adding this

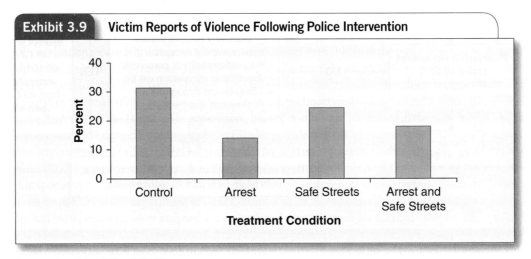

Exhibit 3.9 **Victim Reports of Violence Following Police Intervention**

Source: Adapted from Miller 2003:704.

requirement to a research project can dramatically reduce participation, because many parents simply do not bother to respond to mailed consent forms. For example, Sloboda and colleagues (2009) used an active consent procedure for gaining parental consent along with student assent: Parents and students both had to sign forms before the student could participate. The result was that only 58% of the 34,000 eligible seventh-grade students were enrolled in the study.

When Tricia Leakey and her colleagues (2004) were conducting research on a smoking prevention effort for middle school students, they were creative in getting parental consent forms returned. When the project began in the seventh grade, the researchers gave students project information and a consent card to take home to their parents. A pizza party was then held in every class where at least 90% of the students returned a signed consent card. In subsequent follow-ups in the eighth grade, a reminder letter was sent to parents whose children had previously participated. Classes with high participation rates also received a candy thank you. As Exhibit 3.10 shows, the result was a very high rate of participation.

IRBs sometimes allow the use of a "passive consent" procedure—students can participate as long as their parents do not return a form indicating their lack of consent—and this can result in much higher rates of participation. In fact, based on Article 12 of the 1989 United Nations Convention on the Rights of the Child (UNCROC), which acknowledged that children are people who have a right to be heard, there has been an increased push for children to have their voices heard in research. Janis Carroll-Lind, James Chapman, and Juliana Raskauskas in New Zealand (2011) attempted just that when they surveyed children aged 9 to 13 years about their experiences with violence. They utilized a passive consent procedure that facilitated the right of children to report on their experiences of violence. To defend their use of this method, they stated,

> The Ethics Committee carefully weighed and gave credence to the issue of children's rights to protection and acknowledged and confirmed Article 12 of the UNCROC that grants children the right to speak on matters that concern them. Active consent could have compromised both of these rights. The view was held that protecting the rights of children was more important than parental rights to privacy regarding abuse in the home. (p. 7)

Research With Prisoners: Because individuals under the supervision of a correctional system are under constraints that could affect their ability to voluntarily consent to participate in research, there are also special

Exhibit 3.10	**Parental Consent Response Rates and Outcomes**					

Survey	Population Size[a]	Consent to Parents[b]	Consent Returned[c]	Refused Consent[d]	Consent to Participate	Student Assent "Yes"[e]
Seventh-grade baseline[f]	4,741	4,728	89.5% (*n* = 4,231)	7.3% (*n* = 310)	92.7% (*n* = 3,921)	99.4% (*n* = 3,716)
Eighth-grade baseline[g]	4,222	421	58.0% (*n* = 244)	11.9% (*n* = 29)	88.1% (*n* = 215)	99.0% (*n* = 3,235)
Eighth-grade follow-up[g]	3,703	177	41.8% (*n* = 74)	5.4% (*n* = 4)	94.6% (*n* = 70)	98.7% (*n* = 2,999)

Source: Leakey, Tricia, Kevin B. Lunde, Karin Koga, and Karen Glanz. 2004. "Written Parental Consent and the Use of Incentives in a Youth Smoking Prevention Trial: A Case Study From Project SPLASH." *American Journal of Evaluation* 25:509–523.

Note: Parents who had refused participation at the previous survey point were again contacted for permission at the next survey point.

[a] Number of students who were enrolled in the program varies over time depending on classroom enrollment and teacher participation rates.

[b] Number of consent forms that were handed out at each time period to new students.

[c] Out of the total number of consent forms distributed.

[d] Out of the total number of consent forms returned.

[e] Out of all students who had parental consent and were present on the day of the survey.

[f] Project staff explained and distributed consent on site.

[g] Teachers explained and distributed consent.

protections for these populations. The U.S. Department of Health and Human Services (DHHS) has imposed strict limits on the involvement of prisoners as research subjects unless the research is material to their lives as prisoners. The term *prisoner* is defined by DHHS (McGough 2015) as follows:

> A prisoner means any individual involuntarily confined or detained in a penal institution. The term is intended to encompass individuals sentenced to such an institution under criminal or civil statue, individuals detained in other facilities by virtue of statues or commitment procedures which provide alternatives to criminal prosecution or incarceration in a penal institution, and individuals detained pending arraignment, trial, or sentencing. (p. 2)

Included are those in hospitals or alcohol and drug treatment facilities under court order. Individuals in work-release programs and in at-home detention programs also qualify as prisoners. The definition applies to minors as well as to adults.

Although regulations restrict participation of prisoners to research that is material to their lives, this actually includes a great deal of research. For example, they can participate in research examining many issues, including but not limited to the following: research on the possible causes, possible effects, and processes of incarceration and of criminal behavior; research on conditions particularly affecting prisoners as a class, such as diseases like hepatitis and substance abuse; and research that has the intent of improving their health and well-being.

Voluntary consent is an important issue with research involving prisoners. IRBs ensure that the decision to take part in research can have no effect on an inmate's future treatment and/or parole decision. The use of incentives for prisoners is also judged differently than the use of incentives for the general population. For example, while a $10 incentive to participate may not seem like a lot to someone not in prison, the maximum wage in many state prisons is only $1 per day, so a $10 incentive is a great deal indeed! In research one of the authors just completed on factors related to desistance from substance abuse and crime, former inmates who were not currently under correctional supervision were given $100 to travel to the research office for a three-hour interview, and those who were still in prison were provided $20 in their prison spending accounts for a comparable interview (Bachman et al. 2013). The IRB in this case deemed that giving current inmates $100 (as former inmates were given) would unduly influence them to participate in the study, since this amount was comparable to five month's pay in prison.

In sum, research involving children or prisoners represents special cases for IRBs to consider when evaluating the benefits and potential harms of a study. Typically, when proposals come before IRBs that involve these special populations, special representatives ensure their rights are protected.

Case Study

Sexual Solicitation of Adolescents and Milgram Revisited

After reading this chapter, you may think that the ethical dilemmas from the past have been remedied by the new regulations and oversights. However, research organizations and IRBs around the world have to make decisions every day about whether the benefits of research outweigh the risks imposed to human subjects. For researchers interested in examining criminal, deviant, or otherwise hidden subcultures, obtaining informed consent is often a dubious enterprise. In addition, the growth of the World Wide Web has provided new frontiers for observing and engaging in online communications in such forums as blogs and online chat rooms. In fact, David Calvey has described the cyber world as "a covert playground, where social researchers typically 'lurk' in order to explore this area" (Calvey 2014, 546). This research has generated renewed debate about informed consent and deception. Of course, some researchers contend that covert research that does not obtain voluntary consent is necessary and justified, because the information would otherwise be closed to research, or because alerting participants that they are being studied would change their behavior or put researchers at risk (Pearson 2009). A few contemporary case studies will illuminate these ethical dilemmas well.

The first research example comes from studies examining chat rooms and pedophilia. Research indicates that sexual or romantic relationships between adults and adolescents sometimes are initiated in Internet chat rooms. In fact, reality television shows like *To Catch a Predator* impersonate underage people to solicit male adults over the Internet. Of course, many police organizations including the FBI utilize such methods, and investigative journalists, like those who developed *To Catch a Predator*, do not have to go through an IRB for permission.

But what about researchers who do? To more fully understand these chat room solicitations, Emilia Bergen and her colleagues (2013) examined how adult male chat room visitors reacted to children and adolescents (they were adults posing as children) in three chat rooms. They wanted to determine whether the age of the child affected whether the adults continued to engage in sexual conversation or pursued a meeting after finding out the ages of the impersonated children. The impersonators pretended to be either 10, 12, 14, 16, or 18 years of age. The researchers hypothesized that the older the impersonated child was, the more likely it was that adult males would express sexual interest and suggest meeting offline. All chat rooms were free and did not require registration, and one had a homosexual orientation while the other two were heterosexual in nature. Results indicated that the adult males were more likely to engage in sexual conversation and that face-to-face meetings were more likely to be suggested for impersonators who were 16 or older. Moreover, almost half of the adult males (46%) stopped the conversation after they learned that the impersonator was 10 or 12. However, quite disturbingly, one in five adult males continued sexual conversations even when impersonators divulged their age to be under 13. This research confirmed previous research findings that sexual predators are more likely to solicit older adolescents; however, it revealed that there is a nontrivial percentage of predators who are not deterred from soliciting children as young as 10 years of age.

Was this knowledge worth the lack of informed consent and deception in the research? Bergen and her colleagues (2013) were aware of the ethical dilemmas but concluded that

> the value of the results from the present study would be higher than the possible harm. . . . Also, it should be noted, that we had no means (nor any interest in) gaining any information that could lead to a positive identification of those engaging in conversation, thus ensuring absolute anonymity in the study. (p. 108)

Do you agree?

You may also be surprised to learn that a few IRBs have allowed both Milgram's obedience experiment and Zimbardo's prison experiment to be replicated with the addition of more human subject protections. For example, Jerry Burger replicated Milgram's experiment with several modifications (Burger 2009). In Burger's experiment, the following protections were implemented: (1) No subject was allowed to go beyond the 150-volt mark, (2) a two-step screening process was used to exclude any individuals who might have a negative reaction to the experience, (3) participants were told at least three times that they could withdraw from the study at any time and still receive their $50 for participation, (4) participants were monitored by a clinical psychologist to identify excessive stress, and (5) participants were told immediately after the experiment that the "learner" had received no shocks. After all of these safeguards were implemented, the IRB at Santa Clara University, where Dr. Burger is a faculty member, approved the project. It is somewhat troubling that results indicated that obedience rates in this 2006 replication were only slightly lower than those Milgram found. In fact, the majority of both men and women continued after the limit of 150 volts was reached. Burger illuminated the importance of his findings by concluding, "Although one must be cautious when making the leap from laboratory studies to complex social behaviors like genocide, understanding the social psychological factors that contribute to people acting in unexpected and unsettling ways is important" (Burger 2009, 10). If you had been serving on an IRB, would you have determined that the benefits of this study outweighed the potential costs?

▣ Conclusion

The extent to which ethical issues are a problem for researchers and their subjects varies dramatically with the type of research design. Survey research, in particular, creates few ethical problems. In fact, researchers from the Survey Research Center at the University of Michigan's Institute for Social Research interviewed a representative national sample of adults and found that 68% of those who had participated in a survey were somewhat or very interested in participating in another; the more times respondents had been interviewed, the more willing they were to participate again. Presumably, they would have felt differently if they had been treated unethically (Reynolds 1979). On the other hand, some experimental studies in the social sciences that have put people in uncomfortable or embarrassing situations have generated vociferous complaints and years of debate about ethics (Reynolds 1979; Sjoberg 1967).

The evaluation of ethical issues in a research project should be based on a realistic assessment of the overall potential for harm and benefit to research subjects rather than an apparent inconsistency between any particular aspect of a research plan and a specific ethical guideline. For example, full disclosure of "what is really going on" in an experimental study is unnecessary if subjects are unlikely to be harmed. Nevertheless, researchers should make every effort to foresee all possible risks and to weigh the possible benefits of the research against these risks. They should consult with individuals with different perspectives to develop a realistic risk-benefit assessment, and they should try to maximize the benefits to, as well as minimize the risks for, subjects of the research (Sieber 1992).

Ultimately, these decisions about ethical procedures are not just up to you, as a researcher, to make. Your university's IRB sets the human subjects protection standards for your institution and will require that researchers—even, in most cases, students—submit their research proposal to the IRB for review. So we leave you with the instruction to review the human subjects guidelines of the ACJS or other professional association in your field, consult your university's procedures for the conduct of research with human subjects, and then proceed accordingly.

Key Terms

> Review key terms with eFlashcards. SAGE edge™

Highlights

- Philip Zimbardo's prison simulation study and Stanley Milgram's obedience experiments led to intensive debate about the extent to which deception could be tolerated in social science research and about how harm to subjects should be evaluated.
- Egregious violations of human rights by researchers, including scientists in Nazi Germany and researchers in the Tuskegee syphilis study, led to the adoption of federal ethical standards for research on human subjects.
- The 1979 Belmont Report developed by a national commission established three basic ethical standards for the protection of human subjects: respect for persons, beneficence, and justice.
- The Department of Health and Human Services adopted in 1991 a Federal Policy for the Protection of Human Subjects. This policy requires that every institution seeking federal funding for biomedical or behavioral research on human subjects have an institutional review board to exercise oversight.
- The ACJS standards for the protection of human subjects require avoiding harm, obtaining informed consent, avoiding deception except in limited circumstances, and maintaining privacy and confidentiality.
- Scientific research should maintain high standards for validity and be conducted and reported in an honest and open fashion.
- Effective debriefing of subjects after an experiment can help reduce the risk of harm due to the use of deception in the experiment.
- Regulations protect special populations, including children and prisoners, whose voluntary consent is sometimes difficult to ensure.

Exercises

> Test your understanding of chapter content. Take the practice quiz. ⑤SAGE edge™

1. Should criminologists be permitted to conduct replications of Zimbardo's prison simulation? Of Milgram's obedience experiments? Can you justify such research as permissible within the current ACJS ethical standards? If not, do you believe that these standards should be altered so as to permit this type of research?

2. How do you evaluate the current ACJS ethical code? Is it too strict, too lenient, or just about right? Are the enforcement provisions adequate? What provisions could be strengthened?

3. Why does unethical research occur? Is it inherent in science? Does it reflect "human nature"? What makes ethical research more or less likely?

4. Does debriefing solve the problem of subject deception? How much must researchers reveal after the experiment is over as well as before it begins?

5. What policy would you recommend that researchers such as Sherman and Berk (1984) follow in reporting the results of their research? Should social scientists try to correct misinformation in the popular press about their research, or should they just focus on what is published in academic journals? Should researchers speak to audiences like police conventions in order to influence policies related to their research results?

6. Investigate the standards and operations of your university's IRB. Interview one IRB member and one researcher whose research has been reviewed by the IRB (after receiving the appropriate permissions!). How well do typical IRB meetings work to identify the ethical issues in proposed research? Do researchers feel that their proposals are treated fairly? Why or why not?

7. Now go to the book's study site at **edge.sagepub.com/bach manprccj6e** and choose the Learning From Journal Articles option. Read one article based on research involving human subjects. What ethical issues did the research pose, and how were they resolved? Does it seem that subjects were appropriately protected?

Developing a Research Proposal

Now it's time to consider the potential ethical issues in your proposed study and the research philosophy that will guide your research. The following exercises involve very critical decisions for your research.

1. List the elements in your research plans that an IRB might consider to be relevant to the protection of human subjects. Rate each element from 1 to 5, where 1 indicates no more than a minor ethical issue, and 5 indicates a major ethical problem that probably cannot be resolved.

2. Write one page for the application to the IRB that explains how you will ensure that your research adheres to each relevant ASA standard.

3. Draft a consent form to be administered to your subjects when they enroll in your research. Use underlining and margin notes to indicate where each standard for informed consent statements is met.

Web Exercises

1. The Collaborative Institutional Training Initiative (CITI) offers an extensive online training course in the basics of human subjects protection issues. Go to the public access CITI site at www.citiprogram.org/rcrpage.asp?affiliation=100 and complete the course in social and behavioral research. Write a short summary of what you have learned.

2. Philip Zimbardo provides extensive documentation about the Stanford Prison Experiment at www.prisonexperiment.org. Read several documents that you find on this website and write a short report about them.

3. Read the entire ACJS Code of Ethics at www.acjs.org. Discuss the meaning of each research standard.

SPSS or Excel Exercises

Data for Exercise	
Dataset	**Description**
2013 YRBS.sav	The 2013 YRBS, short for Youth Risk Behavior Survey, is a national study of high school students. It focuses on gauging various behaviors and experiences of the adolescent population, including substance use and some victimization.
Variables for Exercise	
Variable Name	**Description**
state	The state in which the respondent lives
schoolname	The name of the school the respondent went to
qn23	Dichotomy based on how respondents answer a question about whether they have been forced to have sex on a date in the past year, where 1 = yes and 0 = no
qn49	Dichotomy based on whether respondent smoked marijuana in the past month, where 1 = yes and 0 = no

This time we'll be using the YRBS 2013 subsample, which is a survey of high school students all around the United States. This survey was given to students in a classroom filled with their peers under the supervision of a trained survey administrator.

1. Let's say we'd like to see if individuals from different schools and states have higher or lower rates of sexual victimization. First, make a frequency table (analyze->descriptives->frequencies) of the variables state and schoolname. What do you see? Why do you think that the results look this way? How does this apply to what you've been reading about research ethics?

2. Calculate a frequency table for the variable qn23, forced to have sex on a date.

   a. First, what sort of ethical considerations need to be made when asking a question like this? Bear in mind that this survey was given to students in a classroom filled with their peers under the supervision of a trained survey administrator. Consider, for instance, what the participant must be told before the survey, the setting the survey occurs in, and how datasets will be released to researchers.

   b. What does this frequency table tell us about the incidence of sexual assault in the country?

   c. Consider the questions in Part 2a (above) again. Do you think the results in Part 2b might have been different if those ethical considerations hadn't been made? If you do, how so?

   d. What about in the case of qn49—used marijuana in the past month?

3. Make a cross-tabulation of the relationship between gender and qn23. This is process explained in detail in the SPSS exercises for Chapter 2.

   a. How would a positivist interpret these results? A post-positivist?

   b. What do you think an interpretivist would say to both the positivist and postpositivist?

Section II: Fundamentals of Research

CHAPTER 4

Conceptualization and Measurement

ubstance abuse is a social problem of remarkable proportions. About 18 million Americans have an alcohol use disorder (Grant et al. 2004; Hasin et al. 2007; NIAAA 2013), and about 80,000 die every year from alcohol-related causes (NIAAA 2013). While in college, four out of ten students binge drink (Wechsler et al. 2002), and about one out of three could be diagnosed as alcohol abusers (Knight et al. 2002). Drinking is a factor in almost half of on-campus sexual assaults (Sinozich and Langton 2014), and almost one in four victims of violence in the general population perceive their attackers to have been under the influence of drugs and/or alcohol. And finally, almost half of jail inmates report having alcohol dependence or abuse problems (Karberg and James 2005). All told, the annual costs of prevention and treatment for alcohol and drug abuse exceed $340 billion in the United States (Miller and Hendrie 2008). Across the globe, alcohol misuse results in about 2.5 million deaths annually (WHO 2013).

With all of this these facts, we have presented several concepts including *alcohol, college students,* and *alcohol dependence.* While we all have our own ideas about what these concepts mean, do we all have the same idea in mind when we hear these terms? For example, are community colleges classified within the term *college?* How is alcohol abuse different from dependence?

Whether your goal is to examine the factors related to criminal offending, to deliver useful services, or to design effective social policies, at some point, you will probably need to read the research literature on substance abuse. Every time you begin to review or design relevant research, you will have to answer two questions: The first concerns conceptualization: "What is meant by *substance abuse* in this research?" The second concerns measurement: "How was substance abuse measured?" Both questions must be answered to evaluate the validity of substance abuse research. You cannot make sense of the results of a study until you know how the concepts were defined and measured. Nor are you ready to begin a research project until you have defined your concepts and constructed valid measures of them. Measurement validity is essential to successful research; in fact, without valid measures, it is fruitless to attempt to achieve the other two aspects of validity: causal validity (see Chapter 6) and generalizability (see Chapter 5).

In this chapter, we first address the issue of conceptualization, using substance abuse and related concepts as examples. We also provide examples of the conceptualization process for other terms like *street gangs* and *inmate misconduct.* We then focus on measurement, reviewing first how measures of substance abuse have been constructed using available data (i.e. arrest data), questions on surveys, observations, and less direct and unobtrusive measures. Then we explain how to assess the validity and reliability of these measures. The final topic is the level of measurement reflected in different measures. By chapter's end, you should have a good understanding of measurement, the first of the three legs on which a research project's validity rests.

回 Concepts

Every concept requires an explicit definition before it is used in research, because we cannot otherwise be certain that all readers will share the same definition. It is even more important to define concepts that are somewhat abstract or unfamiliar. When we refer to concepts such as *poverty,* or *social control,* or *strain,* we cannot be certain that others know exactly what we mean.

Many high school and college students have become familiar with the term *binge drinking,* but you may be surprised to learn that even researchers do not agree on how to measure it. The definition that Henry Wechsler et al. (2002) used is "heavy episodic drinking"; more specifically, "we defined binge drinking as the consumption of at least 5 drinks in a row for men or 4 drinks in a row for women during the 2 weeks before completion of the questionnaire" (p. 205). While this definition is widely accepted among social researchers, the National Institute on Alcoholism and Alcohol Abuse (College Alcohol Study 2008) provides a more precise definition: "A pattern of drinking alcohol that brings blood alcohol concentration to 0.08 grams percent or above." Most researchers consider the so-called 5/4 definition (5 drinks for men; 4 for women) to be a reasonable approximation to this more precise definition. We can't say either of these definitions is "correct," or even that one is "better." However, if we were to conduct research on the topic of binge drinking, we would need to specify what we mean when we use the term and be sure that others know that definition. And of course, the definition has to be useful for our purposes: A definition based solely on blood alcohol concentration will not be useful if we are not taking blood measures.

We call binge drinking a **concept**—a mental image that summarizes a set of similar observations, feelings, or ideas. To make that concept useful in research (and even in ordinary discourse), we have to define it. Many concepts are used

Concept: A mental image that summarizes a set of similar observations, feelings, or ideas.

It is usually a good idea to try to measure variables at the highest level of measurement possible. The more information available, the more ways we have to compare cases. We also have more possibilities for statistical analysis with quantitative variables than with qualitative variables. Thus, if doing so does not distort the meaning of the concept that is to be measured, measure at the highest level possible. For example, even if your primary concern is only to compare teenagers with young adults, measure age in years rather than in categories; you can always combine the ages later into categories corresponding to teenager and young adult.

Be aware, however, that other considerations may preclude measurement at a high level. For example, many people are very reluctant to report their exact incomes, even in anonymous questionnaires. So asking respondents to report their income in categories (such as under $10,000, $10,000–$19,999, $20,000–$29,999, etc.) will result in more responses, and thus more valid data, than asking respondents for their income in dollars.

> **Interval–ratio level of measurement:** A measurement of a variable in which the numbers indicating the variable's values represent fixed measurement units, but there may be no absolute, or fixed, zero point.

Often, researchers treat variables measured at the interval and ratio levels as comparable. They then refer to this as the **interval–ratio level of measurement**. You will learn in Chapter 14 that different statistical procedures are used for variables with fixed measurement units, but it usually doesn't matter whether there is an absolute zero point.

🔲 Did We Measure What We Wanted to Measure?

Do the operations developed to measure our concepts actually do so? Are they valid? If we have weighed our measurement options, carefully constructed our questions and observational procedures, and carefully selected indicators from the available data, we should be on the right track. We cannot have much confidence in a measure until we have empirically evaluated its validity. Additionally, we must also evaluate its reliability (consistency).

Measurement Validity

> **Measurement validity:** The type of validity that is achieved when a measure measures what it is presumed to measure.

In Chapter 2 you learned that **measurement validity** refers to the extent to which measures indicate what they are intended to measure. We want to discuss it in more detail here along with the ways validity can be assessed.

We briefly discussed the difference between official police reports and survey data in Chapter 1. We noted that official reports underestimate the actual amount of offending because a great deal of offending behavior never comes to the attention of police (Mosher et al. 2002). There is also evidence that arrest data often reflect the political climate and police policies as much as they do criminal activity. For example, let's suppose we wanted to examine whether illicit drug use was increasing or decreasing since the advent of the United States' "War on Drugs," which heated up in the 1980s and is still being fought today. During this time, arrest rates for drug offenses soared, giving the illusion that drug use was increasing at an epidemic pace. However, self-report surveys that asked citizens directly about their drug use during this time period found that use of most illicit drugs was actually declining or had stayed the same (Regoli and Hewitt 1994). In your opinion, then, which measure of drug use, the UCR or self-report surveys, was more valid? The extent to which measures indicate what they are intended to measure can be assessed with one or more of four basic approaches: face validation, content validation, criterion validation, and construct validation. Whatever the approach to validation, no one measure will be valid for all times and places. For example, the validity of self-report measures of substance abuse varies with such factors as whether the respondents are sober or intoxicated at the time of the interview, whether the measure refers to recent or lifetime abuse, and whether the respondents see their responses as affecting their chances at receiving housing, treatment, or some other desired outcome (Babor, Stephens, and Marlatt 1987). In addition, persons with severe mental illness are, in general, less likely to respond accurately (Corse, Hirschinger, and Zanis 1995). These types of possibilities should always be considered when evaluating measurement validity.

Face Validity

Researchers apply the term **face validity** to the confidence gained from careful inspection of a concept to see if it is appropriate "on its face," simply whether it appears to measure what it intends. For example, if college students' alcohol consumption is what we are trying to measure, asking for student's favorite color seems unlikely on its face to tell us much about their drinking patterns. A measure with greater face validity would be a count of how many drinks they have consumed in the past week.

> **Face validity:** The type of validity that exists when an inspection of the items used to measure a concept suggests that they are appropriate "on their face."

Although every measure should be inspected in this way, face validation, on its own, is not the gold standard of measurement validity. The question "How much beer or wine did you have to drink last week?" may look valid on its face as a measure of frequency of drinking, but people who drink heavily tend to underreport the amount they drink. So the question would be an invalid measure in a study that includes heavy drinkers.

Content Validity

Content validity establishes that the measure covers the full range of the concept's meaning. To determine that range of meaning, the researcher may solicit the opinions of experts and review literature that identifies the different aspects of the concept.

> **Content validity:** The type of validity that establishes a measure covers the full range of the concept's meaning.

An example of a measure that covers a wide range of meaning is the Michigan Alcoholism Screening Test (MAST). The MAST includes 24 questions representing the following subscales: recognition of alcohol problems by self and others; legal, social, and work problems; help seeking; marital and family difficulties; and liver pathology (Skinner and Sheu 1982). Many experts familiar with the direct consequences of substance abuse agree that these dimensions capture the full range of possibilities. Thus, the MAST is believed to be valid from the standpoint of content validity.

Criterion Validity

Consider the following scenario: when people drink an alcoholic beverage, the alcohol is absorbed into their blood and then gradually metabolized (broken down into other chemicals) in their liver (National Institute on Alcohol Abuse and Alcoholism [NIAAA] 1997). The alcohol that remains in their blood at any point, unmetabolized, impairs both thinking and behavior (NIAAA 1994). As more alcohol is ingested, cognitive and behavioral consequences multiply. These biological processes can be identified with direct measures of alcohol concentration in the blood, urine, or breath. Questions about alcohol consumption, on the other hand, can be viewed as attempts to measure indirectly what biochemical tests measure directly.

Criterion validity is established when the scores obtained on one measure can be accurately compared to those obtained with a more direct or already validated measure of the same phenomenon (the criterion). A measure of blood-alcohol concentration or a urine test could serve as the criterion for validating a self-report measure of drinking, as long as the questions we ask about drinking refer to the same time period. Observations of substance use by friends or relatives could also, in some circumstances, serve as a criterion for validating self-report substance use measures.

> **Criterion validity:** The type of validity that is established by comparing the scores obtained on the measure being validated to those obtained with a more direct or already validated measure of the same phenomenon (the criterion).

Criterion validation studies of substance abuse measures have yielded inconsistent results. Self-reports of drug use agreed with urinalysis results for about 85% of the drug users who volunteered for a health study in several cities (Weatherby et al. 1994). On the other hand, the posttreatment drinking behavior self-reported by 100 male alcoholics was substantially less than the drinking behavior observed by the alcoholics' friends or relatives (Watson et al. 1984). Such inconsistent findings can occur because of differences in the adequacy of measures across settings and populations. This underscores our point that you cannot assume that a measure that was validated in one study is also valid in another setting or with a different population.

It is important to know exactly what population a sample can represent when you select or evaluate sample components. In a survey of "adult Americans," the general population may reasonably be construed as all residents of the United States who are at least 18 years old. But always be alert to ways in which the population may have been narrowed by the sample selection procedures. For example, if the survey was conducted in English only, it would represent only English-speaking residents of the United States. The population for a study is the aggregation of elements that we actually focus on and sample from, not some larger aggregation that we really wish we could have studied.

Some populations, such as the homeless, are not identified by a simple criterion such as a geographic boundary or an organizational membership. Let's say we were interested in victimizations experienced by the homeless population. In this case, a clear definition of the homeless population is difficult but quite necessary. In research, anyone should be able to determine what population was actually studied. However, early studies of homeless persons "did not propose definitions, did not use screening questions to be sure that the people they interviewed were indeed homeless, and did not make major efforts to cover the universe of homeless people" (Burt 1996, 15). For example, some studies relied on homeless persons in only one shelter. The result was "a collection of studies that could not be compared" (Burt 1996, 15). Several studies of homeless persons in urban areas addressed the problem by employing a more explicit definition of the population: People are homeless if they have no home or permanent place to stay of their own (renting or owning) and no regular arrangement to stay at someone else's place (Burt 1996). Even this more explicit definition still leaves some questions unanswered: What is a regular arrangement? How permanent does a permanent place have to be? The more complete and explicit the definition of the population from which a sample is selected, the more precise our generalizations from a sample to that population can be.

Evaluate Generalizability

After we clearly define the population we will sample, we need to determine the scope of the generalizations we will seek to make from our sample. Let us say we were interested in the extent to which high school youth are fearful of being attacked or harmed at school or going to and from their schools. It would be easy to go down to the local high school and hand out a survey asking students to report their levels of fear in these situations. But what if our local high school were located in a remote and rural area of Alaska? Would this sample reflect levels of fear perceived by suburban youth in California or urban youth in New York City? Obviously not. Often, regardless of the sample utilized, researchers will go on to talk about how "this percentage of high school students is fearful," or "freshman students are more fearful than seniors," as if their study results represent all high school students. Many researchers (and most everyone else, for that matter) are eager to draw conclusions about all individuals they are interested in, not just their samples. Generalizations make their work (and opinions) sound more important. If every high school student were like every other one, generalizations based on observations of one high school student would be valid. But of course, that is not the case.

As we noted in Chapter 2, generalizability has two aspects. Can the findings from a sample of the population be generalized to the population from which the sample was selected? **Sample generalizability** refers to the ability to generalize from a sample, or subset, of a larger population to that population itself. This is the most common meaning of generalizability. Can the findings from a study of one population be generalized to another, somewhat different population? This is **cross-population generalizability** and refers to the ability to generalize from findings about one group, population, or setting to other groups, populations, or settings (see Exhibit 5.2). In this book, we use the term **external validity** to refer only to cross-population generalizability, not to sample generalizability.

Sample generalizability: Exists when a conclusion based on a sample, or subset, of a larger population holds true for that population.

Cross-population generalizability (external validity): Exists when findings about one group, population, or setting hold true for other groups, populations, or settings.

Generalizability is a key concern in research design. We rarely have the resources to study the entire population that is of interest to us, so we have to select cases to study that will allow our findings to be generalized to the population of interest. We can never be sure that our propositions will hold under all conditions, so we should be cautious in generalizing to populations that we did not actually sample.

This chapter primarily focuses on the problem of sample generalizability: Can findings from a sample be generalized to the population from which the sample

| Exhibit 5.2 | **Sample and Cross-Population Generalizability** |

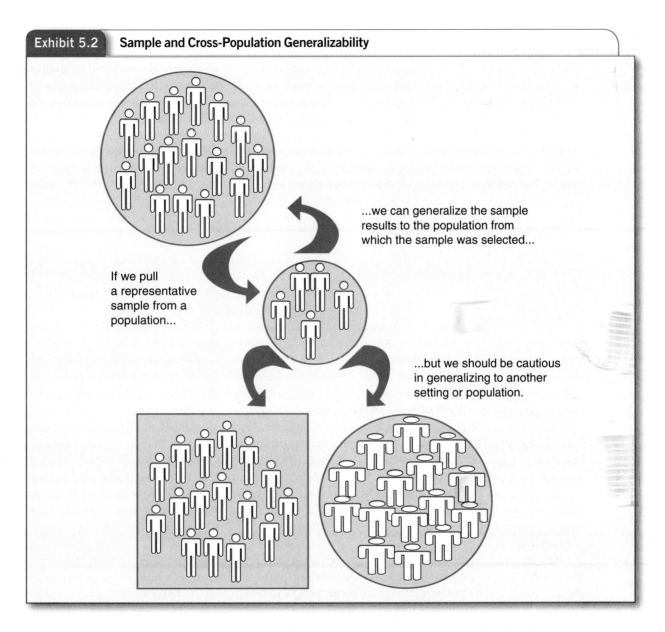

...we can generalize the sample results to the population from which the sample was selected...

If we pull a representative sample from a population...

...but we should be cautious in generalizing to another setting or population.

was drawn? This is the most basic question to ask about a sample, and social research methods provide many tools to address it.

Sample generalizability depends on sample quality, which is determined by the amount of sampling error. **Sampling error** can generally be defined as the difference between the characteristics of a sample and the characteristics of the population from which it was selected. The larger the sampling error, the less representative the sample, and thus the less generalizable the findings. To assess sample quality when you are planning or evaluating a study, ask yourself these questions:

- From what population were the cases selected?
- What method was used to select cases from this population?
- Do the cases that were studied represent, in the aggregate, the population from which they were selected?

> **Sampling error:** Any difference between the characteristics of a sample and the characteristics of the population from which it was drawn. The larger the sampling error, the less representative the sample is of the population.

Target population: A set of elements larger than or different from the population sampled and to which the researcher would like to generalize study findings.

In reality, researchers often project their theories onto groups or populations much larger than, or simply different from, those they have actually studied. The **target population** is a set of elements larger than or different from the population that was sampled and to which the researcher would like to generalize any study findings. When we generalize findings to target populations, we must be somewhat speculative. We must carefully consider the claim that the findings can be applied to other groups, geographic areas, cultures, or times.

Because the validity of cross-population generalizations cannot be tested empirically, except by conducting more research in other settings, we do not focus much attention on this problem here. We will return to the problem of cross-population generalizability in Chapter 7, which addresses experimental research.

Assess Population Diversity

Sampling is unnecessary if all the units in the population are identical. Physicists do not need to select a representative sample of atomic particles to learn about basic physical processes. They can study a single atomic particle, because it is identical to every other particle of its type. Similarly, biologists do not need to sample a particular type of plant to determine whether a given chemical has toxic effects on it. The idea is "if you've seen one, you've seen 'em all."

What about people? Certainly all people are not identical, nor are animals in many respects. Nonetheless, if we are studying physical or psychological processes that are the same among all people, sampling is not needed to achieve generalizable findings. Psychologists and social psychologists often conduct experiments on college students to learn about processes that they think are identical for all individuals. They believe that most people will have the same reactions as the college students if they experience the same experimental conditions. Field researchers who observe group processes in a small community sometimes make the same assumption.

There is a potential problem with this assumption, however. There is no way to know if the processes being studied are identical for all people. In fact, experiments can give different results depending on the type of people studied or the conditions for the experiment. Milgram's (1965) classic experiments on obedience to authority, among the most replicated experiments in the history of social psychological research, illustrate this point very well. The Milgram experiments tested the willingness of male volunteers in New Haven, Connecticut, to comply with instructions from an authority figure to give electric shocks to someone else, even when these shocks seemed to harm the person receiving them. In most cases, the volunteers complied. Milgram concluded that people are very obedient to authority.

Were these results generalizable to all men, to men in the United States, or to men in New Haven? We have confidence in these findings because similar results were obtained in many replications of the Milgram experiments when the experimental conditions and subjects were similar to those studied by Milgram. Other studies, however, showed that some groups were less likely to react so obediently. Given certain conditions, such as another subject in the room who refused to administer the shocks, subjects were likely to resist authority.

So what do the experimental results tell us about how people will react to an authoritarian movement in the real world, when conditions are not so carefully controlled? In the real social world, people may be less likely to react obediently. Other individuals may argue against obedience to a particular leader's commands, or people may see, on TV, the consequences of their actions. But alternatively, people may be even more obedient to authority than the experimental subjects, as they get swept up in mobs or are captivated by ideological fervor. Milgram's research gives us insight into human behavior, but there is no guarantee that what he found with particular groups in particular conditions can be generalized to the larger population (or to any particular population) in different settings.

Accurately generalizing the results of experiments and of participant observation is risky, because such research often studies a small number of people who do not represent a particular population. Researchers may put aside concerns about generalizability when they observe the social dynamics of specific clubs or college dorms or when they conduct a controlled experiment that tests the effect of, say, a violent movie on feelings for others. Nonetheless, we should still be cautious about generalizing the results of such studies.

But what if your goal is not to learn about individuals, but about the culture or subculture in a society or group? The logic of sampling does not apply if the goal is to learn about culture that is shared across individuals:

When people all provide the same information, it is redundant to ask a question over and over. Only enough people need to be surveyed to eliminate the possibility of errors and to allow for those who might diverge from the norm. (Heise 2010, 15)

If you are trying to describe a group or society's culture, you may choose individuals for the survey based on their knowledge of the culture, not as representatives of a population of individuals (Heise 2010). In this situation, what is important about the individuals surveyed is what they have in common, not their diversity.

Keep these exceptions in mind, but the main point is that social scientists rarely can skirt the problem of demonstrating the generalizability of their findings. If a small sample has been studied in an experiment or a field research project, the study should be replicated in different settings or, preferably, with a **representative sample** of the population to which generalizations are sought (see Exhibit 5.3). The social world and the people in it are just too diverse to be considered *identical units* in most respects. Social psychological experiments and small field studies have produced good social science, but they need to be replicated in other settings, with other subjects, to claim any generalizability. Even when we believe that we have uncovered basic social processes in a laboratory experiment or field observation, we should be very concerned with seeking confirmation in other samples and in other research.

> **Representative sample:** A sample that looks like the population from which it was selected in all respects that are potentially relevant to the study. The distribution of characteristics among the elements of a representative sample is the same as the distribution of those characteristics among the total population. In an unrepresentative sample, some characteristics are overrepresented or underrepresented, and sampling error emerges.

Consider a Census

In some circumstances, researchers can bypass the issue of generalizability by conducting a **census** studying the entire population of interest rather than drawing a sample. The federal government tries to do this every 10 years with the U.S. Census. A census can also include studies of all the employees (or students) in small organizations (or universities), studies comparing all 50 states, and studies of the entire population of a particular type of organization in a particular area. However, in all these instances, except for the U.S. Census, the population studied is relatively small.

> **Census:** Research in which information is obtained through the responses that all available members of an entire population give to questions.

The reason that social scientists don't often attempt to collect data from all the members of some large population is simply that doing so would be too expensive and time-consuming—and they can do almost as well with a sample. Some social scientists conduct research with data from the U.S. Census, but the government collects the data and our tax dollars pay for the effort to get one person in about 134 million households to answer 10 questions. To conduct the 2010 census, the U.S. Census Bureau spent more than $5.5 billion and hired 3.8 million people (U.S. Bureau of the Census 2010a, 2010b).

Even if the population of interest for a survey is a small town of 20,000 or students in a university of 10,000, researchers will have to sample. The costs of surveying just thousands of individuals far exceed the budgets for most research projects. In fact, even the U.S. Bureau of the Census cannot afford to have everyone answer all the questions that should be covered in the census. So it draws a sample. Every household must complete a short version of the census (it had seven questions in 2000), and a sample consisting of one in six households must complete a long form (with 53 additional questions) (Rosenbaum 2000).

Another costly fact is that it is hard to get people to complete a survey. Even the U.S. Bureau of the Census (1999) must make multiple efforts to increase the rate of response in spite of the federal law requiring all citizens to complete their census questionnaire. After spending $167 million on publicity (Forero 2000), the bureau still planned up to six attempts to contact each household that did not respond by mail (U.S. Bureau of the Census 2000).

In most situations, then, it is much better to select a representative sample from the total population so that there are more resources for follow-up procedures that can overcome reluctance or indifference about participation.

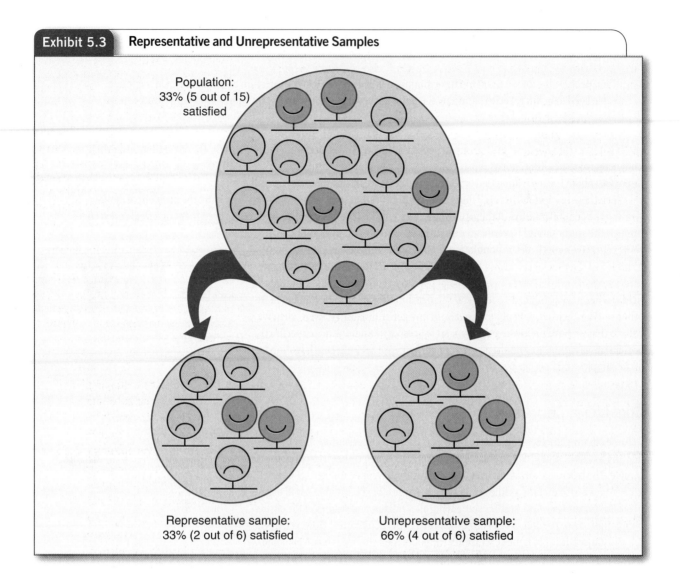

| Exhibit 5.3 | Representative and Unrepresentative Samples |

Population:
33% (5 out of 15)
satisfied

Representative sample:
33% (2 out of 6) satisfied

Unrepresentative sample:
66% (4 out of 6) satisfied

回 Sampling Methods

Probability sampling methods: Sampling methods that rely on a random, or chance, selection method so that the probability of selection of population elements is known.

Nonprobability sampling methods: Sampling methods in which the probability of selection of population elements is unknown.

As you can probably guess, the most important feature to know about a sample is whether it is truly representative of the population from which it was selected. Sampling methods that allow us to know in advance how likely it is that any element of a population will be selected for the sample are **probability sampling methods**. Sampling methods that do not reveal the likelihood of selection in advance are **nonprobability sampling methods**.

Probability sampling methods rely on a random selection procedure. In principle, this is the same as flipping a coin to decide which person wins and which one loses. Heads and tails are equally likely to turn up in a coin toss, so both persons have an equal chance to win. That chance, or the **probability of selection**, is 1 out of 2, or .5.

Flipping a coin is a fair way to select one of two people, because the selection process harbors no systematic bias. You might win or lose the coin toss, but you know that the outcome was due simply to chance, not to bias (unless your opponent tossed a two-headed coin!). For the same reason, rolling a six-sided die is a fair way to choose one of six possible outcomes (the odds of selection are 1 out of 6, or .17). Dealing out a hand after shuffling a deck of cards is a fair way to allocate sets of cards in a poker game. (The odds of each person getting a particular outcome, such as a full house or a flush, are the same.) Similarly, state lotteries use a random process to select winning numbers. Thus, the odds of winning a lottery, the probability of selection, are known even though they are very small (perhaps 1 out of 1 million) compared to the odds of winning a coin toss. As you can see, the fundamental strategy in probability sampling is the **random selection** of elements into the sample. When a sample is randomly selected from the population, every element has a known and independent chance of being selected into the sample.

There is a natural tendency to confuse the concept of probability, in which cases are selected only on the basis of chance, with a haphazard method of sampling. On first impression, leaving things up to chance seems to imply the absence of control over the sampling method. But to ensure that nothing but chance influences the selection of cases, the researcher must actually proceed very methodically and leave nothing to chance except the selection of the cases themselves. The researcher must carefully follow controlled procedures if a purely random process is to occur. In fact, when reading about sampling methods, do not assume that a random sample was obtained just because the researcher used a random selection method at some point in the sampling process. Look for these two particular problems: selecting elements from an incomplete list of the total population, and failing to obtain an adequate response rate (say, only 45% of the people who were asked to participate actually agreed).

If the sampling frame, or list from which the elements of the population are selected, is incomplete, a sample selected randomly from the list will not be random. How can it be when the sampling frame fails to include every element in the population? Even for a simple population like a university's student body, the registrar's list is likely to be at least a bit out of date at any given time. For example, some students will have dropped out, but their status will not yet be officially recorded. Although you may judge the amount of error introduced in this particular situation to be negligible, the problems are greatly compounded for a larger population. The sampling frame for a city, state, or nation is always likely to be incomplete because of constant migration into and out of the area. Even unavoidable omissions from the sampling frame can bias a sample against particular groups within the population.

An inclusive sampling frame may still yield systematic bias if many sample members cannot be contacted or refuse to participate. **Nonresponse** is a major hazard in survey research, because individuals who do not respond to a survey are likely to differ systematically from those who take the time to participate. You should not assume that findings from a randomly selected sample will be generalizable to the population from which the sample was selected if the rate of nonresponse is considerable (certainly not if it is much above 30%).

Probability Sampling Methods

Probability sampling methods are those in which the probability of selection is known and is not zero (so there is some chance of selecting each element). These methods randomly select elements and therefore have no **systematic bias**; nothing but chance determines which elements are included in the sample. This feature of probability samples makes them much more desirable than nonprobability samples when the goal is to generalize to a larger population.

Probability of selection: The likelihood that an element will be selected from the population for inclusion in the sample. In a census of all the elements of a population, the probability that any particular element will be selected is 1.0, because everyone will be selected. If half the elements in the population will be sampled on the basis of chance (say, by tossing a coin), the probability of selection for each element is one half, or .5. When the size of the desired sample as a proportion of the population decreases, so does the probability of selection.

Random selection: The fundamental element of probability samples; the essential characteristic of random selection is that every element of the population has a known and independent chance of being selected into the sample.

Nonresponse: People or other entities who do not participate in a study although they are selected for the sample.

Systematic bias: Overrepresentation or underrepresentation of some population characteristics in a sample resulting from the method used to select the sample; a sample shaped by systematic sampling error is a biased sample.

Research in the News

For Further Thought ?

FERGUSON POLICE AND RACIAL BIAS

This article reports the finding from a U.S. Justice Department study that investigated the arrest trends in the Ferguson police department after the Ferguson, Missouri, police killing of Michael Brown. After analyzing police records for the years 2012 through 2014, the report concluded that blacks were more likely than whites to be stopped and arrested for many offenses. For example, a black motorist who was pulled over was twice as likely to be searched compared to a white motorist, despite the fact that searches of white drivers were more likely to uncover drugs or other contraband. The report concluded that Mr. Brown's death was not the cause of the racial unrest in the city; it was simply the "spark that ignited years of pent-up tension and animosity in the area."

1. The reaction of a former mayor of Ferguson was highlighted in the news article as noting that the Justice Department's report was based on incomplete data, because it did not take into account the number of people from surrounding towns who visit Ferguson to shop. How could this issue be controlled in the analysis of the police data?

2. If you were a researcher, how would you measure Ferguson citizens' degree of trust in the police? What hypothesis would you state regarding the variables of race and trust in police?

Source: Apuzzo, Matt. 2015. "Ferguson Police routinely Violate Rights of Blacks, Justice Department Finds. *New York Times,* March 3. http://mobile .nytimes.com/2015/03/04/us/justice-department-finds-pattern-of-police-bias-and-excessive-force-in-ferguson.html?_r=0.

Even though a random sample has no systematic bias, it certainly will have some sampling error due to chance. The probability of selecting a head is .5 in a single toss of a coin and in 20, 30, or however many tosses of a coin you like. Be aware, however, that it is perfectly possible to toss a coin twice and get a head both times. The random sample of the two sides of the coin is selected in an unbiased fashion, but it still is unrepresentative. Imagine randomly selecting a sample of 10 people from a population comprising 50 men and 50 women. Just by chance, it is possible that your sample of 10 people will include seven women and only three men. Fortunately, we can determine mathematically the likely degree of sampling error in an estimate based on a random sample (as you will see later in this chapter), assuming that the sample's randomness has not been destroyed by a high rate of nonresponse or by poor control over the selection process.

In general, both the size of the sample and the homogeneity (sameness) of the population affect the degree of error due to chance; the proportion of the population that the sample represents does not. To elaborate:

The larger the sample, the more confidence we can have in the sample's representativeness of the population from which it was drawn. If we randomly pick five people to represent the entire population of our city, our sample is unlikely to be very representative of the entire population in terms of age, gender, race, attitudes, and so on. But if we randomly pick 100 people, the odds of having a representative sample are much better; with a random sample of 1,000, the odds become very good indeed.

The more homogeneous the population, the more confidence we can have in the representativeness of a sample of any particular size. Let us say we plan to draw samples of 50 from each of two communities to estimate mean family income. One community is very diverse, with family incomes ranging from $12,000 to $85,000. In the more homogeneous community, family incomes are concentrated in a narrower range, from $41,000 to $64,000. The estimated average family income based on the sample from the homogeneous community is more likely to be representative than is the estimate based on the sample from the more heterogeneous community. With less variation, fewer cases are needed to represent the larger population.

The fraction of the total population that a sample contains does not affect the sample's representative-ness, unless that fraction is large. We can regard any sampling fraction under 2% with about the same degree of confidence (Sudman 1976). In fact, sample representativeness is not likely to increase much until the sampling fraction is quite a bit higher. Other things being equal, a sample of 1,000 from a population of 1 million (with a sampling fraction of 0.001, or 0.1%) is much better than a sample of 100 from a population of 10,000 (although the sampling fraction is 0.01, or 1%, which is 10 times higher). The size of a sample is what makes representativeness more likely, not the proportion of the whole that the sample represents.

Polls that predict presidential election outcomes illustrate both the value of random sampling and the problems that it cannot overcome. In most presidential elections, pollsters have accurately predicted the outcomes of the actual vote by using random sampling and, these days, phone interviewing to learn which candidate voters intend to choose. Exhibit 5.4 shows how close these sample-based predictions have been in the last 12 contests. The big exception was the 1980 election, when a third-party candidate had an unpredicted effect. Otherwise, the small discrepancies between the votes predicted through random sampling and the actual votes can be attributed to random error. In 2008, the final Gallup prediction of 55% for Obama was within 2 percentage points of his winning total of 53%. Because they do not disproportionately select particular groups within the population, random samples that are successfully implemented avoid systematic bias. The four most common methods for drawing random samples are simple random sampling, systematic random sampling, stratified random sampling, and multistage cluster sampling.

Simple Random Sampling

Simple random sampling requires a procedure that generates numbers or identifies cases strictly on the basis of chance. As you know, flipping a coin and rolling a die can be used to identify cases strictly on the basis of chance, but these procedures are not very efficient tools for drawing a sample. A **random number table**, which can be obtained from many websites, simplifies the process considerably. The researcher numbers all the elements in the sampling frame and then uses a systematic procedure for picking corresponding numbers from the random number table. (Exercise 2 at the end of the chapter explains the process step by step.) Alternatively, a researcher may use a lottery procedure. Each case number is written on a small card, and then the cards are mixed up and the sample is selected from the cards.

When a large sample must be generated, these procedures are very cumbersome. Fortunately, a computer program can easily generate a random sample of any size. The researcher must first number all the elements to be sampled (the sampling frame) and then run the computer program to generate a random selection of the numbers within the desired range. The elements represented by these numbers are the sample.

Organizations that conduct phone surveys often draw random samples with another automated procedure called **random digit dialing (RDD)**. A machine dials random numbers within the phone prefixes corresponding to the area in which the survey is to be conducted. RDD is particularly useful when a sampling frame is not available. The researcher simply replaces any inappropriate numbers (e.g., those no longer in service or for businesses) with the next randomly generated phone number.

Exhibit 5.4 Election Outcomes: Predicted and Actual

Winner (Year)	Polls (%)	Result (%)
Kennedy (1960)	51	50
Johnson (1964)	64	61
Nixon (1968)[b]	43	43
Nixon (1972)	62	62
Carter (1976)	48	50
Reagan (1980)[b]	47	51
Reagan (1984)	59	59
Bush (1988)	56	54
Clinton (1992)[b]	49	43
Clinton (1996)[b]	52	50
Bush, G. W. (2000)[b]	48	50
Bush, G. W. (2004)[b]	49	51
Obama (2008)[b]	55	53
Obama (2012)[a]	54	51.1

Source: Gallup Poll Accuracy Record, 12-13-00, http://www.gallup.com/poll/111742/Obamas-Road-White-House-Gallup-Review.aspx for the 2008 presidential election. Copyright © 2008 Gallup, Inc. All rights reserved.

a. Final Gallup Poll prior to the election.
b. There was also a third-party candidate.

Simple random sampling: A method of sampling in which every sample element is selected only on the basis of chance, through a random process.

Random number table: A table containing lists of numbers that are ordered solely on the basis of chance; it is used for drawing a random sample.

Random digit dialing (RDD): The random dialing by a machine of numbers within designated phone prefixes, which creates a random sample for phone surveys.

As the fraction of the population that has only cell phones has increased (40% in 2013), it has become essential to explicitly sample cell phone numbers as well as landline phone numbers (McGeeney and Keeter 2014). Those who use cell phones only tend to be younger, more male, more single, more likely to be black or Hispanic, and less likely to vote compared with those who have a landline phone. As a result, failing to include cell phone numbers in a phone survey can introduce bias (Christian et al. 2010). In fact, in a 2008 presidential election survey, those who use only cell phones were less likely to be registered voters than were landline users but were considerably more favorable to Obama than landline users (Keeter 2008).

In the National Intimate Partner and Sexual Violence Survey (NISVS) conducted by the Centers for Disease Control and Prevention (CDC), both landline and cell phone databases of adult U.S. residents were selected through an RDD random sampling method (Black et al. 2011). You will learn more about this survey in Chapter 8.

The probability of selection in a true simple random sample is equal for each element. If a sample of 500 is selected from a population of 17,000 (i.e., a sampling frame of 17,000), then the probability of selection for each element is 500 out of 17,000, or .03. Every element has an equal and independent chance of being selected; these odds are just like the odds in a toss of a coin (1 in 2) or a roll of a die (1 in 6). Thus, simple random sampling is an equal probability of selection method (EPSEM).

Replacement sampling: A method of sampling in which sample elements are returned to the sampling frame after being selected, so they may be sampled again. Random samples may be selected with or without replacement.

Simple random sampling can be done either with or without replacement sampling. In **replacement sampling**, each element is returned to the sampling frame from which it is selected so that it may be sampled again. In sampling without replacement, each element selected for the sample is then excluded from the sampling frame. In practice it makes no difference whether sampled elements are replaced after selection, as long as the population is large and the sample is to contain only a small fraction of the population.

For the CDC's NISVS study, noninstitutionalized (e.g., not in nursing homes, prison, and so on) English- and/or Spanish-speaking residents aged 18 and older were randomly selected through an RDD sampling method in 2010. A total of 9,970 women and 8,079 men were selected. Approximately, 45% of the interviews were conducted by landline and 55% by cell phone. The final sample represented the U.S. population very well. For example, the proportion of the sample by gender, race/ethnicity, and age in the NISVS sample was very close to the sample proportions for the U.S. population as a whole.

How does this sample strike you? Let us assess sample quality using the questions posed earlier in the chapter:

- *From what population were the cases selected?* There is a clearly defined population: the adult residents of the continental United States (who live in households with phones).

- *What method was used to select cases from this population?* The case selection method is a random selection procedure, and there are no systematic biases in the sampling.

- *Do the cases that were studied represent, in the aggregate, the population from which they were selected?* The findings are very likely to represent the population sampled, because there were no biases in the sampling and a very large number of cases were selected. However, it must be remembered that an average of 30% of those selected for interviews could not be contacted or chose not to respond. This rate of nonresponse may have created a small bias in the sample for several characteristics.

We also must consider the issue of cross-population generalizability. Do findings from this sample have implications for any larger group beyond the population from which the sample was selected? Because a representative sample of the entire U.S. adult population was drawn, this question has to do with cross-national generalizations.

Systematic random sampling: A method of sampling in which sample elements are selected from a list or from sequential files, with every *n*th element being selected after the first element is selected randomly within the first interval.

Systematic Random Sampling

Systematic random sampling is a variant of simple random sampling and is a little less time consuming. When you systematically select a random sample, the first element is selected randomly from a list or from sequential files, and then every *n*th element is systematically selected thereafter. This is a convenient method for drawing a random sample when the population elements are arranged sequentially. It is particularly efficient when the elements are not actually printed (i.e., there is no sampling frame) but instead are represented by folders in filing cabinets.

Systematic random sampling requires three steps:

Sampling interval: The number of cases between one sampled case and the next in a systematic random sample.

1. The total number of cases in the population is divided by the number of cases required for the sample. This division yields the **sampling interval**, the number of cases from one sampled case to another. If 50 cases are to be selected out of 1,000, the sampling interval is 20 (1,000/50 = 20); every 20th case is selected.

2. A number between 1 and 20 (the sampling interval) is selected randomly. This number identifies the first case to be sampled, counting from the first case on the list or in the files.

3. After the first case is selected, every nth case is selected for the sample, where n is the sampling interval. If the sampling interval is not a whole number, the size of the sampling interval is systematically varied to yield the proper number of cases for the sample. For example, if the sampling interval is 30.5, the sampling interval alternates between 30 and 31.

In almost all sampling situations, systematic random sampling yields what is essentially a simple random sample. The exception is a situation in which the sequence of elements is affected by **periodicity**; that is, the sequence varies in some regular, periodic pattern. The list or folder device from which the elements are selected must be truly random in order to avoid sampling bias. For example, we could not have a list of convicted felons sorted by offense type, age, or some other characteristic of the population. If the list is

Periodicity: A sequence of elements (in a list to be sampled) that varies in some regular, periodic pattern.

sorted in any meaningful way, this will introduce bias to the sampling process, and the resulting sample is not likely to be representative of the population. But in reality, periodicity and the sampling interval are rarely the same.

Stratified Random Sampling

Although all probability sampling methods use random sampling, some add steps to the sampling process to make sampling more efficient or easier. Samples are easier to collect when they require less time, money, or prior information.

Stratified random sampling uses information known about the total population prior to sampling to make the sampling process more efficient. First, all elements in the population (i.e., in the sampling frame) are differentiated on the basis of their value on some relevant characteristic. This sorting step forms the sampling strata. Next, elements are sampled randomly from within these strata. For example, race may be the basis for distinguishing individuals in some population of interest. Within each racial category selected for the strata, individuals are then sampled randomly.

Why is this method more efficient than drawing a simple random sample? Well, imagine that you plan to draw a sample of 500 from an ethnically diverse neighborhood. The neighborhood population is 15% African American, 10% Hispanic, 5% Asian, and 70% Caucasian. If you drew a simple random sample, you might end up with disproportionate numbers of each group. But if you created sampling strata based on race and ethnicity, you could randomly select cases from each stratum: 75 African Americans (15% of the sample), 50 Hispanics (10%), 25 Asians (5%), and 350 Caucasians (70%). By using **proportionate stratified sampling**, you would eliminate any possibility of error in the sample's distribution of ethnicity. Each stratum would be represented exactly in proportion to its size in the population from which the sample was drawn (see Exhibit 5.5).

Stratified random sampling: A method of sampling in which sample elements are selected separately from population strata that are identified in advance by the researcher.

Proportionate stratified sampling: Sampling methods in which elements are selected from strata in exact proportion to their representation in the population.

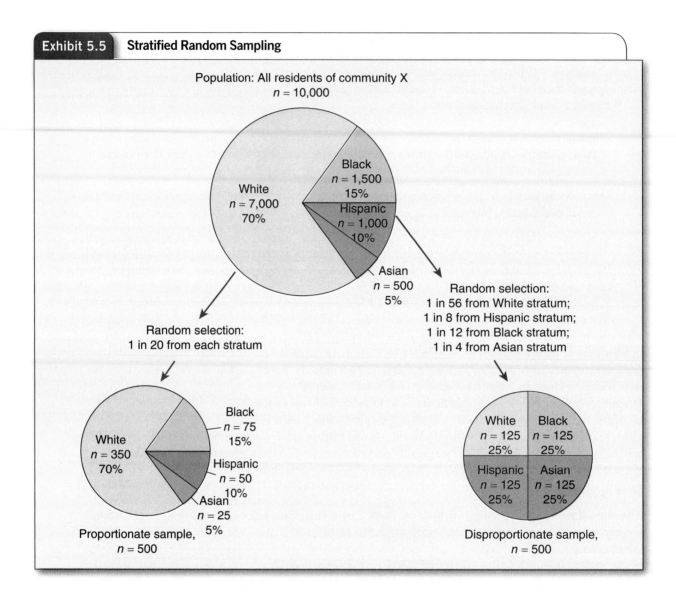

Exhibit 5.5   **Stratified Random Sampling**

Disproportionate stratified sampling:
Sampling in which elements are selected from strata in different proportions from those that appear in the population.

In **disproportionate stratified sampling**, the proportion of each stratum that is included in the sample is intentionally varied from what it is in the population. In the case of the sample stratified by ethnicity, you might select equal numbers of cases from each racial or ethnic group: 125 African Americans (25% of the sample), 125 Hispanics (25%), 125 Asians (25%), and 125 Caucasians (25%). In this type of sample, the probability of selection of every case is known but unequal between strata. You know what the proportions are in the population, so you can easily adjust your combined sample accordingly. For instance, if you want to combine the ethnic groups and estimate the average income of the total population, you would have to weight each case in the sample. The weight is a number you multiply by the value of each case based on the stratum it is in. For example, you would multiply the incomes of all African Americans in the sample by 0.6 (75/125), the incomes of all Hispanics by 0.4 (50/125), and so on. Weighting in this way reduces the influence of the oversampled strata and increases the influence of the undersampled strata to just what they would have been if pure probability sampling had been used.

Why would anyone select a sample that is so unrepresentative in the first place? The most common reason is to ensure that cases from smaller strata are included in the sample in sufficient numbers. Only then can separate statistical estimates and comparisons be made between strata (e.g., between African Americans and Caucasians). Remember that one determinant of sample quality is sample size. The same is true for subgroups within samples. If a key concern in a research project is to describe and compare the incomes of people from different racial and ethnic groups, then it is important that the researchers base the mean income of each group on enough cases to be a valid representation. If few members of a particular minority group are in the population, they need to be oversampled. Such disproportionate sampling may also result in a more efficient sampling design if the costs of data collection differ markedly between strata or if the variability (heterogeneity) of the strata differs.

Multistage Cluster Sampling

Although stratified sampling requires more information than usual prior to sampling (about the size of strata in the population), **multistage cluster sampling** requires less prior information. Specifically, cluster sampling can be useful when a sampling frame is not available, as often is the case for large populations spread across a wide geographic area or among many different organizations. In fact, if we wanted to obtain a sample from the entire U.S. population, there would be no list available. Yes, there are lists in telephone books of residents in various places who have telephones, lists of those who have registered to vote, lists of those who hold driver's licenses, and so on. However, all these lists are incomplete; some people do not list their phone number or do not have a telephone, some people are not registered to vote, and so on. Using incomplete lists such as these would introduce selection bias into our sample.

> **Multistage cluster sampling:** Sampling in which elements are selected in two or more stages, with the first stage being the random selection of naturally occurring clusters and the last stage being the random selection of multilevel elements within clusters.

> **Cluster:** A naturally occurring, mixed aggregate of elements of the population.

In such cases, the sampling procedures become a little more complex, and we usually end up working toward the sample we want through a series of steps or stages (hence the name multistage!). First, researchers extract a random sample of groups or clusters of elements that are available, and then they randomly sample the individual elements of interest from within these selected clusters. So what is a cluster? A **cluster** is a naturally occurring, mixed aggregate of elements of the population, with each element appearing in one and only one cluster. Schools could serve as clusters for sampling students, blocks could serve as clusters for sampling city residents, counties could serve as clusters for sampling the general population, and businesses could serve as clusters for sampling employees.

Drawing a cluster sample is at least a two-stage procedure. First, the researcher draws a random sample of clusters. A list of clusters should be much easier to obtain than a list of all the individuals in each cluster in the population. Next, the researcher draws a random sample of elements within each selected cluster. Because only a fraction of the total clusters are involved, obtaining the sampling frame at this stage should be much easier.

In a cluster sample of city residents, for example, blocks could be the first-stage clusters. A research assistant could walk around each selected block and record the addresses of all occupied dwelling units. Or in a cluster sample of students, a researcher could contact the schools selected in the first stage and make arrangements with the registrars to obtain lists of students at each school. Exhibit 5.6 displays the multiple stages of a cluster sample.

Exhibit 5.6 **Multistage Cluster Sampling**

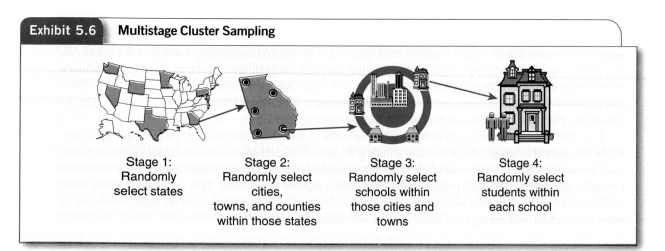

Stage 1:
Randomly
select states

Stage 2:
Randomly select
cities,
towns, and counties
within those states

Stage 3:
Randomly select
schools within
those cities and
towns

Stage 4:
Randomly select
students within
each school

crime rate in his state (Archibold 2010), and sociologist Robert J. Sampson (2008) draws attention to the rising level of immigration in cities through the 1990s to help explain the national decline in the crime rate. Criminal justice advocates in Texas point to the state's investment in community treatment and diversion programs (Grissom 2011). Police officials in New York City point to the effectiveness of CompStat, the city's computer program that indicates to the police where crimes are clustering (Dewan 2004a:A25; Dewan 2004b:A1; Kaplan 2002:A3), but other New Yorkers credit the increase in the ranks of New York's police officers because of its Safe Streets, Safe Cities program (Rashbaum 2002). Yet another possible explanation in New York City is the declining level of crack cocaine use (Dewan 2004b:C16). But then should we worry about the increasing number of drug arrests nationally (Bureau of Justice Statistics 2011) and a rise in abuse of prescription drugs (Goodnough 2010)? For cautionary lessons, should we look to Japan, where the crime rate rose sharply after being historically very low (Onishi 2003)? Clearly, to explain changes in the rate of serious crime, we must design our research strategies carefully.

In this chapter, we first discuss the meaning of causation from two different perspectives—nomothetic and idiographic—and then review the criteria for achieving causally valid explanations. During this review, we give special attention to several key distinctions in research design that are related to our ability to come to causal conclusions: the use of an experimental or nonexperimental design and reliance on a cross-sectional or longitudinal design. By the end of the chapter, you should have a good grasp of the different meanings of causation and be able to ask the right questions to determine whether causal inferences are likely to be valid. You also may have a better answer about the causes of crime and violence.

▣ Causal Explanation

A cause is an explanation for some characteristic, attitude, or behavior of groups, individuals, or other entities (such as families, organizations, or cities) or for events. Most social scientists seek causal explanations that reflect tests of the types of hypotheses with which you are familiar (see Chapter 2). In these tests, the independent variable is the

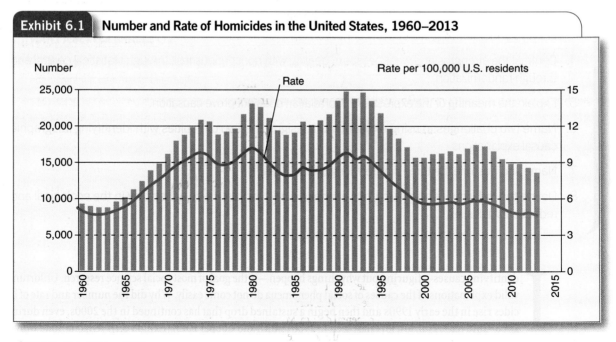

Exhibit 6.1 **Number and Rate of Homicides in the United States, 1960–2013**

Source: Smith and Cooper 2013.

presumed cause, and the dependent variable is the potential effect. For example, does problem-oriented policing (independent variable) reduce violent crime (dependent variable)? Does experiencing abuse as a child (independent variable) increase the likelihood that you will be a violent adult (dependent variable)? This type of causal explanation is termed *nomothetic*.

A different type of cause is the focus of some qualitative research (see Chapter 9) and our everyday conversations about causes. In this type of causal explanation, termed *idiographic*, individual events or the behavior of individuals are explained with a series of related, prior events. For example, you might explain a particular crime as resulting from several incidents in the life of the perpetrator that resulted in a tendency toward violence, coupled with stress resulting from a failed marriage and a chance meeting.

Quantitative (Nomothetic) Causal Explanation

A **nomothetic causal explanation** is one involving the belief that variation in an independent variable will be followed by variation in the dependent variable, when all other things are equal (*ceteris paribus*), or when all other potentially influential conditions and factors are taken into consideration. For instance, researchers might claim that the likelihood of committing violent crimes is higher for individuals who were abused as children than it would be if these same individuals had not been abused as children. Or, researchers might claim that the likelihood of committing violent crimes is higher for individuals exposed to media violence than it would be if these same individuals had not been exposed to media violence. The situation as it would have been in the absence of variation in the independent variable is termed the **counterfactual** (see Exhibit 6.2).

> **Nomothetic causal explanation:** A type of causal explanation involving the belief that variation in an independent variable will be followed by variation in the dependent variable, when all other things are equal.

Of course, the fundamental difficulty with this perspective is that we never really know what would have happened at the same time to the same people (or groups, cities, and so on) if the independent variable had not varied, because it did. We cannot rerun real-life scenarios (King, Keohane, and Verba 1994). We could observe the aggressiveness of people's behavior before and after they were exposed to media violence. But this comparison involves an earlier time period, when, by definition, the people and their circumstances were not exactly the same.

> **Example of a nomothetic causal effect:** Individuals arrested for domestic assault tend to commit fewer subsequent assaults than do similar individuals who are accused in the same circumstances but not arrested.

Fortunately, we can design research to create conditions that are comparable indeed so that we can confidently assert our conclusions *ceteris paribus*. We can examine the impact on the dependent variable of variation in the independent variable alone, even though we will not be able to compare the same people at the same time in exactly the same circumstances except for the variation in the independent variable. And by knowing the ideal standard of comparability, we can improve our research designs and strengthen our causal conclusions even when we cannot come so close to living up to the meaning of *ceteris paribus*.

> **Ceteris paribus:** Latin term meaning "all other things being equal."

> **Counterfactual:** The outcome that would have occurred if the subjects who were exposed to the treatment actually were not exposed but otherwise had had identical experiences to those they underwent during the experiment.

Quantitative researchers seek to test nomothetic causal explanations with either experimental or nonexperimental research designs. However, the way in which experimental and nonexperimental designs attempt to identify causes differs quite a bit. It is very hard to meet some of the criteria for achieving valid nomothetic causal explanations using a nonexperimental design. Most of the rest of this chapter is devoted to a review of these causal criteria and a discussion of how experimental and nonexperimental designs can help establish them.

Exhibit 6.2 | The Counterfactual in Causal Research

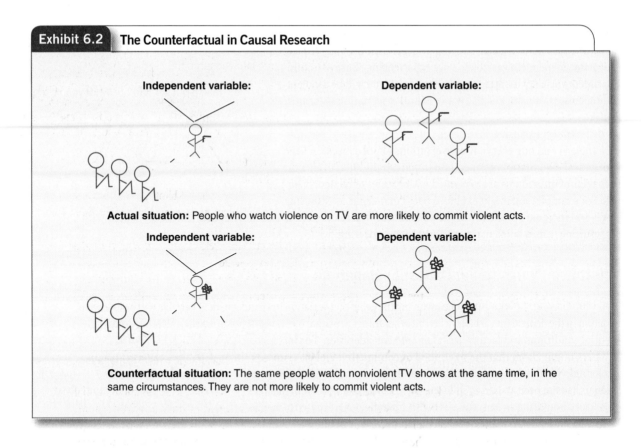

Actual situation: People who watch violence on TV are more likely to commit violent acts.

Counterfactual situation: The same people watch nonviolent TV shows at the same time, in the same circumstances. They are not more likely to commit violent acts.

Qualitative (Idiographic) Causal Explanation

Idiographic causal explanation: An explanation that identifies the concrete, individual sequence of events, thoughts, or actions that resulted in a particular outcome for a particular individual or that led to a particular event; may be termed an individualist or historicist explanation.

The other meaning of the term *cause* is one that we have in mind very often in everyday speech. This is **idiographic causal explanation**: the concrete, individual sequence of events, thoughts, or actions that resulted in a particular outcome for a particular individual or that led to a particular event (Hage and Meeker 1988). An idiographic explanation also may be termed an *individualist* or a *historicist explanation*.

Causal effect (idiographic perspective): When a series of concrete events, thoughts, or actions result in a particular event or individual outcome.

A **causal effect** from an **idiographic perspective** includes statements of initial conditions and then relates a series of events at different times that led to the outcome, or causal effect. This narrative, or story, is the critical element in an idiographic explanation, which may therefore be classified as narrative reasoning (Richardson 1995). Idiographic explanations focus on particular social actors, in particular social places, at particular social times (Abbott 1992). Idiographic explanations are also typically very concerned with **context**, with understanding the particular outcome as part of a larger set of interrelated circumstances. Idiographic explanations thus can be termed holistic.

Context: A focus of causal explanation; a particular outcome is understood as part of a larger set of interrelated circumstances.

Elijah Anderson's (1990) field research in a poor urban community produced a narrative account of how drug addiction can result in a downward slide into residential instability and crime:

When addicts deplete their resources, they may go to those closest to them, drawing them into their schemes. . . . The family may put up with the person for a while. They provide money if they can. . . . They come to realize that the person is on drugs. . . . Slowly the reality sets in more and more completely, and the family becomes drained of both financial and emotional resources. . . . Close relatives lose faith and begin to see the person as untrustworthy and weak. Eventually the addict begins to "mess up" in a variety of ways, taking furniture from the house [and] anything of value. . . . Relatives and friends begin to see the person . . . as "out there" in the streets. . . . One deviant act leads to another. (pp. 86–87)

> **Example of an idiographic causal effect:**
> An individual is neglected by his parents. He comes to distrust others, has trouble maintaining friendships, has trouble in school, and eventually gets addicted to heroin. To support his habit, he starts selling drugs and is ultimately arrested and convicted for drug trafficking.

An idiographic explanation like Anderson's (1990) pays close attention to time order and causal mechanisms. Nonetheless, it is difficult to make a convincing case that one particular causal narrative should be chosen over an alternative narrative (Abbott 1992). Does low self-esteem result in vulnerability to the appeals of drug dealers, or does a chance drug encounter precipitate a slide in self-esteem? The prudent causal analyst remains open to alternative explanations.

Idiographic explanation is deterministic, focusing on what caused a particular event to occur or what caused a particular case to change. As in nomothetic explanations, idiographic causal explanations can involve counterfactuals, by trying to identify what would have happened if a different circumstance had occurred. But unlike in nomothetic explanations, in idiographic explanations, the notion of a probabilistic relationship, an average effect, does not really apply. A deterministic cause has an effect in the case under consideration.

▣ Criteria and Cautions for Nomothetic Causal Explanations

Mark Twitchell wanted to be a filmmaker and become famous. One of the short movies he made was about a serial killer. Twitchell also was a big fan of the TV show *Dexter,* a drama about a serial killer. In 2008, he advanced this fiction to real life when he posed as a woman on a dating website to lure Johnny Altinger on a date. When Altinger showed up for the date on October 8, 2008, he was killed and dismembered. Fortunately, the murder was discovered before Twitchell could kill again. Not surprisingly, after his arrest, Twitchell became known as the "Dexter Killer" ("The Mark Twitchell Case" 2015). As frequently happens, some attributed Twitchell's violence to media portrayals of violence, in this case, to the series *Dexter.* How would you evaluate this claim? What evidence do we need to develop a valid conclusion about a hypothesized causal effect? Imagine a friend saying, after reading about the incident, "See, media violence causes people to commit crimes." Of course, after reading Chapter 1 you would not be so quick to jump to such a conclusion. "Don't overgeneralize," you would remind yourself. When your friend insists, "But I recall that type of thing happening before," you might even suspect selective observation. As a blossoming criminological researcher, you now know that if we want to have confidence in the validity of our causal statements, we must meet a higher standard.

How research is designed influences our ability to draw causal conclusions. In this section, we will introduce the features that need to be considered in a research design in order to evaluate how well it can support nomothetic causal conclusions.

Five criteria must be considered when deciding whether a causal connection exists. When a research design leaves one or more of the criteria unmet, we may have some important doubts about causal assertions the researcher may have made. The first three of the criteria are generally considered the necessary and most important basis for identifying a nomothetic causal effect: empirical association, appropriate time order, and nonspuriousness. The other two criteria, identifying a causal mechanism and specifying the context in which the effect occurs, can also considerably strengthen causal explanations, although many do not consider them to be requirements for establishing a causal relationship.

Conditions necessary for determining causality:

1. Empirical association
2. Appropriate time order
3. Nonspuriousness

prison, we would satisfy the time order requirement even if we were to measure education at the same time we measure recidivism after release. However, if there is a possibility that some respondents went back to school after prison release, the time order requirement would not be satisfied.

We believe that respondents can give us reliable reports of what happened to them or what they thought at some earlier point in time. The reliability of recall is based on many factors, including how far back in time respondents are queried and also the events they are asked to recall.

Our measures are based on records that contain information on cases in earlier periods. Government, agency, and organizational records are an excellent source of time-ordered data after the fact. However, sloppy record keeping and changes in data-collection policies can lead to inconsistencies, which must be taken into account. Another weakness of such archival data is that they usually contain measures of only a fraction of the variables that we think are important. This caution applies to the arrest records obtained by Lo and colleagues (Lo, Kim, and Cheng 2008) described in the next section. For example, their research did not obtain arrest records from states other than Ohio, and for this reason, they may have missed important incidents that could have affected their results.

We know that the value of the dependent variable was similar for all cases prior to the treatment. For example, we may hypothesize that an anger management program (independent variable) improves the conflict resolution abilities (dependent variable) of individuals arrested for intimate partner assault. If we know that none of the arrested individuals could employ verbal techniques for resolving conflict prior to the training program, we can be confident that any subsequent variation in their ability to do so did not precede exposure to the training program. This is one way that traditional experiments establish time order: Two or more equivalent groups are formed prior to exposing one of them to some treatment.

Case Study Using Life Calendars

Do Offenders Specialize in Different Crimes?

Life calendar: An instrument that helps respondents recall events in their past by displaying each month of a given year along with key dates noted within the calendar, such as birthdays, arrests, holidays, anniversaries, et cetera.

Arrestee Drug Abuse Monitoring (ADAM): A U.S. monitoring program that uses standardized drug-testing methodologies and predictive models to measure the consequences of drug abuse within each state and across state boundaries.

Anchors: Key dates of important events like birthdays that help trigger recall for respondents.

Lo and colleagues (2008) provide an interesting example of the use of such retrospective data. The researchers wanted to examine the characteristics of offenders that would lead them to repeat certain crimes. Specifically, they wanted to know if the type of crime committed early in someone's life was a reliable predictor of offenses committed later. Stated differently, do offenders specialize in different types of crime? Lo et al. obtained official arrest records from the age of 18 to the time of the study (typically around age 25) for a sample of young offenders who were incarcerated in county jails in Ohio. They then asked the inmates to reconstruct their drug and alcohol use, among other things, monthly for the same time period using a **life calendar** instrument based on the **Arrestee Drug Abuse Monitoring (ADAM)** interview schedule. This life calendar instrument helps respondents recall events in their past by displaying each month of a given year along with key dates noted within the calendar, such as birthdays, arrests, holidays, anniversaries, and so on. Respondents are given a calendar that displays these key dates, typically called **anchors**, and then are asked to recall the variables of interest (i.e., drug use, victimizations) that also occurred during the specified time frame. The use of a life calendar has been shown to improve the ability of respondents to recall events in the past compared to the use of basic questions without a calendar (Belli, Stafford, and Alwin 2009).

Results of the research by Lo et al. (2008) were somewhat mixed regarding offender specialization. Most offenders engaged in a variety of offenses prior to their current arrest. However, compared to drug and property offenders, violent offenders were more likely to specialize, as they were the most likely to have had violent arrest records prior to their current offenses.

It is important to note that retrospective data like these are often inadequate for measuring variation in past psychological states or behaviors, because what we recall about our feeling or actions in the past is likely to be influenced by what we feel in the present. For example, retrospective reports by both adult alcoholics and their parents appear to greatly overestimate the frequency of childhood problems (Vaillant 1995). People cannot report reliably the frequency and timing of many past events, from hospitalization to hours worked. However, retrospective data tend to be reliable when they concern major, persistent experiences in the past, such as what type of school someone went to or how a person's family was structured (Campbell 1992).

Longitudinal Designs

In longitudinal research, data are collected at two or more points in time and, for this reason, can be ordered in time. By measuring the value of cases on an independent variable and a dependent variable at different times, the researcher can determine whether variation in the independent variable precedes variation in the dependent variable.

In some longitudinal designs, the same sample (or panel) is followed over time; in other designs, sample members are rotated or completely replaced. The population from which the sample is selected may be defined broadly, as when a longitudinal survey of the general population is conducted. Or the population may be defined narrowly, as when members of a specific age group are sampled at multiple points in time. The frequency of follow-up measurement can vary, ranging from a before-and-after design with just one follow-up to studies in which various indicators are measured every month for many years.

Collecting data at two or more points in time can prove difficult for a number of reasons—lack of long-term funding, not being able to locate the original participants, and so on. But think of the many research questions that really should involve a much longer follow-up period: Does community-oriented policing decrease rates of violent crime? What is the impact of job training in prison on recidivism rates? How effective are batterer-treatment programs for individuals convicted of intimate partner assault? Do parenting programs for young mothers and fathers reduce the likelihood of their children becoming delinquent? It is safe to say that we will never have enough longitudinal data to answer many important research questions. Nonetheless, the value of longitudinal data is so great that every effort should be made to develop longitudinal research designs when they are appropriate for the research question asked. The following discussion of the three major types of longitudinal designs will give you a sense of the possibilities (see Exhibit 6.7).

Repeated Cross-Sectional Designs

Studies that use a **repeated cross-sectional design**, also known as **trend studies**, have become fixtures of the political arena around election time. Particularly in presidential election years, we accustom ourselves to reading weekly or even daily reports on the percentage of the population that supports each candidate. Similar polls are conducted to track sentiment on many other social issues like attitudes toward marijuana legalization and trust in the police.

> **Repeated cross-sectional design (trend study):** A type of longitudinal study in which data are collected at two or more points in time from different samples of the same population.

| Exhibit 6.7 | Three Types of Longitudinal Design |

Repeated cross-sectional surveys are conducted as follows:

1. A sample is drawn from a population at Time 1, and data are collected from the sample.

2. As time passes, some people leave the population, and others enter it.

3. At Time 2, a different sample is drawn from this population.

These features make the repeated cross-sectional design appropriate when the goal is to determine whether a population has changed over time. Has racial tolerance increased among Americans in the past 20 years? Are prisons more likely to have drug-treatment programs available today than they were in the 1950s? These questions concern changes in the population as a whole, not changes in individuals within the population. We want to know whether racial tolerance increased in society, not whether this change was due to migration that brought more racially tolerant people into the country or to individual U.S. citizens becoming more tolerant. We are asking whether state prisons overall are more likely to have drug-treatment programs available today than they were a decade or two ago, not whether any such increase was due to an increase in prisoner needs or to individual prisons changing their program availability. When we do need to know whether individuals in the population changed, we must turn to a panel design.

Fixed-Sample Panel Designs

Fixed-sample panel design (panel study): A type of longitudinal study in which data are collected from the same individuals—the panel—at two or more points in time. In another type of panel design, panel members who leave are replaced with new members.

Panel designs allow us to identify changes in individuals, groups, or whatever we are studying. This is the process for conducting **fixed-sample panel designs**, also known as **panel studies**:

1. A sample (called a panel) is drawn from a population at Time 1, and data are collected from the sample.

2. As time passes, some panel members become unavailable for follow-up, and the population changes.

3. At Time 2, data are collected from the same people as at Time 1 (the panel), except for those people who cannot be located.

Because a panel design follows the same individuals, it is better than a repeated cross-sectional design for testing causal hypotheses.

Case Study

Offending Over the Life Course

Sampson and Laub (1993) used a fixed-sample panel design to investigate the effect of childhood deviance on adult crime. They studied a sample of white males in Boston when the subjects were between 10 and 17 years old and then followed up when the subjects were in their adult years. Data were collected from multiple sources, including the subjects themselves and criminal justice records. Sampson and Laub found that children who had been committed to a correctional school for persistent delinquency were much more likely than other children in the study to commit crimes as adults: 61% were arrested between the ages of 25 and 32, compared to 14% of those who had not been in correctional schools as juveniles. In this study, juvenile delinquency unquestionably occurred before adult criminality. If the researchers had used a cross-sectional design to study the past of adults, the juvenile delinquency measure might have been biased by memory lapses, by self-serving recollections about behavior as juveniles, or by loss of agency records.

If you now wonder why not every longitudinal study is designed as a panel study, you have understood the advantages of panel designs. However, remember that this design does not in itself establish causality. Variation in both the independent variable and the dependent variables may be due to some other variable, even to earlier variation in what is considered the dependent variable. In the example in Exhibit 6.8, there is a hypothesized association between delinquency in the 11th grade and grades obtained in the 12th grade (the dependent variable). The time order is clear. However, both variables are consequences of grades obtained in the 7th grade. The apparent effect of 11th-grade delinquency on 12th-grade grades is spurious because of variation in the dependent variable (grades) at an earlier time.

Panel designs are also a challenge to implement successfully, and often are not even attempted, because of two major difficulties:

Expense and attrition. It can be difficult, and very expensive, to keep track of individuals over a long period, and inevitably the proportion of panel members who can be located for follow-up will decline over time. Panel studies often lose more than one quarter of their members through attrition (Miller 1991), and those who are lost are often not necessarily like those who remain in the panel. As a result, a high rate of subject attrition may mean that the follow-up sample will no longer be representative of the population from which it was drawn and may no longer provide a sound basis for estimating change. Subjects who were lost to follow-up may have been those who changed the most, or the least, over time. For example, between 5% and 66% of subjects are lost in substance abuse prevention studies, and the dropouts typically begin such studies with higher rates of tobacco and marijuana use (Snow, Tebes, and Arthur 1992).

It does help to compare the baseline characteristics of those who are interviewed at follow-up with characteristics of those lost to follow-up. If these two groups of panel members were not very different at baseline, it is less likely that changes had anything to do with characteristics of the missing panel members. Even better, subject attrition can be reduced substantially if sufficient staff can be used to keep track of panel members. In their panel study, Sampson and Laub (1993) lost only 12 of the juveniles in the original sample (8 if you do not count those who died).

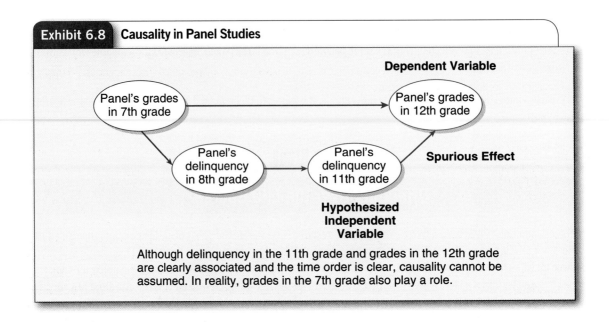

Exhibit 6.8 Causality in Panel Studies

Dependent Variable

Panel's grades in 7th grade → Panel's grades in 12th grade

Panel's delinquency in 8th grade → Panel's delinquency in 11th grade

Spurious Effect

Hypothesized Independent Variable

Although delinquency in the 11th grade and grades in the 12th grade are clearly associated and the time order is clear, causality cannot be assumed. In reality, grades in the 7th grade also play a role.

Subject fatigue. Panel members may grow weary of repeated interviews and drop out of the study, or they may become so used to answering the standard questions in the survey that they start giving stock answers rather than actually thinking about their current feelings or actions (Campbell 1992). This is called the problem of **subject fatigue**. Fortunately, subjects do not often seem to become fatigued in this way, particularly if the researchers have maintained positive relations with the subjects.

Because panel studies are so useful, social researchers have developed increasingly effective techniques for keeping track of individuals and overcoming subject fatigue. But when resources do not permit use of these techniques to maintain an adequate panel, repeated cross-sectional designs usually can be employed at a cost that is not a great deal higher than that of a one-time-only cross-sectional study. The payoff in explanatory power should be well worth the cost.

Subject fatigue: Problems caused by panel members growing weary of repeated interviews and dropping out of a study or becoming so used to answering the standard questions in the survey that they start giving stock or thoughtless answers.

Event-Based Designs

In an **event-based design**, often called a **cohort study**, the follow-up samples (at one or more times) are selected from the same **cohort**: people who all have experienced a similar event or a common starting point. Examples include the following:

Event-based design (cohort study): A type of longitudinal study in which data are collected at two or more points in time from individuals in a cohort.

- *Birth cohorts*: those who share a common period of birth (those born in the 1940s, 1950s, 1960s, etc.)
- *Seniority cohorts*: those who have worked at the same place for about 5 years, about 10 years, and so on
- *School cohorts*: freshmen, sophomores, juniors, and seniors

Cohort: Individuals or groups with a common starting point. Examples of cohorts include the college class of 1997, people who graduated from high school in the 1980s, General Motors employees who started work between 1990 and 2000, and people who were born in the late 1940s or the 1950s (the baby boom generation).

An event-based design can be a type of repeated cross-sectional design or a type of panel design. In an event-based repeated cross-sectional design, separate samples are drawn from the same cohort at two or more different times. In an event-based panel design, the same individuals from the same cohort are studied at two or more different times.

Determining Causation Using Nonexperimental Designs

How well do the research designs just described satisfy the criteria necessary to determine causality? Although it is relatively easy to establish that an empirical association exists between an independent and a dependent variable in these designs, the other criteria are much more difficult to assess.

Case Study

Gender, Social Control, and Crime

Let us first illustrate the importance of time order and nonspuriousness using research that has examined the factors related to the gender and crime relationship. Based on both victimization data and official police reports, data indicate that males commit the majority of all crimes. Why is this? Gottfredson and Hirschi's (1990) general theory of crime (GTC) contends that the reason males engage in more criminality is that they have lower levels of self-control than females. The researchers also contend that socialization of children by parents is the primary factor in the development of self-control. However, based on a critique of the GTC by Miller and Burack (1993) and the power-control theory (Hagan, Gillis, and Simpson 1985), Blackwell and Piquero (2005) hypothesized that the power relationships that exist between parents in a household (e.g., patriarchy) would also affect the socialization experiences of boys and girls and ultimately their levels of self-control.

To summarize briefly, Blackwell and Piquero (2005) examined the factors related to self-control acquisition in childhood using a sample of adults. Using this same sample of adults, they then examined the extent to which low-self control predicted the propensity for criminal offending. In a nutshell, they sought to explain the origins of self-control as well as the effects of self-control on criminal offending and how all this may be different for males and females from patriarchal families and for males and females from more egalitarian families. Using a random sample of 350 adults from Oklahoma City, Oklahoma, they found that there were indeed differences in the way power relationships between parents affected the acquisition of self-control for males and females. They also found, however, that there were essentially no differences in the ability of self-control to predict criminal aspirations; males and females with low self-control were more likely to self-report that they would engage in criminal behavior than their higher-self-control counterparts.

Do these findings establish that low self-control leads to crime through poor socialization of children by parents? Well, there are many assumptions being made here that we hope you can see right away. First, this study relied on the recollections of adults about their childhood socialization. It also assumed that levels of low self-control were subsequent to parental socialization and came before individuals' aspirations to offend (time order). This may very well be the case. It may be that those adults who were more likely to offend had inadequate socialization, which created low self-control. However, it may also be that offending behavior during their adolescence led to weak attachments to family and high attachments to other delinquent peers like themselves, which also decreased levels of self-control. In this case, the delinquent offending and peer associations would be a third variable responsible for both the low self-control and the criminal aspirations in adulthood (spurious relationship). The problem, of course, is that with cross-sectional data like these, the correct time order cannot be established, and it is difficult to control for the effects of all important factors. To reduce the risk of spuriousness, Blackwell and Piquero (2005) used the technique of **statistical control**. However, they still stated clearly the need for longitudinal research, "Future research should attempt to examine the changing nature of parental socialization and self-control across gender in longitudinal studies" (2005, 15).

> **Statistical control:** A technique used in nonexperimental research to reduce the risk of spuriousness. One variable is held constant so the relationship between two or more other variables can be assessed.

Example of statistical control: Blackwell and Piquero (2005) found that self-control predicted criminal aspirations for individuals at all levels of income (a control variable). So an individual's level of income could not have caused the association between self-control and criminal aspirations.

Similarly, Sampson and Raudenbush (1999) designed their study, in part, to determine whether the apparent effect of visible disorder on crime—the "broken windows" thesis—was spurious due to the effect of informal social control. Exhibit 6.9 shows how statistical control was used to test this possibility. The data for all neighborhoods show that neighborhoods with much visible disorder had higher crime rates than those with less visible disorder. However, when we examine the relationship between visible disorder and neighborhood crime rates separately for neighborhoods with high and low levels of informal social control—that is, when we statistically control for social control level—we see that the crime rate no longer varies with visible disorder. Therefore, we must conclude that the apparent effect of "broken windows" was spurious due to level of informal social control. Neighborhoods with low levels of social control were more likely to have high levels of visible social and physical disorder, and they were also more likely to have a high crime rate, but the visible disorder itself did not alter the crime rate.

Intervening variables: Variables that are influenced by an independent variable and in turn influence variation in a dependent variable, thus helping to explain the relationship between the independent and dependent variables.

Our confidence in causal conclusions based on nonexperimental research also increases with identification of a causal mechanism. These mechanisms are called **intervening variables** in nonexperimental research and help us understand how variation in the independent variable results in variation in the dependent variable. For example, in a study that reanalyzed data from Glueck and Glueck's (1950) path-breaking study of juvenile delinquency, Sampson and Laub (1993) found that children who grew up with such structural disadvantages as family poverty and geographic mobility were more likely to become juvenile delinquents. Why did this occur? Their analysis indicated that these structural disadvantages led to lower levels of informal social control in the family (less parent-child attachment, less maternal supervision, and more erratic or harsh discipline). Lower levels of informal social control resulted in a higher probability of delinquency (see Exhibit 6.10). Informal social control intervened in the relationship between structural context and delinquency.

Of course, identification of one (or two or three) intervening variables does not end the possibilities for clarifying the causal mechanisms. You might ask why structural disadvantage tends to result in lower levels of family social control or how family social control influences delinquency. You could then conduct research to identify the mechanisms that link, for example, family social control and juvenile delinquency. (Perhaps the children feel they are not cared for, so they become less concerned with conforming to social expectations.) This process could go on and on. The

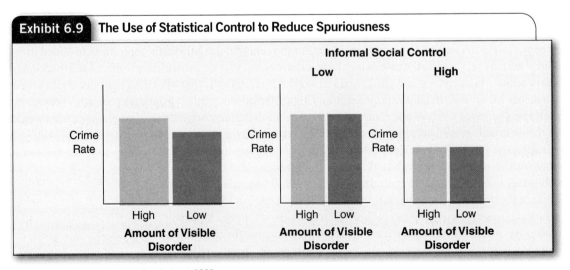

Exhibit 6.9   The Use of Statistical Control to Reduce Spuriousness

Source: Based on Sampson and Raudenbush 1999.

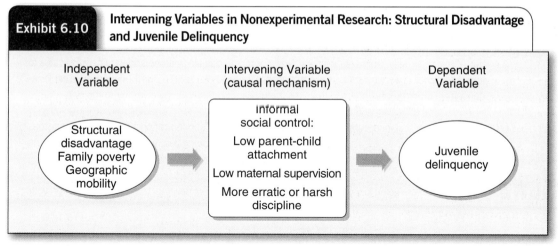

Exhibit 6.10 Intervening Variables in Nonexperimental Research: Structural Disadvantage and Juvenile Delinquency

Source: Based on Sampson and Laub 1993.

point is that identification of a mechanism through which the independent variable influences the dependent variable increases our confidence in the conclusion that a causal connection does indeed exist.

When you think about the role of variables in causal relationships, do not confuse variables that cause spurious relationships with variables that intervene in causal relationships, even though both are third variables that do not appear in the initial hypothesis. Intervening variables help explain the relationship between the independent variable (juvenile delinquency) and the dependent variable (adult criminality).

Nonexperimental research can be a very effective tool for exploring the context in which causal effects occur. Administering surveys in many different settings and to different types of individuals is usually much easier than administering various experiments. The difficulty of establishing nonspuriousness does not rule out using nonexperimental data to evaluate causal hypotheses. In fact, when enough nonexperimental data are collected to allow tests of multiple implications of the same causal hypothesis, the results can be very convincing (Freedman 1991).

In any case, nonexperimental tests of causal hypotheses will continue to be popular, because the practical and ethical problems in randomly assigning people to different conditions preclude testing many important hypotheses with an experimental design. Just remember to carefully consider possible sources of spuriousness and other problems when evaluating causal claims based on individual nonexperimental studies.

Units of Analysis and Errors in Causal Reasoning

In criminological research, we obtain samples from many different units, including individuals, groups, cities, prisons, countries, and so on. When we make generalizations from a sample to the population, it is very important to keep in mind the units under study, which are referred to as the **units of analysis**. These units of analysis are the level of social life on which the research question is focused, such as individuals, groups, or nations.

> **Units of Analysis:** The level of social life on which a research question is focused, such as individuals.

Individual and Group Units of Analysis

In many research studies, the units of analysis are individuals. The researcher may collect survey data from individuals, analyze the data, and then report on how many individuals felt socially isolated and whether recidivism by individuals related to their feelings of social isolation. Data are collected from individuals, and the focus of analysis is on the individual.

Research in the News

For Further Thought ?

HOW TO REDUCE CRIME

Social science researchers are looking at New York City's decline in crime and incarceration rates to find the answer to "what works?" Researchers are trying to pull apart a number of possible explanations, from demographic shifts to policing strategies. Experiments reviewed by Anthony A. Braga, Andrew V. Papachristos, and David M. Hureau suggest that "hot-spot" policing may be the solution to reducing crime and incarceration. Hot-spot policing involves concentrating extra policing resources in narrowly defined areas with high rates of crime and then being very aggressive in issuing tickets and making arrests. However, there is as yet no consensus about how to implement this strategy.

1. If you were going to evaluate the effectiveness of hot spot policing, how would you design your study?

2. Pose a research question that would extend research on hot-spot policing.

Source: Tierney, John. 2013. "Prison Population Can Shrink When Police Crowd the Streets." *New York Times*, January 26, p. A1.

In other instances, however, the units of analysis may instead be groups, such as families, schools, prisons, towns, states, or countries. For example, a researcher may collect data from town and police records on the number of DUI accidents and the presence or absence of a server liability law, which makes those who serve liquor liable for accidents caused by those they served. The researcher can then analyze the relationship between server liability laws and the frequency of accidents due to drunk driving (perhaps also taking into account town population). Because the data describe the towns, towns are the units of analysis.

In some studies, groups are the units of analysis, but data are collected from individuals. For example, Sampson, Raudenbush, and Earls (1997) studied influences on violent crime in Chicago neighborhoods. Collective efficacy was one variable they hypothesized as an influence on the neighborhood crime rate. This variable was a characteristic of the neighborhood residents who were likely to help other residents and were trusted by other residents, so they measured this variable in a survey of individuals. The responses of individual residents about their perceptions of their neighbors' helpfulness and trustworthiness were averaged to create a collective efficacy score for each neighborhood. It was this neighborhood measure of collective efficacy that was used to explain variation in the rate of violent crime between neighborhoods. The data were collected from individuals and were about individuals, but they were combined or aggregated to describe neighborhoods. The units of analysis were thus groups (neighborhoods).

Units of observation: The cases about which measures actually are obtained in a sample.

In a study such as this, we can distinguish the concept of units of analysis from the **units of observation**. Data were collected from individuals, the units of observation, and then the data were aggregated and analyzed at the group level. In most studies, however, the units of observation and the units of analysis are the same. For example, Yili Xu, Mora Fiedler, and Karl Flaming (2005), in collaboration with the Colorado Springs Police Department, surveyed a stratified random sample of 904 residents to test whether their sense of collective efficacy and other characteristics would predict their perceptions of crime, fear of crime, and satisfaction with police. Their data were collected from individuals and analyzed at the individual level. They concluded that collective efficacy was not as important as in Sampson et al.'s (1997) study.

The important point is to know when this is true. A conclusion that crime increases with joblessness could imply that individuals who lose their jobs are more likely to commit a crime, that a community with a high unemployment rate is likely to have a high crime rate, or both. Whether we are drawing conclusions from data or interpreting others' conclusions, we have to be clear about which relationship is referenced.

We also have to know what the units of analysis are to interpret statistics properly. Measures of association tend to be stronger for group-level than for individual-level data, because measurement errors at the individual level tend to cancel out at the group level (Bridges and Weis 1989).

The Ecological Fallacy and Reductionism

Researchers should make sure that their causal conclusions reflect the units of analysis in their study. Conclusions about processes at the individual level should be based on individual-level data; conclusions about group-level processes should be based on data collected about groups. When this rule is violated, we can often be misled about the existence of an association between two variables.

A researcher who draws conclusions about individual-level processes from group-level data is constructing an **ecological fallacy** (see Exhibit 6.11). The conclusions may or may not be correct, but we must recognize that group-level data do not describe individual-level processes. For example, a researcher may examine prison employee records and find that the higher the percentage of correctional workers without college education in prisons, the higher the rate of inmate complaints of brutality by officers in prisons. But the researcher would commit an ecological fallacy if she then concluded that individual correctional officers without a college education were more likely to engage in acts of brutality against inmates. This conclusion is about an individual-level causal process (the relationship between the education and criminal propensities of individuals), whereas the data describe groups (prisons). It could actually be that college-educated officers are the ones more likely to commit acts of brutality. If more officers in prison are not college educated, perhaps the college-educated officers feel they would not be suspected.

> **Ecological fallacy:** An error in reasoning in which incorrect conclusions about individual-level processes are drawn from group-level data.

Conversely, when data about individuals are used to make inferences about group-level processes, a problem occurs that can be thought of as the mirror image of the ecological fallacy: the **reductionist fallacy,** or **reductionism,** also known as the *individualist fallacy* (see Exhibit 6.11). For example, a reductionist explanation of individual violence would focus on biological factors, such as genes or hormones, rather than on the community's level of poverty. William Wilson (1987) also notes that we can be misled into concluding from individual-level data that race has a causal effect on violence. Although African Americans may be disproportionately represented in arrest statistics, they are also disproportionately represented in poor communities. That is, they are significantly more likely to live in communities with concentrated disadvantage compared to whites. The concentration of African Americans in poverty areas, not the race or other characteristics of the individuals in these areas, may be the cause of higher rates of violence. Explaining violence in this case requires community-level data.

> **Reductionist fallacy (reductionism):** An error in reasoning that occurs when incorrect conclusions about group-level processes are based on individual-level data.

The fact that errors in causal reasoning can be made should not deter you from conducting research with aggregate data, nor should it make you unduly critical of researchers who make inferences about individuals on the basis of aggregate data. When considered broadly, many research questions point to relationships that could be manifested in many ways and on many levels. The study of urban violence by Sampson et al. (1997) is a case in point. Their analysis involved only aggregate data about cities,

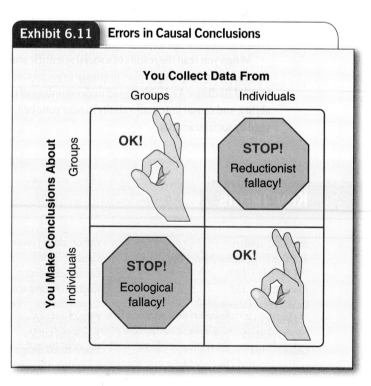

Exhibit 6.11   Errors in Causal Conclusions

CHAPTER 7

Experimental Designs

LEARNING OBJECTIVES

1. List the essential components of a true experimental design.

2. Identify the consequences of using random assignment in an experiment.

3. Distinguish the concepts of random assignment (randomization) and random sampling.

4. Explain the advantages and disadvantages of using quasi-experimental and experimental designs.

5. Define five of the threats to internal validity in research designs, and explain the extent to which each is a source of concern in true experimental designs.

6. Compare the influences on external validity (generalizability) in experimental design to those on internal validity (causal validity).

7. Discuss the most distinctive ethical challenges in experimental research.

8. Understand how factorial surveys and the Solomon four-group design increase sample generalizability.

At the end of 2013, an estimated 6,899,000 people were under the supervision of adult correctional systems in the United States. The majority of these were on probation or parole, but 2,220,300 people were incarcerated in prisons or local jails (Glaze and Kaeble 2014). The large prison population coupled with lawsuits has prompted most correctional institutions to begin classifying inmates into different security levels (e.g., minimum, maximum) based on objective criteria such as the severity of their offenses, their previous records, and so forth. Obviously, the security level of an institution in which an inmate is classified will affect his or her incarceration experience. For example, someone who is assigned to a maximum-security prison instead of one with a lower level of security will also have differential access to things like mental health services, drug treatment programs, and vocational training (Brennan and Austin 1997).

But is the classification of inmates also related to their behavior while incarcerated? Do those assigned to maximum-security prisons engage in more misconduct compared to inmates assigned to less secure facilities? How

176

could you answer this question? If you compared rates of misconduct across prison settings, you would not have the answer, because the inmates may be very different to begin with; that is, the people assigned to maximum security prisons may be different from those assigned to medium security prisons to begin with. For this reason, any differences you observe in misconduct could be attributable to these "before incarceration" differences, not to the type of facility in which they are housed.

In the previous chapter, you learned that experimental research provides the most powerful design for testing nomothetic causal hypotheses. This chapter examines experimental methodology in more detail. You will learn to distinguish different types of experimental designs (which include true experiments and quasi-experiments), to evaluate the utility of particular designs for reaching causally valid conclusions, to identify problems of generalizability with experiments, and to consider ethical problems in experimentation. We will also return to the relationship between prison security level and inmate misconduct later in the chapter.

回 History of Experiments

Experimentation has always been a key method of scientific research. A famous experiment, perhaps the first, was conducted by Archimedes in 230 BC when he tested the way in which levers balance weights. In 1607, Galileo conducted experiments by dropping weights to test the theory of falling bodies. By the mid-1800s, the use of experiments in the rapidly growing fields of scientific research was well established (Willer and Walker 2007).

Successful experiments measure variables precisely and control the conditions in which a hypothesis is tested. Conducting the research in a laboratory setting—often a specially designed room in a university—can permit exacting control over every detail. Experimental researchers thus remove sources of variability that are not relevant to the specific hypothesis being tested.

Experimental research by social scientists, including those interested in criminological and criminal justice related issues, have made important contributions to understanding the social world since the middle years of the 20th century. In fact, there is a journal titled *The Journal of Experimental Criminology*, there is a Division of Experimental Criminology in the American Society of Criminology, and there is an Institute of Experimental Criminology at Cambridge University (http://www.crim.cam.ac.uk/research/experiments/). In sum, while many think that experiments remain in the domains of physics or psychology, experimental methods are being increasingly used in all social science research.

回 True Experiments

Recall from the previous chapter that **true experiments** must have at least three things:

> **True experiment:** Experiment in which subjects are assigned randomly to an experimental group that receives a treatment or other manipulation of the independent variable and a comparison group that does not receive the treatment or receives some other manipulation. Outcomes are measured in a posttest.

1. Two comparison groups, one receiving the experimental condition (e.g., treatment or intervention) and the other receiving no treatment or intervention or another form of experimental condition.

2. Random assignment to the two (or more) comparison groups.

3. Assessment of change in the dependent variable for both groups after the experimental condition has been received.

The combination of these features permits us to have much greater confidence in the validity of causal conclusions than is possible with other research designs. As you learned in Chapter 6, two more features further enhance our confidence in the validity of an experiment's findings:

1. Identification of the causal mechanism

2. Control over the context of an experiment

You will learn more about each of these key features of experimental design as you review examples of experimental studies. We will use simple diagrams to help describe and compare the experiments' designs. These diagrams also show at a glance how well suited any experiment is to identifying causal relationships, by indicating whether the experiment has a comparison group, a pretest and a posttest, and randomization.

Experimental and Comparison Groups

> **Experimental group:** In an experiment, the group of subjects that receives the treatment or experimental manipulation.

> **Control or comparison group:** The group of subjects who are either exposed to a different treatment than the experimental group or who receive no treatment at all.

> **Treatment:** The manipulation that exposes subjects in an experiment to a particular value of the independent variable.

True experiments must have at least one **experimental group** (subjects who receive some treatment) and at least one **control or comparison group** (subjects to whom the experimental group can be compared). The control group differs from the experimental group by one or more independent variables, whose effects are being tested. In other words, the difference between the two groups is that the experimental group receives the treatment or condition we are interested in, whereas the comparison group does not.

In many experiments, the independent variable indicates the presence or absence of something, such as receiving a treatment program or not receiving it. This **treatment** can be thought of as the independent variable. In these experiments, the comparison group, consisting of the subjects who do not receive the treatment, is termed a control group. You learned in Chapter 6 that an experiment can have more than two groups. There can be several treatment groups, corresponding to different values of the independent variable, and several comparison groups, including a control group that receives no treatment.

Pretest and Posttest Measures

> **Posttest:** Measurement of an outcome (dependent) variable after an experimental intervention or after a presumed independent variable has changed for some other reason.

> **Pretest:** Measurement of an outcome (dependent) variable prior to an experimental intervention or change in a presumed independent variable for some other reason. The pretest is exactly the same "test" as the posttest, but it is administered at a different time.

All true experiments have a **posttest**—that is, measurement of the outcome in both groups after the experimental group has received the treatment. In fact, we might say that any hypothesis-testing research involves a posttest. The dependent variable is measured after the independent variable has had its effect, if any. True experiments also may have **pretests** that measure the dependent variable prior to the experimental intervention. A pretest is exactly the same as the posttest, just administered before the treatment. Strictly speaking, a true experiment does not require a pretest, but having pretest scores has many advantages. They provide a direct measure of how much the experimental and comparison groups changed over time. They allow the researcher to verify that randomization was successful (that chance factors did not lead to an initial difference between the groups). In addition, by identifying subjects' initial scores on the dependent variable, a pretest provides a more complete picture of the conditions in which the intervention had (or did not have) an effect (Mohr 1992).

An experiment may have multiple posttests and perhaps even multiple pretests. Multiple posttests can identify just when the treatment has its effect and for how long. They are particularly important for treatments delivered over time (Rossi and Freeman 1989).

How do we know the control and experimental groups are equivalent before the treatment if we do not have a pretest? When researchers use random assignment to the experimental and comparison groups, the groups' initial scores on the dependent variable and on all other variables are very likely to be similar. Any difference in outcome between the experimental and comparison groups is therefore likely to result from the intervention (or to other processes occurring during the experiment), and the likelihood of a difference just on the basis of chance can be calculated. This is fortunate, because the dependent variable in some experiments cannot be measured in a pretest. We talk more about random assignment next.

Random Assignment

Random assignment, sometimes referred to as randomization, is what makes the comparison group in a true experiment such a powerful tool for identifying the effects of the treatment. If subjects are randomly assigned to either the experimental group or the comparison group, then a researcher can assume that the only difference between the two groups is that the experimental group received

> **Random assignment:** A procedure by which each experimental and control group subject is placed in a group randomly.

the treatment or intervention and the comparison group did not. Thus, a randomly assigned comparison group can provide a good estimate of the counterfactual, the outcome that would have occurred if the subjects had not been exposed to the treatment but had otherwise equal experiences (Mohr 1992; Rossi and Freeman 1989). If the comparison group differed from the experimental group in any way other than not receiving the treatment (or receiving a different treatment), a researcher would not be able to determine the unique effects of the treatment.

Assigning subjects randomly to the experimental and comparison groups ensures that systematic bias does not affect the assignment of subjects to groups. But of course, random assignment cannot guarantee that the groups are perfectly identical at the start of the experiment. Similar to random selection in sampling, random assignment removes bias from the assignment process but only by relying on chance, which itself can result in some intergroup differences. Fortunately, researchers can use statistical methods to determine the odds of ending up with groups that differ on the basis of chance alone; these odds are low even for groups of moderate size.

Although the two procedures are similar, it is important to note here that random assignment of subjects to experimental and comparison groups is not the same as random sampling of individuals from a larger population (see Exhibit 7.1). In fact, random assignment (randomization) does not help ensure that the research subjects are representative of some larger population; that is the goal of random sampling. What random assignment does by creating two or more equivalent groups is useful for ensuring internal validity, not generalizability.

Random assignment does share with random sampling the use of a chance selection method. In random assignment, a random procedure is used to determine the group into which each subject is placed. In random sampling, a random procedure is used to determine which cases are selected for the sample. The random procedure of tossing a coin, using a random number table, or generating random numbers with a computer can be similar in both random assignment and random sampling.

Matching is another procedure sometimes used to equate experimental and comparison groups, but by itself, it is a poor substitute for randomization. Matching of individuals in a treatment group with those in a comparison group might involve pairing persons on the basis of similarity of gender, age, year in school, or some other characteristic. The basic problem is that, as a practical matter, individuals can be matched on only a few characteristics; unmatched differences between the experimental and comparison groups may still influence outcomes. However, matching combined with randomization can reduce the possibility of differences due to chance. For example, if individuals are matched by gender and age, then the members of each matched pair are randomly assigned to the experimental and comparison groups, and the possibility of differences due to chance in the gender and age composition of the groups is minimized (see Exhibit 7.2). Matching is also used in some quasi-experimental designs when randomization is not possible, as you will see later in this chapter.

> **Matching:** A procedure for equating the characteristics of individuals in different comparison groups in an experiment. Matching can be done on either an individual or an aggregate basis. For individual matching, individuals who are similar in terms of key characteristics are paired prior to assignment, and then each member of each pair is assigned to a different group. For aggregate matching, groups are chosen for comparisons that are similar in terms of the distribution of key characteristics.

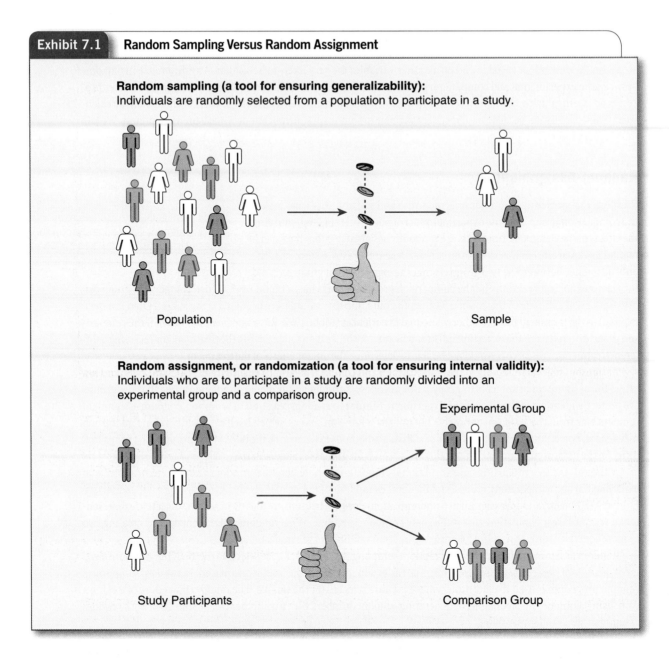

Exhibit 7.1   **Random Sampling Versus Random Assignment**

Random sampling (a tool for ensuring generalizability):
Individuals are randomly selected from a population to participate in a study.

Population   Sample

Random assignment, or randomization (a tool for ensuring internal validity):
Individuals who are to participate in a study are randomly divided into an
experimental group and a comparison group.

                                             Experimental Group

Study Participants   Comparison Group

We have already discussed two true experimental designs in this text: the Bushman experiment on media violence (for review, see Bushman and Huesmann 2012) and the Sherman and Berk (1984) experiment on the effects of arrest on intimate partner violence. Both are graphically displayed for you now in Exhibit 7.3. As you can see, in the Bushman experiment of media violence and aggression, the experimental design included a pretest. In this experiment, undergraduate college students were randomly assigned to experimental and control groups.

Recall from the last chapter that subjects in both groups were required to perform a learning task with a fake partner. In the task, subjects were to administer noises as a form of punishment to their partners when their partners gave an incorrect answer. The noise level was the operationalization of aggression for the experiment. The louder the noises administered, the higher the aggression score. Both experimental and control group subjects thus received a pretest score on their aggressiveness.

| Exhibit 7.2 | Experimental Design Combining Matching and Random Assignment |

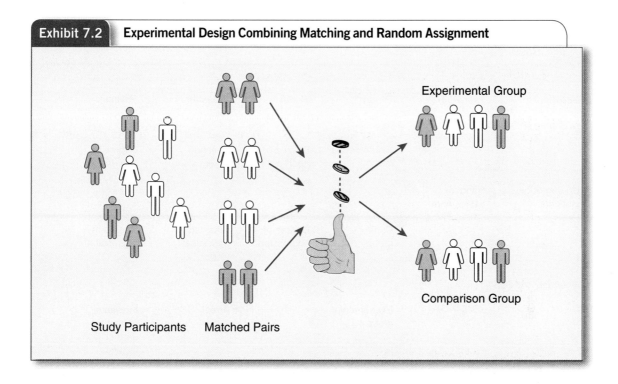

Subjects in both groups then watched a videotape; experimental group subjects watched a violent video, whereas control group subjects watched a nonviolent video. After viewing of the tapes, aggression levels were then similarly measured in the posttests. Using this design, Bushman was not only able to measure differences in aggression after the treatment (viewing the videotapes), but he was also able to determine whether aggression levels for the experimental and control subjects differentially changed from pretest to posttest. This illustrates the advantage of utilizing pretest measures in an experimental design.

The bottom panel of Exhibit 7.3 depicts the Sherman and Berk (1984) experiment. This study can be considered a **field experiment** because it was conducted in a real-world setting. Many of the experiments related to criminal justice–related issues are field experiments. The subjects for the Sherman and Berk experiment were all reported offenders of misdemeanor intimate partner assault in Minneapolis,

Field experiment: An experimental study conducted in a real-world setting.

Minnesota, during the time of the experiment. The experimental treatment was arrest, and the control treatment was separation and no arrest. The key to this experimental design was that incidents were randomly assigned to the arrest and nonarrest conditions. That is, when an officer arrived at the scene, he or she randomly assigned offenders to the treatment based on a randomly color-coded police record sheet. For example, if an officer arrived at the scene and the next sheet in his book was pink, he would make an arrest; if the sheet was white, he would not make an arrest. The posttest measurement was recidivism. If those offenders who were arrested were less likely than nonarrested offenders to have assaulted their partners six months after the incident, this decreased rate of assault could be attributed to the treatment of arrest. This, of course, is what happened.

Throughout the remainder of this chapter, you will learn more about each of these key features of experimental design. To help you understand the variability across different experimental designs, we will incorporate the use of simple diagrams. These diagrams also show at a glance just how well suited any experiment is to identifying causal relations, by indicating whether it has a comparison group, a pretest and a posttest, and random assignment. We will now turn to the question that we asked at the beginning of the chapter, "Does the type of security classification inmates are given affect their behavior?"

Exhibit 7.3	**Experimental Design Used in the Bushman (2012) and Sherman and Berk (1984) Research**

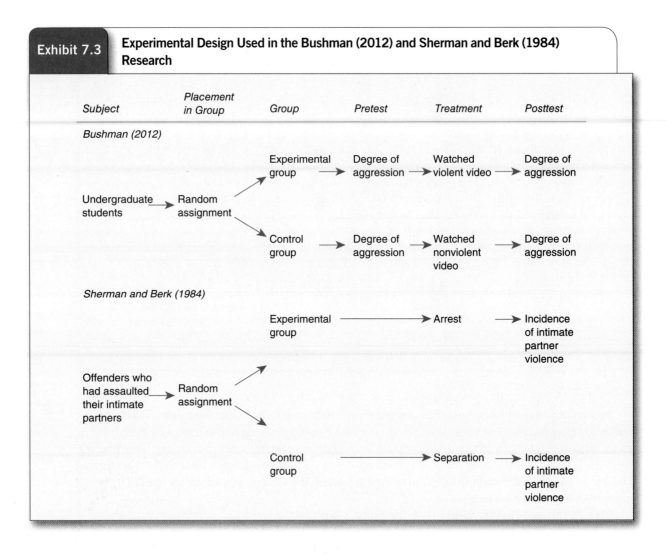

Case Study

Prison Classification and Inmate Behavior

There is wide variability in the criteria used to classify prisoners across states. Regardless of how these classifications are made, once these labels are assigned, they have the effect that all labels have: They attach various expectations to prisoners. Bench and Allen (2003) state,

> An offender classified as maximum security instantly obtains an image of one who is hard to handle, disrespectful of authority, prone to fight with other inmates, and at a high risk for escape. In contrast, an offender classified as medium security is generally regarded as more manageable, less of an escape risk, and not requiring as much supervision as a maximum-security offender. (p. 369)

To examine whether prison classification actually affected inmate behavior, Bench and Allen (2003) obtained a random sample of 200 inmates admitted to the Utah State Prison who had been classified as maximum security following their initial assessment based on the following criteria: severity of current crime, expected length of incarceration, criminal violence history, escape history, prior institutional commitment, age, history of institutional adjustment, and substance abuse history.

From this group, inmates were randomly assigned to either an experimental group, in which inmates were reclassified to medium security status, or to a control group, in which inmates retained their maximum security status. The independent variable, then, was security classification. The dependent variable was the number of disciplinary infractions, or sanctions for violation of prison rules, received by each group. The severity of infractions were weighted to control for their (e.g., possession of unauthorized food was weighted lower than assaulting another inmate). The primary hypothesis was that the experimental group, those reclassified as medium security, would have a lower number of disciplinary infractions compared to the control group, the inmates who retained their maximum-security classification. A diagram depicting the experiment is provided in Exhibit 7.4. Results indicated that inmates reclassified to medium security did not receive a lower number of infractions; both groups received about the same number of disciplinary infractions, regardless of security classification. Policy implications are obvious. Bench and Allen (2003) state,

> Maximum-security offenders who stand out on a number of dimensions such as length of sentence, severity of offense, prior incarcerations, and propensity for violence can be housed in medium-security environments with no increased risk of disciplinary involvement. . . . In addition, institutions that are considering expansion should give careful consideration to how much room actually is needed for costly maximum-security housing. (p. 378)

To help you understand the procedures involved in true experimental designs, we will describe a very novel experiment conducted by Devah Pager (2007) that investigated the effects of having a criminal record on employment opportunities.

| Exhibit 7.4 | Experiment Examining the Effect of Prison Classification on Inmate Behavior (Bench and Allen 2003) |

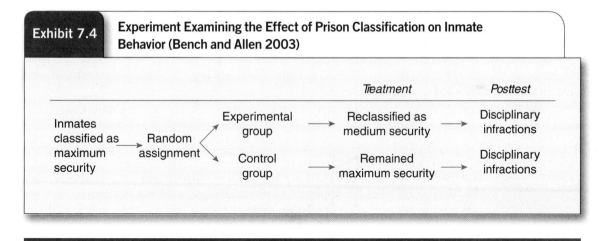

Case Study

The Effect of Incarceration on Employment

One recent innovative field experiment was conducted by Devah Pager (2007) to determine the effects of incarceration on the likelihood of obtaining employment. This is an extremely important research question, because the prison population in the United States has vastly increased over the past 30 years. The vast majority of the over 2 million individuals incarcerated in correctional facilities will eventually return to their communities. In fact, over 650,000 inmates reenter society every year in the United States (Bureau of Justice Statistics 2011). In addition to the laws barring exoffenders in some states from obtaining employment in certain sectors, reentering offenders also face other obstacles in finding a job.

How could we determine the effects of a formal record on the likelihood of getting a job? Well, we could examine employer attitudes about hiring exoffenders through a survey, but as you now know, this would not help us isolate a causal relationship between having a record and getting a job. We could interview offenders reentering the community to find out about their experiences, but this too would tell us only about a few individuals' experiences. The best way to determine the effects of a criminal record on employment chances would be to conduct a field experiment.

Pager (2007) was interested in the negative consequences that being incarcerated had on future employment opportunities. She designed a field experiment in which pairs of applicants, one who had a criminal record and one who did not, applied for real jobs. Her study used two male teams of applicants, one team composed of two African Americans and one team composed of two whites. These individuals were actually college students in Milwaukee, Wisconsin, whom Pager refers to as "testers." The testers were matched on the basis of age, physical appearance, and general style of self-presentation, and all were assigned fictitious résumés that reflected equivalent levels of education (all had a high school education) and equivalent levels of steady work experience. However, one tester within each team was randomly assigned to have a criminal record and the other was not. The criminal record consisted of a felony drug conviction and 18 months of served prison time. This assignment rotated each week of the study (e.g., one individual played the job applicant with a record one week, and the other did so the next week) to control for unobserved differences between team members. Same-race testers (one with a criminal record and one without) applied for the same job, one day apart. The black team applied for a total of 200 jobs, and the white team applied for a total of 150 jobs.

The primary outcome of the study was the proportion of applications that elicited either callbacks from employers or on-the-spot job offers. The testers went through intensive training to become familiar with their assumed profiles and to respond similarly to potential interview questions. For this reason, the only difference between the two testers on each race team was that one had a criminal record and the other didn't. Because there was random assignment to these two conditions and the other characteristics of the testers were essentially the same, the differences observed in the percentage of callbacks between team members can be assumed to be related to the criminal record only and not to other factors. This study is diagrammed in Exhibit 7.5.

The results of Pager's (2007) field experiment were stark. Testers with a criminal record were one-half to one-third less likely to receive a callback from employers, and the effect was even more pronounced for black

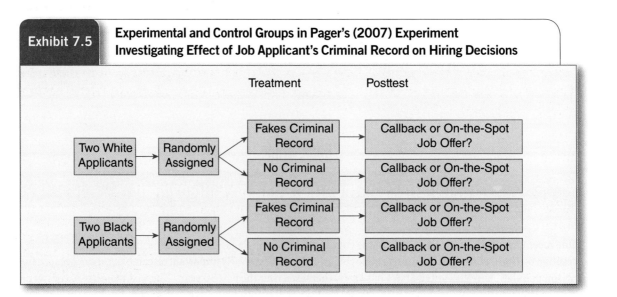

Exhibit 7.5 **Experimental and Control Groups in Pager's (2007) Experiment Investigating Effect of Job Applicant's Criminal Record on Hiring Decisions**

Source: Based on Pager, D. 2007. *Marked: Race, Crime and Finding Work in an Era of Mass Incarceration.* Chicago: University of Chicago Press.

applicants. Pager concludes, "Mere contact with the criminal justice system in the absence of any transformative or selective effects severely limits subsequent job prospects. The mark of a criminal record indeed represents a powerful barrier to employment" (p. 145). With such a powerful randomly assigned field experiment, the internal (causal) validity of these findings is strong. The implications of these results when generalized to the hundreds of thousands of offenders who attempt to reenter society from prison each year are troubling indeed.

Summary: Causality in True Experiments

The studies by Pager (2007) and Bench and Allen (2003) were both true experiments because they had at least one experimental and one comparison group to which subjects were randomly assigned. The researchers also compared variation in the dependent variables after variation in the independent variables.

Let's examine how well these true experiments meet the criteria for identifying a nomothetic cause:

Association between the hypothesized independent and dependent variables. As you have seen, experiments can provide unambiguous evidence of association by comparing the distribution of the dependent variable (or its average value) between the experimental and comparison groups.

Time order of effects of one variable on the others. Unquestionably, the faked criminal record or lack thereof came before the job offers in the Pager (2007) study, and the reclassification came before disciplinary infractions in the Bench and Allen (2003) experiment. In true experiments, randomization to the experimental and comparison groups equates the groups at the start of the experiment, so time order can be established by comparing posttest scores between the groups. However, experimental researchers include a pretest when possible so that equivalence of the groups at baseline can be confirmed and the amount of change can be compared between the experimental and comparison groups. Bushman (Bushman and Huesmann 2012) included a pretest in his experiment examining the effects of watching media violence on individual aggression.

Nonspurious relationships between variables. Nonspuriousness is difficult—some would say impossible—to establish in nonexperimental designs. The random assignment of subjects to experimental and comparison groups is what makes true experiments such powerful designs for testing causal hypotheses. Randomization controls for the host of possible extraneous influences that can create misleading, spurious relationships in both experimental and nonexperimental data. If we determine that a design has used randomization successfully, we can be much more confident in the resulting causal conclusions. For example, the only thing that was different between the job applicants in Pager's (2007) study was they randomly faked having a criminal record. Everything else was virtually identical. For this reason, the fact that those who faked a criminal record (drug conviction) were less likely to be offered a job can be attributable only to the presence of the criminal record.

▣ Quasi-Experiments

Often, testing a hypothesis with a true experimental design is not feasible. Such a test may be too costly, take too long to carry out, be inappropriate for the particular research problem, or presume ability to manipulate an intervention that already has occurred. To overcome these problems yet still benefit from the logic of the experimental method, researchers may use designs that retain several components of experimental design but differ in other important details.

Usually, the best alternative to an experimental design is a **quasi-experimental design**, maximizing internal validity. Although it is not defined consistently by all

Quasi-experimental design: A research design in which there is a comparison group that is comparable to the experimental group in critical ways, but subjects are not randomly assigned to the comparison and experimental groups.

Cohort: Individuals or groups with a common starting point. Examples of cohorts include the college class of 1997, people who graduated from high school in the 1980s, General Motors employees who started work between 1990 and 2000, and people who were born in the late 1940s or the 1950s (the baby boom generation).

Nonequivalent control group design: A quasi-experimental design in which there are experimental and comparison groups that are designated before the treatment occurs but are not created by random assignment.

Before-and-after design: A quasi-experimental design may consist of before-and-after comparisons of the experimental group, but has no control group.

Ex post facto control group design: Nonexperimental design in which comparison groups are selected after the treatment, program, or other variation in the independent variable has occurred.

experts, in a quasi-experimental design the comparison group is predetermined to be comparable to the treatment group in critical ways, such as eligibility for the same services or membership in the same school or **cohort** (Rossi and Freeman 1989). However, because subjects are *not* randomly assigned to the comparison and experimental groups, these research designs are "quasi"-experimental. In other quasi-experimental designs, there may be just one group that is monitored before and after a treatment is delivered and no comparison group. In both cases, we cannot be as confident in their causal conclusions as we can with true experimental designs.

The following are the three major types of quasi-experimental designs (others can be found in Cook and Campbell 1979 or Mohr 1992):

- **Nonequivalent control group designs** have experimental and comparison groups designated before the treatment occurs that are not created by random assignment.

- **Before-and-after designs** have a pretest and posttest but no comparison group. In other words, the subjects exposed to the treatment served, at an earlier time, as their own controls.

- **Ex post facto control group designs**, like nonequivalent control group designs, have experimental and comparison groups that are not created by random assignment. But unlike the groups in nonequivalent control group designs, the groups in ex post facto designs are designated after the treatment or intervention has occurred. For this reason, some researchers consider this design to be nonexperimental, not even quasi-experimental.

Nonequivalent Control Group Designs

In this type of quasi-experimental design, a comparison group is selected to be as comparable as possible to the treatment group. Two selection methods can be used:

Individual matching. Individual cases in the treatment group are matched with similar individuals in the comparison group. A Mexican American male about 20 years old who is assigned to the treatment group may be matched with another Mexican American male about 20 years old who is assigned to the comparison group. The problem with this method is determining in advance which variables should be used for matching. It is also unlikely that a match can be found for all cases. However, in some situations matching can create a comparison group that is very similar to the experimental group. For example, some studies of the effect of Head Start, the government program that prepares disadvantaged toddlers for school, used participants' siblings as the comparison group. The members of the control group were thus similar to the experimental group to the extent that siblings are similar to one another.

Aggregate matching. Matching in the aggregate means finding a group with similar distributions on key variables, such as average age, percentage of females, and so on. In this way, a comparison group is identified that matches the treatment group in the aggregate rather than for each individual case. In most situations when random assignment is not possible, this method of matching makes sense. For this design to be considered even quasi-experimental, individuals cannot choose which group to join or where to seek services. In other words, the subjects cannot opt for or against the experimental treatment.

Case Study

The Effectiveness of Drug Courts

The study of the effectiveness of a drug court on recidivism by Listwan et al. (2003) illustrates a quasi-experimental nonequivalent control group design. Their quasi-experimental design is diagrammed in Exhibit 7.6. Reflecting the priority that policymakers place on controlling drug use and drug-related crime, drug courts have become extremely popular in the United States. They emerged as an alternative to correctional prison- and jail-based responses to addicted offenders and generally rely on community-based treatment models. The assumption behind the drug court movement is that drug users and their drug-related crimes will increasingly clog the courts and fill our jails and prisons if their addictions are not remedied. Although drug court programs vary tremendously across jurisdictions, they generally integrate alcohol and drug treatment services with justice system case processing. In addition, they are designed to decrease case-processing time, alleviate the demand of drug-related cases on the court, and decrease jail and prison commitments, all of which are supposed to decrease the cost of controlling drug offenders.

Listwan and her colleagues (2003) examined whether participants in the Hamilton County Drug Court program in Cincinnati, Ohio, had lower rates of recidivism for both drug-related and other offenses. Exhibit 7.6 illustrates that two groups were compared: those who participated in the drug court (experimental group) and those who were eligible but did not receive the drug court treatment services or the additional court supervision (control group). Importantly, the offenders were *not* randomly assigned to these groups. The researchers simply stated, "Members of the [control group] . . . either refused drug treatment or were refused by the drug court team" (Listwan et al. 2003, 396). Unfortunately, many evaluations of this nature do not have the ability to employ random assignment, thereby diluting the ability to determine the causal relationship between the treatment and the results. The researchers did examine the potential differences between the two groups and determined that they did not significantly differ in terms of age, race, education, or prior arrest for a drug-related offense, but the experimental group had a higher number of women and people with other prior records not related to drugs. Arrest and incarceration records for the participants were collected for up to four years after the program, but results were mixed. While participation in the program decreased the probability that offenders would be rearrested for drug-related offenses, it did not decrease the likelihood that they would be rearrested for other offenses.

Before-and-After Designs

The common feature of before-and-after designs is the absence of a comparison group. All cases are exposed to only the experimental treatment. The basis for comparison is provided by the pretreatment measures in the experimental group. These designs are useful for studies of interventions that are experienced by virtually every element in some population.

The simplest type of before-and-after design is the **fixed-sample panel design (panel study)**. A panel design involves only one pretest and one posttest. It does not qualify as a quasi-experimental design, because comparing subjects

Fixed-sample panel design (panel study): A type of longitudinal study in which data are collected from the same individuals—the panel—at two or more points in time. In another type of panel design, panel members who leave are replaced with new members.

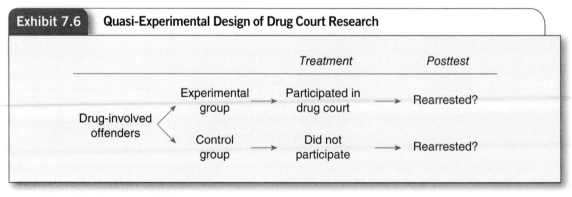

Exhibit 7.6 | **Quasi-Experimental Design of Drug Court Research**

		Treatment		Posttest
Drug-involved offenders	Experimental group →	Participated in drug court →	Rearrested?
	Control group →	Did not participate →	Rearrested?

Source: Adapted from Listwan et al. 2003.

to themselves at only one earlier point in time does not provide an adequate comparison group. Many influences other than the experimental treatment may affect a subject following the pretest. Consequently, if there is a change in the dependent variable from pre- to postmeasures, we cannot be certain that the treatment itself is the sole cause of this change. Other before-and-after designs use repeated pretest and posttest measurements, such as the one we will see next to examine the effects of the Youth Criminal Justice Act in Canada.

Case Study

The Effects of the Youth Criminal Justice Act

Carrington and Schulenberg's (2008) study of the effect of the Youth Criminal Justice Act (YCJA) of 2002 in Canada on police discretion with apprehended young offenders illustrates a **time series design,** often called a **repeated measures panel design**. This design typically includes many pretest and posttest observations that allow the researcher to study the process by which an intervention or a treatment has an impact over time. First, some background. One of the major objectives of the YCJA, which came into effect in 2003 in Canada, was to reduce the number of referrals to youth court. The YCJA generally requires police officers who are considering charging a minor with a crime to first consider extralegal judicial measures such as giving the youth an informal warning.

Time series design (repeated measures panel design): A quasi-experimental design consisting of many pretest and posttest observations of the same group.

To examine the effects of the YCJA, Carrington and Schulenberg (2008) examined the number of juveniles who were apprehended and charged from January 1, 1986, through December 31, 2006. The Canadian Uniform Crime Reporting Survey captures the number of minors who were charged, as well as the number who were "chargeable" but not charged. The researchers note, "A change in the charge ration, or proportion of chargeable youth who were charged, is an indication of a change in the use of police discretion with apprehended youth" (Carrington and Schulenberg 2008, 355). To control for the actual crime rate of youth, the researchers also examined per capita ratios. Exhibit 7.7 displays the annual rates per 100,000 young persons who were (a) apprehended (i.e., chargeable), (b) charged, and (c) not charged. This clearly shows that the YCJA may have had the intended effect. Of course, the study design leaves open the possibility that something else in 2003 may have happened to effect this change in formal charges against juveniles. However, because there was no known event that could have had such a national impact, the conclusion that this effect is attributable to the YCJA is more plausible. As you can see, this time series design is particularly useful for studying the impact of new laws or social programs that affect everyone and can be readily assessed by ongoing measurement.

Exhibit 7.7	**Results From a Repeated Measures Panel Design Used to Examine the Efficacy of the Youth Criminal Justice Act**

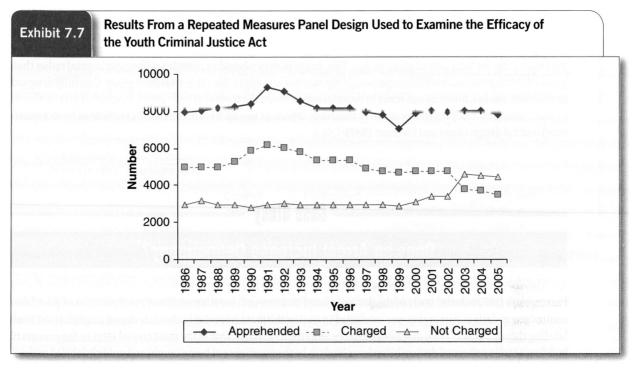

Source: From Canadian Centre for Justice Statistics and adapted from Carrington and Schulenberg 2008.

Case Study

Reduced Caseload and Intensive Supervision in Probation

Probation and parole professionals often contend that supervision outcomes would improve if caseloads were reduced, but research findings for this contention are inconsistent. For example, Jalbert and her colleagues (2010) studied the effect of reduced caseload size and intensive supervision on probation outcomes using a regression-discontinuity design. The probation office they examined identified the probationers most at risk of reoffending using a risk assessment tool that classifies probationers' risk of recidivism. Those with a high score on the measure are assigned to the highest level of supervision, called intensive supervision probation (ISP). This assessment tool score was used by Jalbert as the assignment variable. The researchers wanted to know if recidivism was actually different for those assigned to ISP compared to those assigned to a "high-normal" supervision caseload. Jalbert et al. describe their rationale for using the regression-discontinuity design as follows: "The inference about treatment effectiveness is based on a comparison of the outcomes for offenders who are at the margins: those offenders who just failed to qualify for ISP and those offenders who just qualified for ISP" (2010, 239). Results indicated that offenders supervised on both ISP and high-normal caseloads had high rates of recidivism; over two-thirds were arrested for some new charge during or after supervision, although most of these offenses were minor public order offenses. At a six-month follow-up, however, ISP reduced the likelihood of criminal recidivism compared to offenders assigned to the high-normal supervision. Importantly, the researchers also determined that ISP did *not* increase the likelihood of probationers receiving technical violations.

Importantly, valid statistical data on the prevalence of these victimizations, including defining the characteristics of those most affected (e.g., subgroups by race/ethnicity and age), is the first step in preventing them. Two federal agencies have attempted to measure both rape and intimate partner violence, the Centers for Disease Control and Prevention (CDC) and the U.S. Department of Justice's Bureau of Justice Statistics (BJS). The CDC-sponsored survey is called the *National Intimate Partner and Sexual Violence Survey* (NISVS), and the BJS sponsored survey, which measures most other forms of crime victimization, is called the *National Crime Victimization Survey* (NCVS). As we will see in this chapter, the survey questions used by the two agencies are quite different, despite the fact that they are attempting to measure the same things.

After an initial review of the reasons for using survey methods, we explain the major steps in questionnaire design and then consider the features of four types of surveys, highlighting the unique problems of each and suggesting possible solutions. Important ethical issues are discussed in the final section. By the chapter's end, you should be well on your way to becoming an informed consumer of survey reports and a knowledgeable developer of survey designs. In addition, you will become a more informed student of the methodological issues surrounding the measurement of violent victimization in the United States.

▣ Survey Research in the Social Sciences

Survey research: Research in which information is obtained from a sample of individuals through their responses to questions about themselves or others.

Survey research involves the collection of information from a sample of individuals through their responses to questions. Not only is survey research one of the most popular methods for science research, many newspaper editors, political pundits, and marketing gurus have turned to survey research because it is an efficient method for systematically collecting data from a broad spectrum of individuals and social settings. In fact, surveys have become such a vital part of our nation's social fabric that we cannot assess much of what we read in the newspaper or see on TV without having some understanding of this method of data collection (Converse 1984).

Attractive Features of Survey Research

Regardless of its scope, survey research owes its continuing popularity to three features: versatility, efficiency, and generalizability.

Versatility

The first and foremost reason for the popularity of survey methods is their versatility. Researchers can ask respondents questions about almost any topic you can imagine. Although a survey is not the ideal method for testing all hypotheses or learning about every social process, a well-designed survey can enhance our understanding of just about any social issue. In fact, there is hardly any topic of interest to social scientists that has not been studied at some time with survey methods.

Computer technology has made surveys even more versatile. Computers can be programmed so that different types of respondents are asked different questions. Short videos or pictures can be presented to respondents on a computer screen. An interviewer may give respondents a laptop on which to record their answers to sensitive personal questions, such as about illegal activities, so that not even the interviewer will know what they said (Tourangeau 2004).

Efficiency

Surveys also are popular because data can be collected from many people at relatively low cost and, depending on the survey design, relatively quickly. For example, the NISVS relies on a random digit dialing telephone survey of both landlines and cell phones. These one-shot telephone interviews can cost as little as $30 per respondent (Ross 1990). Large, mailed surveys are less expensive, at $10 to $15 per potential respondent, but the cost can increase greatly when intensive follow-up efforts are made. Surveys of the general population using personal interviews are much more expensive, and can be extremely costly per survey respondent when lengthy travel or repeat visits are needed to connect with respondents (Groves and Cork 2008). As you would expect, phone surveys are the quickest survey method, which accounts for their popularity.

Surveys are efficient research methods because many variables can be measured without substantially increasing the time or cost of data collection. Mailed questionnaires can include up to 10 pages of questions before respondents lose interest (and before more postage must be added). The maximum time limit for phone surveys seems to be about 45 minutes. In-person interviews can last much longer, taking more than an hour. For example, the NISVS asks approximately 60 questions to assess intimate partner violence, sexual violence, and stalking over the lifetime and during the 12 months prior to the interview.

Of course, the efficiency of the surveys can be attained only in a place with a reliable communications infrastructure (Labaw 1980). A reliable postal service, required for mail surveys, has generally been available in the United States, and phone surveys can be effective in the United States because 95% of its households have phones (Czaja and Blair 1996). Also important to efficiency are the services of the many survey organizations that provide the trained staff and the proper equipment for conducting high-quality surveys. Crime surveys in nonwestern countries still must rely on personal interviews (WHO 2010).

Generalizability

Survey methods lend themselves to probability sampling from large populations. Thus, survey research is very appealing when sample generalizability is a central research goal. In fact, survey research is often the only means available for developing a representative picture of the attitudes and characteristics of a large population.

Surveys also are the research method of choice when cross-population generalizability is a primary concern. They allow a range of social contexts and subgroups to be sampled, and the consistency of relationships can be examined across the various subgroups.

Still, challenges remain. For example, although only 14% of U.S. households had no Internet access at home or work in 2013, the persons in these households tended to be older, poorer, and less educated than those who were "connected" (Pew Research Center 2014). Another challenge in survey research is the growing foreign-born population in the United States, 13% in 2012, which requires foreign-language versions of survey forms. If surveys cannot be provided in a variety of languages, results may not be generalized to the entire population (Grieco et al. 2012).

The Omnibus Survey

Most surveys are directed at a specific research question. In contrast, an **omnibus survey** covers a range of topics of interest to different social scientists. It has multiple sponsors or is designed to generate data useful to a broad segment of the social science community rather than answer one particular research question.

> **Omnibus survey:** A survey that covers a range of topics of interest to different social scientists.

One of the most successful omnibus surveys is the General Social Survey (GSS) of the National Opinion Research Center at the University of Chicago. Today, the GSS is administered every two years as a 90-minute interview to a probability sample of almost 3,000 Americans. It includes more than 500 questions about background characteristics and opinions, with an emphasis on social stratification, race relations, family issues, law and social control, and morale. It explores political views, work experiences, social ties, news sources, and views on law, health, and religion. Questions and topic areas are chosen by a board of overseers drawn from the best survey researchers.

Consider just a few of the differences between everyday conversations and standardized surveys. Survey questions must be asked of many people, not just one person:

- The same survey questions must be used with each person, not tailored to the specifics of a given conversation.

- Survey questions must be understood in the same way by people who differ in many ways.

- You will not be able to rephrase a survey question if someone does not understand it, because that would alter the question, and it would not be the same as the one posed to other participants.

- Survey respondents do not know you, and so cannot be expected to share the nuances of expression that you and those close to you use to communicate.

These features make a survey very different from natural conversation and make question writing a challenging and important task for survey researchers.

Questions must be very clear and specific about what is being asked of respondents. Note the differences in specificity between the rape-screening questions used by the NISVS and the NCVS displayed in Exhibits 8.1 and 8.2. It is logical that the multiple, behaviorally specific questions from the NISVS will be associated with greater disclosure by survey respondents compared to the one question about sexual intercourse posed by the NCVS. Research has shown that questions that are written with more behavior-specific language, such as those used by the NISVS, result in much better recall by respondents of these types of victimizations compared to the questions used by the NCVS (Bachman et al. 2013; Fisher 2009).

Exhibit 8.2 **Screening Questions for Sexual Violence From the CDC-Sponsored National Intimate Partner and Sexual Violence Survey**

How many people have ever...

a. exposed their sexual body parts to you, flashed you, or masturbated in front of you?
b. made you show your sexual body parts to them? Remember, we are only asking about things that you didn't want to happen.
c. made you look at or participate in sexual photos or movies?
d. harassed you while you were in a public place in a way that made you feel unsafe?
e. kissed you in sexual way? Remember, we are only asking about things that you didn't want to happen.
f. fondled or grabbed your sexual body parts?

When you were drunk, high, drugged, or passed out and unable to consent, how many people ever...

a. had vaginal sex with you? By vaginal sex, we mean that {if female: a man or boy put his penis in your vagina} {if male: a women or girl made you put your penis in her vagina}
b. {if male} made you perform anal sex, meaning that they made you put your penis into their anus?
c. made you receive anal sex, meaning they put their penis into your anus?
d. made you perform oral sex, meaning that they put their penis in your mouth or made you penetrate their vagina or anus with your mouth?
e. made you receive oral sex, meaning that they put their mouth on your {if male: penis} {if female: vagina} or anus?

How many people have ever used physical force or threats to physically harm you to make you...

a. have vaginal sex?
b. {if male} perform anal sex?

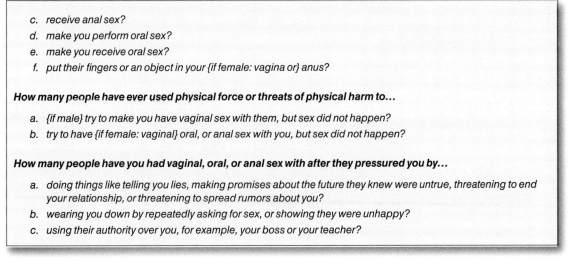

c. *receive anal sex?*

d. *make you perform oral sex?*

e. *make you receive oral sex?*

f. *put their fingers or an object in your {if female: vagina or} anus?*

How many people have ever used physical force or threats of physical harm to...

a. *{if male} try to make you have vaginal sex with them, but sex did not happen?*

b. *try to have {if female: vaginal} oral, or anal sex with you, but sex did not happen?*

How many people have you had vaginal, oral, or anal sex with after they pressured you by...

a. *doing things like telling you lies, making promises about the future they knew were untrue, threatening to end your relationship, or threatening to spread rumors about you?*

b. *wearing you down by repeatedly asking for sex, or showing they were unhappy?*

c. *using their authority over you, for example, your boss or your teacher?*

In addition to writing clear and meaningful questions, there are several other rules to follow and pitfalls to avoid that we will highlight in the next section.

Avoid Confusing Phrasing and Vagueness

Good grammar is a basic requirement for clear questions. Clearly and simply phrased questions are most likely to have the same meaning for different respondents. So, be brief and to the point. The wordier and longer the question, the more likely you to lose the respondent's attention and focus.

Virtually all questions about behavior and feelings will be more reliable if they refer to specific times or events (Turner and Martin 1984). Without a **reference period,** or time frame around which a question is being asked, a researcher will not know how to interpret an answer. For example, the question "How often do you carry a method of self-protection such as pepper spray?" will produce answers

> **Reference period:** A time frame in which a survey question asks respondents to place a particular behavior (e.g., in the last six months).

that have no common reference period and can therefore not be reliably compared to answers from other respondents. A more specific way to ask the question is "In the last month, how many days did you carry a method of self-protection such as pepper spray?"

In general, research shows that the longer the reference period, the greater the underreporting of a given behavior (Cantor 1984, 1985; Kobelarcik et al. 1983). As a general rule, when respondents are being asked about mundane or day-to-day activities, reference periods should be no longer than "in the past month." However, when rare events are being measured, such as experiences with victimizations, "in the last 6 months," as utilized by the NCVS Survey, or "in the past 12 months," as used by the National Violence Against Men and Women survey (NVAMW, a precursor to the NISVS), are both more appropriate. By using longer reference periods like this, we will more likely capture these rarer events.

Avoid Negatives and Double Negatives

Picture yourself answering the following question: "Do you disagree that juveniles should not be tried as adults if they commit murder?" It probably took a long time for you to figure out if you would actually agree or disagree with this statement, because it is written as a **double-negative question.** For example, if you think juveniles who commit murder should be tried as adults, you would actually agree with this statement. Even questions that are written with a single negative are usually difficult to answer. For example, suppose you were asked to respond to "I can't stop thinking about a terrorist attack happening" using a

> **Double-negative question:** A question or statement that contains two negatives, which can muddy the meaning.

five-point response set of "very rarely" to "very often." A person who marks "very rarely" is actually saying, "I very rarely can't stop thinking about the terrorist attacks on 9/11." Confusing, isn't it? Even the most experienced survey researchers can unintentionally make this mistake.

Avoid Double-Barreled Questions

> **Double-barreled question:** A single survey question that actually asks two questions but allows only one answer.

When a question is really asking more than one question, it is called a **double-barreled question**. For example, the statement "I believe we should stop spending so much money building prisons and put it into building more schools" is really asking respondents two different questions. Some respondents may believe we should stop building so many prisons but may not want the revenue to go into building more schools. Double-barreled questions can also show up in the response categories. For example, the item below is really asking two questions:

Do you know anyone who has ever used cocaine?

_____Yes _____No _____I have used cocaine

Avoid Making Either Disagreement or Agreement Disagreeable

People often tend to "agree" with a statement just to avoid seeming disagreeable. You can see the impact of this human tendency in a Michigan Survey Research Center survey that asked who was to blame for crime and lawlessness in the United States (Schuman and Presser 1981). When one question stated that individuals were more to blame than social conditions, 60% of the respondents agreed. But when the question was rephrased so respondents were asked, in a balanced fashion, whether individuals or social conditions were more to blame, only 46% chose individuals.

You can take several steps to reduce the likelihood of agreement bias. As a general rule, you should impartially present both sides of attitude scales in the question itself: "In general, do you believe that *individuals* or *social conditions* are more to blame for crime and lawlessness in the United States?" (Dillman 2000, 61–62). The response choices themselves should be phrased to make each one seem as socially approved, or as "agreeable," as the others. You should also consider replacing the word "agree" with a range of response alternatives. For example, the question, "To what extent do you support or oppose mandatory background checks for all people who want to buy a firearm?" (response choices range from "strongly support" to "strongly oppose") is probably a better approach than the question, "To what extent do you agree or disagree with the statement 'Mandatory background checks for all people who want to buy a firearm is worthy of support'?" (response choices range from "strongly agree" to "strongly disagree").

When an illegal or socially disapproved behavior or attitude is the focus, we have to be concerned that some respondents will be reluctant to agree that they have ever done or thought such a thing. In this situation, the goal is to write a question and response choices that make agreement seem acceptable, or at the very least, not stigmatizing. For example, Dillman (2000) suggests that we ask, "Have you ever taken anything from a store without paying for it?" rather than "Have you ever shoplifted something from a store?" (p. 75). Asking about a variety of behaviors or attitudes that range from socially acceptable to socially unacceptable will also soften the impact of agreeing with those that are socially unacceptable.

Additional Guidelines for Fixed-Response Questions

Creating questions that are clear and meaningful is only half of the formula to creating a good survey instrument. The choices you provide respondents in fixed-choice questions are also important. In this section, we provide you with several rules that will help ensure that the response choices you provide to your questions will also be clear, concise, and exhaustive.

Response Choices Should Be Mutually Exclusive

When you want respondents to make only one choice, the fixed-response categories must not overlap. For example, if you were interested in the ways foot patrol officers spent their time while working, you might ask the following question:

On average, how much time do you spend on the job each week taking care of traffic violations?

- Less than 1 hour

- 1–3 hours

- 3–6 hours

- 6–10 hours

- 10 hours or more

The choices provided for respondents in this question are not **mutually exclusive responses**, because they overlap. Which choice would an officer select if he or she spent three hours a week on traffic violations? Choices that are mutually exclusive would look like this:

> **Mutually exclusive responses:** Response choices on a survey that do not overlap.

- 1 hour or less

- 2–3 hours

- 4–6 hours

- 7–10 hours

- 11 hours or more

Make the Response Categories Exhaustive

In addition to mutual exclusivity, fixed-response categories must also allow all respondents to select an option. Consider the same research question about foot patrol officers. Suppose we asked a question such as this:

In what activity do you spend the most time in an average week on the job?

_____Traffic violations

_____Disturbance-related issues

_____Felony arrests

_____Misdemeanor arrests

Regardless of how exhaustive we think the response categories are, there must always be an option for respondents who require another choice. Response categories can easily be made **exhaustive** if respondents are provided with a choice labeled:

> **Exhaustive responses:** Response choices on a survey in which every case can be classified as having one attribute.

_____ Other, please specify: _____

Note, however, that "Other" should be used only after you have included all options that you believe to be relevant. Otherwise, a large percentage of respondents will select the "Other" category and you will have to spend time coding their responses.

Utilize Likert-Type Response Categories

Likert-type responses: Survey responses in which respondents indicate the extent to which they agree or disagree with statements.

Likert-type responses generally ask respondents to indicate the extent to which they agree or disagree with statements. Why the name? Well, this format is generally believed to have been developed by Rensis Likert in the 1930s. Likert-type response categories list choices for respondents to select their level of agreement with a statement and may look something like this:

"Three-strikes" laws that increase penalties for individuals convicted of three or more felonies will help decrease the crime rate.

1	2	3	4
Strongly Agree	Agree	Disagree	Strongly Disagree

Minimize Fence Sitting and Floating

Two related problems in question writing stem from some respondents' desires to choose an acceptable or socially desirable answer and from other respondents who want to get through the survey as fast as possible. There is no uniformly correct solution to these problems, so you must carefully select an alternative.

Fence sitters: Survey respondents who see themselves as being neutral on an issue and choose a middle (neutral) response that is offered.

Fence sitters are people who see themselves as neutral in their attitudes toward a particular issue. If you are truly interested in those who do not have strong feelings on an issue, one alternative is to provide a neutral or undecided response option. The disadvantage to these options is that they may encourage some respondents to take the easy way out rather than really thinking about their feelings. This alternative may also provide an out for respondents who do not want to reveal how they truly feel about an issue. On the other hand, not providing respondents who really have no opinion on an issue with an option such as "undecided" can be very frustrating and may encourage them to leave the item blank altogether. Whatever you decide, it is generally a good idea to provide respondents with instructions that ask them to "select the choice in each item that most closely reflects your opinion." This should help make all respondents feel more comfortable about their answers, particularly those who only slightly feel one way or the other.

Floaters: Survey respondents who provide an opinion on a topic in response to a closed-ended question that does not include a "don't know" option, but will choose "don't know" if it is available.

Floaters are respondents who choose a substantive answer even when they do not know anything about a particular question. For example, research has shown that a third of the public will provide an opinion on a proposed law they know nothing about if they are not provided with a "don't know" response option (Schuman and Presser 1981). Of course, providing a "don't know" option has the same disadvantage as providing a neutral response option; its inclusion leads some people to take the easy way out.

If you are really interested in informed opinions about an issue, it is best to provide detailed information about that issue when asking a question. For example, let us say we were interested in attitudes about the treatment of juvenile offenders by the criminal justice system. Suppose we asked respondents to provide their opinion on the following statement: "The Juvenile Justice Bill before Congress will help reduce crime committed by juveniles." Do you know what the Juvenile Justice Bill is? If we did not provide a "don't know" option, respondents who knew nothing about the Juvenile Justice Bill would be forced to select a response that would not be meaningful and may bias the results of the entire survey. Instead of a "don't know" option, another way to handle the problem is to provide details of the issue you are interested in. For example, you could tell respondents that one component of the bill encourages states to adjudicate all juvenile homicide offenders 13 years of age or older as adults and then ask respondents their opinion about this particular issue. If you are truly interested in the extent to which respondents have knowledge about a particular issue and you want to include a "don't know" response, it should be set apart from the other choices so that respondents do not mistake it as a neutral or undecided choice. Of course, as with all questions, there should be clear instructions about what the response options actually mean. For example, if you wanted to examine citizens' knowledge and opinion about the independent counsel statute, you could ask this question:

Instructions: For each statement, check the box that best indicates the extent to which you agree with the statement. If you do not have enough information about a statement to determine your level of agreement, leave the boxes blank and put an X next to "don't know."

I think the independent counsel law should remain as it is.

- strongly agree

- agree

- disagree

- strongly disagree

- don't know

Utilize Filter Questions

The use of filter questions is important to ensure that questions are asked only of relevant respondents. For example, if you are interested in the utilization of police services by robbery victims, you would first need to establish victimization with a **filter question**. These filter questions create **skip patterns**. For example, respondents who answer no to one question are directed to skip ahead to another question, but respondents who answer yes go on to the **contingent question** or questions. That's why these questions are called contingent questions. Skip patterns should be indicated clearly with arrows or other directions in the questionnaire, as demonstrated in Exhibit 8.3.

Filter question: A survey question used to identify a subset of respondents who then are asked other questions.

Skip patterns: The unique combination of questions created in a survey by filter questions and contingent questions.

Contingent questions: Questions that are asked of only a subset of survey respondents.

Combining Questions Into Indexes

Measuring variables with single questions is very popular. Public opinion polls based on answers to single questions are reported frequently in newspaper articles and TV newscasts: "Do you favor or oppose the policy for . . . ?" "If you had to vote today, for which candidate would you vote?" The primary problem with using a single question is that if respondents misunderstand the question or have some other problem with the phrasing, there is no way to tell. Single questions are prone to this **idiosyncratic variation**, which occurs when individuals' responses vary because of their reactions to particular words or ideas

Idiosyncratic variation: Variation in responses to questions that is caused by individuals' reactions to particular words or ideas in the question instead of by variation in the concept that the question is intended to measure.

in the question. Differences in respondents' backgrounds, knowledge, and beliefs almost guarantee that they will understand the same question differently. If some respondents do not know some of the words in a question, we may misinterpret their answers—if they answer at all. If a question is too complex, respondents may focus on different parts of the question. If prior experiences or culturally biased orientations lead different groups in the sample to interpret questions differently, answers will not have a consistent meaning, because the question meant something different to each respondent.

If just one question is used to measure a variable, the researcher may not realize respondents had trouble with a particular word or phrase in the questions. Although writing carefully worded questions will help reduce idiosyncratic variation, when measuring concepts, the best option is to devise an index of multiple rather than single questions.

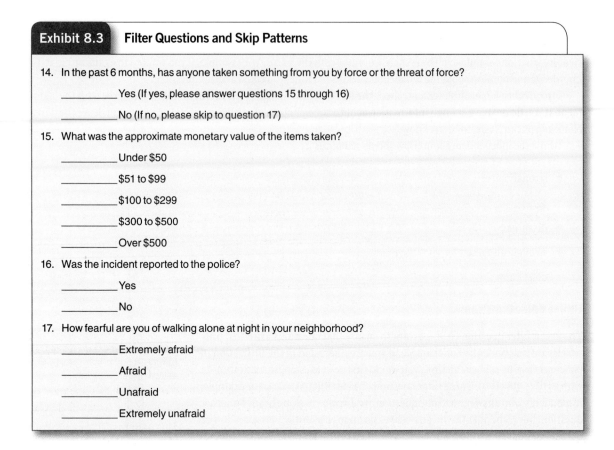

Exhibit 8.3   **Filter Questions and Skip Patterns**

14. In the past 6 months, has anyone taken something from you by force or the threat of force?

_____ Yes (If yes, please answer questions 15 through 16)

_____ No (If no, please skip to question 17)

15. What was the approximate monetary value of the items taken?

_____ Under $50

_____ $51 to $99

_____ $100 to $299

_____ $300 to $500

_____ Over $500

16. Was the incident reported to the police?

_____ Yes

_____ No

17. How fearful are you of walking alone at night in your neighborhood?

_____ Extremely afraid

_____ Afraid

_____ Unafraid

_____ Extremely unafraid

When several questions are used to measure one concept, the responses may be combined by taking the sum or average of the responses. A composite measure based on this type of sum or average is called an **index** or a **scale**. The idea is that idiosyncratic variation in response to single questions will average out, so the main influence on the combined measure will be the concept focused on by the questions. In addition, the index can be considered a more complete measure of the concept than can any one of the component questions.

Index: The sum or average of responses to a set of questions about a concept.

Scale: A composite measure of one concept created from a series of two or more questions.

Reliability measures: Special statistics that help researchers decide whether responses are consistent.

Creating an index, however, is not just a matter of writing a few questions that seem to focus on one concept. Questions that seem to you to measure a common concept might seem to respondents to concern several different issues. The only way to know that a given set of questions does effectively form an index is to administer the questions in a pretest to people similar to the sample you plan to study. If a common concept is being measured, people's responses to the different questions should display some consistency. Special statistics called **reliability measures** help researchers decide whether responses are consistent. Most respondent attitudes are complex and consist of many elements.

Be aware of response sets when constructing an index measuring attitudes. For example, some people tend to agree with almost everything asked of them, whereas others tend to disagree. Still others are prone to answer neutrally to everything if given the option. To decrease the likelihood of this happening, it is a good idea to make some statements both favorable and unfavorable to a particular attitude to vary the response choices and still reach an understanding of individuals' opinions. In this way, respondents are forced to be more careful in their responses to individual items. Exhibit 8.4 displays a hypothetical set of questions designed to solicit respondents' attitudes toward police in their community.

Exhibit 8.4   **Items in an "Attitude Toward Police" Index**

1. Police officers are generally fair to all people regardless of their race or ethnicity.

    _____Strongly Agree _____ Agree _____Disagree _____Strongly Disagree

2. Police officers are given too much freedom to stop and frisk community residents.

    _____Strongly Agree _____ Agree _____Disagree _____Strongly Disagree

3. If someone resisted arrest, even a little, most police officers would become assaultive if they thought they could get away with it.

    _____Strongly Agree _____ Agree _____Disagree _____Strongly Disagree

4. Police officers put their lives on the line every day trying to make it safe for residents of this community.

    _____Strongly Agree _____ Agree _____Disagree _____Strongly Disagree

5. The majority of police officers have lied under oath at least once.

    _____Strongly Agree _____ Agree _____Disagree _____Strongly Disagree

6. The majority of police officers are honest and fair.

    _____Strongly Agree _____ Agree _____Disagree _____Strongly Disagree

---

When scoring an index or scale made up of both favorable and unfavorable statements, you must remember to reverse code the unfavorable items. For example, marking "strongly agree" to the first item in Exhibit 8.4 should not be scored the same as a "strongly agree" response to the second item.

Due to the popularity of survey research, indexes already have been developed to measure many concepts, and some of these indexes have proved to be reliable in a range of studies. It usually is much better to use these indexes to measure concepts than to try to devise new questions to form a new index. As noted earlier in this chapter, the use of a preexisting measure both simplifies the work involved in designing a study and facilitates a comparison of findings to those obtained in previous studies.

One index available in the NCVS is designed to measure what is referred to in criminological literature as *routine activities*. To explain crime victimization, the routine activities theory focuses on the circumstances in which crimes are committed rather than on the circumstances of the offender. According to Cohen and Felson (1979), each criminal act requires the convergence of three elements: likely and motivated offenders, suitable targets, and an absence of capable guardians to prevent the would-be offenders from committing the crime. Thus, the routine patterns of work, play, and leisure time affect the convergence in time and place of the motivated offenders, the suitable targets, and the absence of guardians. To measure the extent to which respondents engage in routine activities away from the home, the NCVS asks three questions that are displayed in Exhibit 8.5. These questions measure different types of activities people routinely engage in away from the home. When combined, these three questions create a better measure of an individual's activities away from the home than would a single question.

Another example of an index is that used to measure student perceptions of tolerance for substance abuse on college campuses (Core Institute 1994). An excerpt from this is shown in Exhibit 8.6. Alone, no single question would be sufficient to capture the overall tolerance of substance abuse on campus. A person's total response to these questions is likely to provide a more accurate indication of tolerance for substance abuse than would a single, general question such as, "Do students on this campus feel that drinking or using drugs is okay?"

The advantages of using indexes rather than single questions to measure important concepts are very clear, and for this reason, surveys often include multiple questions to measure one concept. The following are three cautions to consider when using indexes:

Questionnaire structure. Survey designs also differ in the extent to which the content and order of questions are structured in advance by the researcher. Most mailed, group, phone, and electronic surveys are highly structured, fixing in advance the content and order of questions and response choices. Some of these types of surveys, particularly mailed surveys, may include some open-ended questions (where respondents write in their answers rather than checking off one of several response choices). In-person interviews are often highly structured, but they may include many questions without fixed response choices. Moreover, some interviews may proceed from an interview guide rather than a fixed set of questions. In these relatively unstructured interviews, the interviewer covers the same topics with respondents but varies questions according to the respondent's answers to previous questions. Extra questions are added as needed to clarify or explore answers to the most important questions.

Setting. Most mail and electronic questionnaires and phone interviews are intended for completion by only one respondent. The same is usually true of in-person interviews, although sometimes researchers interview several family members at once. On the other hand, a variant of the standard survey is a questionnaire distributed simultaneously to a group of respondents, who complete the survey while the researcher (or assistant) waits. Students in classrooms are typically the group involved, although this type of group distribution also occurs in surveys administered to employees and members of voluntary groups.

Cost. As mentioned earlier, in-person interviews are the most expensive type of survey. Phone interviews are much less expensive, but surveying by mail is cheaper yet. Electronic surveys are now the least expensive method because there are no interviewer costs, no mailing costs, and, for many designs, almost no costs for data entry. Of course extra staff time and expertise is required to prepare an electronic questionnaire.

Because of their different features, the five designs vary in the types of errors to which they are most prone and the situations in which they are most appropriate. The rest of this section focuses on the unique advantages and disadvantages of each design.

Mailed, Self-Administered Surveys

Mailed (self-administered) survey: A survey involving a mailed questionnaire to be completed by the respondent.

A **mailed (self-administered) survey** is conducted by mailing a questionnaire to respondents, who then administer the survey themselves. The principal drawback in using this method of survey administration is the difficulty maximizing the response rate—we have to rely on people to voluntarily return the surveys! The final response rate is unlikely to be much above 80% and almost surely will be below 70% unless procedures to maximize the response rate are precisely followed. A response rate below 60% is a disaster, and even a 70% response rate is not much more than minimally acceptable. It is hard to justify the representativeness of the sample if more than a third of those surveyed fail to respond.

Some ways to maximize the response rate (Fowler 1988; Mangione 1995; Miller 1991) include the following:

- Make the questionnaire attractive, with plenty of white space.

- Use contingent questions and skip patterns infrequently. When they are necessary, guide respondents visually through the pattern.

- Make individual questions clear and understandable to all the respondents. No interviewers will be on hand to clarify the meaning of the questions or probe for additional details.

- Use no more than a few open-ended questions. Respondents are likely to be put off by the idea of having to write out answers.

- Include a personalized and professional cover letter. Using an altruistic appeal (informing respondents that their response will do some good) seems to produce a response rate 7% higher than indicating that respondents will receive something for their participation.

- Have a credible research sponsor. According to one investigation, a sponsor known to respondents may increase the rate of response by as much as 17%. The next most credible sponsors are the state headquarters of an organization and then other people in a similar field. Publishing firms, college professors or students, and private associations elicit the lowest response rates.

- Write an identifying number on the questionnaire so you can determine who the nonrespondents are.

- A small incentive can help. Even a coupon or ticket worth $2 can be enough to increase the response rate.

- Include a stamped, self-addressed return envelope with the questionnaire.

Most important, use follow-up mailings to encourage initial nonrespondents to return a completed questionnaire. Dillman (2000) recommends a standard procedure for follow-up mailings:

1. Send a reminder postcard, thanking respondents and reminding nonrespondents, to all sample members two weeks after the initial mailing.

2. Send a replacement questionnaire with a new cover letter only to nonrespondents about three or four weeks after the initial mailing.

3. Send another replacement questionnaire with a new cover letter eight weeks after the initial mailing by certified mail if possible. (It's pretty expensive.) If enough time and resources are available for telephone contacts or in-person visits for interviews, they will also help.

Related to the threat of nonresponse in mailed surveys is the hazard of incomplete response. Some respondents may skip some questions or just stop answering questions at some point in the questionnaire. Fortunately, this problem does not often occur with well-designed questionnaires. Potential respondents who decide to participate in the survey will usually complete it. But there are many exceptions to this observation, since questions that are poorly written, too complex, or about sensitive personal issues simply turn off some respondents. Revising or eliminating such questions during the design phase should minimize the problem.

Many researchers continue to rely on mailed surveys because they are relatively inexpensive, and respondents are free to answer questions at their leisure, without the scrutiny of a survey administrator.

Group-Administered Surveys

A **group-administered survey** is completed by individual respondents assembled in a group. The response rate is not usually a concern in surveys that are distributed and collected in a group setting, because most group members will participate. The difficulty with this method is that assembling a group is seldom feasible because it requires a captive audience. Individuals going about their daily activities are usually not amenable to group-administered surveys. With the exception of students, employees, members of the armed forces, and some institutionalized populations, most populations cannot be sampled in such a setting.

> **Group-administered survey:** A survey that is completed by individual respondents who are assembled in a group.

One issue of special concern with group-administered surveys is the possibility that respondents will feel coerced to participate and as a result will be less likely to answer questions honestly.

Also, because administering a survey to a group probably requires the approval of the group's supervisor, and because such surveys are often conducted on the organization's premises, respondents may infer that the researcher is not at all independent of the sponsor. Even those who volunteer may still feel uncomfortable answering all questions, which may bias their responses. No complete solution to this problem exists, but it helps to make an introductory statement that emphasizes the researcher's independence, assures respondents that their surveys will be completely anonymous, and gives participants a chance to ask questions about the survey.

Surveys by Telephone

Phone survey: A survey in which interviewers question respondents over the phone and then record their answers.

In a **phone survey**, interviewers question respondents over the phone and then record respondents' answers. Phone interviewing has become a very popular method of conducting surveys in the United States because almost all families have phones. But two matters may undermine the validity of a phone survey: not reaching the proper sampling units and not getting enough complete responses to make the results generalizable.

Reaching Sampling Units

Today, drawing a random sample is easier than ever due to random digit dialing (RDD) (Lavrakas 1987). A machine calls random phone numbers within designated exchanges, regardless of whether the numbers are published. When the machine reaches an inappropriate household (such as a business in a survey directed to the general population), the phone number is simply replaced with another. Also, several recent surveys have used both landline and cell phone databases to capture individuals who no longer have landlines.

To ensure cell phone–only households were also included in the sample, NISVS interviews were conducted both by landline and cell phone. The NISVS used random digit dialing conducted in all 50 states and the District of Columbia, so estimates of victimization could be aggregated up to the state level of analysis. This allowed both individual- and state-level prevalence rates to be calculated. Regardless of how individuals are contacted, the interviewers must also ask a series of questions at the start of the survey to ensure that they are speaking to the appropriate member of the household.

Maximizing Response to Phone Surveys

Three issues require special attention in phone surveys. First, because people often are not home, multiple callbacks will be necessary for many sample members. In addition, interviewers must be prepared for distractions if the respondent is interrupted by other household members. Sprinkling interesting questions throughout the questionnaire may help maintain respondent interest. In general, rapport between the interviewer and the respondent is likely to be lower with phone surveys than in-person interviews, as respondents may tire and refuse to answer all the questions (Miller 1991).

The number of callbacks needed to reach respondents by telephone has increased greatly in the past 20 years, with increasing numbers of single-person households, dual-earner families, and out-of-home activities. The growth of telemarketing has also created another problem for telephone survey researchers: Individuals are more accustomed to just "saying no" to calls from strangers or simply use their answering machines or caller ID mechanism to screen unwanted calls (Dillman 2000). The response rates for most phone surveys, even those sponsored by the U.S. government, have been decreasing over the past two decades. For example, the individual response rate for the NCVS was 91% in 1996, but by 2007, it had fallen to 85% (Groves and Cork 2008). Cell phone users are also harder (and more costly) to contact in phone surveys. Households with a cell phone but no landline tend to be younger, so the rate of phone survey participation is declining even more among those 18 to 34 years of age (Keeter 2008).

Response rates by age of respondent from the NCVS indicate that age is a factor. As you can see in Exhibit 8.11, persons 24 years of age or younger were much less likely to volunteer for the telephone interview compared to older persons. In fact, it can be seen that as age of respondents increased, so did response rates.

Phone surveyors also must cope with difficulties due to the impersonal nature of phone contact. Visual aids cannot be used, so the interviewer must be able to verbally convey all information about response choices and skip patterns. With phone surveys, instructions for the interviewer must clarify how to ask each question, and the response choices must be short.

| Exhibit 8.11 | NCVS Response Rates by Age, 2011 Through 2013 |

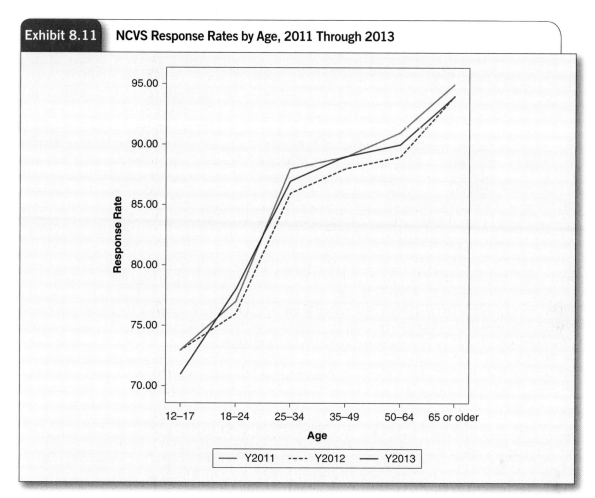

Source: Adapted from National Crime Victimization Survey: Technical Documentation, http://www.bjs.gov/content/pub/pdf/ncvstd13.pdf.

Careful interviewer training is essential for phone surveys. Below is a brief description of how SRBI interviewers were trained before conducting the NVAMW Survey:

Because of the complexity of the survey, only the most experienced SRBI interviewers worked on the survey. Before fielding the survey, interviewers received specialized training on the general principles of survey research and the requirements of the study at hand. Interviewers were also trained to recognize and respond appropriately to cues that the respondent may have been concerned about being overheard. Telephone numbers of local support services (e.g., domestic violence shelters, rape crisis hotlines, child protective services) were offered to respondents who disclosed current abuse or appeared in distress. (Tjaden and Thoennes 1998)

Procedures can be standardized more effectively, quality control maintained, and processing speed maximized when phone interviewers are assisted by computers. This **computer-assisted telephone interview** has become known as

Computer-assisted telephone interview (CATI): A telephone interview in which a questionnaire is programmed into a computer, along with relevant skip patterns that must be followed. It essentially combines the tasks of interviewing, data entry, and some data cleaning.

CATI, and most large surveys are now performed in this way. There are several advantages to using CATI, but perhaps the foremost advantage is that data collection and data entry can occur concurrently. Second, the CATI system has several machine edit features that help minimize data entry error. For example, by automatically assigning single-punch fields of appropriate width for each data item in the questionnaire, the CATI system eliminates the possibility of over-punching and the possibility of including blanks as legitimate values. Third, by programming the skip patterns into its data entry program, the CATI system ensures that the aggregated database is comprehensive and accurate.

Computer interactive voice response (IVR): Software that uses a touch-tone telephone to interact with people in order to acquire information or enter data into a database.

One method that avoids the interviewer altogether is **computerized interactive voice response (IVR)** survey technology. In an IVR survey, respondents receive automated calls and answer questions by pressing numbers on their touch-tone phones or speaking numbers that are interpreted by computerized voice recognition software. These surveys can also record verbal responses to open-ended questions for later transcription. Although they present some difficulties when many answer choices must be used or skip patterns must be followed, IVR surveys have been used successfully with short questionnaires and when respondents are highly motivated to participate (Dillman 2000). When these conditions are not met, potential respondents may be put off by the impersonality of this computer-driven approach.

In summary, phone surveying is the best method to use for relatively short surveys of the general population. Response rates in phone surveys tend to be very high, often above 80%, because few individuals will hang up on a polite caller or refuse to answer questions (at least within the first 30 minutes or so).

In-Person Interviews

In-person interview: A survey in which an interviewer questions respondents and records their answers.

What is unique to the **in-person interview**, compared to the other survey designs, is the face-to-face social interaction between interviewer and respondent. If financial resources are available for hiring interviewers to go out and personally conduct the surveys with respondents, in-person interviewing is often the best way to conduct a survey.

Although time-consuming and costly, in-person interviewing has several advantages. Response rates are higher for this survey design than for any other when potential respondents are approached by a courteous interviewer. For example, respondents for the NCVS actually stay in the sample for three years. The first of their surveys is performed in person. This is one reason the NCVS obtains a very high response rate—approximately 95%. In addition, in-person interviews can be much longer than mailed or phone surveys, and the questionnaire can be complex, with both open-ended and closed-ended questions and frequent branching patterns. The order in which questions are read and answered can be controlled by the interviewer, and the physical and social circumstances of the interview can be monitored. Last, respondents' interpretations of questions can be probed and clarified.

However, researchers must be alert to some special hazards due to the presence of an interviewer. Respondents should experience the interview process as a personalized interaction with an interviewer who is very interested in their experiences and opinions. At the same time, every respondent should have the same interview experience and be asked the same questions in the same way by the same type of person, who reacts similarly to the answers. Therein lies the researcher's challenge: to plan an interview process that will be personal, engaging, consistent, and nonreactive, and to hire interviewers who can carry out the plan. Without a personalized approach, the rate of response will be lower, and answers will be less thoughtful and potentially less valid. Without a consistent approach, information obtained from different respondents will not be comparable, because it is less reliable and less valid.

Balancing Rapport and Control

Adherence to some basic guidelines for interacting with respondents can help interviewers maintain an appropriate balance between personalization and standardization:

- Project a professional image in the interview, that of someone who is sympathetic to the respondent but nonetheless has a job to do.

- Establish rapport at the outset by explaining what the interview is about and how it will work and by reading the consent form. Ask the respondent if he or she has any questions or concerns, and respond to these honestly and fully. Emphasize that everything the respondent says is confidential.

- During the interview, ask questions at a close but not intimate distance. Stay focused on the respondent, and be certain your posture conveys interest. Maintain eye contact, respond with appropriate facial expressions, and speak in a conversational tone of voice.

- Be sure to maintain a consistent approach; deliver each question as written and in the same tone of voice. Listen empathically, but avoid self-expression or loaded reactions.

- Repeat questions if the respondent is confused. Use nondirective probes such as, "Can you tell me more about that?" for open-ended questions.

As with phone interviewing, computers can be used to increase control of the in-person interview. In a **computer-assisted personal interviewing (CAPI)** project, interviewers carry a laptop computer programmed to display the interview questions and process the responses that the interviewer types in, as well as to check that these responses fall within the allowed ranges. Interviewers seem to like CAPI, and the data obtained are at least as good in quality as those obtained in a noncomputerized interview (Shepherd et al. 1996). **Computer-assisted self-interviewing (CASI)** is also an alternative. With audio-CASI, respondents interact with a computer-administered questionnaire by using a mouse and following audio instructions delivered via headphones. Audio-CASI is considered the most reliable way to administer questionnaires that probe sensitive or potentially stigmatizing information, such as offending or victimization information (Miller et al. 1998; Tourangeau and Smith 1996; Turner et al. 1998). Wolff et al. (2006) used this technology to obtain information about the physical and sexual victimization experiences of male and female state prison inmates. They explain,

> **Computer-assisted personal interview (CAPI):** An interview in which the interviewer carries a laptop computer programmed to display the interview questions and to process the responses that the interviewer types in, as well as to check that these responses fall within the allowed ranges.

> **Computer-assisted self-interview (CASI):** A system within which respondents interact with a computer-administered questionnaire by using a mouse and following audio instructions delivered via headphones.

> The survey was administered using audio-CASI (computed assisted self interviewing) and was available in English and Spanish. There were 30 computer stations set up at each facility and members of the research team were available to answer any questions and assist with the technology as needed. (p. 1350)

The presence of an interviewer may make it more difficult for respondents to give honest answers to questions about sensitive personal matters. If you are not using a CASI, interviewers may hand respondents a separate, self-administered questionnaire containing the more sensitive questions. After answering these questions, the respondent can then seal the separate questionnaire in an envelope so that the interviewer does not know the answers.

Although in-person interview procedures are typically designed with the expectation that the interview will involve only the interviewer and the respondent, one or more other household members are often within earshot. This is particularly problematic if you are asking respondents about issues related to other family members, such as victimizations by family members. Although the NVAMW survey interviewed only one member of each household, the NCVS interviews all members of a selected household. Thus, all family members are asked the same set of screening questions regarding

Research in the News

For Further Thought ?

THE RISE OF CELL PHONE–ONLY HOUSEHOLDS IS AFFECTING SURVEYS

An article in the *New York Times* in 2014 reported on the problem that cell phones, and cell phone-only users, are having on obtaining poll results that are generalizable to the entire population in the United States. It noted that over 90% of Americans had cell phones, and that about 40% had eliminated their landlines entirely. The problem with random digit dialing using a cell phone list, the article noted, is that individuals can move with them across cities and states. The question remains: How many cell phones in a sample are enough?

1. If you were going to conduct a telephone survey, how would you select your sample to ensure generalizability?

2. Should survey researchers now consider sampling in multiple ways, for example, both electronically and via the telephone? If so, what types of issues should be considered when comparing results across two survey modes of administration? Do you think use of two modes would affect responses to questions soliciting information on sensitive issues like victimization?

Source: Thee-Brenan, Megan. 2014. "How the Rise of Cellphones Affects Surveys." *New York Times,* July 10. http://www.nytimes.com/2014/07/11/upshot/-how-the-rise-of-cellphones-affects-surveys.html?abt=0002&abg=0.

their victimization experiences with both known and unknown offenders. Even though respondents are instructed to reschedule a telephone or personal interview for a more convenient time (e.g., when others are not present), this situation may nevertheless prevent some respondents from disclosing incidents of violence to interviewers, particularly those incidents perpetrated by intimate partners within the household.

Maximizing Response to Interviews

Even if the right balance is struck between maintaining control over interviews and achieving good rapport with respondents, in-person interviews can still have a problem. Due to the difficulty of catching all the members of a sample, response rates may suffer. As we noted in Chapter 5, many households are screening their calls and have little tolerance for unwanted solicitations.

Several factors affect the response rate in interview studies. Households with young children or elderly adults tend to be easier to contact, whereas single-person households are more difficult to reach (Groves and Couper 1998). Refusal rates vary with some respondent characteristics. People with less education participate somewhat less in surveys of political issues (perhaps because they are less aware of current political issues). Less education is also associated with higher rates of "don't know" responses (Groves 1989). High-income persons tend to participate less in surveys about income and economic behavior (perhaps because they are suspicious about why others want to know about their situation). Unusual strains and disillusionment in a society can also undermine the general credibility of research efforts and the ability of interviewers to achieve an acceptable response rate. These problems can be lessened with an advance letter introducing the survey project and by multiple contact attempts throughout the day and evening, but they cannot entirely be avoided (Fowler 1988; Groves and Couper 1998).

Electronic Surveys

Electronic survey (web-based survey): A survey that is sent and answered by computer, either through e-mail or on the web.

Electronic surveys have become increasingly useful for two reasons: growth in the fraction of the population using the Internet, and technological advances that make the design of electronic surveys, often done using the web or e-mail, relatively easy.

However, it is still not possible to obtain a true representative sample of the U.S. population on the web, since not everyone is connected or has access to the Internet. While many specific populations have very high rates of Internet use, such as professional groups, middle-class communities, members of organizations, and, of course, college students, coverage still remains a major problem with many populations

(Tourangeau et al. 2012). About one quarter of U.S. households are not connected to the Internet (File 2013), so it is not yet possible to survey directly a representative sample of the U.S. population on the web. Rates of Internet usage also are much lower in other parts of the world, with a worldwide average of 34.3% and rates as low as 15.6% in Africa and 27.5% averaged across all of Asia. Households without Internet access also tend to be older, poorer, and less educated than are those that are connected, so web surveys of the general population can result in seriously biased estimates (File 2013; Pew Research Center 2013). Coverage problems can be compounded in web surveys because of much lower rates of survey completion: It is just too easy to stop working on a web survey—much easier than it is to break off interaction with an interviewer (Tourangeau et al. 2012).

The extent to which the population of interest is connected to the web is the most important consideration when deciding whether to conduct a survey through the web. Other considerations that may increase the attractiveness of a web survey include a need for a large sample, desire for a rapid turnaround, a need to collect sensitive information that might be embarrassing to acknowledge in person, the availability of an e-mail list of the population, and the extent to which the interactive and multimedia features will enhance interest in the survey (Sue and Ritter 2012). Jennie Connor, Andrew Gray, and Kypros Kypri (2010) achieved a 63% response rate with a web survey about substance use that began with an initial e-mail invitation to a representative sample of undergraduate students at six New Zealand campuses.

There are several different approaches to conducting web-based surveys, each with unique advantages and somewhat different effects on the coverage problem. Many web-based surveys begin with an e-mail message to potential respondents that contains a direct link to the survey website. If a defined population with known e-mail addresses is to be surveyed, a researcher can send e-mail invitations to a representative sample without difficulty. To ensure that the appropriate people respond to a web-based survey, researchers may require that respondents enter a PIN (personal identification number) to gain access to the survey (Dillman 2000). However, lists of unique e-mail addresses for the members of defined populations generally do not exist outside of organizational settings. Many people have more than one e-mail address, and often there is no apparent link between an e-mail address and the name or location of the person it is assigned to. As a result, there is no available method for drawing a random sample of e-mail addresses for people from any general population, even if the focus is only on those with Internet access (Dillman 2007).

Some web surveys are instead linked to a website that is used by the intended population, and everyone who visits that site is invited to complete the survey. Although this approach can generate a very large number of respondents, the resulting sample will necessarily reflect the type of people who visit that website (middle-class, young North Americans) and thus be a biased representation of the larger population (Dillman 2000). Some control over the resulting sample can be maintained by requiring participants to meet certain inclusion criteria (Selm and Jankowski 2006).

Coverage bias can also be a problem with web surveys that are designed for a population with high levels of Internet use. If the topic of the survey leads some people to be more likely to respond on the web, the resulting sample can be very unrepresentative. William Wells, Michael Cavanaugh, Jeffrey Bouffard, and Matt Nobles (2012) identified this problem in a comparison of attitudes of students responding to a web survey about gun violence with students at the same university who responded to the same survey administered in classes. Here is their e-mail introducing their survey to potential respondents:

> Recently, in response to shootings on university campuses like Virginia Tech and Northern Illinois University, several state legislatures (South Dakota, Texas, Washington) have begun debating whether to change rules banning students and employees from carrying concealed weapons on campus. This is an important public safety issue and the faculty in [name of student's university] are interested in knowing how people on this campus feel about it.

Students who responded to the web survey were much more likely to support the right to carry concealed weapons on campus than were those who responded in the classroom survey. In general, having a more extreme attitude motivated people to participate.

Some web surveys are designed to reduce coverage bias by providing computers and Internet connections to those who do not have them. This design-based recruitment method begins by contacting people by phone and providing those who agree to participate with whatever equipment they lack. This approach considerably increases the cost of the survey, so it is normally used as part of creating the panel of respondents who agree to be contacted for multiple surveys over time. The start-up costs can then be spread across many surveys. Of course, coverage bias is not as important when a convenience sample will suffice for an exploratory survey about some topic. Audrey Freshman (2012) used a web survey of a convenience sample to study symptoms of posttraumatic stress disorder (PTSD) among victims of the convicted white collar criminal Bernie Madoff.

> This convenience, nonprobability sample was solicited via direct link to the study placed in online Madoff survivor support groups and comment sections of newspapers and blogs dealing with the event. The study announcement encouraged victims to forward the link to other former investors who might be interested in responding to the survey, thereby creating a snowball effect. The link led directly to a study description and enabled respondents to give informed consent prior to study participation. Participants were assured of anonymity of their responses and were instructed how to proceed in the event of increased feelings of distress as a result of study material. The survey was presumed to take approximately five to 10 minutes to complete. (p. 41)

Although a majority of respondents met clinical criteria for a diagnosis of PTSD, there is no way to know if this sample represents the larger population of Madoff's victims.

In contrast to problems of coverage, web surveys have some unique advantages for increasing measurement validity (Selm and Jankowski 2006; Tourangeau et al. 2012). Questionnaires completed on the web can elicit more honest reports of illicit behavior and of victimization as compared with phone interviews (Parks, Pardi, and Bradizza 2006). They are relatively easy to complete, as respondents simply click on response boxes, and the survey can be programmed to move each respondent easily through sets of questions, not presenting questions that do not apply to the respondent. Pictures, sounds, and animation can be used as a focus of particular questions, and graphic and typographic variation can be used to enhance visual survey appeal. Definitions of terms can pop up when respondents scroll over them (Dillman 2007). Using these features, a skilled web programmer can generate a survey layout with many attractive features that make it more likely that respondents will give their answers—and have a clear understanding of the question (Smyth et al. 2004). Responses can quickly be checked to make sure they fall within the allowable range. Because answers are recorded directly in the researcher's database, data entry errors are almost eliminated, and results can be reported quickly.

There are many free online services to aid you in developing a web survey, like SurveyMonkey. However, many universities have also subscribed to more sophisticated survey engines such as Qualtrics. For example, the Center for Drug and Health Studies at the University of Delaware conducted a college risk behavior survey using Qualtrics. Exhibit 8.12 displays one screen of the survey, which was devoted to ascertaining the extent to which students engaged in all types of risky behavior, including drinking and driving, using drugs, cheating, victimization, stealing, fighting, gambling, and illegally downloading material. Notice that the top of the screen told respondents how much of the survey they had left before they were finished. To enhance their response rate, the researchers offered students who completed the survey a $5 voucher that could be used at any university eating establishment.

Mixed-Mode Surveys

Survey researchers increasingly are combining different survey designs. **Mixed-mode surveys** allow the strengths of one survey design to compensate for the weaknesses of another and can maximize the likelihood of securing data from different types of respondents. For example, a survey may be sent electronically to sample members who have e-mail addresses and be mailed to those who do not. Alternatively, nonrespondents in a mailed survey may be interviewed in person or over the phone. As noted previously, an interviewer may use a self-administered questionnaire and a computer assisted self-interview (CASI) to present sensitive questions to a respondent.

> **Mixed-mode survey:** Surveys that are conducted by more than one method, allowing the strengths of one survey design to compensate for the weaknesses of another and maximizing the likelihood of securing data from different types of respondents; for example, nonrespondents in a mailed survey may be interviewed in person or over the phone.

Mixing survey designs like this makes it possible that respondents will give different answers to different questions because of the mode in which they are asked, rather than because they actually

Exhibit 8.12 | **A Page From the College Risk Behavior Survey**

UNIVERSITY OF DELAWARE
2009 College Survey

Your responses to the previous section have been recorded.
You are 95% finished with this survey.
This is the final set of questions!

How often have you done the following:

	Never	Before, but not in the past year	A few times in the past year	1-3 times in the past month	4-8 times in the past month	9 or more times in the past month
Cheated on a test	○	○	○	○	○	○
Plagiarized/copied a paper	○	○	○	○	○	○
Threatened someone	○	○	○	○	○	○
Hit someone	○	○	○	○	○	○
Entered a building/vehicle I should not have been in	○	○	○	○	○	○
Stolen money	○	○	○	○	○	○
Stolen something other than money	○	○	○	○	○	○
Vandalized property other than your own	○	○	○	○	○	○
Committed fraud/forgery (includes using fake ID)	○	○	○	○	○	○
Carried a weapon	○	○	○	○	○	○
Drove under the influence of alcohol	○	○	○	○	○	○
Drove under the influence of marijuana or other drugs	○	○	○	○	○	○

[Next Section]

Survey Powered By Qualtrics

have different opinions. However, use of what Dillman (2000) calls "unimode design" reduces this possibility substantially. A unimode design uses questions and response choices that are least likely to yield different answers according to the survey mode that is used. Unimode design principles include use of the same question structures, response choices, and skip instructions across modes, as well as using a small number of response choices for each question.

A Comparison of Survey Designs

Which survey design should be used when? Group-administered surveys are similar in most respects to mailed surveys, except they require the unusual circumstance of having access to the sample in a group setting. We therefore do not need to consider this survey design by itself; what applies to mailed survey designs applies to group-administered survey designs, with the exception of sampling issues. Thus, we can focus our comparison on the four survey designs that involve the use of a questionnaire with individuals sampled from a larger population: mailed surveys, phone surveys, in-person surveys, and electronic surveys. Exhibit 8.13 summarizes their strong and weak points.

desirability. Officers took my presence for granted in the briefing room, the hallways, the interview rooms, and in the field, including me in jokes and informal conversation in the coffee shop. (p. 235)

Generally, in social settings involving many people, an observer may not attract attention. On the other hand, when the social setting involves few people and observing is apparent rather than camouflaged, or when the observer differs in obvious respects from the participants, the complete observer is more likely to have an impact.

Participation and Observation

Most field researchers adopt a role that involves some active participation in the setting. Usually they inform at least some group members of their research interests, but then they participate in enough group activities to develop trust and rapport with members and to gain a direct sense of what group members experience. This is not an easy balancing act:

The key to participant observation as a fieldwork strategy is to take seriously the challenge it poses to participate more, and to play the role of the aloof observer less. Do not think of yourself as someone who needs to wear a white lab coat and carry a clipboard to learn about how humans go about their everyday lives. (Wolcott 1995, 100)

Observational studies are generally conducted over a long period of time. For example, in his classic study of corner gangs and other social organizations in the poor Boston community he called Cornerville, Whyte (1943) spent a large part of nearly four years trying to be accepted by the community and seen as a good fellow. He describes his efforts:

My aim was to gain an intimate view of Cornerville life. My first problem, therefore, was to establish myself as a participant in the society so that I would have a position from which to observe. I began by going to live in Cornerville, finding a room with an Italian family. . . . It was not enough simply to make the acquaintance of various groups of people. The sort of information that I sought required that I establish intimate social relations, and that presented special problems. Since illegal activities are prevalent in Cornerville, every new-comer is under suspicion. . . . I put in a great deal of time simply hanging around with them [the men] and participating in their various activities. This active participation gave me something in common with them so that we had other things to talk about besides the weather. (pp. v–vii)

During the three years that Rios spent in Oakland conducting his research, it was inevitable that he became a participant as well as an observer. For example, one day while walking home after school with a boy Rios called Slick, they were approached by a patrol car, which followed them. Slick recognized the officer as the one who had recently beaten up another boy named Marquil in a McDonald's parking lot during lunch hour. Rios writes,

I turned to Slick and told him, "Let's just keep walking. We'll be fine." The officer continued to follow us, driving slowly behind us. Slick became paranoid, turned around, and gave the officer a dirty look. I turned to look. The officer, a White man with a shaved head in his thirties, looked at us, grinned, and drove off. Police officers played crafty cat-and-mouse games in which the boys remained in constant fear of being humiliated, brutalized, or arrested. (p. 81)

On one occasion, Rios was even arrested. While he was sitting in a park with several of the youth, a police car approached. Rios and the other boys except one pulled their hands out of the pockets and "stood in a position of submission, with our hands open to show that we didn't have a weapon," while a boy Rios called Spider kept his hands in his pockets. The officers, one white and one Latino, got out and said, "Face the wall" (Rios 2011, 126). The officers searched everyone, and because Spider had a pocket knife in his pocket, he was arrested. When Rios asked the officers why they were stopped in the first place, he was handcuffed and arrested, too.

Embedded into the community as Rios was, he witnessed life as it happened, which included youth-on-youth violence as well as harassment and abuse by the police. During his observational time, he witnessed over 40 citations imposed by the police on the boys in his study. These were usually for minor things like loitering, not wearing a properly fitted bicycle helmet, or disturbing the peace. Rios never participated in violence, but sometimes he intervened to stop it.

Disclosing your research to participants as Rios did has two clear ethical advantages. Because group members know the researcher's real role in the group, they can choose to keep some information or attitudes hidden. By the same token, the researcher can decline to participate in unethical or dangerous activities without fear of exposing his or her identity.

Most field researchers who opt for disclosure get the feeling that, after they have become known and at least somewhat trusted figures in the group, their presence does not have a palpable effect on members' actions. The major influences on individual actions and attitudes are past experiences, personality, group structure, and so on, and these continue to exert their influence even when an outside observer is present. The participant observer can presumably be ethical about identity disclosure and still observe the natural social world. Of course, the argument is less persuasive when the behavior to be observed is illegal or stigmatized, giving participants reason to fear the consequences of disclosure to any outsider. In practice, it can be difficult to maintain a fully open research role even in a setting without these special characteristics.

Even when researchers maintain a public identity as researchers, the ethical dilemmas arising from participation in group activities do not go away. In fact, researchers may have to prove themselves to group members by joining in some of their questionable activities. Experienced participant observers try to lessen some of the problems of identity disclosure by evaluating both their effect on others in the setting and the effect of others on the observers. The observers must write about these effects throughout the time they are in the field and as they analyze their data. While in the field they must preserve some regular time when they can concentrate on their research and schedule occasional meetings with other researchers to review the fieldwork. Participant observers modify their role as circumstances seem to require, perhaps not always disclosing their research role at casual social gatherings or group outings but always informing new members of their role.

Covert Participation

To lessen the potential for reactive effects and to gain entry to otherwise inaccessible settings, some field researchers have adopted the role of covert participant. By doing so, they keep their research secret and do their best to act like other participants in a social setting or group. **Covert participation** is also known as **complete participation**. Laud Humphreys (1970) served as a "watch queen" so that he could learn about men engaging in homosexual acts in a public restroom. Randall Alfred (1976) joined a group of Satanists to investigate group members and their interaction. Erving Goffman (1961) worked as a state hospital assistant while studying the treatment of psychiatric patients.

> **Covert (complete) participation:** A role in field research in which the researcher does not reveal his or her identity as a researcher to those who are observed. The covert participant has adopted the role of a "complete participant."

Although the role of covert participant lessens some of the reactive effects encountered by the complete observer, covert participants confront other problems. The following are a few examples:

- *Covert participants cannot openly take notes or use any obvious recording devices.* They must write up notes based solely on memory and must do so at times when it is natural for them to be away from group members.

- *Covert participants cannot ask questions that will arouse suspicion.* Thus, they often have trouble clarifying the meaning of other participants' attitudes or actions.

- *The role of covert participant is difficult to play successfully.* Covert participants will not know how regular participants act in every situation in which the researchers find themselves. Regular participants enter the observed situation with social backgrounds and goals different from those of the researchers, whose spontaneous reactions to every event are unlikely to be consistent with those of the regular participants. Suspicion that a researcher is not "one of us" may then have reactive effects, obviating the value of complete participation (Erikson 1967). In his study of the Satanists, for example, Alfred (1976) pretended to be a regular group participant until he completed his research, at which time he informed the group leader of his covert role. Rather than act surprised, the leader told Alfred that he had long considered Alfred to be strange, not like the others. We will never be certain how Alfred's observations were affected.

- *Covert participants must keep up the act at all times while in the setting under study.* Researchers may experience enormous psychological strain, particularly in situations where they are expected to choose sides in intragroup conflict or to participate in criminal or other acts. Of course, some covert observers may become so wrapped up in their role that they adopt not just the mannerisms but also the perspectives and goals of the regular participants; they "go native." At this point, they abandon research goals and cease to critically evaluate their observations.

As you learned in Chapter 3, ethical issues have been at the forefront of the debate over the strategy of covert participation. Erikson (1967) argues that covert participation is by its very nature unethical and should not be allowed except in public settings. Covert researchers cannot anticipate the unintended consequences (e.g. gang violence) of their actions for research subjects, Erikson points out. If others suspect the researcher's identity, or if the researcher contributes to, or impedes, group action, these consequences can be adverse. In addition, other social research is harmed when covert research is disclosed, either during the research or upon its publication, because distrust of social scientists increases and future access to research opportunities may decrease.

But a total ban on covert participation would "kill many a project stone dead" (Punch 1994, 90). For example, when studying the behavior of male-for-male escorts, Pruitt (2008) contends that "it is unlikely that many escorts would respond to an e-mail from a self-identified Sociologist" (p. 71). In fact, he demonstrated that escorts who received an e-mail from a sociologist asking them about their business responded 15% of the time, while escorts who received the same e-mail message that he sent as a potential client received a response 60% of the time. These findings, Pruitt believes, support his contention that certain populations would be inaccessible without using deception.

Others agree. "The crux of the matter is that some deception, passive or active, enables you to get at data not obtainable by other means" (Punch 1994, 91). Therefore, some field researchers argue that covert participation is legitimate in certain circumstances. If researchers maintain the confidentiality of others, keep their commitments to them, and do not directly lie to the participants, some degree of deception may be justified in exchange for the knowledge gained (Punch 1994). According to the American Sociological Association's (1999) ethical guidelines, which are followed by the American Society of Criminology (see Chapter 3), deceptive techniques may be used only if researchers have determined that their use will not be harmful to research participants; if their use is justified by the study's prospective scientific, educational, or applied value; and if equally effective alternative procedures that do not use deception are not feasible. Or, on rare occasions, sociologists may need to conceal their identity in order to undertake research that could not practically be carried out were they to be known as researchers. Under such circumstances, sociologists undertake the research if it involves no more than minimal risk for the research participants and if they have obtained approval to proceed in this manner from an institutional review board (IRB).

What this means for contemporary research is that it is more difficult to get covert observational studies approved by an IRB than it once was. This has created what David Calvey calls a "submerged yet creative tradition" within the field of criminology (Calvey 2014, 541). Importantly, Calvey also cautions that there is not always a clear divide between covert and overt research. For example, the boys Rios shadowed in Oakland were aware of his status as a researcher, but all of the people Rios encountered during his field work were not. In fact, it would be virtually impossible to continually make everyone aware of your role without completely changing the social world you are studying. A brief case study of research that examined football (soccer) hooligans in the UK is an excellent example that we will highlight next.

―――――――――――――――――――― **Case Study** ――――――――――――――――――――

The Researcher as Hooligan

A riot after a sporting event is not a new phenomenon (Exhibit 9.3). In fact, at this writing, the most recent sporting event riot to result in injuries and arrests to occur in the United States just happened near the University of Kentucky (UK) campus after the UK Wildcats lost to the University of Wisconsin in the NCAA basketball semifinals. Long-term trends in violent riots indicate, however, that riots are equally likely to occur after wins (Bialik 2015). How do these riots happen, and what kinds of people get involved? To find out, Geoff Pearson (2009) engaged in covert participation in the illegal behavior of English football (soccer) supporters, commonly referred to as *hooligans.* He was interested not only in individual and group behavior, but in police responses to this behavior as well (Pearson 2009). He first attempted to interview self-professed hooligans about their behavior, but he found that their reports were unreliable, with nonviolent fans often exaggerating their violent behavior, and violent fans often downplaying theirs because they feared being reported.

To obtain more valid information about the culture of hooliganism, Pearson began to study this social world as a covert participant. He stated, "The only way I could gain an understanding of the 'lifeworld' of the subjects was to fully immerse myself in the group's activities through participant observation" (p. 246). He spent three years as part of a fan club—for an English football club—that regularly engaged in a wide range of low-level criminal offenses, including drinking and drug offenses, disorderly and threatening behavior, damage to property, and sometimes assaults. In his research, Pearson committed minor offenses, which "the majority of the research subjects were committing and that I considered necessary to carry out the research" (p. 247). He justified his covert participation by saying he believed soccer hooligans have been misunderstood and subject to "serious injustices and maltreatment by those in authority" (p. 249).

After Pearson's original study, he collaborated with Clifford Stott (Stott and Pearson 2007) to more formally observe the English fans in other countries during the European Championships, beginning in 2000. Although they also interviewed and conducted focus groups with fans, they still relied heavily on covert participation. They explained,

> By taking part in the activities of a crowd, rather than merely watching in a detached way, researchers gain a better idea about the feelings and psychological reactions of those within it.... Being at the center of the crowd gives researchers the opportunity to see especially subtle changes in mood and behavior, which can be the difference between peaceful good humor and disorder. (p. 212)

What they learned provided important information on how law enforcement could more effectively curtail the violence that often erupted during and after soccer matches. Among many other findings, they concluded,

> Where police forces adopt a more targeted, proactive and less confrontational approach, the risk that these sections of the England fan base pose is clearly and self-evidently decreased. But when police forces adopt a more traditional approach [confrontational], this risk manifests itself sometimes in major incidents of disorder and high numbers of arrests. (p. 326)

Entering the Field

Entering the field or the setting under investigation is a critical stage in a participant observation project, as the introduction can shape many subsequent experiences. Some background work is necessary before entering the field, at least enough to develop a clear understanding of what the research questions are likely to be and to review one's personal stance toward the people and problems likely to be encountered. Rios had lived in the flatlands of Oakland, California, where he conducted his study, but he still spent a great deal of time learning about the community context he was about

| Exhibit 9.3 | **Soccer Hooligans Assaulting A Rival Fan After Match** |

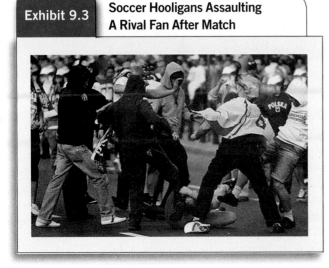

to enter. In fact, his book *Punished* (2011) provides a detailed discussion of the political and structural conditions of the community under study. Among many other statistics that described policies relevant to his study, he noted,

> From 2002 to 2005 Oakland continued to focus on punitive social control in attempts to reduce the crime rate. The city prioritized funding for law enforcement, resulting in declines in spending for educational and social programs. In 2002, Oakland spent $128,331 per law-enforcement employee; by 2005, this rate had increased to $190,140. This approach was further evidenced in the demands made by the Oakland City Council to the city's new chief of police: "You said you can't arrest our way out of this problem. Well you sure better try. We all have our jobs to do and your job is to arrest people." (p. 34)

Examining the larger community context as Rios did was an important component to understand how community factors related to the individual lives of his study participants.

Developing trust with at least one member of the research setting is another necessity in qualitative research. Such a person can become a valuable informant throughout the project, and most participant observers make a point of developing trust with at least one informant in a group under study.

In short, field researchers must be very sensitive to the impression they make and the ties they establish when entering the field. This stage of research lays the groundwork for collecting data from people who have different perspectives and for developing relationships that the researcher can use to overcome the problems that inevitably arise in the field.

Developing and Maintaining Relationships

Researchers must be careful to manage their relationships in the research setting so they can continue to observe and interview diverse members of the social setting throughout the long period typical of participant observation (Maxwell 1996). Making valid observations, of course, would be impossible if researchers do not have the trust of the people whom they are studying.

Rios (2011) originally recruited participants in his study from a youth leadership organization and community center in Oakland. The boys were 'at-promise' ('at-risk') young men, ages fourteen to seventeen, who had previously been arrested" (p. 10). Because he had formally lived in the area and was only 25 years old when he began his research, Rios probably had a relatively easy time developing trust and rapport with his participants. In fact, he stated,

> Many of the boys acknowledged me as someone they could trust and look up to. The majority referred to me as "O. G. Vic." "O. G." stands for "original gangster." This label is often ascribed to older members of the neighborhood who have proven themselves and gained respect on the street and, as a result, are respected by younger residents. I told the young men not to consider me an O. G. since I believed, and still do, that I did not deserve the label. My belief was that any researcher who considered himself an O. G. was being deceptive. . . . At the time of the study, I was a graduate student with many privileges that many of these young people did not have. I was an "outsider" as much as an "insider." (p. 13)

While having personal knowledge or experience with a social setting certainly helps researchers gain entry into that world, many researchers who have not had backgrounds with their areas of study have also been successful.

For example, Jody Miller (2000) describes her efforts to develop trust with the female gang members she interviewed for her book *One of the Guys*:

> First, my research approach proved useful for establishing rapport. The survey began with relatively innocuous questions (demographics, living arrangements, attitudes toward school) and slowly made the transition from these to more sensitive questions about gang involvement, delinquency, and victimization. In addition, completing the survey interview first allowed me to establish a relationship with each young woman, so that when we completed the in-depth interview, there was a preexisting level of familiarity between us. . . . In addition, I worked to develop trust in the young women I interviewed through my efforts to protect their confidentiality. (pp. 29–30)

Sampling People and Events

Decisions to study one setting or several settings and to pay attention to specific people and events will shape field researchers' ability to generalize about what they have found as well as the confidence that others can place in the results of their study. Limiting a particular study to a single setting allows a more intensive portrait of actors and activities in that setting but also makes generalization of the findings questionable.

It is easy to be reassured by information indicating that a typical case was selected for study or that the case selected was appropriate in some way for the research question. We also must keep in mind that many of the most insightful participant observation studies were conducted in only one setting and draw their credibility precisely from the researcher's thorough understanding of that setting. Nonetheless, studying more than one case or setting almost always strengthens the causal conclusions and makes the findings more generalizable (King, Keohane, and Verba 1994).

Most qualitative researchers utilize a purposive sampling technique (Chapter 5), often adding a snowball aspect by asking respondents to recommend others. Rios added a snowball sample component to the original participants he obtained from the community center. He stated, "With snowball sampling, I was able to uncover a population of young men who were surrounded by or involved in crime and who had consistent interaction with police" (2011, p. 11).

Theoretical sampling is a systematic approach to sampling in participant observational research (Glaser and Strauss 1967). Decker and Van Winkle (1996) used this technique to ensure that various subgroups such as those identified by race, sex, and type of gang were represented within their sample. When field researchers discover in an investigation that particular processes seem to be important, implying that certain comparisons should be made or that similar instances should be checked, the researchers then modify their settings and choose new individuals, as diagrammed in Exhibit 9.4 (Ragin 1994). Based on the existing literature and anecdotal knowledge, Decker and Van Winkle knew that not all gang members were young minority-group males. They describe their strategy to obtain a full range of gang members for their sample as follows:

> **Theoretical sampling:** A sampling method recommended for field researchers by Glaser and Strauss (1967). A theoretical sample is drawn in a sequential fashion, with settings or individuals selected for study as earlier observations or interviews indicate that these settings or individuals are influential.

> We aggressively pursued leads for female gangs and gang members as well as opportunities to locate older and nonblack gang members. These leads were more difficult to find and often caused us to miss chances to interview other gang members. Despite these "missed opportunities," our sample is strengthened in that it more accurately represents the diverse nature of gangs and gang members in St. Louis. (p. 43)

The resulting sample of gang members in Decker and Van Winkle's (1996) study represented 29 different gangs. Thus, Decker and Van Winkle's ability to draw from different gangs in developing conclusions gives us greater confidence in their studies' generalizability.

A: No.

Q: What is marijuana then?

A: I don't know.

Q: What is weed?

A: Stuff you smoke. (p. 92)

Tape recorders commonly are used to record intensive interviews. Most researchers who have tape-recorded interviews feel that tape-recording does not inhibit most interviewees and, in fact, is routinely ignored. The occasional respondent who is very concerned with his or her public image may speak "for the tape recorder," but such individuals are unlikely to speak frankly in any research interview. In any case, constant note taking during an interview prevents adequate displays of interest and appreciation by the interviewer and hinders the degree of concentration that results in the best interviews.

Of course, there are exceptions to every rule. Fenno (1978) presents a compelling argument for avoiding the tape recorder when interviewing public figures who are concerned with their public image:

> My belief is that the only chance to get a nonroutine, nonreflexive interview [from many of the members of Congress] is to converse casually, pursuing targets of opportunity without the presence of a recording instrument other than myself. If [worse] comes to worst, they can always deny what they have said in person; on tape they leave themselves no room for escape. I believe they are not unaware of the difference. (p. 280)

Combining Participant Observation and Intensive Interviewing

Many large research projects aimed at uncovering detailed information about a particular phenomenon combine the qualitative research techniques of participant observation and intensive interviewing. As we have already seen, Victor Rios (2011) combined these methods, as did Susan Miller (1999) in her study of community policing. In fact, Miller contends that the information obtained from both methodologies was vital to her conclusions. For example, the observational component of Miller's research shows how traditional patrol officers' perceptions and experiences differ from those of neighborhood patrol officers. Her observations also uncovered how rarely the paths of patrol officers crossed with their community policing counterparts. These limited interactions contributed, Miller believed, to patrol officers' misconceptions about community policing. Patrol officers believed that neighborhood police officers did not do real police work and spent too much time responding to residents and political needs, not to crime-fighting goals.

While both male and female patrol officers would engage in masculine teasing while in the field, such as talking about their physical fitness and shooting ability, during the one-on-one interviews, she discovered a more gendered nature of the patrol officers' perceptions and experiences:

> Even though the patrolwomen joined in the banter and told their share of crime-fighting war stories [in the field], it became clear during one-on-one conversations with them they dropped their aggressive facade when their actions were less visible to other patrol officers. The women were more than superficially involved in some of the local people's lives, particularly with the children. (p. 176)

▣ Focus Groups

Focus groups are groups of individuals that are formed by a researcher and then led in group discussion of a topic. The researcher asks specific questions and guides the discussion to ensure that group members address these questions, but the resulting information is qualitative and relatively unstructured. Unlike most other survey designs, focus groups do not involve representative samples; instead, a few individuals are recruited for the group who have the time to participate and who share key characteristics with the target population. Focus groups have their roots in the interviewing techniques developed in the 1930s by sociologists and psychologists who were dissatisfied with traditional surveys. Traditionally, in a questionnaire survey, subjects are directed to consider certain issues and particular response options in a predetermined order. The spontaneous exchange and development of ideas that characterize social life outside the survey situation are lost, as are, some social scientists fear, the prospects for validity.

Focus groups were used by the military in World War II to investigate morale and then were popularized by the great American sociologist Robert K. Merton and two collaborators, Marjorie Fiske and Patricia Kendall, in *The Focused Interview* (1956). But marketing researchers were the first to adopt focus groups as a widespread methodology. Marketing researchers use focus groups to investigate likely popular reactions to possible advertising themes and techniques. Their success has prompted other social scientists to use focus groups to evaluate social programs and to assess social needs (Krueger 1988).

Most focus groups involve seven to ten people, a number that facilitates discussion by all in attendance. Although participants usually do not know one another, they are chosen so that they are relatively homogeneous, which tends to reduce their inhibitions in discussion. Of course, the characteristics of individuals that determine their inclusion are based on the researcher's conception of the target population for the study. Focus group leaders must begin the discussion by creating the expectation that all will participate and that the researcher will not favor any particular perspective or participant.

Focus groups are interviewed to collect qualitative data using open-ended questions posed by the researcher (or group leader). Thus, a focused discussion mimics the natural process of forming and expressing opinions and may give some sense of validity. The researcher may also want to conduct a more traditional survey, asking a representative sample of the target population to answer closed-ended questions, to weigh the validity of data obtained from the focus group. No formal procedure exists for determining the generalizability of focus group answers, but the careful researcher should conduct at least several focus groups on the same topic and check for consistency in the findings as a partial test of generalizability.

Like other field research techniques, focus group methods share an emphasis on discovering unanticipated findings and exploring hidden meanings. Although they do not provide a means for developing reliable, generalizable results (the traditional strong suits of survey research), focus groups can be an indispensable aid for developing hypotheses and survey questions, for investigating the meaning of survey results, and for quickly identifying the range of opinion about an issue.

--- **Case Study** ---

An Analysis of Police Searches

Racial profiling has generally been defined as the use of race as a key factor in deciding whether to make a traffic stop (Williams and Stahl 2008). As a response to lawsuits alleging racial profiling, many state and local law enforcement agencies have been mandated or have volunteered to collect traffic stop data to monitor the behavior of officers to determine the extent of such profiling. However, to actually determine if racial minorities like African Americans are stopped for speeding more than whites, researchers would first have to determine the percentage of African American drivers relative to white drivers who were actually driving along a given highway, and then the percentage of these motorists who were actually speeding, to get a true base rate of speeding per population group. This would entail many hours of monitoring a given highway during various times of day. While some researchers have actually collected these data, Williams and Stahl decided to examine whether race was a determining factor in the search process, not in the original police stop.

The questions they asked were, "Who is being searched, and what are the results of these searches?" Using data collected in 24 local Kentucky law enforcement agencies along with two state agencies, they concluded that of the motorists pulled over on the interstate for compliance and courtesy stops, African American and Hispanic motorists were significantly more likely to be searched compared to white motorists. To test the second question, they examined whether there were differences in positive search results (e.g., finding contraband) across race/ethnic groups. Not surprisingly, based on other research, there was no statistical difference in the likelihood that white, African American, or Hispanic motorists who were searched had illegal material. In fact, although the difference was not

In any case, no field research project should begin if some participants clearly will suffer serious harm by being identified in project publications.

Confidentiality is particularly important if the research is uncovering deviant or illegal behavior. In his research in Oakland, it was almost inevitable that Rios (2011) would witness illegal activity and/or be told about past criminal behavior. However, he told the boys he was not there to study their criminality. He stated,

> This could put them in danger if the records would ever end up with the police. Inevitably I would witness and hear a plethora of stories about crime. Later I would find myself reminding the young men not to provide me with details about the crimes that they had committed. (p. 170)

As we discussed in Chapter 3, researchers are not generally compelled to report past offending behavior to authorities unless information is reported that indicates a research subject intends to harm himself or herself or others in the future.

Appropriate Boundaries

This is an ethical issue that cuts across several of the others, including identity disclosure, subject well-being, and voluntary participation. You probably are familiar with this issue in the context of guidelines for professional practice: Therapists are cautioned to maintain appropriate boundaries with patients; teachers must maintain appropriate boundaries with students. This is a special issue in qualitative research, because it often involves lessening the boundary between the "researcher" and the research "subject." Qualitative researchers may seek to build rapport with those they plan to interview by expressing an interest in their concerns and conveying empathy for their situation. Is this just "faking friendship" for the purpose of the research? Jean Duncombe and Julie Jessop (2002) posed the dilemma clearly in a book chapter titled "'Doing Rapport' and the Ethics of 'Faking Friendship.'"

> With deeper rapport, interviewees become more likely to explore their more intimate experiences and emotions. Yet they also become more likely to discover and disclose experiences and feelings which, upon reflection, they would have preferred to keep private from others . . . or not to acknowledge even to themselves. (p. 112)

Researcher Safety

Research "in the field," whether researchers are studying gang life or anything else, should not begin until any potential risks to researcher safety have been evaluated. Qualitative methods may provide the only opportunity to learn about organized crime in Russian ports (Belousov et al. 2007), street crime in the Dominican Republic (Gill 2004), or the other studies examined in this chapter, but they should not be used if the risks to the researchers are unacceptably high. Safety needs to be considered at the time the research is designed, not as an afterthought on arriving in the research site. As Hannah Gill learned in the Dominican Republic, such advance planning can require more investigation than just reading the local newspapers: "Due to the community's marginality, most crimes, including murders, were never reported in newspapers, making it impossible to have known the insecurity of the field site ahead of time" (p. 2).

But being realistic about evaluating risk does not mean simply accepting misleading assumptions about unfamiliar situations or communities. For example, reports of a widespread breakdown in law and order in New Orleans were broadcast repeatedly after Hurricane Katrina, but researchers found that most nontraditional behavior in that period was actually "prosocial," rather than antisocial (Rodríguez, Trainor, and Quarantelli 2006):

> One group named itself the "Robin Hood Looters." The core of this group consisted of eleven friends who, after getting their own families out of the area, decided to remain at some high ground and, after the floodwaters

rose, commandeered boats and started to rescue their neighbors. . . . For about two weeks they kept searching in the area. . . . They foraged for food and water from abandoned homes, and hence their group name. Among the important norms that developed were that they were going to retrieve only survivors and not bodies and that group members would not carry weapons. The group also developed informal understandings with the police and the National Guard. (p. 91)

These ethical issues cannot be evaluated independently. The final decision to proceed must be made after weighing the relative benefits and risks to participants. Few qualitative research projects will be barred by consideration of these ethical issues, except for those involving covert participation. The more important concern for researchers is to identify the ethically troublesome aspects of their proposed research, resolve them before the project begins, and act on new ethical issues as they come up during the project. Combining methods is often the best strategy.

🔲 Conclusion

Qualitative research allows the careful investigator to obtain a richer and more intimate view of the social world than can be achieved with more structured methods. It is not hard to understand why so many qualitative studies have become classics in the literature. And the emphases in qualitative research on inductive reasoning and incremental understanding help stimulate and inform other research approaches. Exploratory research to chart the dimensions of previously unstudied social settings and intensive investigations of the subjective meanings that motivate individual action are particularly well served by the techniques of participant observation, intensive interviewing, and focus groups.

The very characteristics that make qualitative research techniques so appealing restrict their use to a limited set of research problems. It is not possible to draw representative samples for study using participant observation, and for this reason the generalizability of any particular field study's results cannot really be known. Only the accumulation of findings from numerous qualitative studies permits confident generalization, but here again the time and effort required to collect and analyze the data make it unlikely that many particular field research studies will be replicated.

Even if qualitative researchers made an effort to replicate key studies, their notion of developing and grounding explanations inductively in the observations made in a particular setting would hamper comparison of findings. Measurement reliability is thereby hindered, as are systematic tests for the validity of key indicators and formal tests for causal connections.

In the final analysis, qualitative research involves a mode of thinking and investigating different from that used in experimental and survey research. Qualitative research is inductive and idiographic; experiments and surveys tend to be conducted in a deductive, quantitative framework. Both approaches can help social scientists learn about the social world; the proficient researcher must be ready to use either. Qualitative data are often supplemented with many quantitative characteristics or activities. And as you have already seen, quantitative data are often enriched with written comments and observations, and focus groups have become a common tool of survey researchers seeking to develop their questionnaires. Thus, the distinction between qualitative and quantitative research techniques is not always clear-cut.

Key Terms ▸ Review key terms with eFlashcards. **⑤SAGE** edge™

CHAPTER 10

Analyzing Content

Secondary Data Analysis, Comparative Analysis, Content Analysis, Crime Mapping, and Big Data

---

LEARNING OBJECTIVES

1. Understand the importance of comparative research along with the difficulties in measurement across contexts.

2. Explain how secondary data analysis is different from the methods we have already examined in this book.

3. Describe the steps necessary when performing a content analysis.

4. Describe the different research questions crime mapping can answer.

5. Understand how computer technology has ushered in our ability to analyze big data and the effects this has had on criminal justice–related research.

6. Describe the strengths and limitations of conducting secondary data analysis.

The research methods we have examined so far in this text have relied on researchers collecting the data or information themselves. Increasingly, however, those interested in criminological research questions are relying on data previously collected by other investigators (Riedel 2000). As we noted in Chapter 1, this is referred to as secondary data analysis. **Secondary data analysis** is simply the act of collecting or analyzing data that were originally collected by someone else at another time (Riedel 2000). Thus, if a researcher goes to a police department and personally compiles information from police reports to examine a research question, she is still engaging in secondary data analysis because the police records were originally collected prior to her own research.

Secondary data analysis has a long history. Since the latter part of the 17th century, people have been monitoring the state of their localities by examining rates of population, mortality, marriage, disease, climate, and crime. Adolphe Quételet, an ambitious Belgian mathematician, was one of the first to show that the annual number of murders reported in France from 1826 to 1831 was relatively constant and, further, that the proportion of murders committed with guns, swords, knives, stones, kicks and punches, and strangulation was also relatively constant. He concluded that although we may not know who will kill whom by what means, we do know, with a high degree of probability, that a certain number of murders of a certain type will happen every year in France (Menand 2001). This was one of the first attempts to apply the methods of science to social phenomena. You are also probably familiar with Émile Durkheim's ([1951] 1987) use of official statistics on suicide rates in different areas to examine the relationship between religion and suicide.

In this chapter, we will tell you about a number of datasets, including surveys and official records that are publicly available for research purposes. Then we will examine several research methods that rely on secondary data, including historical events research, cross-cultural research, content analysis, and crime mapping. And finally, because using data originally gathered for other purposes poses unique concerns for a researcher, we will spend the latter part of the chapter highlighting these methodological issues.

Secondary data analysis: Analysis of data collected by someone other than the researcher or the researcher's assistant.

▣ Analyzing Secondary Data

In general, there are four major types of secondary data: surveys, official statistics, official records, and other historical documents. Although a dataset can be obtained by an agreement between two or more researchers, many researchers obtain data through the Inter-University Consortium for Political and Social Research (ICPSR) (www.icpsr.umich.edu). Data stored at ICPSR primarily include surveys, official records, and official statistics. ICPSR stores data and information for nearly 5,000 sources and studies, including those conducted independently and those conducted by the U.S. government. Riedel (2000) has documented the majority of datasets that are available from ICPSR and that are appropriate for crime research, including the following:

Census enumerations: historical and contemporary population characteristics. The most well-known datasets within this category are the surveys conducted every decade by the Bureau of the Census. Linking information from this dataset (e.g., neighborhood characteristics including such things as poverty and residential mobility) to crime data at the same level (e.g., census block, county) has provided researchers with a rich source of data to test theories of crime.

The National Archive of Criminal Justice Data (NACJD). The Bureau of Justice Statistics and National Institute of Justice cosponsored NACJD, which provides more than 600 criminal justice data collections to the public. A sample of these datasets includes the following:

wealthier jurisdictions tended to have significantly more police employees per 100 index crimes compared to poorer areas. This finding runs counter to the contention that cities generally allocate police resources equitably. Thacher (2011) states, "Police protection has become more concentrated in the most advantaged communities—those with the highest per-capita incomes and the largest share of white residents" (p. 286). What has changed, Thacher believes, are the crime rates. For example, when police protection per capita (number of individuals in jurisdiction) is examined, it becomes evident that police protection has not changed much since 1970 across jurisdictions. However, because crime has become more concentrated in the poorest communities during that time, police resources per crime have become less egalitarian. What does this mean in the real world?

> The result is a growing workload disparity between rich and poor jurisdictions. In rich jurisdictions, each police officer has responsibility for fewer and fewer crimes over time, while in poor jurisdictions this part of the police workload has either remained constant or grown. (Thacher 2011, 289)

▣ Comparative Methods

The limitations of examining data from a single location have encouraged many social scientists to turn to comparisons among many geographical entities, and comparative research increased recently. As noted in the 2001 American Academy of Criminal Justice Sciences' Presidential Address by Richard Bennett (2004), **comparative research** in criminal justice and criminology took on new importance after the terrorist attacks on September 11, 2001. Bennett described two types of comparative research:

1. Research that seeks to understand the structure, nature, or scope of a nation's or nations' criminal justice systems or rates of crime is **descriptive comparative research**.

2. Research that seeks to understand how national systems work and the factors related to their operations is **analytic comparative research**.

Comparative research: Research comparing data from more than one time period and/or more than one nation.

Descriptive comparative research: Research that seeks to understand the structure, nature, or scope of a nation's or nations' criminal justice systems or rates of crime.

Analytic comparative research: Research that seeks to understand how national systems work and the factors related to their operations.

Transnational research: Research that explores how cultures and nations deal with crime that transcends their borders.

There is also variability in the scope of comparative research. Studies can analyze single nations, make a comparison across several nations, or conduct **transnational research**, which generally explores how cultures and nations deal with crime that transcends their borders. Investigating terrorism is one emerging form of transnational research. Bennett (2004) noted,

One of the outcomes of the terrorist attacks in 2001 was a shocking awareness that terrorism is international and inextricably tied to transnational criminal activity. . . . We need to understand how criminal and terrorist organizations fund themselves and exploit our inability to link and analyze criminal activity that transcends national borders. (p. 8)

Although comparative methods are often associated with cross-national comparisons, research examining smaller aggregates such as states and cities can also be subsumed under the comparative research umbrella. Comparative research methods allow for a broader vision about social relations than is possible with cross-sectional research limited to one location.

Case Study

Homicide Across Nations

One of the first large comparative research projects undertaken in criminology was the development of the Comparative Crime Data File (CCDF), which was created by Archer and Gartner (1984). Archer and Gartner articulated the need for comparative research in the field succinctly:

> The need for cross-national comparisons seems particularly acute for research on crime and violence since national differences on these phenomena are of a remarkable magnitude. In some societies, homicide is an hourly, highly visible, and therefore somewhat unexceptional cause of death. In other nations, homicides are so infrequent that, when they do occur, they receive national attention and lasting notoriety. (p. 4)

The CCDF continues to be updated, but it originally contained crime and violence data from 110 nations and 44 major international cities covering the period from approximately 1900 to 1970. In their work, Archer and Gartner (1984) examined many research questions using the CCDF. One of these questions was related to the idea that war might increase the level of postwar homicide within nations involved in wars. There are several theoretical models that speculate about the possible effects of wars on postwar violence within a nation. For example, the social solidarity model posits a wartime *decrease* in violence because of the increase in social solidarity among a nation's citizenry. At a more individual level, the violent veteran model predicts that postwar levels of violence within a nation will *increase* as a result of the violent acts of returning war veterans. At a societal level, the legitimization of violence model postulates that during a war, a society reverses its prohibitions against killing and instead honors acts of violence that would be regarded as murderous in peacetime. This social approval or legitimation of violence, this model predicts, may produce a lasting reduction of inhibitions against taking human life, even after the war, thereby increasing levels of violence within nations.

To examine the effects of war on postwar violence, Archer and Gartner (1984) compared national rates of homicide before and after many wars, both small and large, including the two world wars. Exhibit 10.2 displays the increase or decrease of homicide rates in combatant nations and a sample of control nations that were not involved in World War I and World War II. The researchers also controlled for a number of other factors related to war, including the number of combat deaths in war, whether nations were victorious or defeated, and whether the nation's postwar economics were improved or worsened, and for several types of homicide offenses committed by both men and women. The researchers found that most combatant nations in their analysis experienced substantial postwar increases in their rates of homicide after both small and large wars. Archer and Gartner (1984) concluded,

> The one model that appears to be fully consistent with the evidence is the legitimation of violence model, which suggests that the presence of authorized or sanctioned killing during war has a residual effect on the level of homicide in peacetime society. (p. 96)

More recently, Savage, Bennett, and Danner (2008) examined the relationship between social welfare spending and homicide. Does welfare spending encourage dependency and weaken personal initiative, thereby increasing crime, or does it redress the imbalance of opportunities available in society and alleviate the resulting tensions that arise from such inequality, thereby decreasing crime? When looking at variation in welfare spending across localities in the United States, evidence tends to support the latter. Savage et al. (2008) used a dataset called the Correlates of Crime (COC), which contains data for a sample of 52 diverse nations from every region of the globe for 1960 through 1984. It includes data from the International Criminal Police Organization (Interpol), the United Nations (UN), the World Bank (WB), the International Labour Organization (ILO), and other sources.

Exhibit 10.2	Homicide Rate Changes in Combatant and Control Nations After World War I and World War II

Combatant Nations		
Rates Decreased	*Rates Remained Unchanged*	*Rates Increased*
Australia (I)	England (I)	Belgium
Canada (I)	France (I)	Bulgaria
Hungary (I)	S. Africa (I)	Germany
Finland (II)	Canada (II)	Italy (I)
N. Ireland (II)		Japan (I)
U.S. (II)		Portugal (I)
		Scotland (I)
		U.S. (I)
		Australia (II)
		Denmark (II)
		England (II)
		France (II)
		Italy (II)
		Japan (II)
		Netherlands (II)
		New Zealand (II)
		Norway (II)
		Scotland (II)
		S. Africa (II)
Control Nations		
Rates Decreased	*Rates Remained Unchanged*	*Rates Increased*
Norway (I)	Ceylon (I)	Finland (I)
Ceylon (II)	Chile (1)	Thailand (I)
Chile (II)	Netherlands (I)	Colombia (II)
El Salvador (II)		Sweden (I)
Ireland (II)		Turkey (II)
Switzerland (II)		
Thailand (II)		

Source: From *Violence and Crime in Cross-National Perspective* by Archer, D. & Gartner, R. Copyright © 1984. Reprinted with permission of Yale University Press.

Social welfare spending was operationalized as the amount of governmental spending in U.S. dollar equivalents for social welfare programs per person, adjusted to 1980 dollars. The variable was computed by dividing the total amount of social welfare spending per country per year by the population and further dividing it by the consumer price index. Savage et al. (2008) also controlled for other factors, including the gross domestic product (GDP), the percent of the population residing in urban areas, female labor force participation, and unemployment, among others. In addition to rates of homicide, they used rates of theft as another dependent variable. Over the time period studied, they found that social welfare spending was negatively related to both theft and homicide; that is, as social welfare spending increased, rates of these crimes generally decreased.

Research in the News

DATA ON RAPE IN THE EUROPEAN UNION DIFFICULT TO COMPARE

Most data available for the European Union nations, of which there are 27, are relatively easy to compare. But information on rape and domestic violence is different. In fact, most individual EU member states that do collect such data often have generally relied on police reports, not on surveys. Countries that are working hard to improve conditions for rape victims and victims of intimate partner violence tend to have increasing rates of victimization, because more victims are willing to come forward. Comparing the true magnitude of victimization for these crimes across EU countries is virtually impossible.

For Further Thought?

1. How would the different cultures across countries affect how survey researchers could ask questions to estimate the prevalence of rape and other sexual assault victimizations?

2. Would cultural differences affect the way individuals respond to surveys like this across countries? How so? Is it possible to compare estimates of rape and intimate partner violence across countries?

Source: Loftus, Louise. 2011. "Data on Rape in E.U. Difficult to Compare." *New York Times*, October, 24. http://www.nytimes.com/2011/10/25/world/europe/data-on-rape-in-eu-difficult-to-compare.html.

Content Analysis

Do media accounts of crime, such as newspaper and television news coverage, accurately portray the true nature of crime? The methodologies discussed thus far may not be helpful for answering this question. **Content analysis**, or "the systematic, objective, quantitative analysis of message characteristics" (Neuendorf 2002, 1) would be an appropriate tool. Using this method, we can learn a great deal about popular culture and many other issues through studying the characteristics of messages delivered through the mass media and other sources.

> **Content analysis:** A research method for systematically analyzing and making inferences from text.

The goal of a content analysis is to develop inferences from text (Weber 1990). You can think of a content analysis as a "survey" of some documents or other records of prior communication. In fact, a content analysis is a survey designed with fixed-choice responses so that it produces quantitative data that can be analyzed statistically. This method was first applied to the study of newspaper and film content and then developed systematically for the analysis of Nazi propaganda broadcasts in World War II, but it can also be used to study historical documents, records of speeches, and other "voices from the past" (Neuendorf 2002).

away from the feature itself. When certain motivated offenders interact with suitable targets, the risk of crime and victimization conceivably increases. But, when motivated offenders interact with suitable targets at certain places, the risk of criminal victimization is even higher. Similarly, when certain motivated offenders interact with suitable targets at places that are not conducive to crime, the risk of victimization is lowered.

Using data from many sources, RTM statistically computes the probability of particular kinds of criminal behavior occurring in a place. For example, Exhibit 10.9 displays a risk-terrain map that was produced for Irvington, New Jersey. From the map, you can see that several variables were included in the model predicting the potential for shootings to occur, including the presence of gangs and drugs, along with other infrastructure information such as the location of bars and liquor stores. Why were these some of the factors used? Because previous research and police data indicated that shootings were more likely to occur where gangs, drugs, and these businesses were present. This does not mean that a shooting will occur in the high-risk areas, it only means that it is more likely to occur in these areas compared to other areas. RTM is considered a use of big data because it examines multiple datasets that share geographic location as a common denominator.

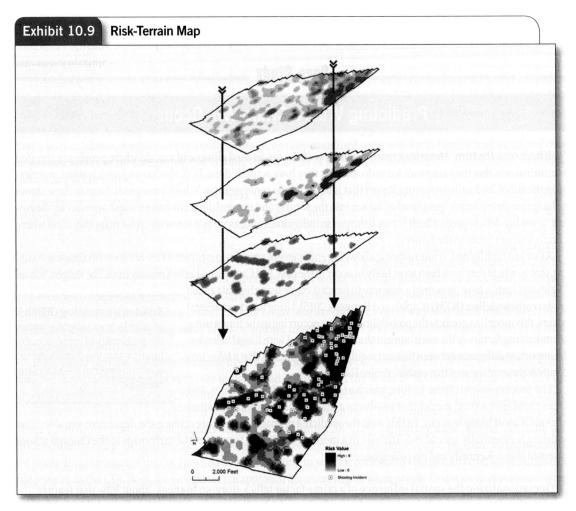

Exhibit 10.9   **Risk-Terrain Map**

Source: Obtained from personal correspondence with Leslie Kennedy and Joel Caplan.

————————————————— **Case Study** —————————————————

Predicting Recidivism With Big Data

As you learned in Chapter 2, the Minneapolis Domestic Violence Experiment and the National Institute of Justice's Spousal Abuse Replication Project, which were experiments to determine the efficacy of different approaches to reducing recidivism for intimate partner violence (IPV), changed the way IPV was handled by law enforcement agencies across the United States and across the globe. No longer were parties simply separated at the scene, but mandatory arrest policies were implemented in many jurisdictions across the country, which "swamped the system with domestic violence cases" (Williams and Houghton 2004, 438). In fact, some states now see thousands of perpetrators arrested annually for assaults against their intimate partners. Many jurisdictions are attempting to more objectively determine whether these perpetrators present a risk of future violence should they be released on parole or probation.

Kirk Williams developed one instrument to determine this risk, which is called the Revised Domestic Violence Screening Instrument (DVSI-R) (Williams 2012). To determine the effectiveness of the DVSI-R in predicting recidivism, Stansfield and Williams (2014) used a huge dataset that would be deemed big data, since it contains information on 29,317 perpetrators arrested on family violence charges in 2010 in Connecticut and is continuously updated for recent arrests and convictions. To measure the risk of recidivism for new family violence offenses (NFVO), the DVSI-R includes eleven items; seven measure the behavioral history of the perpetrator, including such things as prior nonfamily assaults, arrests, or criminal convictions; prior family violence assaults, threats, or arrests; prior violations of protection orders; the frequency of family violence in the previous six months; and the escalation of family violence in the past six months. The other four items include substance abuse, weapons or objects used as weapons, children present during violent incidents, and employment status. The range of the DVSI-R is from 0 to 28, with 28 representing the highest risk score.

To examine how the DVSI-R predicted future arrests, Stansfield and Williams (2014) used two measures of recidivism during an 18-month follow-up: rearrests for NFVOs, and rearrests for violations of protective or restraining orders only. Results indicated that of the over 29,000 cases, nearly one in four (23%) perpetrators were rearrested, with 14% of those rearrested for a violation of a protective order. Perpetrators who had higher DVSI-R risk scores were more likely to be rearrested compared to those with lower risk scores. As you can see, using big data to improve decision making by criminal justice professionals is not a thing of the future, it is happening now. The availability of big data and advanced computer technologies for its analysis mean that researchers can apply standard research methods in exciting new ways, and this trend will only continue to grow.

▣ Methodological Issues When Using Secondary Data

Each of the methods we have discussed in this chapter presents unique methodological challenges. For example, in comparative research, small numbers of cases, spotty historical records, variable cross-national record-keeping practices, and different cultural and linguistic contexts limit the confidence that can be placed in measures, samples, and causal conclusions. Just to identify many of the potential problems for a comparative research project requires detailed knowledge of the times and of the nations or other units investigated (Kohn 1987). This requirement often serves as a barrier to in-depth historical research and to comparisons between nations.

Analysis of secondary data presents several challenges, ranging from uncertainty about the methods of data collection to the lack of maximal fit between the concepts that the primary study measured and each of the concepts that are the focus of the current investigation. Responsible use of secondary data requires a good understanding of the primary data source. The researcher should be able to answer the following questions (most of which were adopted from Riedel 2000 and Stewart 1984):

1. What were the agency's goals in collecting the data? If the primary data were obtained in a research project, what were the project's purposes?

Method of agreement: A method proposed by John Stuart Mill for establishing a causal relation, in which the values of cases that agree on an outcome variable also agree on the value of the variable hypothesized to have a causal effect, whereas they differ in terms of other variables.

Deterministic causal approach: An approach in which there is a relationship between an independent and a dependent variable; the independent variable has an effect on the dependent variable in every case under consideration.

systems are compared in terms of four socioeconomic variables hypothesized by different theories to influence violent crime. If the nations differ in terms of three of the variables but are similar in terms of the fourth, this is evidence that the fourth variable influences violent crime.

The features of the cases selected for comparison have a large impact on the ability to identify influences using the method of agreement. Cases should be chosen for their difference in terms of key factors hypothesized to influence the outcome of interest and their similarity on other, possibly confounding factors (Skocpol 1984). For example, in order to understand how unemployment influences violent crime, you would need to select cases for comparison that differ in unemployment rates so that you could then see if they differ in rates of violence (King et al. 1994).

This **deterministic causal approach** (Ragin 1987) requires that there be no deviations from the combination of factors that are identified as determining the outcome for each nation. Yet there are likely to be exceptions to any explanatory rule that we establish (Lieberson 1991). A careful analyst will evaluate the extent to which exceptions should be allowed in particular analyses.

With these cautions in mind, the combination of historical and comparative methods allows for rich descriptions of social and political processes in different nations or regions as well as for causal inferences that reflect a systematic, defensible weighing of the evidence. Data of increasingly good quality are available on a rapidly expanding number of nations, creating many opportunities for comparative research. We cannot expect one study comparing the histories of a few nations to control adequately for every plausible alternative causal influence, but repeated investigations can refine our understanding and lead to increasingly accurate causal conclusions (King et al. 1994).

Ethical Issues When Analyzing Available Data and Content

Freedom of Information Act (FOIA): This federal law stipulates that all persons have a right to access all federal agency records unless the records are specifically exempted.

When analyzing historical documents or quantitative data collected by others, the potential for harm to human subjects that can be a concern when collecting primary data is greatly reduced. It is still, however, important to be honest and responsible in working out arrangements for data access and protection. Researchers who conclude that they are being denied access to public records of

Exhibit 10.10	John Stuart Mill's Method of Agreement

Variable	Case 1	Case 2	Case 3
A	Different	Different	Different
B	Different	Same	Same
C	Different	Different	Different
D[a]	Same	Same	Same
Outcome	Same	Same	Same

Source: Adapted from Skocpol 1984, 379.

a. D is considered the cause of the outcome.

the federal government may be able to obtain the data by filing a **Freedom of Information Act (FOIA)** request. The FOIA stipulates that all persons have a right to access all federal agency records unless the records are specifically exempted (Riedel 2000). Researchers who review historical or government documents must also try to avoid embarrassing or otherwise harming named individuals or their descendants by disclosing sensitive information.

Subject confidentiality is a key concern when original records are analyzed. Whenever possible, all information that could identify individuals should be removed from the records to be analyzed so that no link is possible to the identities of living subjects or the living descendants of subjects (Huston and Naylor 1996). When you use data that have already been archived, you need to find out what procedures were used to preserve subject confidentiality. The work required to ensure subject confidentiality probably will have been done for you by the data archivist. For example, ICPSR examines carefully all data deposited in the archive for the possibility of disclosure risk. All data that might be used to identify respondents are altered to ensure confidentiality, including removal of information such as birth dates or service dates, specific incomes, or place of residence that could be used to identify subjects indirectly (see www.icpsr.umich.edu/icpsrweb/ICPSR/access/restricted/). If all information that could be used in any way to identify respondents cannot be removed from a dataset without diminishing dataset quality (such as by preventing links to other essential data records), ICPSR restricts access to the data and requires that investigators agree to conditions of use that preserve subject confidentiality.

It is not up to you to decide whether there are any issues of concern regarding human subjects when you acquire a dataset for secondary analysis from a responsible source. The institutional review board (IRB) for the protection of human subjects at your college or university or other institution has the responsibility to decide whether it needs to review and approve proposals for secondary data analysis. The federal regulations are not entirely clear on this point, so the acceptable procedures will vary among institutions based on what their IRBs have decided.

Ethical concerns are multiplied when surveys are conducted or other data are collected in other countries. If the outside researcher lacks much knowledge of local norms, values, and routine activities, the potential for inadvertently harming subjects is substantial. For this reason, cross-cultural researchers should spend time learning about each of the countries in which they plan to collect primary data and establish collaborations with researchers in those countries (Hantrais and Mangen 1996). Local advisory groups may also be formed in each country so that a broader range of opinion is solicited when key decisions must be made. Such collaboration can also be invaluable when designing instruments, collecting data, and interpreting results.

▣ Conclusion

The easy availability for secondary analyses of datasets collected in thousands of social science investigations is one of the most exciting features of social science research in the 21st century. You can often find a previously collected dataset that is suitable for testing new hypotheses or exploring new issues of interest. Moreover, the research infrastructure that has developed at ICPSR and other research consortia, both in the United States and internationally, ensures that a great many of these datasets have been carefully checked for quality and archived in a form that allows easy access.

Comparative social science investigations use a variety of techniques that range from narrative histories having much in common with qualitative methods to analyses of secondary data that in many respects are like traditional survey research. They encourage intimate familiarity with the course of development of the nations studied and thereby stimulate inductive reasoning about the interrelations among different historical events. Comparative methods require attention to causal context, with a particular focus on the ways in which different cultures and social structures may result in different effects on other variables.

Many social scientists now review available secondary data before they consider collecting new data with which to investigate a particular research question. Even if you do not leave this course with a plan to become a social scientist yourself, you should now have the knowledge and skills required to find and use secondary data and to review analyses of big data to answer your own questions about the social world.

The average implementation scale score for all cities was 1.22. This is relatively low considering the possible high score was equal to 9, indicating that many of the strategies that may have been implemented across the CAGI sites were not. Still, when this implementation scale was used to predict gun homicide rates across cities, the CAGI was found to have reduced gun homicides by about 12%. When McGarrell and his colleagues (2013) examined the types of programs that had the most effect on gun homicides, law enforcement strategies appeared to have the largest effect. These law enforcement strategies included comprehensive police partnerships and proactive enforcement strategies like directed patrols, anti-gang ordinances, and comprehensive gun tracing. Unfortunately, these strategies affected only the gun homicide rate in the short term and did not have a sustained impact.

When process evaluations reveal that a program or policy is not being implemented as planned, or they reveal a problem in implementation, these findings can often be used to help shape or refine the program. In this case, the term **formative evaluation** may be used instead of process evaluation (Rossi and Freeman 1989). Formative evaluation procedures that are incorporated into the initial development of the service program can specify the treatment process and lead to changes in recruitment procedures, program delivery, or measurement tools (Patton 2002).

Formative evaluation: Process evaluation that is used to shape and refine program operations.

Process evaluation can employ a wide range of methods. Program coverage can be monitored through program records, participant surveys, community surveys, or utilizers versus dropouts and ineligibles. Service delivery can be monitored through service records completed by program staff, a management information system maintained by program administrators, or reports by program recipients (Rossi and Freeman 1989).

Qualitative methods are often a key component of process evaluation studies because they can be used to elucidate and improve understanding of internal program dynamics, even those that were not anticipated (Patton 2002; Posavac and Carey 1997). Qualitative researchers may develop detailed descriptions of how program participants engage with each other, how the program experience varies for different people, and how the program changes and evolves over time.

The Evaluation of Impact or Outcomes

If a process study shows that the implementation of the program has been delivered to the target population as planned, the next role for an evaluator is to assess the extent to which the program achieved its goals. "Did the program work?" "Did the program have the intended consequences?" This question should by now be familiar to you; stated more like a research question we are used to, "Did the treatment or program (independent variable) effect change in the dependent variable?" It all comes back to the issue of causality. This part of the research is variously called **impact analysis** or **impact evaluation**.

Impact evaluation (impact analysis): Analysis of the extent to which a treatment or other service has the intended effect.

The bulk of the published evaluation studies in our field are devoted to some type of impact assessment. Have new seat belt laws (independent variable) increased rates of seat belt usage (dependent variable)? Have rape reform statutes increased the willingness of rape victims to report their victimizations to police? Are boot camps more likely to reduce recidivism among juveniles compared to more traditional juvenile detention settings? Have mandatory minimum sentencing guidelines decreased the probability that extralegal factors such as sex and race will affect an individual's sentence? The list could go on and on.

Case Study

How Does the Risk Skills Training Program (RSTP) Compare to D.A.R.E.?

The Risk Skills Training Program (RSTP) was designed for adolescents to target multiple risk behaviors, such as drinking and drug use, and to change their personal beliefs about such behavior. Elizabeth D'Amico and Kim Fromme (2002) studied the impact of the RSTP and how it compared to the impact of the Drug Abuse Resistance Education–Abbreviated (D.A.R.E.-A) program, as well as how outcomes for students in both of these programs compared to outcomes for students who received no programming (a control group).

To evaluate the efficacy of these programs in reducing drinking and drug use, they randomly selected 150 students to participate in their study. These 150 students were randomly assigned to one of the two experimental groups: 75 students received RSTP programming, and 75 students received the D.A.R.E.-A programming. Another 150 students were randomly selected to participate in the study but received no programming. The students received a pretest assessment before the programs were implemented, and two posttest assessments, which took place at two and six months after the programs had begun.

The impacts (dependent variables) D'Amico and Fromme (2002) examined included positive and negative "alcohol expectancies" (the anticipated effects of drinking) as well as perceptions of peer risk taking and actual alcohol consumption. They found that negative alcohol expectancies increased for the RSTP group in the posttest but not for the D.A.R.E.-A group or the control group, while weekly drinking and "positive expectancies" for drinking outcomes actually *increased* for the D.A.R.E.-A group and the control group by the six-month posttest but not for the RSTP group (see Exhibit 11.4).

You should recognize the design used by D'Amico and Fromme as a true experimental design (see Chapters 6 and 7). This is the preferred method for maximizing internal validity—that is, for making sure your causal claims about program impact are justified. Cases are assigned randomly to one or more experimental treatment groups and to a control group so that there is no systematic difference among the groups at the outset. The goal is to achieve a fair, unbiased test of the program itself so that the judgment about the program's impact is not influenced by differences among the types of people who are in the different groups. It can be a difficult goal to achieve, because the usual practice in social programs is to let people decide for themselves whether they want to enter a program and also to establish eligibility criteria that ensure that people who enter the program are different from those who do not (Boruch 1997). In either case, a selection bias is introduced.

Of course, program impact may also be evaluated with quasi-experimental designs (see Chapter 7) or survey or field research methods, without a randomized experimental design. But if current participants who are already in a program are compared to nonparticipants, it is unlikely that the treatment group will be comparable to the control group. Participants will probably be a selected group, different at the outset from nonparticipants. As a result, causal conclusions about program impact will be on much shakier ground. For instance, when a study at New York's maximum-security prison for women found that "Income Education [i.e., college-level classes] Is Found to Lower Risk of New Arrest," the conclusions were immediately suspect: The research design did not ensure that the women who enrolled in the prison classes were the same as those who had not enrolled in the classes, "leaving open the possibility that the results were due, at least in part, to self-selection, with the women most motivated to avoid re-incarceration being the ones who took the college classes" (Lewin 2001:A18).

Impact analysis is an important undertaking that fully deserves the attention it has been given in government program funding requirements. However, you should realize that more rigorous evaluation designs are less likely to conclude that a program has the desired effect; as the standard of proof goes up, success is harder to demonstrate. We will provide other case studies of impact evaluations at the end of the chapter.

Exhibit 11.4 Impact of Risk Skills Training Program (RSTP), D.A.R.E.-A.

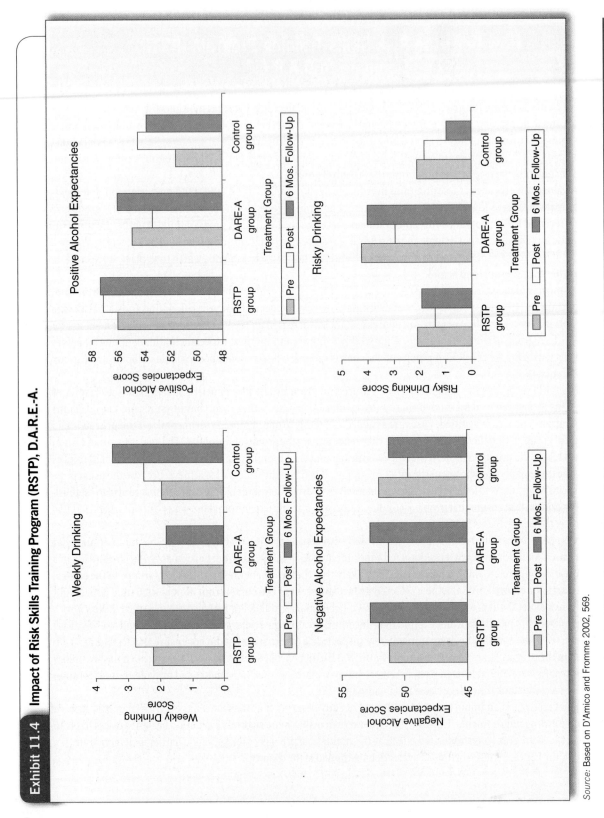

Source: Based on D'Amico and Fromme 2002, 569.

The Evaluation of Efficiency

Whatever the program's benefits, are they sufficient to offset the program's costs? Are the taxpayers getting their money's worth? What resources are required by the program? These efficiency questions can be the primary reason that funders require evaluation of the programs they fund. As a result, **efficiency analysis**, which compares program effects to costs, is often a necessary component of an evaluation research project.

> **Efficiency analysis:** A type of evaluation research that compares program costs to program effects. It can be either a cost-benefit analysis or a cost-effectiveness analysis.

A **cost-benefit analysis** must identify the specific program costs and the procedures for estimating the economic value of specific program benefits. This type of analysis also requires that the analyst identify whose perspective will be used in order to determine what can be considered a benefit rather than a cost. Program clients may have a different perspective on these issues than will taxpayers or program staff.

A **cost-effectiveness analysis** focuses attention directly on the program's outcomes rather than on the economic value of those outcomes. In a cost-effectiveness analysis, the specific costs of the program are compared to the program's outcomes, such as the number of jobs obtained, the extent of improvement in reading scores, or the degree of decline in crimes committed. For example, one result might be an estimate of how much it cost the program for each job obtained by a program participant.

> **Cost-benefit analysis:** A type of evaluation research that compares program costs to the economic value of program benefits.

Social science training often does not include much attention to cost-benefit analysis, so it can be helpful to review possible costs and benefits with an economist or a business school professor or student. Once potential costs and benefits have been identified, they must be measured. It is a need highlighted in recent government programs:

> **Cost-effectiveness analysis:** A type of evaluation research that compares program costs to actual program outcomes.

> The Governmental Accounting Standards Board's (GASB) mission is to establish and improve standards of accounting and financial reporting for state and local governments in the United States. . . . The new reporting will provide information that citizens and other users can utilize to gain an understanding of the financial position and cost of programs for a government and a descriptive management's discussion and analysis to assist in understanding a government's financial results. (Campbell 2002, 1)

Case Study

Cost-Benefit Analysis of Therapeutic Communities

A study of therapeutic communities provides a clear illustration. A therapeutic community is an alternative to the traditional correctional response to drug addiction, which is typically incarceration for those convicted of either the possession or trafficking of illegal substances. In therapeutic communities, abusers participate in an intensive, structured living experience with other addicts who are attempting to stay sober. Because the treatment involves residential support as well as other types of services, it can be quite costly. Are those costs worth it?

Stanley Sacks and colleagues (2002) conducted a cost-benefit analysis of a modified therapeutic community (TC). A total of 342 homeless mentally ill chemical abusers were randomly assigned to either a TC or a "treatment-as-usual" comparison group. Employment status, criminal activity, and utilization of health care services were each measured for the three months prior to entering treatment and the three months after treatment ended. Earnings from employment in each period were adjusted for costs incurred by criminal activity and utilization of health care services.

Was it worth it? The average cost of TC treatment for a client was $20,361. In comparison, the economic benefit (based on earnings) to the average TC client was $305,273, which declined to $273,698 after comparing post- to pre-program earnings, but was still $253,337 even after adjustment for costs. The resulting benefit-cost ratio was 13:1, although this ratio declined to only 5.2:1 after further adjustments (for cases with extreme values). Nonetheless, the TC program studied seems to have had a substantial benefit relative to its costs.

The goal of most policymakers, of course, is to offer services that will justify the investment of funds. In a business, these cost-benefit analyses are relatively straightforward. When delivering human services, however, the evaluation of efficiency is a bit trickier, because the benefits are usually hard to convert into a dollar figure. The procedures involved in these types of analyses are highly technical and, for this reason, are beyond the scope of this book. It is important, however, to understand the concept of efficiency analysis. Sherman (1997) succinctly describes the importance of this type of evaluation:

> Even though scientific evaluation results are a key part of rational policy analysis, those results cannot automatically select the best policy. This is due not just to the scientific limitations of generalizing results from one setting to the next. Another reason is that evaluations often omit key data on cost-benefit ratios; the fact that a program is "effective" may be irrelevant if the financial or social costs are too high. (p. 11)

In addition to measuring services and their associated costs, a cost-benefit analysis must be able to make some type of estimation of how clients benefited from the program. Normally, this will involve a comparison of some indicators of client status before and after clients received program services or between a group of clients who received program services and a comparable group who did not.

Design Decisions

Once we have decided on, or identified, the goal or focus for a program evaluation, there are still important decisions to be made about how to design the specific evaluation project. The most important decisions are the following:

- Black box or program theory: Do we care how the program gets results?
- Researcher or stakeholder orientation: Whose goals matter most?
- Simple or complex outcomes: How complicated should the findings be?

Black Box Evaluation or Program Theory?

Black box evaluation: This type of evaluation occurs when an evaluation of program outcomes ignores, and does not identify, the process by which the program produced the effect.

Program theory: A descriptive or prescriptive model of how a program operates and produces its effects.

Theory-driven evaluation: A program evaluation that is guided by a theory that specifies the process by which the program has an effect.

The meat and potatoes of most evaluation research involves determining whether a program has the intended effect. If the effect occurred, the program "worked"; if the effect didn't occur, then, some would say, the program should be abandoned or redesigned. In this approach, the process by which a program has an effect on outcomes is often treated as a **black box**; that is, the focus of the evaluation researcher is on whether cases seem to have changed as a result of their exposure to the program, between the time they entered the program as inputs and when they exited the program as outputs (Chen 1990). The assumption is that program evaluation requires only the test of a simple input/output model. There may be no attempt to open the black box of the program process.

If an investigation of program process is conducted, a program theory may be developed. A **program theory** describes what has been learned about how the program has its effect. When a researcher has sufficient knowledge before the investigation begins, outlining a program theory can help guide the investigation of program process in the most productive directions. This is termed a **theory-driven evaluation**.

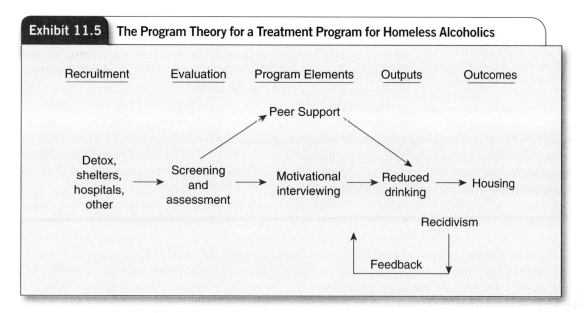

Exhibit 11.5 The Program Theory for a Treatment Program for Homeless Alcoholics

A program theory specifies how the program is expected to operate and identifies which program elements are operational (Chen 1990). In addition, a program theory specifies how a program is to produce its effects and so improves understanding of the relationship between the independent variable (the program) and the dependent variable (the outcome or outcomes). For example, Exhibit 11.5 illustrates the theory for an alcoholism treatment program. It shows that persons entering the program are expected to respond to the combination of motivational interviewing and peer support. A program theory can also decrease the risk of failure when the program is transported to other settings, because it will help identify the conditions required for the program to have its intended effect.

Program theory can be either descriptive or prescriptive (Chen 1990). Descriptive theory specifies what impacts are generated and how they occur. It suggests a causal mechanism, including intervening factors, and the necessary context for the effects. Descriptive theories are generally empirically based. On the other hand, prescriptive theory specifies what ought to be done by the program and is not actually tested. Prescriptive theory specifies how to design or implement the treatment, what outcomes should be expected, and how performance should be judged. Comparison of the descriptive and prescriptive theories of the program can help identify implementation difficulties and incorrect understandings that can be corrected (Patton 2002).

Researcher or Stakeholder Orientation?

Whose prescriptions specify how the program should operate, what outcomes it should try to achieve, or who it should serve? Most social science research assumes that the researcher specifies the research questions, the applicable theory or theories, and the outcomes to be investigated. Social science research results are most often reported in a professional journal or at professional conferences, where scientific standards determine how the research is received. In program evaluation, however, the research question is often set by the program sponsors or the government agency that is responsible for reviewing the program. In consulting projects for businesses, the client—a manager, perhaps, or a division president—decides what question researchers will study. It is to these authorities that research findings are reported. Most often this authority also specifies the outcomes to be investigated. The first evaluator of the evaluation research is the funding agency, then, not the professional social science community. Evaluation research is research for a client, and its results may directly affect the services, treatments, or even punishments (e.g., in the case of prison studies) that program users receive. In this case, the person who pays the piper gets to call the tune.

Should the evaluation researcher insist on designing the evaluation project and specifying its goals, or should she accept the suggestions and adopt the goals of the funding agency? What role should the preferences of program staff or clients play? What responsibility does the evaluation researcher have to politicians and taxpayers when evaluating government-funded programs? The different answers that various evaluation researchers have given to these questions are reflected in different approaches to evaluation (Chen 1990).

Stakeholder approaches (responsive evaluation): An orientation to evaluation research that expects researchers to be responsive primarily to the people involved with the program.

Stakeholder approaches encourage researchers to be responsive to program stakeholders (so this approach is also termed **responsive evaluation**). Issues for study are to be based on the views of people involved with the program, and reports are to be made to program participants (Shadish, Cook, and Leviton 1991). The program theory is developed by the researcher to clarify and develop the key stakeholders' theory of the program (Shadish et al. 1991). As noted above, in one stakeholder approach, termed *utilization-focused evaluation*, the evaluator forms a task force of program stakeholders who help shape the evaluation project so that they are most likely to use its results (Patton 2002). In evaluation research termed *action research* or *participatory research*, program participants are engaged with the researchers as co-researchers and help design, conduct, and report the research. This is similar to participatory action research, which was highlighted in Chapter 1.

In their book, *Fourth Generation Evaluation*, Guba and Lincoln (1989) argue for evaluations oriented toward stakeholders:

> The stakeholders and others who may be drawn into the evaluation are welcomed as equal partners in every aspect of design, implementation, interpretation, and resulting action of an evaluation—that is, they are accorded a full measure of political parity and control . . . determining what questions are to be asked and what information is to be collected on the basis of stakeholder inputs. (p. 11)

Because different stakeholders may differ on their reports about or assessment of the program, there is not likely to be one conclusion about program impact. The evaluators are primarily concerned with helping participants understand the views of other stakeholders and generate productive dialogue. Abma (2005) took this approach in a study of an injury prevention program in the Netherlands:

> The evaluators acted as facilitators, paying deliberate attention to the development of trust and a respectful, open and comfortable climate. . . . Furthermore, the evaluation stimulated a public discourse about issues that were taboo, created a space for reflection, fostered dynamics and motivated participants to think about ways to improve the quality of their teaching practice. (pp. 284–85)

Social science approaches: An orientation to evaluation research that expects researchers to emphasize the importance of researcher expertise and maintenance of autonomy from program stakeholders.

Social science approaches emphasize the importance of researcher expertise and maintenance of some autonomy in order to develop the most trustworthy, unbiased program evaluation. It is assumed that "evaluators cannot passively accept the values and views of the other stakeholders" (Chen 1990, 78). Evaluators who adopt this approach derive a program theory from information they obtain on how the program operates and extant social science theory and knowledge, not from the views of stakeholders. In one somewhat extreme form of this approach, *goal-free evaluation*, researchers do not even permit themselves to learn what goals the program stakeholders have for the program. Instead, the researcher assesses and then compares the needs of participants to a wide array of program outcomes (Scriven 1972). The goal-free evaluator wants to see the unanticipated outcomes and to remove any biases caused by knowing the program goals in advance.

Of course, there are disadvantages to both stakeholder and social science approaches to program evaluation. If stakeholders are ignored, researchers may find that participants are uncooperative, that their reports are unused, and that the next project remains unfunded. On the other hand, if social science procedures are neglected, standards of evidence will be compromised, conclusions about program effects will likely be invalid, and results are unlikely to be generalizable to other settings. These equally undesirable possibilities have led to several attempts to develop more integrated approaches to evaluation research.

Integrative approaches attempt to cover issues of concern to both stakeholders and evaluators, as well as to include stakeholders in the group from which guidance is routinely sought (Chen and Rossi 1987). The emphasis given to either stakeholder or social concern is expected to vary with the specific project circumstances. Integrated approaches seek to balance the goal of carrying out a project that is responsive to stakeholder concerns with the goal of objective, scientifically trustworthy, and generalizable results. When the research is planned, evaluators are expected to communicate and negotiate regularly with key stakeholders and to take stakeholder concerns into account. Findings from preliminary inquiries are reported back to program decision makers so that they can make improvements in the program before it is formally evaluated. When the actual evaluation is conducted, the evaluation research team is expected to operate more autonomously, minimizing intrusions from program stakeholders.

> **Integrative approaches:** An orientation to evaluation research that expects researchers to respond to concerns of people involved with stakeholders as well as to the standards and goals of the social scientific community.

Many evaluation researchers now recognize that they must take account of multiple values in their research and be sensitive to the perspectives of different stakeholders, in addition to maintaining a commitment to the goals of measurement validity, internal validity, and generalizability (Chen 1990). Ultimately, evaluation research takes place in a political context, in which program stakeholders may be competing or collaborating to increase program funding or to emphasize particular program goals. It is a political process that creates social programs, and it is a political process that determines whether these programs are evaluated and what is done with evaluation findings (Weiss 1993). Developing supportive relations with stakeholder groups will increase the odds that political processes will not undermine evaluation practice. You do not want to find out after you are all done that "people operating ineffective programs who depend on them for their jobs" are able to prevent an evaluation report from having any impact ("'Get Tough' Youth Programs Are Ineffective, Panel Says" 2004, 25).

Simple or Complex Outcomes?

Does the program have only one outcome? Unlikely. How many outcomes are anticipated? How many might be unintended? Which are direct consequences of program action, and which are indirect effects that occur as a result of the direct effects (Mohr 1992)? Do the longer-term outcomes follow directly from the immediate program outputs? Does the output (the increase in test scores at the end of the preparation course) result surely in the desired outcomes (increased rates of college admission)? Due to these and other possibilities, the selection of outcome measures is a critical step in evaluation research.

The decision to focus on one outcome rather than another, or on a single outcome or on several, can have enormous implications. When Sherman and Berk (1984) evaluated the impact of an immediate arrest policy in cases of domestic violence in Minneapolis, Minnesota, they focused on recidivism as the key outcome. Similarly, the reduction of recidivism was the single desired outcome of prison "boot camps" opened in the 1990s. Boot camps are military-style programs for prison inmates that provide tough, highly regimented activities and harsh punishment for disciplinary infractions, with the goal of scaring inmates straight. They were very popular in the 1990s, and the researchers who evaluated their impact understandably focused on criminal recidivism.

But these single-purpose programs turned out not to be quite so simple to evaluate. The Minneapolis researchers found that there was no adequate single source for records of recidivism in domestic violence cases, so they had to hunt for evidence from court and police records, follow-up interviews with victims, and family member reports. More easily measured variables, such as partners' ratings of the accused's subsequent behavior, eventually received more attention. Boot camp researchers soon concluded that the experience did not reduce recidivism: "Many communities are wasting a great deal of money on those types of programs" (Robert L. Johnson quoted in "'Get Tough' Youth Programs Are Ineffective, Panel Says" 2004, 25). However, some participants felt the study had missed something:

> [A staff member] saw things unfold that he had never witnessed among inmates and their caretakers. Those experiences profoundly affected the drill instructors and their charges, who still call to talk to the guards they once saw as torturers. Graduation ceremonies routinely reduced inmates, relatives, and sometimes even supervisors to tears. (Latour 2002:B7)

Former boot camp superintendent Michael Corsini compared a Massachusetts boot camp to other correctional facilities and concluded, "Here, it was a totally different experience" (Latour 2002:B7).

Some now argue that the failure of boot camps to reduce recidivism was due to the lack of post-prison support rather than a failure of the camps to promote positive change in inmates. Looking only at recidivism rates would ignore some important positive results.

So in spite of the additional difficulties introduced by measuring multiple outcomes, most evaluation researchers attempt to do so (Mohr 1992). The result usually is a much more realistic, and richer, understanding of program impact.

Of course, there is a potential downside to the collection of multiple outcomes. Policymakers may choose to publicize those outcomes that support their own policy preferences and ignore the rest. Often, evaluation researchers themselves have little ability to publicize a more complete story.

In a sense, all these choices (black box or program theory, researcher or stakeholder interests, simple or complex outcomes) hinge on (a) what your real goals are in doing the project and (b) how able you will be in a research-for-hire setting to achieve those goals. Not every agency really wants to know whether its programs work, especially if the answer is that they don't. Dealing with such issues and the choices they require is part of what makes evaluation research both scientifically and politically fascinating.

▣ Evaluation in Action

—————— Case Study ——————
Problem-Oriented Policing in Violent Crime Areas—A Randomized Controlled Experiment

Several studies have found that over half of all crimes in a city are committed at a few criminogenic places within communities. You learned in Chapter 10 that these places have been called "hot spots" by some criminologists (Sherman, Gartin, and Buerger 1989; Weisburd, Maher, and Sherman 1992). Even within the most crime-ridden neighborhoods, it has been found that crime clusters at a few discrete locations, while other areas remain relatively crime-free. The clustering of violent crime at particular locations suggests that there are important features or dynamics at these locations that give rise to violent situations. For this reason, focused crime prevention efforts should be able to modify these criminogenic conditions and reduce violence.

Problem-oriented policing strategies are increasingly utilized by urban jurisdictions to reduce crime in these high-activity crime places. Problem-oriented policing challenges officers to identify and analyze the causes of problems behind a string of criminal incidents. Once the underlying conditions that give rise to crime problems are known, police officers can develop and implement appropriate responses. Despite the increasing use of problem-oriented policing strategies, however, there has been very little evaluation research conducted to determine whether such strategies are actually effective in decreasing crime rates.

One of the few true experiments to examine the efficacy of problem-oriented policing was conducted by Anthony Braga and his colleagues (1999), and it remains a model evaluation study today. These researchers created a novel field experiment to determine the effectiveness of problem-oriented policing in decreasing the incidence of violent street crime in Jersey City, New Jersey. Recall from Chapter 6 that a true experiment allows researchers to assume that the only systematic difference between a control and an experimental group is the presence of the intervention, in this case the presence or absence of problem-oriented policing strategies.

To determine which places would receive the problem-oriented strategies and which places would not, Braga et al. (1999) used computerized mapping technologies to analyze all robbery and assault incidents and emergency citizen calls for services in Jersey City. These incidents were then matched to intersection areas (the intersection and its four adjoining street segments) and counted. Braga et al. then identified 56 discrete high-activity violent crime places. These 56 places were then matched into 28 pairs. Matching was done on a number of variables, including the primary offenses in each place (e.g., places with lower numbers of robberies and higher numbers of assaults were grouped together), types of problems at a place (e.g., robberies of commuters versus robberies of convenience stores), known dynamics of the place (e.g., the presence of active drug markets), and physical characteristics (e.g., presence of a park or school). A coin was flipped by the researchers to randomly determine which of the places within the pair would receive the problem-oriented policing treatment (experimental places). Remember that a key feature of true experimental designs is this **random assignment**. The places that were not selected from the flip in each pair did not receive the new policing strategies (control places). The design of this experimental evaluation is illustrated in Exhibit 11.6.

> **Random assignment:** A procedure by which each experimental and control group subject or entity or entity is placed in a group randomly.

In each of the experimental places, police officers from the violent crime unit (VCU) of the Jersey City police department established networks consistent with problem-oriented policing. For example, community members were used as information sources to discuss the nature of the problems the community faced, the possible effectiveness of proposed responses, and the assessment of implemented responses. In most places, the VCU officers believed that the violence that distinguished these places from other areas of the city was closely related to the disorder of the place. Although specific tactics varied from place to place, most attempts to control violence in these places were actually targeted at the social disorder problems. For example, some tactics included cleaning up the environment of the place through aggressive order maintenance and making physical improvements such as securing vacant lots or removing trash from the street. Other tactics included aggressive interventions to control the social disorder of a place, such as repeat foot and radio car patrols, dispersing groups of loiterers, and stop-and-frisks of suspicious persons. In addition, in places where drug markets were located, VCU officers increased their investigations to disrupt both the selling and the consumption of illicit drugs. The independent variable or treatment, then, was the use of problem-oriented policing, which comprised a number of specific tactics implemented by police officers to control the physical and social disorder at experimental violent places. In contrast, control places did not receive these problem-solving efforts; they received traditional policing strategies such as arbitrary patrol interventions and routine follow-up investigations by detectives. No problem-oriented strategies were employed.

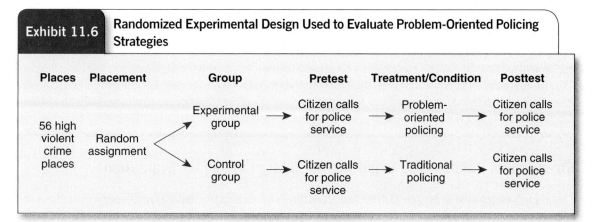

Exhibit 11.6 **Randomized Experimental Design Used to Evaluate Problem-Oriented Policing Strategies**

Places	Placement	Group	Pretest	Treatment/Condition	Posttest
56 high violent crime places	Random assignment	Experimental group	Citizen calls for police service	Problem-oriented policing	Citizen calls for police service
		Control group	Citizen calls for police service	Traditional policing	Citizen calls for police service

Source: Braga et al. 1999.

Braga et al. (1999) examined the efficacy of these problem-oriented policing strategies by using three separate dependent variables. The first two were traditional indicators of crime: incident report data and citizen emergency calls for service within each place. The third variable was a physical observation of each place during the pretest and posttest periods. This variable was used to indicate changes in both physical incivilities at places, such as vacant lots, trash, graffiti, or broken windows; and social incivilities, such as drinking in public and loitering. These variables were measured for six-month preintervention and postintervention periods. If the problem-oriented policing approach was effective, then Braga et al. should have seen a decrease in incidents and emergency calls for service in the experimental areas in the posttest compared to the control areas. They should also have seen decreased signs of physical and social incivilities in the experimental areas compared to the control areas.

Results indicated that the total number of criminal incidents and the total number of citizen calls for service were significantly reduced at the experimental places relative to the control places. This effect was true for most specific crime types examined as well. Examination of the observational data indicated that both physical disorder and social disorder were lower in 91% of the experimental places (10 of the 11 experimental places) relative to their paired control places. Thus, the problem-oriented policing strategies examined in this evaluation research appear to have had a great deal of success in controlling and preventing crime.

Recall from Chapter 7 that although randomized experiments do allow us to determine whether the independent variable had an effect on the dependent variable, they do not tell us why. That is, they do not provide us with information about the causal mechanisms that may be producing this effect. Braga et al. (1999), however, utilized several theories to speculate on how these problem-oriented strategies may have changed the dynamics of a place in ways that resulted in a decrease in crime. For example, based on rational choice theory, which asserts that offenders consider risks, effort, and reward when contemplating criminal acts, the researchers speculated that the increased presence of order maintenance activities at the experimental places may have served as a powerful deterrent by communicating to offenders that disorderly behavior would no longer be tolerated. Braga et al.

> **Mechanism:** A discernible process that creates a causal connection between two variables.

correctly pointed out, however, that the study did not gather data to determine the specific causal **mechanisms** responsible for the reductions found in crime. To do this, other forms of research would be necessary, such as interviewing offenders to determine their perceptions regarding their decisions to offend or to desist from offending in particular places.

What is certain from this research is that problem-oriented policing strategies are more effective in reducing both incidents of violent crime and citizen calls for emergency service than traditional policing strategies. Braga and his colleagues (1999) concluded,

> Law enforcement agencies interested in controlling violence should consider implementing problem-oriented policing programs that focus on the places where violence clusters by developing tailored interventions addressing the underlying conditions and dynamics that give rise to violent situations. (p. 571)

As a follow-up to this classic experiment, a recent review of the literature performed by Braga and his colleagues (2015) indicates the crime reduction efforts that focus on interventions designed to change social and physical disorder more often work to reduce crime compared to aggressive order maintenance strategies that target individual disorderly behaviors (Braga, Welsch, and Schnell 2015).

Strengths of Randomized Experimental Design in Impact Evaluations

The research design used by Braga et al. (1999) meets all three criteria for a true experimental design. First, they used at least two comparison groups. In the Braga et al. research, some communities received the problem-oriented patrol strategies (experimental groups) while the other comparison communities received traditional police patrol (control groups). And finally, the assessment of change in the dependent variables used in their study was performed after the experimental condition (problem-oriented strategies) had been delivered.

Recall the three criteria necessary for establishing a causal relationship between independent and dependent variables (see Chapter 6):

1. Association between the independent and dependent variables
2. Correct time order (the independent variable precedes the dependent)
3. Nonspuriousness (rule out influence of other variables)

Data obtained from a true experimental design provide the best way to determine that all three of these criteria have been met.

Because the communities in the study by Braga et al. (1999) were randomly assigned to receive either problem-oriented or traditional patrol strategies, the relationship found between these strategies (independent variable) and the dependent variables (incidents of crime, etc.) is unambiguous. Braga et al. monitored their dependent variables both before and after the different policing strategies were implemented, so there is also no question that the strategies came before the change in the dependent variable. Finally, the random assignment of the communities to either the problem-oriented or traditional police conditions controlled for a host of possible extraneous influences that may have created spurious relationships.

The extent to which the findings of these studies can be generalized to the larger population, however, is another issue. Can findings by Braga et al. (1999) be generalized to the larger population in New Jersey (sample generalizability) or to other states and communities (external validity)? Issues of sample generalizability, you will recall, are related to selecting a random sample from the population in the first place (random selection), not random assignment. However, because the study by Braga et al. utilized several experimental and control communities, this increases the likelihood that their findings are generalizable to their respective populations. In addition, because the study was a field experiment (i.e., real world) and not in a laboratory, their findings are more likely to be generalizable to the larger population.

▣ Quasi-Experimental Designs in Evaluation Research

We have already learned that many research questions or situations are not amenable to a true experimental design. The same is true in evaluation research. There are many reasons why it may be impossible to use randomized experiments to evaluate the impacts of programs and policies. The primary reason why randomization is not possible in evaluation research is that the program is usually outside the control of the evaluator. As Rossi and Freeman (1989) state, "For political, human subject or other considerations, program staff, sponsors, or other powerful stakeholders resist randomization" (p. 313). Obtaining the cooperation of the program staff and sponsors is often an obstacle in evaluation research. In fact, when there are several locations implementing similar programs, the sites included in an evaluation study may be selected based primarily on the cooperation of the staff and sponsors. For example, in their evaluation study of treatment alternatives to street crime (TASC), Anglin, Longshore, and Turner (1999) state, "The program's ability to negotiate successfully with local officials to ensure their cooperation with evaluation activities was also a condition of study inclusion" (p. 172).

In general, **quasi-experimental designs** are the most powerful alternatives to true randomized experimental designs. The more alike the experimental and control groups are to each other, particularly on characteristics thought to be related to the intervention or treatment, the more confident we can be in a study's findings. In this section, we will discuss two types of quasi-experimental designs that are often utilized in criminology and criminal justice to determine the impacts of programs. To illustrate the first type, a **nonequivalent control group design** (for review of this design, see Chapter 7), we will highlight an evaluation study that examined the effects of conducted energy devices (CEDs) by law enforcement agencies on reducing injuries sustained by both police officers and suspects. The second type of quasi-experimental design we will highlight is the **time series design,** which we will illustrate using a study that examined the effect of alcohol consumption on homicide rates across several nations.

Quasi-experimental design: A research design in which there is a comparison group that is comparable to the experimental group in critical ways, but subjects are not randomly assigned to the comparison and experimental groups.

Nonequivalent control group design: A quasi-experimental design in which there are experimental and comparison groups that are designated before the treatment occurs but are not created by random assignment.

Time series design: A quasi-experimental design consisting of many pretest and posttest observations of the same group.

Case Study

Decreasing Injuries From Police Use of Force

As noted in the introduction of this chapter, although a great deal of media attention has been given to police use of force, there is a dearth of research investigating ways to curtail both injuries and deaths as a result of police-citizen encounters. One weapon, called the conducted energy device (CED or Taser), holds promise to reduce injuries to both officers and suspects. Although there is some controversy about CEDs, including Amnesty International's call for a moratorium on their use until standards can be reached on their safe use, very few research attempts have been undertaken to determine whether the use of CEDs reduce injuries. Bruce Taylor and Daniel Woods (2010) were among the first to compare injury rates of both officers and suspects in law enforcement agencies (LEAs) that used CEDs with a matched sample of LEAs that did not use them. Because they could not randomly assign LEAs to experimental and control conditions, they used a nonequivalent control group experimental design. In 2008, they selected 13 LEAs that could provide data for four years (two years pre- and two years post-CED deployment, and a comparable time period for non-CED sites). To ensure the LEAs were comparable in other ways, they were matched on several criteria, including violent crime levels, violent crime arrests, agency size, and population size of jurisdiction. All LEAs also provided detailed training for their officers on use-of-force issues, regardless of whether they employed CEDs. LEAs that did not use CEDs did use other nonlethal weapons such as pepper spray and batons.

Taylor and Woods (2010) defined use of force by an officer as any

> physical strike or instrumental contact with a person by an officer or any significant physical contact that restricted the movement of a person by an officer, including the discharge of firearms, use of a CED, use of chemical spray, use of any other weapon, choke holds, or hard hands, taking the suspect to the ground, and deployment of a canine. (2010, 268)

Measures included a simple injury variable coded yes or no as well as measures indicating the severity of the injury, whether or not the injury required medical attention, and whether it required hospitalization. The researchers also controlled for other characteristics of each incident, including the suspect's race, gender, and age. After these factors were controlled, results indicated that LEAs that used CEDs had improved safety outcomes compared to the matched non-CED sites on four injury measures: There were reductions in officer injuries overall, suspect severe injuries, and injuries to both officers and suspects that required medical attention. Appropriately, Taylor and Woods (2010) caution that because they did not use a true experimental design, they could not control for all possible unmeasured variables related to injury. However, they conclude, "We have considered various alternative explanations for our results and believe the most plausible explanation is that the availability of CEDs to officers is a key factor in reducing injuries to officers and suspects" (2010, 281).

Case Study

Drinking and Homicide in Eastern Europe

Alcohol consumption has been linked to violence by many researchers, not just in the United States, but in many countries. In fact the World Health Organization (WHO) estimates that nearly one-quarter of homicides are attributable to alcohol worldwide (WHO 2011). Research also reveals that the relationship between alcohol and violence is culturally mediated. That is, if the cultural ethos of getting drunk also involves violence, individuals are more likely to be violent when drunk compared to individuals whose cultural response to alcohol is more lethargic or peaceful. To examine the effects of alcohol consumption on rates of homicide in several Eastern European countries (Russian, Belarus, Poland, former Czechoslovakia, Hungary, and Bulgaria), Bye (2008) examined per capita alcohol consumption and homicide rate data for various time periods, generally from the 1950s through 2002. To measure alcohol consumption, Bye (2008) used annual sales in liters of pure alcohol per inhabitant aged 15 and older, which did not include alcohol made at home. Based on survey data, several of the countries are characterized by heavy and/or binge drinking that often leads to intoxication (e.g., Russia and Belarus), while Poland is characterized by nondaily drinking and irregular binge drinking episodes.

We won't highlight results for all countries, but instead focus on a contrast between Russia and Poland. Exhibits 11.7 and 11.8 display the alcohol sales plotted along with total, male, and female homicide rates over time for Poland and Russia respectively. For Poland, alcohol sales increased steadily until 1980, when pressures from the Solidarity movement introduced rationing and reduced state production of alcohol. Trends in Russia indicate an increasing trend in both alcohol sales and homicide rates until 1985, when policies reduced alcohol availability. After the campaign to reduce alcohol consumption in Russia ended, both alcohol consumption and homicide rates began to increase again. It can also be seen that the relationship between alcohol consumption and homicide in Russia is very consistent: As alcohol sales increase, so do homicide rates. In Poland, however, alcohol consumption remained relatively unchanged during the increase in homicide rates witnessed in the 1990s. Bye's (2008) statistical analyses confirm these descriptive displays. The effect of alcohol consumption on homicide rates was more pronounced in countries with more detrimental drinking patterns, "implying that the relative risk will depend on the patterns of drinking and of behavior associated with drinking in a particular society" (Bye 2008, 24).

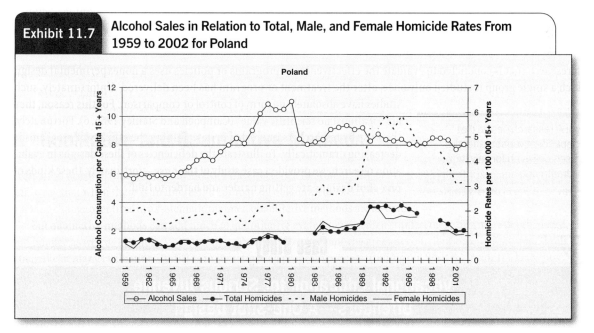

Exhibit 11.7   **Alcohol Sales in Relation to Total, Male, and Female Homicide Rates From 1959 to 2002 for Poland**

Source: Bye, Elin K. 2008. Alcohol and Homicide in Eastern Europe: A Time Series Analysis of Six Countries.

is the combination of those features or some particular features that are responsible for the program's effect, or for the absence of an effect. Lisbeth B. Schorr, director of the Harvard Project on Effective Interventions, and Daniel Yankelovich, president of Public Agenda, put it this way: "Social programs are sprawling efforts with multiple components requiring constant mid-course corrections, the involvement of committed human beings, and flexible adaptation to local circumstances" (Schorr and Yankelovich 2000:A19).

The more complex the social program, the more value qualitative methods can add to the evaluation process. Schorr and Yankelovich (2000) point to the TenPoint Coalition, an alliance of African American ministers who helped reduce gang warfare in Boston through multiple initiatives, "ranging from neighborhood probation patrols to safe havens for recreation" (p. A19). Qualitative methods would help describe a complex, multifaceted program like this.

For the most part, the strengths and weaknesses of methodologies used in evaluation research are those of the methods we have already discussed throughout this text. As Patton (1997) contends, "There are no perfect [evaluation] studies. And there cannot be, for there is no agreement on what constitutes perfection" (p. 23). However, some methods are better able than others for inferring cause and effect. Because the basic question of most impact evaluations is "Does the program (cause) have its intended consequences (effect)?" there are basic methodological criteria we can use to judge the methods discussed in this chapter.

Despite the fact that a randomized experiment is the best way to determine the impact of a program, it is also important to remember that the methodology selected for an evaluation project should be relevant to the policymakers and planners who intend to use the results. Although some researchers vehemently contend that only a randomized experimental design can provide reliable information on the impacts of a program, others just as vehemently disagree. For example, in his utilization-focused method of evaluation, Patton (1997) believes that when making evaluation methods decisions, the primary focus should be on getting the best possible data to answer primary users' questions. This cannot be done without involving them in the decision-making process to begin with. For methods decisions, the emphasis is on the appropriateness of the method to answer the practitioner's questions. Patton contends that only when these decisions are made in collaboration with the primary users will they be perceived as credible and, thus, more likely to be used.

It should also be noted that evaluation research faces obstacles not faced by general social research. We have already highlighted a few of these, including the obstacle of obtaining support and cooperation from program staff and sponsors. In their review of evaluation research on crime prevention programs, Sherman et al. (1997) delineate several other obstacles. For example, one obstacle noted is the structural separation of research and program funding. In everyday life, this often means that an evaluator is brought in after a program has been implemented and asked to assess its consequences. This, of course, leads to several problems. How can the consequences be accurately assessed if the evaluator did not have the opportunity to monitor the dependent variable (outcomes) before the program was started? How can the consequences be accurately assessed if the evaluator had no chance to obtain a comparison group by randomly assigning some units (e.g., individuals or communities) to the program or treatment condition and others elsewhere? To ameliorate this problem, Sherman recommends that Congress produce financial incentives for partnerships to be created between local agencies implementing programs and researchers evaluating them.

▣ Policy Research: Increasing Demand for Evidence-Based Policy

Policy research is a process rather than a method: "a process that attempts to support and persuade actors by providing them with well-reasoned, evidence-based, and responsible recommendations for decision making and action" (Majchrzak and Markus 2014, 3). Because policy research often draws on the findings of evaluation research projects and involves working for a client, as is the case in evaluation research, policy researchers confront many of the same challenges as do evaluation researchers. Because policy researchers must summarize and weigh evidence from a wide range of sources, they need to be familiar with each of the methods presented in this book.

The goal of policy research is to inform those who make policy about the possible alternative courses of action in response to some identified problem, their strengths and weaknesses, and their likely positive and negative effects. Reviewing the available evidence may lead the policy researcher to conclude that enough is known about the issues to develop recommendations without further research, but it is more likely that additional research will be needed using primary or secondary sources. Policy that has been evaluated with a methodologically rigorous design and has been proven effective is sometimes called **evidence-based policy.**

As you have seen in this chapter, evaluation studies come in many forms. A single study, such as the Minneapolis Domestic Violence Experiment (first introduced in Chapter 2), can be very influential and have an enormous effect on police policies. But we have seen that replications of studies answering the same question often result in very different conclusions. Obviously, learning what works should rely on more than one study. Evaluation specialists are increasingly encouraging policymakers to enact evidence-based policies, which are based on a systematic review of all available evidence that assesses what works and what doesn't. Petrosino and Lavenberg (2007) define **systematic reviews** as follows:

> In systematic reviews, researchers attempt to gather relevant evaluative studies, critically appraise them, and come to judgments about what works using explicit, transparent, state-of-the-art methods. In contrast to traditional syntheses, a systematic review will include detail about each stage of the decision process, including the question that guided the review, the criteria for studies to be included, and the methods used to search for and screen evaluation reports. It will also detail how analyses were done and how conclusions were reached.

The reviews often try to quantify the successfulness of particular programs and interventions, sometimes using a technique called meta-analysis, which we describe later. Although these reviews are designed to be objective, there are still controversies surrounding any particular review, including conflict about the inclusion or exclusion of studies and what qualifies as a rigorous study design (e.g., is a true experimental design the only way to determine causality?).

Systematic reviews are increasingly sponsored by both private and government entities. One private organization that has become a leader in publicizing reviews related to criminal justice policy research is the **Campbell Collaboration**. The Campbell Collaboration is an international research network that prepares and disseminates systematic reviews of social science evidence in three fields, including crime and justice, education, and social welfare. The collaboration's mission "is to promote positive social change, by contributing to better-informed decisions and better-quality public and private services around the world" (www.campbellcollaboration. org). All reports are peer reviewed and are available on the collaboration's website. One example from the online Campbell Library (www.campbellcollaboration.org/library.php) is a systematic review by Tolan, Schoeny, and Bass (2008) that examined the impact of mentoring interventions in decreasing delinquency and other problems. If you read the report, you will see that all decisions made by the authors are explicitly stated. For example, they were very specific in their criteria for mentoring, which had to meet four criteria: (1) an interaction between two individuals over an extended period of time; (2) inequality of experience, knowledge, or power between the mentor and mentee, with the mentor possessing the greater share; (3) a mentee in a position to imitate and benefit from the knowledge, skill, ability, or experience of a mentor; and (4) absence of the inequality that typifies other helping relationships and is marked by professional training, certification, or predetermined status differences such as parent-child or teacher-student relationships.

Policy research: A process in which research results are used to provide policy actors with recommendations for action that are based on empirical evidence and careful reasoning.

Evidence-based policy: A policy that has been evaluated with a methodologically rigorous design and has been proven to be effective.

Systematic review: Summary review about the impact of a program wherein the analyst attempts to account for differences across research designs and samples, often using statistical techniques such as a meta-analysis. (p. 1)

Campbell Collaboration: Group producing systematic reviews of programs and policies in many areas, including criminal justice, social work, and education.

When selecting studies for their review, Tolan et al. (2008) also clearly stated four criteria: (1) studies that focused on youth who were at risk for juvenile delinquency or who were currently involved in delinquent behavior; (2) studies that focused on prevention or treatment for those at-risk youth; (3) studies that measured at least one quantitative effect on at least one outcome, including delinquency, substance abuse, academic achievement, or aggression; and (4) studies that were conducted in predominately English-speaking countries reported between 1980 and 2005. As you can see, systematic reviews are, well, extremely systematic! For the record, the review found that there was a modest impact of mentoring in reducing delinquency and aggression, but less of a correlation was found between mentoring and drug use and academic achievement. Meta-analyses, which are often used in systematic reviews, will be discussed in the next chapter.

CAREERS AND RESEARCH

Kristin M. Curtis, MA, Senior Research Program Coordinator, The Senator Walter Rand Institute for Public Affairs at Rutgers University–Camden

Source: Courtesy of Kristin M. Curtis

Kristin Curtis graduated with a master's degree in criminal justice from Rutgers University–Camden in 2010. While a graduate student, she worked on a nationwide research project examining policymaker and practitioner perspectives on sex offender laws, and this experience convinced her that pursuing a career in research was the best fit for her interests and talents. She secured a position at the Walter Rand Institute (WRI) as a graduate project assistant and worked on statewide prisoner reentry studies. Kristin has quickly moved up the ranks at the WRI and in the process has worked on a myriad of criminal justice projects. Her research assignments require varied methodological approaches, including interviews, focus groups, surveys, network analysis, regression models, and geographic information systems (GIS).

One feature of working at WRI that Kristin truly values is the fact that she can participate in other areas of study outside the criminal justice realm. For instance, she has worked on projects that examine the impact of social service organization collaboration on child well-being, financial stability of families, and relationships between children and their caregivers. These projects involve the evaluation of collaborations among social service organizations in multiple New Jersey counties and employ both qualitative and quantitative research methods. Kristin has been at WRI for eight years and still enjoys her position as each day presents new challenges and different tasks, including data collection and analysis, finalizing reports, writing grant proposals for potential new projects, and supervising graduate students.

Kristin has advice for students interested in careers conducting research or using research results:

Locate faculty who engage in research in your areas of interest. Even if you are unsure what your primary research areas are, working on a research project allows you to gain exposure to different research methodologies and techniques (i.e., quantitative and qualitative). You might find you enjoy research and pick up conference presentations and academic publications along the way. Remember, college is an opportunity to explore the different career choices in the world, so take advantage of this.

Basic Science or Applied Research

Now that we have examined evaluation research, you should have an understanding of how this applied research differs from some of the other research studies examined in this book. Alfred Blumstein (2009) has argued that criminologists and other social scientists who do research on criminal justice issues are "constantly in a battle with ideology that argues policy positions from a strongly ideological and moralistic position rather than one based on scientific knowledge of how to be effective in policy" (p. 1). For example, you can find many examples of criminal justice policies that were implemented based on political imperatives that were not based on empirical evidence; these include "three strikes" laws, many drug-related laws including mandatory minimum sentences, sexual offender registry laws, and so on. This reality is being played out at a time when funding agencies are increasingly demanding that policy relevance be addressed in research proposals.

Evaluation research like the studies examined in this chapter and elsewhere in the text seeks to determine whether one program or policy has a more desirable impact than another. This knowledge can then be applied to policy formation and, for this reason, is termed *applied research*. In contrast, **basic science** is generally used for the discipline itself, for advancing general knowledge, and "more precisely for generating and testing hypotheses serving to support, modify or innovate theory" (Junger-Tas 2005, 147). In distinguishing between basic science and applied research, Junger-Tas further explains, "The most important distinction . . . is that the former addresses scientific questions, such as the accu-

> **Basic science:** In contrast to applied research, the main motivation of basic science is to advance general knowledge and/or to test theoretical propositions.

mulation or extension of knowledge, and aims at theoretical conclusions, while the latter addresses political and policy decisions, and as such is action-oriented" (p. 148). Canton and Yates (2008) identify three basic questions that applied criminology should address:

1. What is to be done about offenders?

2. What is to be done about crime?

3. What is to be done on behalf of victims of crime?

Do you think that doing applied research would be good for society as well as for social researchers? Or do you think that a focus on how to improve society might lead social researchers to distort their understanding of how society works? Regardless of your own orientation, you have lots of company in the debate. In the 19th century, sociologist Lester Frank Ward (soon to be the American Sociological Society's first president) endorsed applied research: "The real object of science is to benefit man. A science which fails to do this, however agreeable its study, is lifeless" (Ward 1897, xxvii). But in 1929, American Sociological Society President William Fielding Ogburn urged sociologists to be guided by a basic research orientation: "Sociology as a science is not interested in making the world a better place to live. . . . Science is interested directly in one thing only, to wit, discovering new knowledge" (Ogburn 1930, 300–301).

While many criminological researchers view applied and basic research as complementary, tension between these two orientations has continued ever since these early disputes. For example, Joyner (2003) recently stated,

> I argue that the call for social science research to be "value-free" is untenable and that a legitimate role for the [researcher] involves using one's disciplinary perspective and research to inform program and policy development in an attempt to improve the quality of life for marginalized groups. (p. 5)

Others have articulated warnings about where the demand for policy relevance may lead. For example, even Garvin and Lee (2003), who have engaged in policy-related research of their own, have asked researchers to critically examine the dangers of this increased demand for policy relevance and how these demands might affect research decisions. The first decision that may be affected, of course, is the research question itself. Garvin and Lee state,

> If our gaze leads us to seek only policy-relevant data and findings, what might we overlook? What questions might we *not* ask? . . . We may miss some of the most interesting parts of the work, as well as subtle yet critical power relations, in our hurry to solve problems. More dangerously, we may simply pass over the more challenging research questions because they may not seem policy-relevant at a particular place or time. (p. 44)

Walters (2006) goes even further and argues that to participate in government research is to endorse a biased agenda that omits topics of national and global concern in favor of regulating the poor and the powerless.

Researchers who seek funding for their work are even more constrained by requests for proposals (RFPs) from funding agencies such as the National Institute of Justice, the U.S. Department of Justice's main funding source for research. To obtain funding, researchers must generally fit their research questions into the research needs mandated by funding agencies. Junger-Tas (2005) echoes this danger when he states,

> We have seen successive trends in research topics, which were directly influenced by the agenda of the country's criminal justice administration. This explains the different waves of research on incapacitation and career criminals, followed by research on drugs and now, of course, on organized crime and terrorism. There is indeed a danger in allowing (funding) administrative authorities to decide exclusively on research topics, since this may seriously restrict the field of research. (p. 150)

Clearly, most of us would not be in this discipline if we did not have an inherent desire to help society in some way. In the end, we should constantly reflect on decisions we are making in research and how these decisions may be influenced by external influences. After reading this text, you undoubtedly have a good understanding of the difference between these orientations, but we can't predict whether you'll decide which one is preferable. Perhaps you'll conclude, like we do, that they both have merit.

▣ Ethics in Evaluation

Evaluation research can make a difference in people's lives while it is in progress, as well as after the results are reported. Educational and vocational training opportunities in prison, the availability of legal counsel, and treatment for substance abuse—each is a potentially important benefit, and an evaluation research project can change both the type and the availability of benefits. This direct impact on research participants and, potentially, their families heightens the attention that evaluation researchers have to give to human subjects concerns. Although the particular criteria that are at issue and the decisions that are most ethical vary with the type of evaluation research conducted and the specifics of a particular project, there are always serious ethical as well as political concerns for the evaluation researcher (Boruch 1997; Dentler 2002).

Assessing needs, determining evaluability, and examining the process of treatment delivery have few special ethical dimensions. Cost-benefit analyses in themselves also raise few ethical concerns. It is when program impact is the focus that human subjects considerations multiply. What about assigning persons randomly to receive some social program or benefit? One justification given by evaluation researchers has to do with the scarcity of these resources. If not everyone in the population who is eligible for a program can receive it, due to resource limitations, what could be a fairer way to distribute the program benefits than through a lottery? Random assignment also seems like a reasonable way to allocate potential program benefits when a new program is being tested with only some members of the target recipient population. However, when an ongoing entitlement program is being evaluated and experimental subjects would normally be eligible for program participation, it may not be ethical simply to bar some potential participants from the programs. Instead, evaluation researchers may test alternative treatments or provide some alternative benefit while the treatment is being denied.

There are many other ethical challenges in evaluation research:

- How can confidentiality be preserved when the data are owned by a government agency or are subject to discovery in a legal proceeding?

- Who decides what level of burden an evaluation project may tolerably impose upon participants?

- Is it legitimate for research decisions to be shaped by political considerations?

- Must evaluation findings be shared with stakeholders rather than only with policymakers?

- Is the effectiveness of the proposed program improvements really uncertain?

- Will a randomized experiment yield more defensible evidence than the alternatives?

- Will the results actually be used?

The Health Research Extension Act of 1985 (Public Law 99-158) mandated that the Department of Health and Human Services require all research organizations receiving federal funds to have an institutional review board (IRB) to assess all research for adherence to ethical practice guidelines. We have already reviewed the federally mandated criteria (Boruch 1997):

- Are risks minimized?

- Are risks reasonable in relation to benefits?

- Is the selection of individuals equitable? (Randomization implies this.)

- Is informed consent given?

- Are the data monitored?

- Are privacy and confidentiality ensured?

Evaluation researchers must consider whether it will be possible to meet each of these criteria long before they even design a study.

The problem of maintaining subject confidentiality is particularly thorny, because researchers, in general, are not legally protected from the requirements that they provide evidence requested in legal proceedings, particularly through the process known as "discovery." However, it is important to be aware that several federal statutes have been passed specifically to protect research data about vulnerable populations from legal disclosure requirements. For example, the Crime Control and Safe Streets Act (28 CFR Part 11) includes the following stipulation:

Copies of [research] information [about persons receiving services under the act or the subjects of inquiries into criminal behavior] shall be immune from legal process and shall not, without the consent of the persons furnishing such information, be admitted as evidence or used for any purpose in any action, suit, or other judicial or administrative proceedings. (Boruch 1997, 60)

It is also important to realize that it is costly to society and potentially harmful to participants to maintain ineffective programs. In the long run, at least, it may be more ethical to conduct an evaluation study than to let the status quo remain in place.

🔲 Conclusion

In recent years, the field of evaluation research has become an increasingly popular and active research specialty within the fields of criminology and criminal justice. Many social scientists find special appeal in evaluation research because of its utility.

The research methods applied to evaluation research are not different from those covered elsewhere in this text; they can range from qualitative intensive interviews to rigorous randomized experimental designs. In process evaluations, qualitative methodologies can be particularly advantageous. However, the best method for determining cause and effect, or for determining whether a program had its intended consequences (impacts), is the randomized experimental design. Although this may not always be possible in the field, it is the gold standard with which to compare methodologies used to assess the impacts of all programs and policies.

Key Terms

➤ Review key terms with eFlashcards. ⑤SAGE edge™

Highlights

- Whenever people implement a program for a specific purpose, they pay attention to the consequences of it, although they do not always use rigorous scientific methods to assess these consequences. Evaluation research, however, has been increasingly used since the 1950s to assess the impacts of programs and policies.

- The evaluation process can be modeled as a feedback system, with inputs entering the program, which generates outputs and then outcomes, which feed back to program stakeholders and affect program inputs.

- The evaluation process as a whole, and the feedback process in particular, can be understood only in relation to the interests and perspectives of program stakeholders.

- The process by which a program has an effect on outcomes is often treated as a "black box," but there is good reason to open the black box and investigate the process by which the program operates and produces, or fails to produce, an effect.

- A program theory may be developed before or after an investigation of program process is completed. It may be either descriptive or prescriptive.

- Evaluation research is done for a client, and its results may directly affect the services, treatments, or punishments that program users receive. Evaluation researchers differ in the extent to which they attempt to orient their evaluations to program stakeholders.

- There are five primary types of program evaluation: needs assessment, evaluability assessment, process evaluation (including formative evaluation), impact evaluation (also termed summative evaluation), and efficiency (cost-benefit) analysis.

- The evaluation of need generally aims to describe the nature and scope of the problem along with the target population in need of services.

- The evaluation of process determines the extent to which implementation has taken place, whether the program is reaching the target population, whether the program is actually operating as expected, and what resources are being expended. Qualitative methods are typically utilized in process evaluations.

- Impact evaluations determine whether the program or policy produced the desired outcomes. Quantitative methods are typically utilized in impact evaluations.

- The evaluation of efficiency relates program outcomes to program costs.

- True randomized experiments are the most appropriate method for determining cause and effect and, as such, for determining the impact of programs and policies.

- Evaluation research raises complex ethical issues because it may involve withholding desired social benefits.

- Systematic reviews synthesize the results of the best available research on a given topic using transparent procedures.

- Research seeking to contribute to basic science focuses on expanding knowledge by testing theories and providing results to other researchers. Applied research seeks to have an impact on social practice and to share results with a wide audience.

Exercises

1. Read one of the articles reviewed in this chapter. Fill in the answers to the article review questions (Appendix B) not covered in the chapter. Do you agree with the answers to the other questions discussed in the chapter? Could you add some points to the critique provided by the author of the text or to the lessons on research design drawn from these critiques?

2. Evaluate the ethics of one of the studies reviewed in which human subjects were used. Sherman and Berk's (1984) study of domestic violence raises some interesting ethical issues, but there are also points to consider in most of the other studies. Which ethical guidelines (see Chapter 3) seem most difficult to adhere to? Where do you think the line should be drawn between not taking any risks at all with research participants and developing valid scientific knowledge? Be sure to consider various costs and benefits of the research. Now do the same for one of the articles reviewed in this chapter.

3. Propose a randomized experimental evaluation of a social program with which you are familiar. Include in your proposal a description of the program and its intended outcomes. Discuss the strengths and weaknesses of your proposed design.

4. Identify the key stakeholders in a local social or educational program. Interview several stakeholders to determine their goals for the program and what tools they use to assess goal achievement. Compare and contrast the views of each stakeholder, and try to account for any differences you find.

Developing a Research Proposal

Imagine that you are submitting a proposal to the U.S. Justice Department to evaluate the efficacy of a new treatment program for substance abusers within federal correctional institutions.

1. What would your research question be if you proposed a process evaluation component to your research?

2. For the outcome evaluation, what is your independent variable, and what would your dependent variable be? How would you operationalize both?

3. What type of research design would you propose to address both the process evaluation and outcome evaluation components in your proposal?

Web Exercises

1. Go to the American Evaluation Association website at www.eval.org. Choose "Publications" and then "Guiding Principles for Evaluators." What are the five guiding principles discussed in this document? Provide a summary of each principle.

   a. How adequate are juvenile court records? Go to the Bureau of Justice Statistics website at www.ojp.usdoj.gov/bjs/, find a report that uses juvenile data, and write a brief summary.

   b. Propose a research project to evaluate the adequacy of the juvenile justice system in the collection and maintenance of juvenile law enforcement records and/or juvenile court records.

2. Describe the resources available for evaluation researchers at the following websites: http://ieg.worldbankgroup.org/ and www.wmich.edu/evalctr.

3. Check out the latest information regarding the D.A.R.E. program at www.dare.com. What is the current approach? Can you find information on the web about current research on D.A.R.E.?

4. Go to the Campbell Collaboration website (http://www.campbellcollaboration.org/) and access the library. Find a study that evaluates a topic of interest to you. What were the selection criteria used for the review? How did the researchers operationalize the constructs they were measuring (e.g., mentoring, delinquency, recidivism)? What do they conclude?

5. Evaluation research is a big industry. There are several large research firms that contract with the federal government to evaluate programs and policies. Two examples are the Rand Corporation (www.rand.org) and Abt Associates (www.abtassociates.com/). Check out their websites, and summarize at least one evaluation study related to criminal justice or criminology. What type of evaluation study was it? What methods were used? Were these methods appropriate for the evaluation question? If an outcome evaluation study was conducted, was a true experiment used, or a quasi-experimental design?

Ethics Exercises

1. The Manhattan Bail Project randomly assigned some defendants with strong community ties to be recommended for release without bail and some not to be recommended. There was a very high (99%) rate of appearance at trial for those released without bail, but of course, the researchers did not know that this would be the case before they conducted the study. Would you consider this study design ethical? What if one of the persons in the 1% who did not come to trial murdered someone when he should have been at court? Are there any conditions when randomization should not be permitted when evaluating criminal justice programs?

2. A large body of evaluation research suggested that the D.A.R.E. program was not effective in reducing drug use in schools, but many school and police officials and parents and students insisted on maintaining the program without change for many years. Do you think that government agencies should be allowed to defund programs that numerous evaluations have shown to be ineffective? Should government agencies be *required* to justify funding for social programs on the basis of evaluation results?

3. Imagine that you are evaluating a group home for recently released prison inmates who are reentering their communities. If you learned that a house resident has started using illegal drugs, would you inform the house staff about this? If you learned that a house resident was having a difficult time securing employment and had started cutting herself with a kitchen knife, would you inform house staff about this? If your actions would be different in the two scenarios, why? If your actions would be the same in the two scenarios, why?

SPSS or Excel Exercises

Data for Exercise	
Dataset	**Description**
NCVS lone offender assaults 1992 to 2013.sav	These are data from the National Crime Victimization Survey (NCVS), a nationally representative study of individuals' experience of criminal victimization. This particular dataset contains responses from 1992 to 2013, allowing for larger numbers of uncommon offenses to be used in analyses. It also only includes data from respondents who reported either violent or nonviolent assault by a single offender.
Variables for Exercise	
Variable Name	**Description**
year	The year in which the data were collected. Ranges from 1992 to 2013.
maleoff	The sex of the offender, where 1 = male and 0 = female.
injury	A binary variable indicating whether the respondent was physically injured during the assault, where 1 = injured and 0 = uninjured.
age_r	The age (in years) at which victimization occurred. This variable is cut off at 75.
victimreported	A binary variable indicating whether the respondent reported the victimization to the police.
vic18andover	An age binary, where 0 = victimization occurred when the victim was below 18 years old, and 1 = victimization occurred when the victim was 18 or older.

1. The NCVS has been conducted for many years using roughly the same measures. For this reason, it is an excellent tool for tracking trends over time. To begin with, let's look at this theory: Some criminologists have suggested that as women enter the workforce and adopt more traditionally masculine roles, they also engage in other traditionally masculine behaviors. In particular, they will be more likely to commit crimes!

   a. To test this assertion, we'll check whether assault victims report a male or a female offender at different rates over time. To do this select: graphs->legacy dialogues->line->simple. Then put the variable year in the "category axis" box. In the "line represents" area, select "other statistic" and insert the variable maleoff into the box that lights up. Then select ok.

      i. What is the general trend over time? The Y axis can be multiplied by 100 to get the percentage of offenders who are male.

      ii. Do these results support the theory presented above?

      iii. Look carefully at the scale of your graph. How large are these changes that have occurred over time?

   b. Let's elaborate on these results by looking at whether the trend you saw in Part 1a appears if we distinguish between violent and nonviolent assaults (e.g. verbal assault, threat with a weapon). To do this, go back to the line dialogue and repeat Part 1a. This time, put the variable injured in the "panel by: rows" box. What do you conclude? Does it appear that women are becoming more violent, or are they just more prone to nonviolent assaults?

2. Another application for line graphs is to look at trends across age rather than time. Often we tell our kids that if they are in trouble, they should report it to the police. In the case of assault, are younger individuals reporting their victimizations at the same rate as adults?

   a. First, run a frequency of the variable victimreported. Overall, what proportion of assaults were reported to the police? Take a second to think about the implications of this result. What does it suggest about conclusions based on just police data?

   b. Create a line graph using the instructions in Part 1a. This time, put age_r in the "category axis"; and for "line represents," select "other statistic" and use the variable victimreported.

      i. The X axis of this graph is the age at which the assault occurred. The Y axis reflects the percentage of victims who reported the assault to the police.

      ii. What do you conclude about the relationship between assault reporting and age?

      iii. Why do you think these patterns exist? Are these the same kind of assaults we're seeing among adults?

3. Let's try to explain those results from Part 2a a bit further by looking at the relationship between victim and offender.

   a. Cross-tabulate the variable vic18andover with the variable relationship—be sure to put vic18andover in the column box and to ask for column percentages under the "cell" menu.

   b. Describe your results. Who appears to be assaulting these children at a disproportionately high rate?

   c. Consider these two explanations, and explain which one is appropriate (or whether both are) given these results:

      i. Assaults against children are underreported because family members abuse kids at a higher rate than they abuse adults. Kids do not want to have their parents be arrested, so they do not report.

      ii. Assaults against children are underreported because violence within schools is rarely reported to the police. This is because schools deal with issues in house, and students fear retribution from their assailants if they report the problem.

Results indicated that American Indian communities with higher levels of both social disorganization and economic deprivation also had higher rates of homicide. Bachman (1992) did not find support in her data for the third hypothesis. In addition to guiding her deductive research, the qualitative interview data also provided Bachman's research with a wealth of narratives that added meaning and depth to the statistical relationships that were found at the aggregate level. For example, many homicide offenders revealed what conditions of social disorganization and economic deprivation were like in their own lives. One offender talked about the reality of his disorganized childhood, being placed in multiple foster homes:

> I was pretty much living in foster homes since I was about two. I guess my parents weren't doing too good—you know, drinking and partying. My brother got put into a different foster home, but my sister and I got in the same one. After several moves, we all eventually got placed in the same home. We moved around quite a bit. (p. 38)

Finding support for relationships between the independent and dependent variables at two different levels—the individual level and the community level—provided validity to Bachman's (1992) conclusions that both social disorganization and economic deprivation are related to homicide in American Indian communities. Campbell and Fiske (1959) explain the validity-enhancing qualities of triangulation:

> If a hypothesis can survive the confrontation of a series of complementary methods of testing, it contains a degree of validity unattainable by one tested within the more constricted framework of a single method. . . . Findings from this latter approach must always be subject to the suspicion that they are method-bound: Will the comparison totter when exposed to an equally prudent but different testing method? (p. 82)

Case Study of Embedded Design

Investigating Rape

Testa and colleagues (2011) supplemented their quantitative study of violence against women with a qualitative component, because violence against women is "a complex, multifaceted phenomenon, occurring within a social context that is influenced by gender norms, interpersonal relationships, and sexual scripts" and "understanding of these experiences of violence is dependent on the subjective meaning for the woman and cannot easily be reduced to a checklist" (p. 237). This was an embedded, QUAN(qual), design.

Victims' responses to structured questions indicated an association between alcohol and rape, but when victims elaborated on their experiences in qualitative interviews, their comments led to a new way of understanding this quantitative association. Although this association has often been interpreted as suggesting "impaired judgment" about consent by intoxicated victims, the women interviewed by Testa et al. (2011) all revealed that they had had so much to drink that they were unconscious or at least unable to speak at the time of the rape. Testa and her colleagues concluded that the prevalence of this type of "incapacitated rape" required a new approach to the problem of violence against women (2011, 242):

> Qualitative analysis of our data has resulted in numerous "a-ha" types of insights that would not have been possible had we relied solely on quantitative data analysis (e.g., identification of incapacitated rape and sexual precedence, heterogeneity in the way that sexual assaults arise) and also helped us to understand puzzling quantitative observations. . . . These insights, in turn, led to testable, quantitative hypotheses that supported our qualitative findings, lending rigor and convergence to the process. We never could have anticipated what

these insights would be and that is what is both scary and exhilarating about qualitative data analysis, particularly for a scientist who has relied on quantitative data analysis and a priori hypothesis testing. The lengthy process of reading, coding, rereading, interpreting, discussing, and synthesizing among two or more coders is undeniably a major investment of time.

Testa and her colleagues concluded that insights yielded by the qualitative data analysis fully justified the time-consuming process of reading and rereading interviews, coding text, and discussing and reinterpreting the codes (2011).

▣ Strengths and Limitations of Mixed Methods

Combining qualitative and quantitative methods within one research project can strengthen the project's design by enhancing measurement validity, generalizability, causal validity, or authenticity. At the same time, combining methods creates challenges that may be difficult to overcome and ultimately limit the extent to which these goals are enhanced. This should be your golden rule: *The choice of a data collection method should be guided in large part by the aspect of validity that is of most concern and by the best method for answering your research question!*

As you can see in Exhibit 12.4, none of these methods is superior to the others in all respects, and each varies in its suitability to different research questions and goals. Choosing among them for a particular investigation requires consideration of the research problem, opportunities and resources, prior research, philosophical commitments, and research goals.

True experimental designs are strongest for testing nomothetic causal hypotheses and are most appropriate for studies of treatment effects and for research questions that are believed to involve basic social-psychological processes. Random assignment reduces the possibility of preexisting differences between treatment and comparison groups to small, specifiable, chance levels, so many of the variables that might create a spurious association are controlled. But despite this clear advantage, an experimental design requires a degree of control that cannot always be achieved in other settings. Researchers may be unable to randomly assign participants to groups or have too few participants to assign to groups, and unfortunately, most field experiments also require more access arrangements and financial resources than can often be obtained. In view of these difficulties, quasi- and nonexperimental designs are often used instead, but at the cost of causal validity.

Exhibit 12.4	Comparison of Three General Research Methods			
Design	Measurement Validity	Generalizability	Type of Causal Assertions	Causal Validity
Experiments	+	–[a]	Nomothetic	+
Surveys	+	+/–	Nomothetic	+/–[b]
Participant observation and intensive interviewing	–/+[c]	–	Idiographic	-

[a] Experiments are designed to ensure causal validity, not generalizability.

[b] Surveys are a weaker design for identifying causal effects than true experiments, but use of statistical controls can strengthen causal arguments. Also, if a random sample is used to collect survey data and the response rate is high, only then can results can be generalized to the target population.

[c] Reliability is low compared to surveys, and evaluation of measurement validity is often not possible. However, direct observations may lead to a greater understanding of the concepts being measured.

Surveys typically use standardized, quantitative measures of attitudes, behaviors, or social processes. Closed-ended questions are most common and are well suited for the reliable measurement of variables that have been studied in the past and whose meanings are well understood. Of course, surveys often include measures of many more variables than are included in an experiment, but this feature is not inherent in either design. Many surveys rely on random sampling for their selection of cases from some larger population, and this feature makes them preferable for research that seeks to develop generalizable findings. However, survey questionnaires can measure only what respondents are willing to report; they may not be adequate for studying behaviors or attitudes that are regarded as socially unacceptable. Surveys are also often used to test hypothesized causal relationships. When variables that might create spurious relationships are included in the survey, they can be controlled statistically in the analysis and thus eliminated as rival causal influences.

Qualitative methods such as participant observation and intensive interviewing presume an exploratory measurement approach in which indicators of concepts are drawn from direct observation or in-depth commentary. This approach is most appropriate when it is not clear what meaning people attach to a concept or what sense they might make of particular questions about it. Qualitative methods are also suited to the exploration of new or poorly understood social settings when it is not even clear what concepts would help to understand the situation. Further, these methods are useful in uncovering the process of a program or the implementation of an intervention. They may also be used instead of survey methods when the population of interest is not easily identifiable or seeks to remain hidden. For these reasons, qualitative methods tend to be preferred when exploratory research questions are posed or when new groups are investigated. But, of course, intensive measurement necessarily makes the study of large numbers of cases or situations difficult, resulting in the limitation of many field research efforts to small numbers of people or unique social settings. The individual field researcher may not require many financial resources, but the amount of time required for many field research projects serves as a barrier to many would-be field researchers.

A researcher should always consider whether data of another type should be collected in single-method studies and whether additional research using different methods is needed before the research question can be answered with sufficient confidence. But the potential for integrating methods and combining findings does not decrease the importance of single studies using just one method of data collection. The findings from well-designed studies in carefully researched settings are the necessary foundation for broader, more integrative methods. There is little point in combining methods that are poorly implemented or in merging studies that produced invalid results. Whatever the research question, we should consider the full range of methodological possibilities, make an informed and feasible choice, and then carefully carry out our strategy. As you saw in Chapter 2, research questions are never completely answered. Research findings regarding a particular question are added to the existing literature to inform future research, and the research circle continues.

▣ Comparing Results Across Studies

Meta-Analysis

Meta-analysis: The quantitative analysis of findings from multiple studies.

Meta-analysis is a quantitative method for identifying patterns in findings across multiple studies of the same research question (Cooper and Hedges 1994). Unlike a traditional literature review, which describes previous research studies verbally, meta-analyses treat previous studies as cases whose features are measured as variables and are then analyzed statistically. It is like conducting a survey in which the respondents are previous studies. Meta-analysis shows how evidence about interventions varies across research studies. If the methods used in these studies varied, then meta-analysis can be used to describe how this variation affected study findings. If social contexts or demographic characteristics varied across the studies, then a meta-analysis can indicate how social context or demographic characteristics affected study findings. Meta-analysis often accompanies systematic reviews that summarize what we know about the effectiveness of a particular intervention. By integrating different study samples and controlling for social context and demographic characteristics, meta-analysis enhances the generalizability of the findings. As noted in the last chapter, meta-analyses are often used to provide systematic reviews for evidence-based policies.

Research in the News

ARE YOUTH DESENSITIZED TO VIOLENCE?

Oakland, California, had several shootings of very young victims in 2011. For example, five-year-old Gabriel Martinez Jr. was shot as he played near his father's business. After several years of declining violent crime, shootings in Oakland increased rapidly, with around five people shot or shot at each day. In an article in the *New York Times,* the experts interviewed gave their perceptions of the reasons for the increased violence. For example, Anthony Del Toro of California Youth Outreach said, "To secure a gun in Oakland is like looking for some candy." Another youth worker believed that kids were too desensitized to violence because "young people see it all the time." The police department appeared to blame the budget cuts, which resulted in officer layoffs. How could these beliefs translate into more scientific facts?

For Further Thought

1. What kind of study is needed to determine whether "young people" are "desensitized" to violence?
2. What exactly is meant by the term *expert* in this article?
3. What does the empirical literature reveal about the relationship between law enforcement expenditures and rates of violence?

Source: Walter, Shoshana. 2012. "Shootings Soar in Oakland: Children Often Victims." *New York Times,* January 8, p. A29A.

Meta-analysis can be used when a number of studies have attempted to answer the same research question with similar quantitative methods. It is not typically used for evaluating results from multiple studies that employed different methods or measured different dependent variables. It is also not very sensible to use meta-analysis to combine study results when the original case data from these studies are available and can actually be combined and analyzed together (Lipsey and Wilson 2001). Rather, meta-analysis is a technique to combine and statistically analyze the statistical findings in published research reports.

After a research problem is formulated about prior research, the literature must be searched systematically to identify the entire population of relevant studies. Typically, multiple bibliographic databases are used; some researchers also search for related dissertations and conference papers. Eligibility criteria must be specified carefully to determine which studies to include and which to omit as too different. Mark Lipsey and David Wilson (2001) suggest that eligibility criteria include the following:

- *Distinguishing features.* This includes the specific intervention tested and perhaps the groups compared.

- *Research respondents.* These specify the population to which generalization is sought.

- *Key variables.* These must be sufficient to allow tests of the hypotheses of concern and controls for likely additional influences.

- *Research methods.* Apples and oranges cannot be directly compared, but some trade-off must be made between including the range of studies about a research question and excluding those that are so different in their methods as not to yield comparable data.

- *Cultural and linguistic range.* If the study population is going to be limited to English language publications, or limited in some other way, this must be acknowledged and the size of the population of relevant studies in other languages should be estimated.

- *Time frame.* Social processes relevant to the research question may have changed as a result of historical events or new technologies, so temporal boundaries around the study population must be considered.

- *Publication type.* Will the analysis focus only on published reports in professional journals, or will it include dissertations and/or unpublished reports? (pp. 16–21)

Once the studies are identified, their findings, methods, and other features are coded (e.g., sample size, location of sample, strength of the association between the independent and dependent variables). Statistics are then calculated to identify the average effect of the independent variable on the dependent variable, as well as the effect of methodological and other features of the studies (Cooper and Hedges 1994). The **effect size** statistic is the key to capturing the association between the independent and dependent variables across multiple studies. The effect size statistic is a standardized measure of association—often the difference between the mean of the experimental group and the mean of the control group on the dependent variable, adjusted for the average variability in the two groups (Lipsey and Wilson 2001).

Effect size: A standardized measure of association—often the difference between the mean of the experimental group and the mean of the control group on the dependent variable, adjusted for the average variability in the two groups.

The meta-analytic approach to synthesizing findings from several studies can result in more generalizable findings than those obtained with just one study. Methodological weaknesses in the studies included in the meta-analysis are still a problem; it is only when other studies without particular methodological weaknesses are included that we can estimate effects with some confidence. In addition, before we can place any confidence in the results of a meta-analysis, we must be confident that all (or almost all) relevant studies were included and that the information we need to analyze was included in all (or most) of the studies (Matt and Cook 1994).

One of the challenges of meta-analysis is that the authors of the articles to be reviewed may not always report sufficient information. For example, the study report (whether a journal article or an unpublished report) may not contain information about participant characteristics, an especially important variable if we are to consider the generalizability of the results to different population groups. Littell (2005) noted that to conduct her meta-analysis of multisystemic therapy, she had to contact principal investigators to obtain more information about participant characteristics, interventions, and outcomes.

Case Study of Meta-Analysis

The Effectiveness of Antibullying Programs

The 2013 School Crime Supplement to the National Crime Victimization Survey reported that about 28% of teens between the ages of 12 and 18 had been bullied in the past six months. The effects of bullying are numerous and include perceived risk of harm, behavior problems, negative consequences for school performance, depression, and other physical ailments. There have been many different programs designed to decrease bullying in schools, but the effectiveness of these programs remains largely unknown. To examine the effects of antibullying programs across studies, Ferguson et al. (2007) performed a meta-analysis of randomized experimental studies examining the efficacy of such programs.

Studies included in the Ferguson et al. (2007) meta-analysis had several selection criteria: (a) They had to be published between 1995 and 2006, (b) the outcome variables had to clearly measure some element of bullying behavior toward peers, (c) they had to involve some form of control group to test program effectiveness, (d) the intervention programs had to be school based, and (e) only manuscripts published in peer-reviewed journals were included. Results of the meta-analysis indicated that the impact of antibullying programs ranged from less than 1% for low-risk children to 3.6% for high-risk children. Ferguson and his colleagues (2007) stated, "Thus, it can be said that although anti-bullying programs produce a small amount of positive change, it is likely that this change is too small to be practically significant or noticeable" (p. 408).

Meta-analyses such as this make us aware of how hazardous it is to base understanding of social processes on single studies that are limited in time, location, and measurement. Of course, we need to have our wits about us when we read reports of meta-analytic studies. It is not a good idea to assume that a meta-analysis is the definitive word on a research question just because it cumulates the results of multiple studies.

Meta-analyses and meta-syntheses make us aware of how hazardous it is to base understandings of social processes on single studies that are limited in time, location, and measurement. Although one study may not support the hypothesis that we deduced from what seemed to be a compelling theory, this is not a sufficient basis for discarding the theory itself, nor even for assuming that the hypothesis is no longer worthy of consideration in future research. You can see that a meta-analysis combining the results of many studies may identify conditions for which the hypothesis is supported and others for which it is not.

Case Study of Meta-Analysis

Do Parent Training Programs Prevent Child Abuse?

Brian Lundahl, Janelle Nimer, and Bruce Parsons (2006) were interested in the effect of parent training and parent education programs on reducing risk factors associated with child abuse. In their meta-analysis, they included only studies that met four eligibility criteria: (1) The training was conducted with families in which there were no parent or child developmental or cognitive delays; (2) the training was directed to preventing physical abuse, child neglect, or emotional abuse and not sexual abuse; (3) there was actual training; and (4) pretests and posttests were given to at least five participants. Using three keywords (*child abuse*, *child neglect*, and *parent training*) they searched three databases (ERIC, PsychInfo, and Social Work Abstracts) for any articles published between 1970 and 2004. Of 186 studies, they found 23 that met the eligibility criteria. They coded outcome measures, including parents' emotional adjustment, child-rearing attitudes, child-rearing behaviors, and documented abuse; and they coded moderating and independent variables, including participant characteristics, parent training program characteristics, and the methodological rigor of the studies.

Overall, they found that parent training had a moderate effect and was effective in changing parental beliefs and attitudes toward children, improving parental emotional well-being, altering child-rearing behaviors, and reducing documented abuse. They also found that specific program characteristics influenced these outcomes. For example, programs that included home visitors had a greater impact than programs without home visitors, and programs that did training in both the home and the office were more effective than programs that limited training to one site.

Meta-Synthesis

Meta-synthesis is a related method used to analyze and integrate findings from qualitative studies (Jensen and Allen 1996). This type of analysis requires not just aggregating findings from different qualitative studies, but also reinterpreting the data once it is in aggregate. As with meta-analyses, attention to eligibility criteria for selection into a meta-synthesis is extremely important.

Meta-synthesis: The qualitative analysis of findings from multiple qualitative studies.

Case Study of Meta-Synthesis

Female Drug Dealers

Maher and Hudson (2007) performed a meta-synthesis examining the qualitative literature on women in the illicit drug economy to identify and integrate key themes. The authors spelled out their methods meticulously describing the characteristics they used to select studies that met their criteria. They first searched many databases (e.g., Criminal Justice Abstracts, Sociological Abstracts) for research using various key terms such as *drug market*, *drug economy, women dealing.* Studies were selected only if they "generated findings in relation to female participation in the drug economy," and the "primary data collection used qualitative or ethnographic research" (Maher and Hudson 2007, 809). Of 36 studies located, only 15 met their criteria and provided detailed descriptions of female experiences using field notes or narrative data from transcribed interviews. A sample of the selected studies included in the metasynthesis is shown in Exhibit 12.5.

After reading that qualitative material from the 15 studies examined, Maher and Hudson (2007) identified six themes that captured the nature and experience of women's participation in the illicit drug economy. One of the key findings was that gender-stratified nature of women's involvement; all studies regardless of time or place found that women tended to occupy subordinate roles to men, even those women identified as successful dealers. They also concluded that most women were introduced to dealing through relationships with sex partners. They concluded,

> Our results suggest that while women rely on a diverse range of income sources and juggle different roles both within the drug economy and in relation to dealing and domestic responsibilities, most women in most drug markets remain confined to low level and marginal roles. (Maher and Hudson 2007, 821)

Exhibit 12.5	Example of the Studies for Metasynthesis of Female Drug Dealers	
Author(s)	*Study Location*	*Sample*
Rosenbaum (1981)	San Francisco and New York	100 women
Adler (1985)	Southwest County close to Mexico border	65 dealers/smugglers, 6 women
Miller, E. M. (1986)	Milwaukee	64 women "hustlers"
Waldorf, Reinarman, and Murphy (1991)	San Francisco	80 sellers, 26 female
Taylor (1993)	Glasgow, Scotland	26 women
Maher (1997)	New York	211 women
Dunlap, Johnson, and Maher (1997)	New York	111 dealers, 39 women
Sterk (1999)	Atlanta, Georgia	149 women
Denton (2001)	Melbourne, Australia	16 women recently released from prison

Source: Adapted from Maher and Hudson 2007.

Ethics and Mixed Methods

Researchers who combine methods must be aware of the ethical concerns involved in using each of the separate methods, but there are also some ethical challenges that are heightened in mixed-methods projects. One special challenge is defining the researcher's role in relation to the research participants. Every researcher creates an understanding about his or her role with research participants (Mertens 2012). Researchers using quantitative methods often define themselves as outside experts who design a research project and collect research data using objective procedures that are best carried out without participant involvement. By contrast, qualitative researchers often define themselves as

CAREERS AND RESEARCH

Claire Wulf Winiarek, MA, Director of Collaborative Policy Engagement

Source: Claire Wulf Winiarek

Claire Wulf Winiarek didn't set her sights on research methods as an undergraduate in political science and international relations at Baldwin College, nor as a masters student at Old Dominion University; her goal was to make a difference in public affairs. It still is. She is currently Director of Collaborative Policy Engagement at WellPoint, a Fortune 50 health insurance company based in Indianapolis, Indiana. Her previous positions include working for a Virginia member of the U.S. House of Representatives, coordinating grassroots international human rights advocacy for Amnesty International's North Africa Regional Action Network, and working as director of Public Policy and Research at Amerigroup's Office of Health Reform Integration.

Early in her career, Winiarek was surprised by the frequency with which she found herself leveraging research methods. Whether she is analyzing draft legislation and proposed regulations, determining next year's department budget, or estimating potential growth while making the case for a new program, Winiarek has found that a strong foundation in research methods shapes her success. The increasing reliance of government and its private sector partners on data and evidence-based decision making continues to increase the importance of methodological expertise.

Policy work informed by research has made for a very rewarding career:

The potential for meaningful impact in the lives of everyday Americans is very real at the nexus of government and the private sector. Public policy, and how policy works in practice, has significant societal impact. I feel The potential for meaningful impact in the lives of everyday Americans is very real at the nexus of government and the private sector. Public policy, and how policy works in practice, has significant societal impact. I feel fortunate to help advance that nexus in a way that is informed not only by practice, evidence, and research, but also by the voice of those impacted.

Winiarek's advice for students seeking a career like hers is clear:

The information revolution is impacting all industries and sectors, as well as government and our communities. With this ever-growing and ever-richer set of information, today's professionals must have the know-how to understand and apply this data in a meaningful way. Research methods will create the critical and analytical foundation to meet the challenge, but internships or special research projects in your career field will inform that foundation with practical experience. Always look for that connection between research and reality.

engaging in research in some type of collaboration with the community or group they are studying, with much input from their research participants into the research design and the collection and analysis of research data.

A researcher using mixed methods cannot simply adopt one of these roles: A researcher needs some degree of autonomy when designing quantitative research plans, but a researcher will not be able to collect intensive qualitative data if participants do not accord her or him some degree of trust as an insider. The challenge is compounded by the potential for different reactions of potential participants to the different roles. Authorities who control access to program clients or employees or community members may be willing to agree to a structured survey but not to a long-term engagement with researchers as participant observers, so that a mixed-methods project that spans programs, communities, or other settings may involve a biased sampling for the qualitative component. Natalia Luxardo, Graciela Colombo, and Gabriela Iglesias (2011) confronted this challenge in their study of Brazilian services that provided support to victims of family violence, and as a result, focused their qualitative research on one service that supported the value of giving voice to their service recipients.

Weighing both roles and the best combination of them is critical at the outset of a mixed-methods project, although the dilemma will be lessened if a project uses different researchers to lead the quantitative and qualitative components.

Complex mixed-methods projects in which quantitative surveying is interspersed with observational research or intensive interviews may also require renegotiation of participant consent to the particular research procedures at each stage. As stated by Chih Hoong Sin (2005),

> Different stages and different components of research may require the negotiation of different types of consent, some of which may be more explicit than others. Sampling, contact, re-contact, and fieldwork can be underpinned by different conceptualization and operationalization of "informed consent." This behooves researchers to move away from the position of treating consent-seeking as an exercise that only occurs at certain points in the research process or only for certain types of research. Consent-seeking should not be thought of merely as an event. (p. 290)

In the qualitative component of their study of Brazilian victims of domestic violence, Luxardo and her colleagues (2011) adopted a flexible qualitative interviewing approach to allow participants to avoid topics they did not want to discuss:

> We tried to consider what was important for that adolescent during the interview and, many times, we had to reframe the content of the encounters according to the expectations they had. So, if they were not willing to share during an interview but still had complaints, doubts, or comments to share, we tried to focus on those instead of subtly directing the talk to the arena of the research interests. Moreover, we noticed that some adolescents (most of them migrants from Bolivia) did not feel at ease sharing that kind of information about their lives with a stranger, so we tried not to invade their intimacy by being culturally sensitive; if they did not want to talk, they did not have to do so. (p. 996)

▣ Conclusion

We began this chapter by asking what mixed-methods research has to tell us about our social world. The mixed-methods examples from this chapter demonstrate that a research design is an integrated whole. Designing research means deciding how to measure empirical phenomena, how to identify causal connections, and how to generalize findings—not as separate decisions, but in tandem, with each decision having implications for the others. The choice of a data collection method should be guided in part by the aspect of validity that is of most concern, but each aspect of validity must be considered in attempting to answer every research question. A basic question the researcher must ask is this: Will a mixed-methods approach give a better picture of the research target than a single-method approach? If the answer is yes, then the researcher must consider which combination of methods will offer the best mix of validity, generalizability, and rich, accurate data on the target research question.

The ability to apply diverse techniques to address different aspects of a complex research question is one mark of a sophisticated researcher. Awareness that one study's findings must be understood in the context of a larger body of research is another. And the ability to speculate on how the use of different methods might have altered a study's findings is a prerequisite for informed criticism of research.

Finally, realistic assessment of the weaknesses as well as the strengths of each method of data collection should help you to remember that humility is a virtue in research. Advancement of knowledge and clear answers to specific research questions are attainable with the tools you now have in your methodological toolbox. Perfection, however, is not a realistic goal. No matter what research method we use, our mental concepts cannot reflect exactly what we measured, our notions of causation cannot reveal a tangible causal force, and our generalizations always extend beyond the cases that were actually studied. This is not cause for disillusionment, but it should keep us from being excessively confident in our own interpretations or unreasonably resistant to change. Final answers to every research question we pose cannot be achieved; what we seek are new, ever more sophisticated questions for research.

Key Terms

> Review key terms with eFlashcards. ⑤SAGE edge™

Convergent parallel design 357
Effect Size 366
Embedded design 358
Explanatory sequential design 358

Exploratory sequential design 357
Meta-analysis 364
Meta-synthesis 367
Mixed Methods 356

Multiphase design 358
Pragmatism 357
Transformative design 358
Triangulation 356

Highlights

- Using mixed methods means intentionally combining quantitative and qualitative research methods to study a research question.

- The use of mixed-methods research has been increasing for the past 25 years, primarily because most researchers are convinced that research on most topics can be improved by using mixed methods.

- There are several designs available in mixed-methods research, including those that give equal weight to quantitative and qualitative

methodologies and those that give differential weight to one or the other method.

- Researchers can test statistically for patterns across multiple studies with meta-analysis. This technique can be used only in areas of research in which there have been many prior studies using comparable methods.

- Meta-synthesis is the analysis tool for assessing the results of multiple studies that have relied on qualitative methods.

Exercises

> Test your understanding of chapter content. Take the practice quiz. ⑤SAGE edge™

1. Some research projects use an "inverted pyramid" data collection strategy, with broad, quantitative measures gathered from a large population on top, narrowing to more intensive qualitative measures (focus groups, individual interviews) with a smaller subset of the population at the bottom. Design a research project that resembles such an inverted pyramid, showing what measures and what sample size and research subjects you would use at each level of the design.

2. Think of at least three areas of criminological research where you believe much research has been done—for example, understanding why some people engage in crime. Where are you likely to find such studies? You may wish to start by looking on ERIC, in JSTOR, and in Criminal Justice Abstracts, whichever data base your library has. Do a literature search for this substantive area of inquiry with the words "and 'mixed methods'" to find out about recent research on the topic that has utilized mixed methods. What do you find? Did mixing methods enhance the findings?

3. Testa (Testa et al. 2011) describes her own training in quantitative methods and then highlights some experiences that led her

to integrate qualitative methods into her research. Would you describe your own training in research methods so far as focusing primarily on quantitative or qualitative methods? Have you had any experiences that lead you to consider the "other" methodology?

4. Which of the four types of mixed methods do you feel is likely to be useful for investigating the social world? Would you favor more single method or more mixed-methods studies? Explain your reasoning.

5. Select a public setting in which there are many people on a regular basis, such as a sports game, a theater lobby, a coffee shop, or a popular public park. Observe as an ethnographer for 30 minutes on one day, and then write up your notes. Before your next visit, a day later, develop a systematic observation schedule on which to record observations in the same setting in a structured manner. Record observations using the structured observation form on another day, but in the same place and at about the same time of day. Compare the data you have collected with your ethnographic notes and with your systematic observation notes.

Developing a Research Proposal

Now is the time to mix your methods.

1. Add a component involving a second method to your research proposal. If you already developed alternative approaches in answer to the exercises in earlier chapters, just write a justification for these additions that points out the potential benefits.

2. Consider the possible influences of social context factors on the variables pertinent to your research question. Write a rationale for including a test for contextual influences in your proposed research.

3. Describe a method for studying the contextual influences in Question 2.

Web Exercises

1. Find the website for the online *Journal of Mixed Methods Research* (mmr.sagepub.com). On the home page, click the button "Current Issue." When the table of contents for the current issue comes up, click on the abstracts for three of the articles, and for each article, write down two or more methods that the authors used to conduct their research. Were any methods used in more than one study? Were there any methods you had never heard of before?

2. Go to the home page of the *Journal of Mixed Methods Research*. At the button for "Article Statistics," click on "Most Read." When the most-read article titles come up, read the abstracts for the top five articles. What themes or main points do you see running through these articles? Based on the top five abstracts, write a paragraph or two describing the most important issues currently being discussed or investigated by mixed-methods researchers.

3. Go to the National Criminal Justice Reference Service website (www.ncjrs.gov) and search for the term *mixed methods*. Find at least two studies that have used a mixed-methods approach. What strengths did this approach provide the study compared to using just one of the methods?

Ethics Exercises

1. You learned in this book that Sampson and Raudenbush (1999) had observers drive down neighborhood streets in Chicago and record the level of disorder they observed. What should have been the observers' response if they observed a crime in progress? What if they just suspected that a crime was going to occur? What if the crime was a drug dealer interacting with driver at a curb? What if it was a prostitute soliciting a customer? What, if any, ethical obligation does a researcher studying a neighborhood have to residents in that neighborhood? Should research results be shared at a neighborhood forum or community meeting?

2. Some research investigating the effects of alcohol has actually had research subjects drink to the point of intoxication. If you were a student member of your university's institutional review board, would you vote to approve a study like this? Why or why not? Would you ban an experiment that involves alcohol altogether, or would you set certain criteria for the experimental conditions? What would such criteria be? How about for female students who may be pregnant? Can you think of any other circumstances in which you would allow an experiment involving the administration of illegal drugs?

SPSS or Excel Exercises

Data for Exercise	
Dataset	**Description**
2013 YRBS.sav	The 2013 YRBS, short for Youth Risk Behavior Survey, is a national study of high school students. It focuses on behaviors and experiences of the adolescent population, including substance use and some victimization.
Monitoring the future 2013 grade 10.sav	This dataset contains variables from the 2013 Monitoring the Future (MTF) study. These data cover a national sample of 10th graders, with a focus on monitoring substance use and abuse.

Variables for Exercise	
Variable Name (dataset)	**Description**
qn33 (YRBS)	Binary variable indicating whether the respondent drank any alcohol in the past month, where 1 = yes and 2 = no.
qn43 (YRBS)	Binary variable indicating whether the respondent smoked cigarettes in the past month, where 1 = yes and 2 = no.
sex (YRBS)	Gender of the respondent, where 1 = male and 2 = female.
race4 (YRBS)	Four-category race measure, where 1 = white, 2 = black, 3 = Hispanic, and 4 = other
past30cigs (MTF)	Binary variable indicating whether the respondent smoked cigarettes in the past month, where 1 = yes and 0 = no.
past30drink (MTF)	Binary variable indicating whether the respondent drank any alcohol in the past month, where 1 = yes and 0 = no.
gender (MTF)	Gender of the respondent, where 1 = male and 2 = female.
V1070 (MTF)	Three-category race measure, where 1 = black, 2 = white, and 3 = Hispanic.

1. We won't be able to do anything with mixed-methods data in the sense that we mix qualitative and quantitative data, as such an analysis is not well suited to SPSS and is *very* labor intensive. What we can do is look into triangulating and replicating findings across multiple datasets with similar measures. For this exercise we'll look at whether there are any race and gender differences in smoking and drinking behaviors.

    a. Why would we want to compare results across multiple datasets?

    b. Does this allow us to establish (1) causal relationships, (2) that measures are reliable, or (3) the validity of a measure? Why or why not?

2. The Monitoring the Future dataset is for 10th graders specifically, so you will need to make sure that the 2013 YRBS data has only 10th graders selected as well. To do this, go to "data->select cases->if" and enter "grade=2" into the field. After this is done, we'll look into answering our questions:

    a. First, tabulate the YRBS variables qn33 and qn43, and the MTF variables past30cigs and past30drink.

    b. Do these two datasets agree on the incidence of drinking and smoking? If not, can you think of any reasons they wouldn't agree?

3. Next, let's look at whether we can replicate any relationships across the two datasets, regardless of any differences in prevalence estimates. In particular, I'd like you to look at the relationships between (1) race and gender and (2) drinking and smoking in both datasets. You can look at these relationships using the cross-tabs function we used for the SPSS exercises in Chapter 6 (analyze->descriptives->cross tabs. Make sure to put the independent variable in the column box and to select column cell percentages). The variables for race and gender are race4 and sex, respectively, in the YRBS; and gender and V1070, respectively, in the MTF.

    a. Do you see any consistencies or similarities?

    b. What conclusions do you feel most comfortable making based on these comparisons? What do you think needs additional replication and testing?

Section IV: After the Data Are Collected

CHAPTER 13

Quantitative Data Analysis

LEARNING OBJECTIVES

1. Identify the types of graphs and statistics that are appropriate for analysis of variables at each level of measurement.

2. List the guidelines for constructing frequency distributions.

3. Discuss the advantages and disadvantages of using each of the three measures of central tendency.

4. Understand the difference between the variance and the standard deviation.

5. Define the concept of skewness and explain how it can influence measures of central tendency.

6. Explain how to calculate percentages in a cross-tabulation table and how to interpret the results.

7. Discuss the three reasons for conducting an elaboration analysis.

8. Write a statement based on inferential statistics that reports the confidence that can be placed in a statistical statement of a population parameter.

9. Define the statistics obtained in a multiple regression analysis and explain their purpose.

"Oh no, not data analysis and statistics!" We now hit the chapter that you may have been fearing all along, the chapter on data analysis and the use of statistics. This chapter describes what you need to do after your data have been collected. You now need to analyze what you have found, interpret it, and decide how to present your data so that you can most clearly make the points you wish to make.

What you probably dread about this chapter is something that you either sense or know from a previous course: Studying data analysis and statistics will lead you into that feared world of mathematics. We would like to state at the beginning, however, that you have relatively little to fear. The kind of mathematics required to perform the data analysis tasks in this chapter is minimal. If you can add, subtract, multiply, and divide and are willing to put some effort into carefully reading the chapter, you will do well in the statistical analysis of your data. In fact, it is our position that the analysis of your data will require more in the way of careful and logical thought than in mathematical skill. One helpful way to think of statistics is that it consists of a set of tools that you will use to examine your data to help you answer the questions that motivated your research in the first place. Right now, the toolbox that holds your statistical tools is fairly empty (or completely empty). In the course of this chapter, we will add some fundamental tools to that toolbox. We would also like to note at the beginning that the kinds of statistics you will use on criminological data are very much the same as those used by economists, psychologists, political scientists, sociologists, and other social scientists. In other words, statistical tools are statistical tools, and all that changes is the nature of the problem to which those tools are applied.

This chapter will introduce several common statistics in social research and highlight the factors that must be considered in using and interpreting statistics. Think of it as a review of fundamental social statistics, if you have already studied them, or as an introductory overview, if you have not.

Two preliminary sections lay the foundation for studying statistics. In the first, we will discuss the role of statistics in the research process, returning to themes and techniques you already know. In the second preliminary section, we will outline the process of acquiring data for statistical analysis. In the rest of the chapter, we will explain how to describe the distribution of single variables and the relationships among variables. Along the way, we will address ethical issues related to data analysis. This chapter will be successful if it encourages you to see statistics responsibly and evaluate them critically and gives you the confidence necessary to seek opportunities for extending your statistical knowledge.

It should be noted that, in this chapter, we focus primarily on the use of statistics for descriptive purposes. Those of you looking for a more advanced discussion of statistical methods used in criminal justice and criminology should seek other textbooks (e.g., Bachman and Paternoster 2008). Although many colleges and universities offer social statistics in a separate course, we don't want you to think of this chapter as something that deals with a different topic than the rest of the book. Data analysis is an integral component of research methods, and it's important that any proposal for quantitative research include a plan for the data analysis that will follow data collection.

Frequency distributions: Numerical display showing the number of cases, and usually the percentage of cases (the relative frequencies), corresponding to each value or group of values of a variable.

Cross-tabulation (cross-tab): A bivariate (two-variable) distribution showing the distribution of one variable for each category of another variable.

Descriptive statistics: Statistics used to describe the distribution of and relationship among variables.

Inferential statistics: Mathematical tools for estimating how likely it is that a statistical result based on data from a random sample is representative of the population from which the sample is assumed to have been selected.

▣ Introducing Statistics

Statistics play a key role in achieving valid research results in terms of measurement, causal validity, and generalizability. Some statistics are useful primarily to describe the results of measuring single variables and to construct and evaluate multi-item scales. These statistics include **frequency distributions**, graphs, measures of central tendency and variation, and reliability tests. Other statistics are useful primarily in achieving causal validity, by helping us describe the association among variables and control for, or otherwise take into account, other variables.

Cross-tabulation is one technique for measuring association and controlling other variables and is introduced in this chapter. All these statistics are called **descriptive statistics** because they are used to describe the distribution of and relationship among variables.

You learned in Chapter 5 that it is possible to estimate the degree of confidence that can be placed in generalizations for a sample and for the population from which the sample was selected. The statistics used in making these estimates are called **inferential statistics,** and they include confidence intervals, to which you were exposed in Chapter 5. In this chapter we will refer only briefly to inferential statistics, but we will emphasize later in the chapter their importance for testing hypotheses involving sample data.

Criminological theory and the results of prior research should guide our statistical plan or analytical strategy, as they guide the choice of other research methods. In other words, we want to use the statistical strategy that will best answer our research question. There are so many particular statistics and so many ways for them to be used in data analysis that even the best statistician can become lost in a sea of numbers if she is not using prior research and theorizing to develop a coherent analysis plan. It is also important for an analyst to choose statistics that are appropriate to the level of measurement of the variables to be analyzed. As you learned in Chapter 4, numbers used to represent the values of variables may not actually signify different quantities, meaning that many statistical techniques will be inapplicable. Some statistics, for example, will be appropriate only when the variable you are examining is measured at the nominal level. Other kinds of statistics will require interval-level measurement. To use the right statistic, then, you must be very familiar with the measurement properties of your variables (and you thought that stuff would go away!).

Case Study

The Causes of Delinquency

In this chapter, we will use research on the causes of delinquency for our examples. More specifically, our data will be a subset of a much larger study of a sample of approximately 1,200 high school students selected from the metropolitan and suburban high schools of a city in South Carolina. These students, all of whom were in the 10th grade, completed a questionnaire that asked about such things as how they spent their spare time; how they got along with their parents, teachers, and friends; their attitudes about delinquency; whether their friends committed delinquent acts; and their own involvement in delinquency. The original research study was designed to test specific hypotheses about the factors that influence delinquency. It was predicted that delinquent behavior would be affected by such things as the level of supervision provided by parents, the students' own moral beliefs about delinquency, their involvement in conventional activities such as studying and watching TV, their fear of getting caught, their friends' involvement in crime, and whether these friends provided verbal support for delinquent acts. All these hypotheses were derived from extant criminological theory, theories we have referred to throughout this book. One specific hypothesis, derived from deterrence theory, predicts that youths who believe they are likely to get caught by the police for committing delinquent acts are less likely to commit delinquency than others. This hypothesis is shown in Exhibit 13.1. The variables from this study that we will use in our chapter examples are displayed in Exhibit 13.2.

| Exhibit 13.1 | Hypothesis for Perceived Fear of Being Caught and Delinquency |

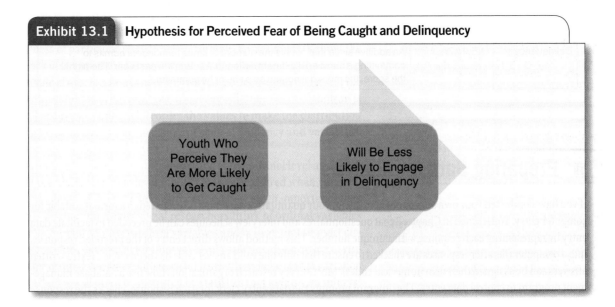

level of measurement. We will touch on some of the details of these issues in the following sections on particular statistical techniques.

We will now examine graphs and frequency distributions that illustrate these three features of shape. Summary statistics used to measure specific aspects of central tendency and variability will be presented in a separate section. There is a summary statistic for the measurement of skewness, but it is used only rarely in published research reports and will not be presented here.

Graphs

It is true that a picture often is worth a thousand words. Graphs can be easy to read, and they very nicely highlight a distribution's shape. They are particularly useful for exploring data, because they show the full range of variation and identify data anomalies that might be in need of further study. And good, professional-looking graphs can now be produced relatively easily with software available for personal computers. There are many types of graphs, but the most common and most useful are bar charts and histograms. Each has two axes, the vertical axis (*y*-axis) and the horizontal axis (*x*-axis), and labels to identify the variables and the values with tick marks showing where each indicated value falls along the axis. The vertical *y*-axis of a graph is usually in frequency or percentage units, whereas the horizontal *x*-axis displays the values of the variable being graphed. There are different kinds of graphs you can use to descriptively display your data, depending upon the level of measurement of the variable.

A **bar chart** contains solid bars separated by spaces. It is a good tool for displaying the distribution of variables measured at the nominal level and other discrete categorical variables, because there is, in effect, a gap between each of the categories. In our study of delinquency, one of the questions asked of respondents was whether their parents knew where the respondents were when the respondents were away from home. We graphed the responses to this question in a bar chart, which is shown in Exhibit 13.3. In this bar chart we report both the frequency count for each value and the **percentage** of the total that each value represents. The chart indicates that very few of the respondents (only 16, or 1.3%) reported that their parents "never" knew where the respondents were when the respondents were not at home. Almost one half (562, or 44.3%) of the youths reported that their parents "usually" knew where the respondents were. What you can also see, by noticing the height of the bars above "usually" and "always," is that most youths report that their parents provide very adequate supervision. You can also see that the most frequent response was "usually" and the least frequent was "never." Because the response "usually" is the most frequent value, it is called the **mode** or modal response. With ordinal data like these, the mode is the most appropriate measure of central tendency (more about this later).

Notice that the cases tend to cluster in the two values of "usually" and "always"; in fact, about 80% of all cases are found in those two categories. There is not much variability in this distribution, then.

A **histogram** is like a bar chart, but it has bars that are adjacent, or right next to each other, with no gaps. This is done to indicate that data displayed in a histogram, unlike the data in a bar chart, are quantitative variables that vary along a continuum (see the discussion of levels of measurement for variables in Chapter 4). Exhibit 13.4 shows a histogram from the delinquency dataset we are using. The variable being graphed is the number of hours per week the respondent reported to be studying. Notice that the cases cluster at the low end of the values. In other words, there are a lot of youths who spend between 0 and 15 hours per week studying. After that, there are only a few cases at each different value, with "spikes" occurring at 25, 30, 38, and 40 hours studied. This distribution is clearly not symmetric. In a symmetric distribution there is a lump of cases or a spike with an equal number of cases to the left and right of that spike. In the distribution shown in Exhibit 13.4, most of the cases are at the left end of the distribution (i.e., at low values), and the distribution trails off on the right side. The ends of a histogram

Bar chart: A graphic for qualitative variables in which the variable's distribution is displayed with solid bars separated by spaces.

Percentage: Relative frequencies, computed by dividing the frequency of cases in a particular category by the total number of cases, and multiplying by 100.

Mode: The most frequent value in a distribution, also termed the probability average.

Histogram: A graphic for quantitative variables in which the variable's distribution is displayed with adjacent bars.

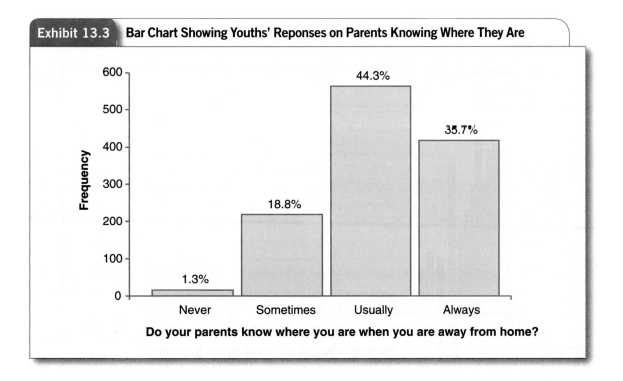

Exhibit 13.3 | **Bar Chart Showing Youths' Reponses on Parents Knowing Where They Are**

Do your parents know where you are when you are away from home?

like this are often called the tail of a distribution. In a symmetric distribution, the left and right tails are approximately the same length. As you can clearly see in Exhibit 13.4, however, the right tail is much longer than the left tail. When the tails of the distribution are uneven, the distribution is said to be asymmetrical or skewed. A skew is either positive or negative. When the cases cluster to the left and the right tail of the distribution is longer than the left, as in Exhibit 13.4, our variable distribution is positively skewed. When the cases cluster to the right side and the left tail of the distribution is long, our variable distribution is negatively skewed.

Positively skewed: Describes a distribution in which the cases cluster to the left and the right tail of the distribution is longer than the left.

If graphs are misused, they can distort, rather than display, the shape of a distribution. Compare, for example, the two graphs in Exhibit 13.5. The first graph shows that high school seniors reported relatively stable rates of lifetime use of cocaine between 1980 and 1985. The second graph, using exactly the same numbers, appeared in a 1986 *Newsweek* article on the coke plague (Orcutt and Turner 1993). To look at this graph, you would think that the rate of cocaine usage among high school seniors

Negatively skewed: A distribution in which cases cluster to the right side, and the left tail of the distribution is longer than the right.

increased dramatically during this period. But, in fact, the difference between the two graphs is due simply to changes in how the graphs are drawn. In the "plague" graph (B), the percentage scale on the vertical axis begins at 15 rather than 0, making what was about a one-percentage-point increase look very big indeed. In addition, omission from the plague graph of the more rapid increase in reported usage between 1975 and 1980 makes it look as if the tiny increase in 1985 were a new, and thus more newsworthy, crisis.

Adherence to several guidelines (Tufte 1983) will help you spot these problems and avoid them in your own work:

- The difference between bars will be exaggerated if you cut off the bottom of the vertical axis and display less than the full height of the bars. Instead, begin the graph of a quantitative variable at 0 on both axes. It may at times be reasonable to violate this guideline, as when an age distribution is presented for a sample of adults, but in this case be sure to mark the break clearly on the axis.

- Bars of unequal width, including pictures instead of bars, can make particular values look as if they carry more weight than their frequency warrants. Always use bars of equal width.

As another example of calculating the frequencies and percentages, suppose we had a sample of 25 youths and asked them their gender. From this group of 25 youths, 13 were male and 12 were female. The frequency of males (symbolized here by f) would be 13 and the frequency of females would be 12. The percentage of males would be 52%, calculated by $f/$ the total number of cases $\times$ 100 (13/25 $\times$ 100 = 52%). The percentage of females would be 12/25 $\times$ 100 = 48%.

In the frequency distribution shown in Exhibit 13.6, you can see that only a very small number (14 out of 1,272) of youths thought that they would experience "no problem" if they were caught and taken to court for drinking liquor under age. You can see that most—in fact, 1,009—of these youths, or 79.3% of them, thought that they would have either "a big problem" or "a very big problem" with this. If you compare Exhibit 13.6 to Exhibit 13.3, you can see that a frequency distribution (see Exhibit 13.6) can provide much of the same information as a graph about the number and percentage of cases in a variable's categories. Often, however, it is easier to see the shape of a distribution when it is graphed. When the goal of a presentation is to convey a general sense of a variable's distribution, particularly when the presentation is to an audience not trained in statistics, the advantages of a graph outweigh those of a frequency distribution.

Exhibit 13.6 is a frequency distribution of an ordinal-level variable; it has a very small number of discrete categories. In Exhibit 13.7, we provide an illustration of a frequency distribution with a continuous quantitative variable. This variable is one we have already looked at and graphed from the delinquency data, the number of hours per week the respondent spent studying. Notice that this variable, like many continuous variables in criminological research, has a large number of values. Although this is a reasonable frequency distribution to construct—you can, for example, still see that the cases tend to cluster in the low end of the distribution and are strung way out at the upper end—it is a little difficult to get a good sense of the distribution of the cases. The problem is that there are too many values to easily comprehend. It would be nice if we could simplify distributions like these that have a large number of different values. Well, we can. We can construct what is called a **grouped frequency distribution**.

Grouped frequency distribution: A frequency distribution in which the data are organized into categories, either because there are more values than can be easily displayed or because the distribution of the variable will be clearer or more meaningful.

Grouped Data

Many frequency distributions, such as those in Exhibit 13.7, and many graphs require grouping of some values after the data are collected. There are two reasons for grouping:

1. There are more than 15–20 values to begin with, a number too large to be displayed in an easily readable table.

2. The distribution of the variable will be clearer or more meaningful if some of the values are combined.

Inspection of Exhibit 13.7 should clarify these reasons. In this distribution it is very difficult to discern any shape, much less the central tendency. What we would like to now do to make the features of the data more visible is change the values into intervals of values, or a range of values. For example, rather than having five separate values of 0, 1, 2, 3, and 4 hours studied per week, we can have a range of values or an interval for the first value, such as 0–4 hours studied. Then we can get a count or frequency of the number of cases (and percentage of the total) that fall within that interval.

Once we decide to group values, or categories, we have to be sure that in doing so we do not distort the distribution. Adhering to the following guidelines for combining values in a frequency distribution will prevent many problems:

- Categories should be logically defensible and preserve the distribution's shape.

- Categories should be mutually exclusive and exhaustive, so every case is classifiable in one and only one category.

- The first interval must contain the lowest value, and the last interval must contain the highest value in the distribution.

Exhibit 13.7	Frequency Distribution With Continuous Quantitative Data: Hours Studied per Week	

Value	Frequency (f)	Percentage (%)
0	38	3.0
1	132	10.4
2	165	13.0
3	116	9.1
4	94	7.4
5	171	13.4
6	92	7.2
7	73	5.7
8	58	4.6
9	16	1.3
10	110	8.6
11	9	0.7
12	40	3.1
13	7	0.6
14	45	3.5
15	32	2.5
16	7	0.6
17	5	0.4
18	4	0.3
19	1	0.1
20	15	1.2
21	8	0.6
22	1	0.1
23	1	0.1
24	4	0.3
25	5	0.4
29	1	0.1
30	8	0.6

(Continued)

(Continued)

Value	Frequency (f)	Percentage (%)
35	1	0.1
37	1	0.1
40	4	0.3
42	1	0.1
50	1	0.1
60	1	0.1
61	1	0.1
65	1	0.1
70	1	0.1
75	1	0.1
80	1	0.1
Total	1,272	100.0

- Each interval width, the number of values that fall within each interval, should be the same size.

- There should be between 7 and 13 intervals. This is a tough rule to follow. The key is not to have so few intervals that your data are clumped or clustered into only a few intervals (you will lose too much information about your distribution) and not to have so many intervals that the data are not much clearer than an ungrouped frequency distribution.

Let us use the data in Exhibit 13.7 on the number of hours studied by these youths to create a grouped frequency distribution. We will follow a number of explicit steps:

Step 1. Determine the number of intervals you think you want. This decision is arbitrary, but try to keep the number of intervals you have in the 7–13 range. For our example, let us say we initially decided we wanted to have 10 intervals. (Note, if you do your frequency distribution and it looks too clustered or there are too many intervals, redo your distribution with a different number of intervals.) Don't worry; there are no hard and fast rules for the correct number of intervals, and constructing a grouped frequency distribution is as much art as science. Just remember that the frequency distribution you make is supposed to convey information about the shape and central tendency of your data.

Step 2. Decide on the width of the interval (symbolized by w). The interval width is the number of different values that fall into your interval. For example, an interval width of 5 has five different values that fall into it, say, the values 0, 1, 2, 3, and 4 hours studied. There is a simple formula to approximate what your interval width should be given the number of intervals you decided on in the first step: Determine the range of the data, where the range is simply the highest score in the distribution minus the lowest score. In our data, with the number of hours studied, the range is 80 because the high score is 80 and the low score is 0, so range = 80 − 0 = 80. Then determine the width of the interval by dividing the range by the number of intervals you want from Step 1. We wanted 10 intervals, so our interval width would be $w_i = 80/10 = 8$. We should therefore have an interval width of 8. If you use this simple formula for determining your interval width and you end up with a decimal, say 8.2 or 8.6, then simply round up or down to an integer.

Step 3. Make your first interval so that the lowest value falls into it. Our lowest value is 0 (for studied 0 hours per week), so our first interval begins with the value 0. Now, if the beginning of our first interval is 0 and we want an interval width of 8, is the last value of our interval 7 (with a first interval of 0–7 hours), or is the last value of our interval 8 (with a first interval of 0–8 hours)? One easy way to make a grouped frequency distribution is to do the following: Take the beginning value of your first interval (in our case, it is 0), and add the interval width to that value (8). This new value is the first value of your next interval. What we know, then, is that the first value of our first interval is 0, and the first value of our second interval is 8 (0–?, 8–?). This must mean that the last value to be included in our first interval is one less than 8, or 7. Our first interval, therefore, includes the range of values 0–7. If you count the number of different values in this interval, you will find that it includes eight different values (0, 1, 2, 3, 4, 5, 6, 7). This is our interval width of 8.

Step 4. After your first interval is determined, the next intervals are easy. They must be the same width and not overlap (mutually exclusive). You must make enough intervals to include the last value in your variable distribution. The highest value in our data is 80 hours per week, so we construct the grouped frequency distribution as follows:

0–7

8–15

16–23

24–31

32–39

40–47

48–55

56–63

64–71

72–79

80–87

Notice that in order to include the highest value in our data (80 hours) we had to make 11 intervals instead of the 10 we originally decided upon in Step 1. No problem. Remember, the number of intervals is arbitrary and this is as much art as science.

Step 5. Count the number or frequency of cases that appear in each interval and their percentage of the total. The completed grouped frequency distribution is shown in Exhibit 13.8. Notice that this grouped frequency distribution conveys the important features of the distribution of these data. Most of the data cluster at the low end of the number of hours studied. In fact, more than two thirds of these youths studied less than 8 hours per week. Notice also that the frequency of cases thins out at each successive interval. In other words, there is a long right tail to this distribution, indicating a positive skew because fewer youths studied a high number of hours. Notice also that the distribution was created in such a way that the interval widths are all the same, and each case falls into one and only one interval (i.e., the intervals are exhaustive and mutually exclusive). We would have run into trouble if we had two intervals like 0–7 and 7–14, because we would not know where to place those youths who spent 7 hours a week studying. Should we put them in the first or second interval? If the intervals are mutually exclusive, as they are here, you will not run into these problems.

Exhibit 13.8	Example of a Grouped Frequency Distribution From Hours Studied	

Value	Frequency (f)	Percentage (%)
0–7	881	69.26
8–15	317	24.92
16–23	42	3.30
24–31	18	1.42
32–39	2	0.16
40–47	5	0.39
48–55	1	0.08
56–63	2	0.16
64–71	2	0.16
72–79	1	0.08
80–87	1	0.08
Total	1,272	100.00

Note: Total may not equal 100.0% due to rounding error.

Summarizing Univariate Distributions

Summary statistics, sometimes called descriptive statistics, focus attention on particular aspects of a distribution and facilitate comparison among distributions. For example, suppose you wanted to report the rate of violent crimes for each city in the United States with over 100,000 in population. You could report each city's violent crime rate, but it is unlikely that two cities would have the same rate, and you would have to report approximately 200 rates, one for each city. This would be a frequency distribution that many, if not most, people would find difficult to comprehend. One way to interpret your data for your audience would be to provide a summary measure that indicates what the average violent crime rate is in large U.S. cities. That is the purpose of the set of summary statistics called measures of *central tendency*. You would also want to provide another summary measure that shows the variability or heterogeneity in your data—in other words, a measure that shows how different the scores are from each other or from the central tendency. That is the purpose of the set of summary statistics called measures of *variation* or *dispersion*. We will discuss each type of measurement in turn.

Measures of Central Tendency

Central tendency is usually summarized with one of three statistics: the mode, the median, or the mean. For any particular application, one of these statistics may be preferable, but each has a role to play in data analysis. To choose an appropriate measure of central tendency, the analyst must consider a variable's level of measurement, the skewness of a quantitative variable's distribution, and the purpose for which the statistic is used. In addition, the analyst's personal experiences and preferences inevitably will play a role.

Mode

The mode is the most frequent value in a distribution. For example, refer to the data in Exhibit 13.8, which shows the grouped frequency distribution for the number of hours studied. The value with the greatest frequency in those data is the interval 0–7 hours; this is the mode of that distribution. Notice that the mode is the most frequently occurring value; it is not the frequency of that value. In other words, the mode in Exhibit 13.8 is 0–7 hours; the mode is not 881, which is the frequency of the modal category. To show how the mode can also be thought of as the value with the highest probability, refer to Exhibit 13.9. Suppose you had this grouped frequency distribution but knew nothing else about each of the 1,272 youths in the study. If you were to pick a case at random from the distribution of 1,272 youths and were asked how many hours the youth studied per week, what would your best guess be? Well, since 881 of the 1,272 youths fall into the first interval of 0–7 hours studied, the probability that a randomly selected youth studied from 0 to 7 hours would be .696 (881/1,272). This is higher than the probability of any other interval. It is the interval with the highest probability because it is the interval with the greatest frequency or mode of the distribution. When a variable distribution has one case or interval that occurs more often than the others, it is called a **unimodal distribution**. The ordinal variable of "parents knowing kids' whereabouts" in Exhibit 13.3 is also unimodal. The category with the highest percentage is "usually."

> **Unimodal distribution:** A distribution of a variable in which there is only one value that is the most frequent.

Sometimes a distribution has more than one mode because there are two values that have the highest frequency. This distribution would be called **bimodal**. Some distributions are trimodal in that there are three distinctively high frequency values. When there is no frequency much higher than another, it is even possible to have a distribution without a mode. In saying that there is no mode, though, you are communicating something very important about the data: that no case is more common than the others. Another potential problem with the mode is that it might happen to fall far from the main clustering of cases in a distribution. It would be misleading in this case, then, to say simply that the variable's central tendency was the same as the modal value.

> **Bimodal distribution:** A distribution that has two nonadjacent categories with about the same number of cases, and these categories have more cases than any other categories.

Nevertheless, there are occasions when the mode is very appropriate. Most important, the mode is the only measure of central tendency that can be used to characterize the central tendency of variables measured at the nominal level. In Exhibit 13.9 we have the frequency distribution of the conviction offense for 1,000 offenders convicted in a criminal court. The central tendency of the distribution is property offense, because more of the 1,000 offenders were convicted of a property crime than any other crime. For the variable "type of offense convicted of," the most common value is property crime. The mode also is often referred to in descriptions

Type of Offense	Frequency (f)
Violent	125
Drug	210
Property	480
Public order	100
Other	85
Total	1,000

Exhibit 13.9 Frequency Distribution of Offense for 1,000 Convicted Offenders

of the shape of a distribution. The terms *unimodal* and *bimodal* appear frequently, as do descriptive statements such as "The typical (most probable) respondent was in her 30s." Of course, when the issue is determining the most probable value, the mode is the appropriate statistic.

Median

The **median** is the score in the middle of a rank-ordered distribution. It is, then, the score or point that divides the distribution in half (the 50th percentile). The median is inappropriate for variables measured at the nominal level because their values cannot be put in ranked order (remember, there is no "order" to nominal-level data), and so there is no meaningful middle position. To determine the median, we simply need to do the following. First, rank-order the values from lowest to highest. Because the median is

> **Median:** The position average, or the point that divides a distribution in half (the 50th percentile).

Exhibit 13.11	Frequency Distribution With Continuous Quantitative Data: Hours Studied per Week

Value	Frequency (f)	Percentage (%)	Cumulative Percentage
0	38	3.0	3.0
1	132	10.4	13.4
2	165	13.0	26.4
3	116	9.1	35.5
4	94	7.4	42.9
5	141	13.4	56.3 (includes 50th percentile)
6	92	7.2	
7	73	5.7	
8	58	4.6	
9	16	1.3	
10	110	8.6	
11	9	0.7	
12	40	3.1	
13	7	0.6	
14	45	3.5	
15	32	2.5	
16	7	0.6	
17	5	0.4	
18	4	0.3	
19	1	0.1	
20	15	1.2	
21	8	0.6	
22	1	0.1	
23	1	0.1	
24	4	0.3	
25	5	0.4	
29	1	0.1	
30	8	0.6	

Value	Frequency (f)	Percentage (%)	Cumulative Percentage
35	1	0.1	
37	1	0.1	
40	4	0.3	
42	1	0.1	
50	1	0.1	
60	1	0.1	
61	1	0.1	
65	1	0.1	
70	1	0.1	
75	1	0.1	
80	1	0.1	
Total	1,272	100.0	

The mean rate of violent crime for these nine U.S. cities, then, is 1,910.7 violent crimes per 100,000 population. When calculating the mean, we do not have to first rank-order the scores. The mean takes every score into account, so it does not matter if we add 3,571 first, in the middle, or last.

Computing the mean requires adding up the values of the cases, so it makes sense to compute a mean only if the values of the cases can be treated as actual quantities—that is, if they reflect an interval or ratio level of measurement, or if they are ordinal and we assume that ordinal measures can be treated as intervals. It would make no sense, however, to calculate the mean for the variable racial or ethnic status. Imagine a group of four people in which there were two Caucasians, one African American, and one Hispanic. To calculate the mean you would need to solve the equation (Caucasian + Caucasian + African American + Hispanic)/4 = ? Even if you decide that Caucasian = 1, African American = 2, and Hispanic = 3 for data entry purposes, it still does not make sense to add these numbers, because they do not represent real numerical quantities. In other words, just because you code Caucasian as "1" and African American as "2," that does not mean that African Americans possess twice the race or ethnicity that Caucasians possess. To see how numerically silly this is, note that we could just as easily have coded African Americans as "1" and Caucasians as "2." Now, with one arbitrary flip of our coding scheme, Caucasians have twice as much race or ethnicity as African Americans. Thus, both the median and the mean are *not* appropriate measures of central tendency for variables measured at the nominal level.

Median or Mean?

Both the median and the mean are used to summarize the central tendency of quantitative variables, but their suitability for a particular application must be carefully assessed.

The key issues to be considered in this assessment are the variable's level of measurement, the shape of its distribution, and the purpose of the statistical summary. Consideration of these issues will sometimes result in a decision to use both the median and the mean and will sometimes result in neither measure being seen as preferable. But in many other situations, the choice between the mean and median will be clear-cut as soon as the researcher takes the time to consider these three issues.

Level of measurement is a key concern, because to calculate the mean, we must add up the values of all the cases, a procedure that assumes the variable is measured at the interval or ratio level. So even though we know that coding Agree as 2 and Disagree as 3 does not really mean that Disagree is one unit more of disagreement than Agree, the mean assumes this evaluation to be true. Calculation of the median requires only that we order the values of cases, so we do not have to make this assumption. Technically speaking, then, the mean is simply an inappropriate statistic for variables measured at the ordinal level (and you already know that it is completely meaningless for nominal variables). In practice, however, many social researchers use the mean to describe the central tendency of variables measured at the ordinal level, for the reasons outlined earlier.

The shape of a variable's distribution should also be taken into account when deciding whether to use the median or the mean. When a distribution is perfectly symmetric (i.e., when the distribution is bell shaped), the distribution of values below the median is a mirror image of the distribution of values above the median, and the mean and median will be the same. But the values of the mean and median are affected differently by skewness, or the presence of cases with extreme values on one side of the distribution but not the other side. The median takes into account only the number of cases above and below the median point, not the value of these cases, so it is not affected in any way by extreme values. The mean is based on adding the value of all the cases, so it will be pulled in the direction of exceptionally high (or low) values. When the value of the mean is larger than the median, we know that the distribution is skewed in a positive direction, with proportionately more cases with lower than higher values. When the mean is smaller than the median, the distribution is skewed in a negative direction.

The differential impact of skewness and/or outliers on the median and the mean can be illustrated with a simple thought exercise. Let's assume your class has 20 people and we ask you each to tell us your family of origin's family

Research in the News

For Further Thought ?

MEDIAN LIFETIME EARNINGS

If you are feeling a bit overwhelmed and wondering whether going to college was worth it, a story from the *Washington Post* will lift your spirits. It highlights a study that utilized census data to investigate the lifetime earnings of people by their level of education. They study also examined the difference in lifetime earnings across many different college majors. If you are taking this class, you are probably not getting your major to make millions of dollars, but to help people and improve society in some way, right? The article presents a bar graph of the "median" lifetime earnings by college major. While engineering and computer science majors are at that top of the pack in terms of earnings, criminal justice and criminology majors are above many majors.

1. Why do you think the research presented median earnings rather than mean earnings over the lifetime?

2. What other statistics would you like to know from this article?

Source: Guo, Jeff. 2014. "Want Proof College is Worth It?" *Washington Post,* September 29. http://www.washingtonpost.com/news/storyline/wp/2014/09/29/want-proof-college-is-worth-it-look-at-this-list-of-the-highest-paying-majors/.

income for the past year. We determine that the mean income for the families for your class members is $72,000. We also find that the median income is $54,000, which tells us that 50% of the families make less than $54,000 and 50% of families make more. Now imagine one of Bill Gate's kids enrolls in the class. Bill Gates is estimated to make over $3.5 billion annually. Wow. That makes the mean income for the class $166,735,238. Clearly, this figure does not represent the "typical" family income any longer. Notice that despite Bill Gates's child entering the class, the median family income would still remain $54,000. As you can see, the median now becomes a much better measure to use when describing the "typical" family income!

Measures of Variation

You have learned that central tendency is only one aspect of the shape of a distribution. Although the measure of center is the most important aspect for many purposes, it is still just a piece of the total picture. A summary of distributions based only on their central tendency can be very incomplete, even misleading. For example, three towns might have the same mean and median crime rate but still be very different in their social character due to the shape of the crime distributions. We show three distributions of community crime rates for three different towns in Exhibit 13.12. If you calculate the mean and median crime rate for each town, you will find that the mean and median crime rate is the same for all three. In terms of its crime rate, then, each community has the same central tendency.

As you can see, however, there is something very different about these towns. Town A is a very heterogeneous town; crime rates in its neighborhoods are neither very homogeneous nor clustered at either the low or high end. Rather, the crime rates in its neighborhoods are spread out from one another. Crime rates in these neighborhoods are, then, very diverse. Town B is characterized by neighborhoods with very homogeneous crime rates; there are no real high or low crime areas, because the rate in each neighborhood is not far from the overall mean of 62.4 crimes per 1,000. Town C is characterized by neighborhoods with either very low crime rates or very high crime rates. Crime rates in the first four neighborhoods are much lower than the mean (62.4 crimes per 1,000), whereas those in the last four neighborhoods much higher than the mean. Although they share identical measures of central tendency, these three towns have neighborhood crime rates that are very different.

The way to capture these differences is with statistical measures of variation. Four popular measures of variation are the range, the interquartile range, the variance, and the standard deviation (which is the most popular measure of variability). To calculate each of these measures, the variable must be at the interval or ratio level. Statistical measures of variation are used infrequently with qualitative variables, so statistical measures will not be presented here.

Range

The **range** is a simple measure of variation, calculated as the highest value in a distribution minus the lowest value:

Range = Highest value − Lowest value

> **Range:** The true upper limit in a distribution minus the true lower limit (or the highest rounded value minus the lowest rounded value, plus one).

It often is important to report the range of a distribution, to identify the whole range of possible values that might be encountered. However, because the range can be drastically altered by just one exceptionally high or low value (called an **outlier**), it does not do an adequate job of summarizing the extent of variability in a distribution. For our three towns in Exhibit 13.12, the range in crime rates for Town A is 89.9 (109.4 − 19.5), for Town B it is 6.9 (65.0 − 58.7), and for Town C it is 106.4 (115.3 − 8.9).

Exhibit 13.12	Neighborhood Crime Rates in Three Different Towns	
Town A	**Town B**	**Town C**
19.5	58.1	8.9
28.2	59.7	15.4
35.7	60.1	18.3
41.9	62.7	21.9
63.2	63.2	63.2
75.8	63.9	103.5
92.0	64.2	104.2
95.7	64.5	110.7
109.4	65.0	105.3

Outlier: An exceptionally high or low value in a distribution.

Interquartile range: The range in a distribution between the end of the first quartile and the beginning of the third quartile.

Quartiles: The points in a distribution corresponding to the first 25% of the cases, the first 50% of the cases, and the top 25% of the cases.

Variance: A statistic that measures the variability of a distribution as the average squared deviation of each score from the mean of all scores.

Interquartile Range

A version of the range statistics, the **interquartile range**, avoids the problem created by unusually high or low scores in a distribution. It is the difference between the scores at the first and third quartiles. **Quartiles** are the points in a distribution corresponding to the first 25% of the cases (the first quartile), the first 50% of the cases (the second quartile), and the first 75% of the cases (the third quartile). You already know how to determine the second quartile, corresponding to the point in the distribution covering half of the cases; it is another name for the median. The first and third quartiles are determined in the same way, but by finding the points corresponding to 25% and 75% of the cases, respectively.

Variance

If the mean is a good measure of central tendency, then it would seem that a good measure of variability would be the distance each score is away from the mean. Unfortunately, we cannot simply take the average distance of each score from the mean. One property of the mean is that it exactly balances negative and positive distances from it, so if we were to sum the difference between each score in a distribution and the mean of that distribution, it would always sum to zero. What we can do, though, is to square the difference of each score from the mean so the distance retains its value. This is the notion behind the variance as a measure of variability.

The **variance** is the average square deviation of each case from the mean, so it takes into account the amount by which each case differs from the mean. The equation to calculate the variance is:

$$s^2 = \frac{\Sigma(x - \overline{X})^2}{N - 1}$$

In words, this formula says to take each score and subtract the mean, then square this difference, then sum all these differences, and then divide this sum by N or the total number of scores. Calculations for the variance for the crime rate data from Town A in Exhibit 13.12 are shown in the table that follows.

x	$(x - \bar{X})$	$(x - \bar{X})^2$
19.5	$(19.5 \sim 62.4) = -42.9$	1,840.41
28.2	$(28.2 \sim 62.4) = -34.2$	1,169.64
35.7	$(35.7 \sim 62.4) = -26.7$	712.89
41.9	$(41.9 \sim 62.4) = -20.5$	420.25
63.2	$(63.2 \sim 62.4) = -0.8$	0.64
75.8	$(75.8 \sim 62.4) = 13.4$	179.56
92.0	$(92.0 \sim 62.4) = 29.6$	876.16
95.7	$(95.7 \sim 62.4) = 33.3$	1,108.89
109.4	$(109.4 \sim 62.4) = 47.0$	2,209.00
	$\Sigma(x - \bar{X}) = 0$	$\Sigma(x - \bar{X})^2 = 8,517.44$

We can now determine that the variance is

$$S^2 = \frac{8,517.44}{8} = 1,064.68$$

The variance of these data, then, is 1,064.68. In "squared deviation units," the variance tells us the amount of variation the distribution has around its mean. We had to square the original deviation units before summing them, because $\Sigma(x - \bar{X})^2 = 0$. For most people, however, it is difficult to grasp "squared deviation units." For this reason, we typically take the square root of this value, called the standard deviation, to bring the variable back to its original units of measurement.

Standard Deviation

The **standard deviation** is simply the square root of the variance. It is the square root of the average squared deviation of each case from the mean:

Standard deviation: The square root of the average squared deviation of each case from the mean.

$$s = \sqrt{\frac{\Sigma(x - \bar{X})^2}{N-1}}$$

To find the standard deviation, then, simply calculate the variance and take the square root. For our example, the standard deviation is

$$s = \sqrt{1,064.68} = 32.62$$

This value tells us that, on average, the neighborhood crime rates in Town A vary 32.62 around their mean of 62.4.

The standard deviation has mathematical properties that make it the preferred measure of variability in many cases. In particular, the calculation of confidence intervals around sample statistics, which you learned about in Chapter 5, relies on an interesting property of normal curves. Areas under the normal curve correspond

In Exhibit 13.14, we report the same data as in Exhibit 13.13, this time switching the rows and the columns. Now, the independent variable (gender) is the column variable, so we calculate our percentage going down each of the two columns. We then compare percentages across rows. For example, we still see that 40.4% of the females were low in delinquency, whereas only 29.6% of the males were. And 42.4% of the males were high in delinquency, but only 32.8% of the females were high in delinquency.

Describing Association

A cross-tabulation table reveals four aspects of the association between two variables:

- *Existence.* Do the percentage distributions vary at all among categories of the independent variable?

- *Strength.* How much do the percentage distributions vary among categories of the independent variable?

- *Direction.* For quantitative variables, do values on the dependent variable tend to increase or decrease with an increase in value of the independent variable?

- *Pattern.* For quantitative variables, are changes in the percentage distribution of the dependent variable fairly regular (simply increasing or decreasing), or do they vary (perhaps increasing, then decreasing, or perhaps gradually increasing, then rapidly increasing)?

Exhibit 13.14 shows that an association exists between delinquency and gender, although we can say only that it is a modest association. The percentage difference at the low and high ends of the delinquency variables is approximately 10 percentage points.

We provide another example of a cross-tabulation in Exhibit 13.15. This is a 3 × 3 table that shows the relationship between how morally wrong a youth thinks delinquency is (the independent variable) and his or her self-reported involvement in delinquency (the dependent variable). This table reveals a very strong relationship between moral beliefs and delinquency. We can see that 5.6% of youths with weak moral beliefs are low on delinquency; this increases to 33.8% for those with medium beliefs and to 62.8% for those with strong moral beliefs. At the high end, over two thirds (72.1%) of those youths with weak moral beliefs are high in delinquency, 29.4% of those with medium moral beliefs are high in delinquency, and only 16.9% of those youths with strong moral beliefs are high in delinquency. Clearly, then, having strong moral beliefs serves to effectively inhibit involvement in delinquent behavior. This is exactly what control theory would have us believe.

Exhibit 13.14   Cross-Tabulation of Respondents' Delinquency by Gender

		Gender		
		Female	Male	Total
Self-Reported Delinquency	Low	275 40.4%	175 29.6%	450
	Medium	182 26.8%	166 28.0%	348
	High	223 32.8%	251 42.4%	474
	Total	680 100%	592 100%	1,272

Exhibit 13.15   **Cross-Tabulation of Respondents' Morals by Delinquency**

| | | \multicolumn{4}{c}{Self-Reported Delinquency} | | | |
		Low	Medium	High	Total
Morals	Weak	20 5.6%	79 22.3%	256 72.1%	355 100%
	Medium	170 33.8%	185 36.8%	148 29.4%	503 100%
	Strong	260 62.8%	84 20.3%	70 16.9%	414 100%
	Total	450	348	474	1,272

Exhibit 13.15 shows an example of a negative relationship between an independent and a dependent variable. As the independent variable increases (i.e., as one goes from weak to strong moral beliefs), the likelihood of delinquency decreases (one becomes less likely to commit delinquency). The independent and dependent variables move in opposite directions, so this is a negative relationship. The pattern in this table is close to what is called monotonic. In a **monotonic relationship**, the value of cases consistently increases (or decreases) on one variable as the value of cases increases (or decreases) on the other variable. *Monotonic* is often defined a bit less strictly, with the idea that as the value of cases on one variable increases (or decreases), the value of cases on the other

> **Monotonic relationship:** A pattern of association in which the value of cases on one variable increases or decreases fairly regularly across the categories of another variable.

variable tends to increase (or decrease), and at least does not change direction. This describes the relationship between moral beliefs and delinquency. Delinquency is most likely when moral beliefs are low, less likely when moral beliefs are medium, and least likely when moral beliefs are strong.

We present another cross-tabulation table for you in Exhibit 13.16. This table shows the relationship between the variable "number of hours studied" and the variable "certainty of punishment" (see Exhibit 13.2). Both variables were originally continuous variables that we recoded into three approximately equal groups for this example. We hypothesize that those youths who study more will have a greater perceived risk of punishment than those who study less, so hours studied is our independent variable and certainty is the dependent variable. Comparing levels of hours studied for those with high certainty, we see that there is not much variation. Of those who did not study very much (0–3 hours), 39.2% were high in perceived certainty. Of those who studied from 4 to 6 hours, 35.6% were high in perceived certainty, and 40.3% of those who studied more than 7 hours per week were high in perceived certainty. Much the same levels prevail at low levels of perceived certainty. Those who do not study very much are no more or less likely to perceive a low certainty of punishment than those who study a lot. Variation in the independent variable, then, is not related to variation in the dependent variable. It looks like there is no association between the number of hours a youth studies and the extent to which he or she thinks punishment for delinquent acts is certain.

You will find when you read research reports and journal articles that social scientists usually make decisions about the existence and strength of association on the basis of more statistics than just percentage differences in a cross-tabulation table. A **measure of association** is a type of descriptive statistic used to summarize the strength of an association. There are many measures of association, some of which are appropriate for variables measured at particular levels. One popular measure of association in cross-tabular analyses with variables measured at the ordinal level is **gamma**. As with many

> **Measure of association:** A type of descriptive statistic that summarizes the strength of an association.

> **Gamma:** A measure of association sometimes used in cross-tabular analyses.

Exhibit 13.17	Cross-Tabulation of Respondents' Gender by Delinquency Within Levels of Parental Supervision

Weak Parental Supervision

Gender		Self-Reported Delinquency			Total
		Low	Medium	High	
	Female	26.1%	27.9%	46.0%	337
	Male	23.2%	27.2%	49.6%	427
	Total				764

$\chi^2 = 1.220$ ($p > .05$), Gamma = .067

Strong Parental Supervision

Gender		Self-Reported Delinquency			Total
		Low	Medium	High	
	Female	54.4%	25.7%	19.8%	343
	Male	46.1%	30.3%	23.6%	165
	Total				508

$\chi^2 = 3.193$ ($p > .05$), Gamma = .136

Extraneous Variables

Another reason for introducing a third variable into a bivariate relationship is to see whether the original relationship is spurious due to the influence of an **extraneous variable**, which is a variable that causes both the independent and dependent variables. The only reason the independent and dependent variables are related, therefore, is that they both are the effects of a common cause (another independent variable).

> **Extraneous variable:** A variable that influences both the independent and dependent variables so as to create a spurious association between them that disappears when the extraneous variable is controlled.

Exhibit 13.18 shows what a spurious relationship would look like. In this case, the relationship between x and y exists only because both are the effects of the common cause z. Controlling for z, therefore, will eliminate the x-y relationship. Ruling out possible extraneous variables will help considerably strengthen the conclusion that the relationship between the independent and dependent variables is causal, particularly if all the variables that seem to have the potential for creating a spurious relationship can be controlled.

Notice that if a variable is acting as an extraneous variable, then controlling for it will cause the original relationship between the independent and dependent variables to disappear or substantially diminish. This was also the empirical test for an intervening variable. Therefore, the difference between intervening and extraneous variables is a logical one and not an empirical one. In both instances, controlling for the third variable will cause the original relationship to diminish or disappear. There should, therefore, be sound theoretical grounds for suspecting that a variable is acting as an intervening variable, explaining the relationship between the independent and dependent variables.

As an example of a possible extraneous relationship, we will look at the association between a youth's perception of the certainty of punishment and self-reported involvement in delinquency. Deterrence theory should lead us to predict a negative relationship between perceived certainty and delinquency. Indeed, this is exactly what we observe in our delinquency data. We will not show you the cross-tabulation table, but when we looked at the relationship between perceived certainty and delinquency, we found that 53.2% of youth who were low in certainty were high in delinquency; 39.1% of those who perceived medium certainty were high in delinquency; and only 23.6% of those who perceived a high certainty of punishment were high in delinquency. Youth who believed they would get caught

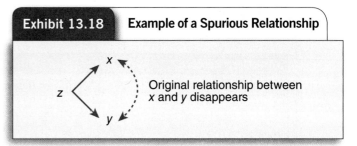

Exhibit 13.18 **Example of a Spurious Relationship**

Original relationship between *x* and *y* disappears

if they engaged in delinquency, then, were less likely to be delinquent. The gamma value for this table was −.382, indicating a moderate negative relationship between perceived certainty and delinquency, exactly what deterrence theory would lead us to expect.

Someone may reasonably argue, however, that this discovered negative relationship may not be causal but instead may be spurious. It could be suggested that what is actually behind this relationship is the extraneous variable, moral beliefs. The argument is that those with strong moral inhibitions against committing delinquent acts think that punishment for morally wrongful actions is certain *and* refrain from delinquent acts. Thus, the observed negative relationship between perceived certainty and delinquency is really due to the positive effect of moral beliefs on perceived certainty and the negative effect of moral beliefs on delinquency (see Exhibit 13.19). If moral beliefs are actually the causal factor at work, then controlling for them will eliminate or substantially reduce the original relationship between perceived certainty and delinquency.

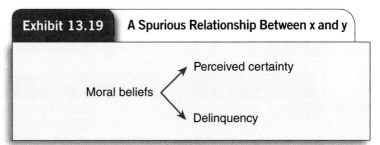

Exhibit 13.19 **A Spurious Relationship Between x and y**

Moral beliefs < Perceived certainty / Delinquency

To look at this possibility, we examined the relationship between perceived certainty and delinquency under three levels of moral beliefs (weak, medium, and strong). The cross-tabulations are shown in Exhibit 13.20. What we can see is that in each of the subtables there is a negative and significant association between the perceived certainty of punishment and delinquency. In two of the three subtables, however, the relationship is weaker than what was in the original table (there the gamma was −.382); we obtained gammas of −.271 and −.197. Under the condition of strong moral beliefs, however, the original relationship is unchanged. What we would conclude from this elaboration analysis is that the variable "moral beliefs" is not acting as a very strong extraneous variable. Although some of the relationship between perceived risk and delinquency is due to their joint relationship with moral beliefs, we cannot dismiss the possibility that the perceived certainty of punishment has a causal influence on delinquent behavior.

Specification

By adding a third variable to an evaluation of a bivariate relationship, the data analyst can also specify the conditions under which the bivariate relationship occurs. A **specification** occurs when the association between the independent and dependent variables varies across the categories of one or more other control variables—that is, when the original relationship is stronger under some condition or conditions of a third variable and weaker under others.

Specification: A type of relationship involving three or more variables in which the association between the independent and dependent variables varies across the categories of one or more other control variables.

In criminology, social learning theory would predict that youths who are exposed to peers who provide verbal support for delinquency are at greater risk for their own delinquent conduct. We found support for this hypothesis in our delinquency dataset. We examined this relationship by recoding into two approximately equal groups the variable FROPINON (see Exhibit 13.2). The first group had weak verbal support from peers, whereas the second group had strong verbal support. Among those youths who reported that their peers provided only weak verbal support for delinquency, 15% were highly delinquent. Among those with strong verbal support from peers, nearly 58% were

Exhibit 13.20	Cross-Tabulation of Perceived Risk by Delinquency Within Levels of Moral Beliefs

Weak Moral Beliefs

		Self-Reported Delinquency			
		Low	Medium	High	Total
Perceived Certainty	Low	3.8%	14.7%	81.4%	156
	Medium	8.6%	27.3%	64.1%	128
	High	4.2%	29.6%	66.8%	71
	Total				355

$\chi^2 = 13.646$ ($p < .001$), Gamma $= -.271$

Medium Moral Beliefs

		Self-Reported Delinquency			
		Low	Medium	High	Total
Perceived Certainty	Low	22.0%	42.5%	35.4%	127
	Medium	33.9%	35.6%	30.5%	174
	High	41.1%	34.2%	24.8%	202
	Total				503

$\chi^2 = 13.646$ ($p < .001$), Gamma $= -.197$

Strong Moral Beliefs

		Self-Reported Delinquency			
		Low	Medium	High	Total
Perceived Certainty	Low	42.7%	28.1%	29.2%	89
	Medium	58.9%	17.7%	23.4%	107
	High	72.9%	18.3%	8.7%	218
	Total				414

$\chi^2 = 13.646$ ($p < .001$), Gamma $= -.393$

highly delinquent. The gamma value for this relationship was .711, a very strong positive relationship. Clearly, then, having friends give you verbal support for delinquent acts (e.g., "it's okay to steal") puts you at risk for delinquency.

It is entirely possible, however, that this relationship exists only when friends' verbal support is backed up by their own behavior. That is, verbal support from our peers might not affect our delinquency when they do not themselves commit delinquent acts or when they commit only a very few. In this case, their actions (inaction in this case) speak louder than their words, and their verbal support does not influence us. When they also commit delinquent acts, however, the verbal support of peers carries great weight.

We looked at this possibility to examine the relationship between friends' verbal support for delinquency and a youth's own delinquency within two levels of friends' behavior (FRBEHAVE; see Exhibit 13.2). We recoded FRBEHAVE into two approximately equal groups. In the first group, fewer of one's friends are delinquent (few delinquent friends) than the other (many delinquent friends). This attempt to specify the relationship between friends' opinions and a youth's own delinquency is shown in Exhibit 13.21. What we see is a little complex. When only a few of a youth's friends are committing delinquent acts, their verbal support still has a significant and positive effect on

Exhibit 13.21	Cross-Tabulation of Friends' Verbal Support by Delinquency Within Levels of Friends' Delinquent Behavior

Few Delinquent Friends

Friends' Verbal Support		Low	Medium	High	Total
	Weak	67.3%	23.8%	8.9%	437
	Strong	44.3%	34.3%	21.4%	140
	Total				577

Self-Reported Delinquency

$\chi^2 = 27.374$ ($p > .001$), Gamma =.416

Many Delinquent Friends

Self-Reported Delinquency

Friends' Verbal Support		Low	Medium	High	Total
	Weak	30.5%	38.5%	31.0%	174
	Strong	7.5%	24.8%	67.4%	521
	Total				695

$\chi^2 = 87.508$ ($p >.001$), Gamma =.608

self-reported delinquency. The gamma value in this subtable is .416, which is moderately strong but less than the original gamma of .771. When many of a youth's friends are delinquent, however, the positive relationship between peers' verbal support and self-reported delinquency is much stronger, with a gamma of .608. The behavior of our peers, then, only weakly specifies the relationship between peer opinion and delinquency. Clearly, then, what our peers say about delinquency matters, even if they are not committing delinquent acts all the time themselves.

Regression and Correlation

Our goal in introducing you to cross-tabulation has been to help you think about the associations among variables and to give you a relatively easy tool for describing association. To read most statistical reports and to conduct more sophisticated analyses of social data, you will have to extend your statistical knowledge. Many statistical reports and articles published in the social sciences use statistical techniques called **regression analysis** and **correlation analysis** to describe the associations among two or more quantitative variables. The terms actually refer to different aspects of the same technique. Statistics based on regression and correlation are used frequently in social science and have many advantages over cross-tabulation—as well as some disadvantages.

We provide only a brief overview of this approach here. Take a look at Exhibit 13.22. It's a plot, termed a *scatterplot*, of the bivariate relationship

Regression analysis: A statistical technique for characterizing the pattern of a relationship between two quantitative variables in terms of a linear equation and for summarizing the strength of this relationship.

Correlation analysis: A standardized statistical technique that summarizes the strength of a relationship between two quantitative variables in terms of its adherence to a linear pattern.

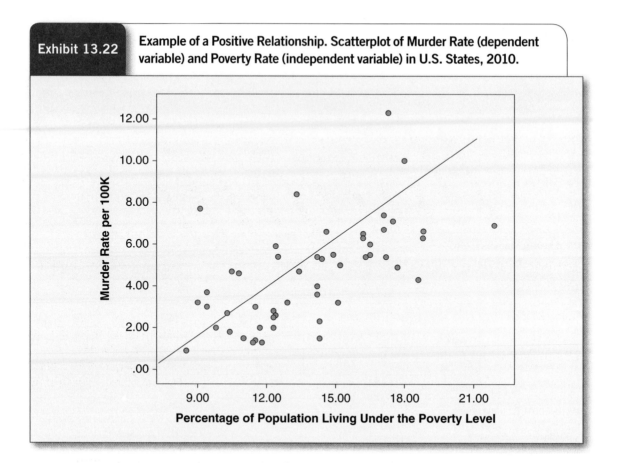

Exhibit 13.22 Example of a Positive Relationship. Scatterplot of Murder Rate (dependent variable) and Poverty Rate (independent variable) in U.S. States, 2010.

between two interval/ratio-level variables. The variables were obtained from a U.S. state-level dataset. The dependent variable, presented on the *y*-axis (vertical) is the murder rate per 100,000 population, and the independent variable, presented on the *x*-axis (horizontal), is the poverty rate (percentage of each state's population living under the poverty level).

You can see that the data points in the scatterplot tend to run from the lower left to the upper right of the chart, indicating a positive relationship. States with higher levels of poverty also tend to have higher rates of murder. This regression line is the "best fitting" straight line for this relationship—it is the line that lies closest to all the points in the chart, according to certain criteria. But you can easily see that quite a few points are pretty far from the regression line.

How well does the regression line fit the points? In other words, how close does the regression line come to the points? (Actually, it's the square of the vertical distance, on the *y*-axis, between the points and the regression line that is used as the criterion.) The **correlation coefficient**, also called *Pearson's r*, or just *r*, gives one answer to that question. The value of *r* for this relationship is .60, which indicates a moderately strong positive linear relationship (if it were a negative relationship,

r would have a negative sign). The value of *r* is 0 when there is absolutely no linear relationship between the two variables, and it is 1 when all the points representing all the cases lie exactly on the regression line (which would mean that the regression line describes the relationship perfectly).

So the correlation coefficient does for two interval/ratio-level variables what gamma does for a cross-tabulation table: It is a summary statistic that tells us about the strength of the association between the two variables. Values of *r* close to 0 indicate that the relationship is weak; values of *r* close to ±1 indicate the relationship is strong—in between there is a lot of room for judgment. You will learn in a statistics course that r^2 is often used

Correlation coefficient (r): A summary statistic that varies from 0 to 1 or –1, with 0 indicating the absence of a linear relationship between two quantitative variables and 1 or –1 indicating that the relationship is completely described by the line representing the regression of the dependent variable on the independent variable.

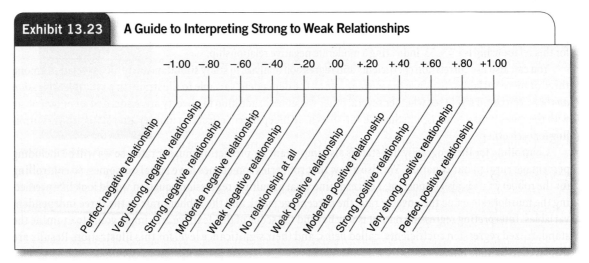

Exhibit 13.23 A Guide to Interpreting Strong to Weak Relationships

instead of *r*. Exhibit 13.23 provides an overview of how to interpret the values of *r*. Although not all possible values of *r* are displayed in Exhibit 13.23, it highlights how the use of adjectives can describe various values between 0 and 1.

An example of a negative relationship is shown in Exhibit 13.24, where we provide a scatterplot of the robbery rate in states (dependent variable) on the *y*-axis and the percentage of each state's population that resides in rural

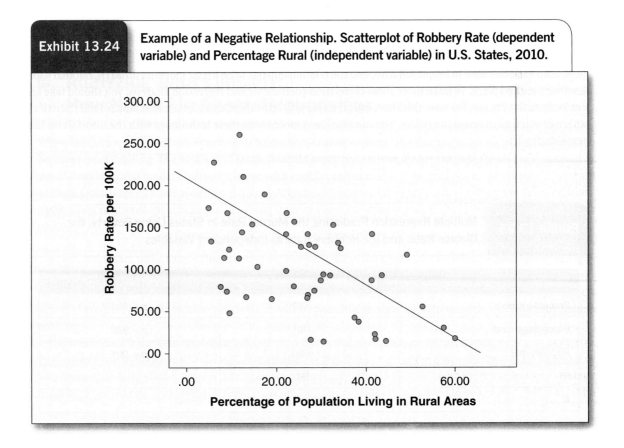

Exhibit 13.24 Example of a Negative Relationship. Scatterplot of Robbery Rate (dependent variable) and Percentage Rural (independent variable) in U.S. States, 2010.

reported that they were serendipitous. Subsequent researchers can try to deductively test the ideas generated by our explorations.

We also have to be honest about the limitations of using survey data to test causal hypotheses. The usual practice for those who seek to test a causal hypothesis with nonexperimental survey data is to test for the relationship between the independent and dependent variables, controlling for other variables that might possibly create spurious relationships. This is what we did by examining the relationship between the perceived certainty of punishment and delinquency while controlling for moral beliefs. But finding that a hypothesized relationship is not altered by controlling for just one variable does not establish that the relationship is causal, nor does controlling for two, three, or many more variables. There always is a possibility that some other variable that we did not think to control, or that was not even measured in the survey, has produced a spurious relationship between the independent and dependent variables in our hypothesis (Lieberson 1985). We must always think about the possibilities and be cautious in our causal conclusions.

▣ Conclusion

This chapter has demonstrated how a researcher can describe phenomena in criminal justice and criminology, identify relationships among them, explore the reasons for these relationships, and test hypotheses about them. Statistics provide a remarkably useful tool for developing our understanding of the social world, a tool that we can use to test our ideas and generate new ones.

Unfortunately, to the uninitiated, the use of statistics can seem to end debate right there; you cannot argue with the numbers. But you now know better than that. The numbers will be worthless if the methods used to generate the data are not valid, and the numbers will be misleading if they are not used appropriately, taking into account the type of data to which they are applied. And even assuming valid methods and proper use of statistics, there is one more critical step, for the numbers do not speak for themselves. Ultimately, it is how we interpret and report the numbers that determines their usefulness. It is this topic we turn to in the next chapter.

Key Terms ➤ Review key terms with eFlashcards. ⑤SAGE edge™

Highlights

- Data collection instruments should be precoded for direct entry, after verification, into a computer. All data should be cleaned during the data entry process.

- Use of secondary data can save considerable time and resources but may limit data analysis possibilities.

- Bar charts, histograms, and frequency polygons are useful for describing the shape of distributions. Care must be taken with graphic displays to avoid distorting a distribution's apparent shape.

- Frequency distributions display variation in a form that can be easily inspected and described. Values should be grouped in frequency distributions in a way that does not alter the shape of the distribution. Following several guidelines can reduce the risk of problems.

- Summary statistics are often used to describe the central tendency and variability of distributions. The appropriateness of using the mode, mean, and median for a description varies with a variable's level of measurement, the distribution's shape, and the purpose of the summary.

- The variance and standard deviation summarize variability around the mean. The interquartile range is usually preferable to the range to indicate the interval spanned by cases, due to the effect of outliers on the range. The degree of skewness of a distribution is usually described in words rather than with a summary statistic.

- Cross-tabulations should normally be divided into percentages within the categories of the independent variable. A cross-tabulation can be used to determine the existence, strength, direction, and pattern of an association.

- Elaboration analysis can be used in cross-tabular analysis to test for spurious and intervening relationships and to identify the conditions under which relationships occur.

- Inferential statistics are used with sample-based data to estimate the confidence that can be placed in a statistical estimate of a population parameter. Estimates of the probability that an association between variables may have occurred on the basis of chance are also based on inferential statistics.

- Regression analysis is a statistical method for characterizing the relationship between two or more quantitative variables with a linear equation and for summarizing the extent to which the linear equation represents that relationship. Correlation coefficients summarize the fit of the relationship to the regression line.

Exercises

> Test your understanding of chapter content. Take the practice quiz. **$SAGE** edge™

1. Create frequency distributions from lists in the Federal Bureau of Investigation (FBI) Uniform Crime Reports on characteristics of arrestees in at least 100 cases (cites). You will have to decide on grouping schemes for the distribution of data for variables such as race, age, and crime committed, and how to deal with outliers in the frequency distribution.

   a. Decide what summary statistics to use for each variable of interest. How well were the features of each distribution represented by the summary statistics? Describe the shape of each distribution.

   b. Propose a hypothesis involving two of these variables, and develop a cross-tabulation to evaluate the support for this hypothesis.

   c. Describe each relationship in terms of the four aspects of an association, after making percentages within each table within the categories of the independent variable. Which hypotheses appear to have been supported?

2. Become a media critic. For the next week, scan a newspaper or some magazines for statistics related to crime or criminal victimization. How many can you find using frequency distributions, graphs, and the summary statistics introduced in this chapter? Are these statistics used appropriately and interpreted correctly? Would any other statistics have been preferable or useful in addition to those presented?

3. The table that follows shows a frequency distribution of "trust in people" as produced by SPSS with the General Social Survey data. As you can see, the table includes abbreviated labels for the variable and its response choices, as well as the raw frequencies and three percentage columns. The first percentage column (Percentage) shows the percentage in each category; the next percentage column (Valid Percentage) is based on the total number of respondents who gave valid answers (3,929 in this instance). It is the Valid Percentage column that normally should be used to construct a frequency distribution for presentation. The last percentage column is Cumulative Percentage, adding up the valid percentages from top to bottom.

   Redo the table for presentation, using the format of the frequency distributions presented in the text.

		Frequency	Percentage	Valid Percentage	Cumulative Percentage
Valid	CAN TRUST	1279	28.4		
	CANNOT TRUST	2458	54.5		
	DEPENDS	192	4.3		
	Total	3929	87.1		
		Frequency	Percentage		
Missing	NAP	575	12.7		
	NA	6	.1		
	Total	581	12.9		
Total		4510	100.0		

Developing a Research Proposal

Use the General Social Survey data to add a pilot study to your proposal. A pilot study is a preliminary effort to test out the procedures and concepts that you have proposed to research.

1. Review the GSSCRJ2K variable list, and identify some variables that have at least some connection to your research problem. If possible, identify one variable that might be treated as independent in your proposed research and one that might be treated as dependent.

2. Request frequencies for these variables.

3. Request a cross-tabulation of the dependent variable by the independent variable (if you were able to identify any). If necessary, recode the independent variable to three or fewer categories.

4. Write a brief description of your findings and comment on their implications for your proposed research. Did you learn any lessons from this exercise for your proposal?

Web Exercises

1. Search the web for a crime-related example of statistics. The Bureau of Justice Statistics is a good place to start: www.ojp .usdoj.gov/bjs/. Using the key terms from this chapter, describe the set of statistics you have identified. What phenomena does this set of statistics describe? What relationships, if any, do the statistics identify?

2. Do a web search for information on a criminological subject that interests you. How much of the information that you find relies on statistics as a tool for understanding the subject? How do statistics allow researchers to test their ideas about the subject and generate new ideas? Write your findings in a brief report, referring to the websites that you found.

Ethics Exercises

1. Review the frequency distributions and graphs in this chapter. Change one of these data displays so that you are "lying with statistics."

2. Consider the relationship between gender and delinquency that is presented in Exhibit 13.13. What third variable do you think should be controlled in the analysis to better understand the basis for this relationship? How might criminal justice policies be affected by finding out that this relationship was due to differences in teacher expectations rather than to genetic differences in violence propensity?

SPSS or Excel Exercises

Data for Exercise	
Dataset	**Description**
Youth.sav	This dataset is from a random sample of students from schools in a southern state. While not representative of the United States, it covers a variety of important delinquent behaviors and peer influences.

Variables for Exercise	
Variable Name	**Description**
delinquency	An interval/level variable that measures self-reported delinquency.
D1	A binary variable based on the number of delinquent acts a respondent reported. A 0 indicates that the respondent reported 1 or fewer acts, while 1 indicates 2 or more.

Variables for Exercise	
Variable Name	**Description**
lowcertain_bin	Binary indicator for whether the respondent felt there was certainty that he or she would be punished for delinquent behaviors, where 1 = low certainty and 0 = high certainty.
certain	A scale indicating how likely the individual feels it is that he or she will be punished for delinquent behavior. High values indicate high certainty.

1. For this exercise let's take a look at whether a person's expectation of punishment after Delinquency is associated with the number of deviant behaviors a student engages in, as measured by the variable Delinquency.

   a. Run a frequency of the dependent variable, delinquency, and answer the following questions:

      i. What level of measurement is this item?

      ii. What forms of descriptive analysis are appropriate?

      iii. How would you best represent this data in a graph?

   b. Based on your responses to Part 1a, conduct all appropriate descriptive analyses. Be sure to describe what you can about the data's distribution and what measures of central tendency are most appropriate. If one or another measure may produce misleading results, be sure to caution the reader why.

2. D1 measures delinquency differently than the interval/ratio level variable called Delinquency. Is the variable D1 appropriate for use in an ordinary least squares (OLS) regression analysis? Why or why not? If you have been

- Conception of the researcher as an "instrument," rather than as the designer of objective instruments to measure particular variables
- Sensitivity to context rather than seeking universal generalizations
- Attention to the impact of the researcher's and others' values on the course of the analysis rather than presuming the possibility of value-free inquiry
- A goal of rich descriptions of the world rather than measurement of specific variables

The focus of qualitative data analysis on meaning and in-depth study also makes it a valuable supplement to analyses of quantitative data. Qualitative data can provide information about the quality of standardized case records and quantitative survey measures, as well as offer some insight into the meaning of particular fixed responses.

There are also features of qualitative data analysis that are shared with those of quantitative data analysis. For example, both qualitative and quantitative data analysis can involve making distinctions about textual data. You also know that textual data can be transposed to quantitative data through a process of categorization and counting. Some qualitative analysts also share with quantitative researchers a positivist goal of describing better the world as it "really" is, although others have adopted a postmodern goal of trying to understand how different people see and make sense of the world, without believing that there is any "correct" description.

▣ Techniques of Qualitative Data Analysis

Although there are several different techniques of qualitative data analysis, most approaches share the following:

1. Documentation of the data and the process of data collection
2. Organization/categorization/condensation of the data into concepts
3. Examination and display of relationships among concepts
4. Corroboration/legitimization of conclusions by evaluating alternative explanations, disconfirming evidence, and searching for negative cases
5. Reflection on the researcher's role

Some researchers suggest different steps, or add additional steps, such as developing propositions that reflect the relationships found and making connections with extant theories (see Miles, Huberman, and Saldaña 2014). Exhibit 14.1

Exhibit 14.1 **Components of Qualitative Data Analysis: Interactive Model**

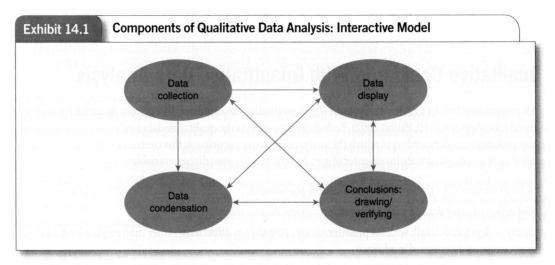

Source: Miles, Huberman, and Saldaña (2014: Chap. 1). Reprinted with permission from SAGE Publications, Inc.

highlights the key techniques and emphasizes the reciprocal relations among them. In qualitative data analysis, condensation of data into concepts may lead to some conclusions and to a particular form of display of relationships among concepts, but the conclusions may then lead to some changes in conceptualization and display, in an iterative process.

Documentation

The first formal analytical step in qualitative analysis for all techniques is **documentation**. The various contacts, interviews, written documents, and whatever it is that preserves a record of what happened all need to be saved and listed. Documentation is critical to qualitative research for several reasons: It is essential for keeping track of what will be a rapidly growing volume of notes, tapes, and documents; it provides a way of developing an outline for the analytic process; and it encourages ongoing conceptualizing and strategizing about the text.

> **Documentation:** A list and/or copy of all contacts, interviews, and written documents that preserves a record of the project.

An excellent example of a documentation guide is provided by Tammy Anderson (2009), who conducted a study of drug use and victimization in nightclub events (e.g., raves, hip-hop, and electronic dance music events) in Philadelphia. When she and her team entered an event for direct observation, they followed a guideline form, which cued the researcher to obtain information about all pertinent data points (see Exhibit 14.2).

Exhibit 14.2 — Example of a Direct Observation Form for Nightclub Observation

1. Site:
2. Period of observation:
3. Type of event:
4. Description of clubber demographics:
5. Description of conversations with clubbers and staff:
6. Description of response to ethnographer's presence, conversations:

Social organization of event	Physical layout (chill areas, dance floor, DJ box, exits, bars)	Utilization of area by clubbers	Clubbers' interactions within areas	Entertainment personnel
Social organization of event II	Staffing patterns	Roles and behaviors	Interaction with clubbers by security, managers, bartenders	Entertainment personnel
Club's cultural ethos	Vibe	Music	Norms	Identity markers or props
Outside support agencies	Public safety	Law enforcement	Medical personnel	
Behaviors at event	Type	Frequency	Impact	
Clubbers' typologies	Dress and props	Status indicators	Clubbing motives	
Drug or alcohol consumption	Clubbers	Staff	Consequences	
Victimization	Observed	Rumored	Victim or offender	Consequences (e.g., clubber and staff reaction)
Personal reflections				

Source: Anderson 2009.

Conceptualization, Coding, and Categorizing

Identifying and refining important concepts is a key part of the iterative process of qualitative research. Sometimes, conceptualizing begins with a simple observation that is interpreted directly, "pulled apart," and then put back together more meaningfully. Stake (1995) provides an example:

> When Adam ran a pushbroom into the feet of the children nearby, I jumped to conclusions about his interactions with other children: aggressive, teasing, arresting. Of course, just a few minutes earlier I had seen him block the children climbing the steps in a similar moment of smiling bombast. So I was aggregating, and testing my unrealized hypotheses about what kind of kid he was, not postponing my interpreting. . . . My disposition was to keep my eyes on him. (p. 74)

The focus in this conceptualization "on the fly" is to provide a detailed description of what was observed and a sense of why that was important.

More often, analytic insights are tested against new observations; the initial statement of problems and concepts is refined; the researcher then collects more data and interacts with the data again; and the process continues. Elijah Anderson (2003) recounts how his conceptualization of social stratification at Jelly's bar developed over a long period of time:

> I could see the social pyramid, how certain guys would group themselves and say in effect, "I'm here and you're there." I made sense of these crowds [initially] as the "respectables," the "non-respectables," and the "near-respectables." . . . Inside, such non-respectables might sit on the crates, but if a respectable came along and wanted to sit there, the lower status person would have to move. (pp. 18–19)

But this initial conceptualization changed with experience, as Anderson (2003) realized that the participants themselves used other terms to differentiate social status: "winehead," "hoodlum," and "regular" (p. 28). What did they mean by these terms? "The 'regulars' basically valued 'decency.' They associated decency with conventionality but also with 'working for a living,' or having a 'visible means of support'" (p. 29). In this way, Anderson progressively refined his concept as he gained experience in the setting.

Jody Miller (2000) provides another excellent illustration of this iterative process of conceptualization in her study of girls in gangs:

> I paid close attention to and took seriously respondents' reactions to themes raised in interviews, particularly instances in which they "talked back" by labeling a topic irrelevant, pointing out what they saw as misinterpretations on my part, or offering corrections. In my research, the women talked back the most in response to my efforts to get them to articulate how gender inequality shaped their experiences in the gang. Despite stories they told to the contrary, many maintained a strong belief in their equality within the gang. Consequently, I developed an entire theoretical discussion around the contradictory operation of gender within the subject. As the research progressed, I also took emerging themes back to respondents in subsequent interviews to see if they felt I had gotten it right. (p. 30)

The process described in this quote illustrates the reflexive nature of qualitative data collection and analysis. In qualitative research, data collection and data analysis are not typically separate activities. This excerpt shows how the researcher first was alerted to a concept by observations in the field and then refined her understanding of this concept by investigating its meaning. By observing the concept's frequency of use, she came to realize its importance.

Examining Relationships and Displaying Data

Examining relationships is the centerpiece of the analytic process, because it allows the researcher to move from simple description of the people and settings to explanations of why things happened as they did with those people in that setting. The process of examining relationships can be captured in a **matrix** that shows how different concepts are connected, or perhaps what causes are linked with what effects.

> **Matrix:** A form that systematically records particular features of multiple cases or instances and how they are related.

Exhibit 14.3 provides an excellent example of a causal model developed by Baskin and Sommers (1998) to explain the desistance process for the sample of violent female offenders they interviewed in the state of New York. They described the process for the women who made it out of their lives of crime as follows:

> Desistance is a process as complex and lengthy as the process of initial involvement. It was interesting to find that some of the key concepts in initiation of deviance—social bonding, differential association, deterrence, age—were equally important in the process of desistance. We see the aging offender take the threat of punishment seriously, reestablish links with conventional society and sever associations with subcultural street elements. We found, too, that the decision to give up crime was triggered by a shock of some sort that was

Exhibit 14.3	The Desistance Process for Violent Female Offenders	
Stage 1: Problems Associated With Criminal Participation	Socially disjunctive experiences	Hitting rock bottom
		Fear of death
		Tiredness
		Illness
	Delayed deterrence	Increased probability of punishment
		Increased difficulty in "doing time"
		Increased severity of sanctions
		Increasing fear
	Assessment	Reappraisal of life and goals
		Psychic change
	Decision	Decision to quit or initial attempts at desistance
		Continuing possibility of criminal participation
Stage 2: Restructuring of Self	Public pronouncement of decision to end criminal participation	Claim to a new identity
Stage 3: Maintenance of the Decision to Stop	Ability to successfully renegotiate identity	Support of significant others
		Integration into new social networks
		Ties to conventional roles
		Stabilization of new social identity

Source: From *Casualties of Community Disorder: Women's Careers in Violent Crime* by Deborah R. Baskin and Ira B. Sommers. Copyright © 1998. Reprinted by permission of Westview Press, a member of Perseus Books Group.

followed by a period of crisis. They arrived at a point at which the deviant way of life seemed senseless. (p. 139)

Corroboration/Authenticating Conclusions

No set standards exist for evaluating the validity or "authenticity" of conclusions in a qualitative study, but the need to consider carefully the evidence and methods on which conclusions are based is just as great as with other types of research. Individual items of information can be assessed in terms of at least three criteria (Becker 1958):

- *How credible was the informant?* Were statements made by someone with whom the researcher had a relationship of trust or by someone the researcher had just met? Did the informant have reason to lie? If the statements do not seem to be trustworthy as indicators of actual events, can they at least be used to help understand the informant's perspective?

- *Were statements made in response to the researcher's questions, or were they spontaneous?* Spontaneous statements are more likely to indicate what would have been said had the researcher not been present.

- *How does the presence or absence of the researcher or the researcher's informant influence the actions and statements of other group members?* Reactivity to being observed can never be ruled out as a possible explanation for some directly observed social phenomenon. However, if the researcher carefully compares what the informant says goes on when the researcher is not present, what the researcher observes directly, and what other group members say about their normal practices, the extent of reactivity can be assessed to some extent.

Tacit knowledge: In field research, a credible sense of understanding of social processes that reflects the researcher's awareness of participants' actions as well as their words, and of what they fail to state, feel deeply, and take for granted.

A qualitative researcher's conclusions should also be assessed by his or her ability to provide a credible explanation for some aspect of social life. That explanation should capture group members' **tacit knowledge** of the social processes that were observed, not just their verbal statements about these processes. Tacit knowledge, "the largely unarticulated, contextual understanding that is often manifested in nods, silences, humor, and naughty nuances," is reflected in participants' actions as well as their words and in what they fail to state but nonetheless feel deeply and even take for granted (Altheide and Johnson 1994). These features are evident in Whyte's (1955) analysis of Cornerville social patterns:

The corner-gang structure arises out of the habitual association of the members over a long period of time. The nuclei of most gangs can be traced back to early boyhood. . . . Home plays a very small role in the group activities of the corner boy. . . . The life of the corner boy proceeds along regular and narrowly circumscribed channels. . . . Out of [social interaction within the group] arises a system of mutual obligations which is fundamental to group cohesion. . . . The code of the corner boy requires him to help his friends when he can and to refrain from doing anything to harm them. When life in the group runs smoothly, the obligations binding members to one another are not explicitly recognized. (pp. 255–57)

Comparing conclusions from a qualitative research project to those obtained by other researchers while conducting similar projects can also increase confidence in their authenticity. Miller's (1999) study of problem-oriented police officers found striking parallels between the ways they defined their masculinity and the processes reported in research about males in nursing and other traditionally female jobs:

In part, male police officers construct an exaggerated masculinity so that they are not seen as feminine as they carry out the social-work functions of policing. Related to this is the almost defiant expression of heterosexuality, so that the men's sexual orientation can never truly be doubted even if their gender roles are contested.

Male patrol officers' language—such as their use of terms like "pansy police" to connote neighborhood police officers—served to affirm their own heterosexuality. . . . In addition, the male officers, but not the women, deliberately wove their heterosexual status into conversations, explicitly mentioning their female domestic partner or spouse and their children. This finding is consistent with research conducted in the occupational field. The studies reveal that men in female-dominated occupations, such as teachers, librarians, and pediatricians, over-reference their heterosexual status to ensure that others will not think they are gay. (p. 222)

Reflexivity

In Chapter 9, we commented on the importance of reflexivity when conducting qualitative research, but reflexivity is also extremely important when analyzing qualitative data. Confidence in the conclusions from a field research study can be strengthened by an honest and informative account about how the researcher interacted with subjects in the field, what problems he or she encountered, and how these problems were or were not resolved. Such a "natural history" of the development of the evidence, sometimes termed **reflexivity**, enables others to evaluate the findings. Such an account is important primarily because of the evolving nature of field research.

> **Reflexivity:** An accounting by a qualitative researcher that describes the natural history of the development of evidence; this enables others to more adequately evaluate the findings.

Qualitative data analysts, more often than quantitative researchers, display real sensitivity to how a social situation or process is interpreted from a particular background and set of values and not simply based on the situation itself (Altheide and Johnson 1994). Researchers are only human, after all, and must rely on their own senses to process information through their own minds. By reporting how and why they think they did what they did, they can help others determine whether, or how, the researchers' perspectives influenced their conclusions.

Anderson's (2003) memoir about the Jelly's bar research illustrates the type of "tracks" that an ethnographer makes as well as how he can describe those tracks. Anderson acknowledges that his tracks began as a child:

> While growing up in the segregated black community of South Bend, from an early age, I was curious about the goings on in the neighborhood, but particularly streets, and more particularly, the corner taverns that my uncles and my dad would go to hang out and drink in. . . . Hence, my selection of Jelly's as a field setting was a matter of my background, intuition, reason, and with a little bit of luck. (pp. 1–2)

Victor Rios was very aware of the effects of his subjective experiences and how they may have affected what he heard and witnessed in the field. He reflected on his goal of producing findings that could be reproduced by others:

> I reflected on my own experience so that I could distinguish between my personal "truths" and the "truths" of others. My goal has been to utilize my experience in the production of knowledge but also to generate a study that could be replicated by anyone who is interested in doing so. . . . I constantly reflected on how I collected data and what consequences, positive or negative, this may have had on my subjects." (2011, 169, 170).

Reflexive thinking like this is extremely important in qualitative analyses and increases the likelihood that findings are both valid and reliable. As we have already learned, replication is a key ingredient of the scientific process.

🔲 Alternatives in Qualitative Data Analysis

The qualitative data analyst can choose from many interesting alternative approaches. Of course, the research question under investigation should shape the selection of an analytic approach, but the researcher's preferences and experiences will inevitably steer the research method selection.

Ethnography

Ethnography: The study of a culture or cultures that some group of people shares, using participant observation over an extended period of time.

As you learned in Chapter 9, an **ethnography** is the study of a culture or cultures that a group of people share (Van Maanen 1995). To understand the ethnographic method, we highlighted a recent ethnography by Victor Rios (2011) in Oakland and the classic study by Elijah Anderson (1999) in Philadelphia. As a method, it usually is meant to refer to the process of participant observation by a single investigator who immerses himself or herself in the group for a long period of time (often a year or more). Ethnographic research can also be called "naturalistic," because it seeks to describe and understand the natural social world as it really is, in all its richness and detail. But there are no particular methodological techniques associated with ethnography, other than just "being there." The analytic process relies on the thoroughness and insight of the researcher to "tell it like it is" in the setting, as he or she experienced it.

In this section, we will examine some alternatives to traditional ethnography, including ethnomethodology, qualitative comparative analysis, narrative analysis, conversation analysis, case-oriented understanding, and grounded theory. These alternative qualitative analysis foundations will give you a good sense of the different possibilities (Patton 2002).

Ethnomethodology

Ethnomethodology: A qualitative research method focused on the way that participants in a social setting create and sustain a sense of reality.

Ethnomethodology focuses on the way that participants construct the social world in which they live, how they "create reality," rather than on describing the social world itself. In fact, ethnomethodologists do not necessarily believe that we can find an objective reality; it is the way that participants come to create and sustain a sense of "reality" that is of interest. In the words of Gubrium and Holstein (1997), in ethnomethodology, as compared to the naturalistic orientation of ethnography,

the focus shifts from the scenic features of everyday life onto the ways through which the world comes to be experienced as real, concrete, factual, and "out there." An interest in members' methods of constituting their world supersedes the naturalistic project of describing members' worlds as they know them. (p. 41)

Unlike the ethnographic analyst, who seeks to describe the social world as the participants see it, the ethnomethodological analyst seeks to maintain some distance from that world. The ethnomethodologist views a "code" of conduct like that described by Anderson (2003) not as a description of a real normative force that constrains social action but as the way that people in the setting create a sense of order and social structure (Gubrium and Holstein 1997). The ethnomethodologist focuses on how reality is constructed, not on what it *is*.

Conversation Analysis

Conversation analysis: Developed from ethnomethodology, this qualitative method focuses on the sequence and details of conversational interaction and on how reality is constructed.

Conversation analysis is a specific qualitative method for analyzing ordinary conversation. Like ethnomethodology, from which it developed, conversation analysis focuses on how reality is constructed, rather than on what it *is*. Three premises guide conversation analysis (Gubrium and Holstein 2000):

1.   Interaction is sequentially organized, and talk can be analyzed in terms of the process of social interaction rather than in terms of motives or social status.

2.   Talk, as a process of social interaction, is contextually oriented; it both is shaped by interaction and creates the social context of that interaction.

3.   These processes are involved in all social interaction, so no interactive details are irrelevant to understanding it.

Consider these premises as you read the following dialogue between British researcher Ann Phoenix (2003) and a boy she called "Thomas" in her study of notions of masculinity, bullying, and academic performance among 11- to 14-year-old boys in 12 London schools.

Thomas: It's your attitude, but some people are bullied for no reason whatsoever just because other people are jealous of them. . . .

Q: How do they get bullied?

Thomas: There's a boy in our year called James, and he's really clever and he's basically got no friends, and that's really sad . . . He gets top marks in every test and everyone hates him. I mean, I like him. (p. 235)

Phoenix (2003) notes that here,

Thomas dealt with the dilemma that arose from attempting to present himself as both a boy and sympathetic to school achievement. He . . . distanced himself from . . . being one of those who bullies a boy just because they are jealous of his academic attainments . . . [and] constructed for himself the position of being kind and morally responsible. (p. 235)

Do you see how Thomas's presentation of himself reflected his interchange with the researcher, as she probed his orientation? Do you imagine that his talk would have been quite different if this conversation had been with other boys? If you can, then you understand the goal of conversation analysis.

Narrative Analysis

Narrative "displays the goals and intentions of human actors; it makes individuals, cultures, societies, and historical epochs comprehensible as wholes" (Richardson 1995, 200). Unlike conversation analysis, which focuses attention on moment-by-moment interchanges, **narrative analysis** focuses on "the story itself," the big picture about experiences or events as participants understand them. It seeks to preserve the integrity of personal biographies or a series of events that cannot adequately be understood in terms of their discrete elements (Riessman 2002). The coding for a narrative analysis is typically of the narratives as a whole, rather than of the different elements within them. The coding strategy revolves around reading the stories and classifying them into general patterns.

> **Narrative analysis:** A form of qualitative analysis in which the analyst focuses on how respondents impose order on the flow of experience in their lives and so make sense of events and actions in which they have participated.

For example, Morrill et al. (2000) read through 254 conflict narratives written by the ninth graders they studied and found four different types of stories:

1. *Action tales*, in which the author represents himself or herself and others as acting within the parameters of taken-for-granted assumptions about what is expected for particular roles among peers.

2. *Expressive tales*, in which the author focuses on strong, negative emotional responses to someone who has wronged him or her.

3. *Moral tales*, in which the author recounts explicit norms that shaped his or her behavior in the story and influenced the behavior of others.

4. *Rational tales*, in which the author represents him- or herself as a rational decision maker navigating through the events of the story.

You can contrast an action tale with the following narrative, which Morrill et al. (2000) classify as a moral tale, in which the students explicitly tell about their moral reasoning, often referring to how normative commitments shape their decision making:

I . . . got into a fight because I wasn't allowed into the basketball game. I was being harassed by the captains that wouldn't pick me and also many of the players. The same type of things had happened almost every day where they called me bad words so I decided to teach the ring leader a lesson. I've never been in a fight before but I realized that sometimes you have to make a stand against the people that constantly hurt you, especially emotionally. I hit him in the face a couple of times and I got respect I finally deserved. (pp. 545–46)

Morrill et al. (2000) summarize their classification of the youth narratives in a simple table that highlights the frequency of each type of narrative and the characteristics associated with each of them (Exhibit 14.4). How does such an analysis contribute to our understanding of youth violence? Morrill et al. (2000) first emphasize that their narratives "suggest that consciousness of conflict among youths—like that among adults—is not a singular entity, but comprises a rich and diverse range of perspectives" (p. 551).

Theorizing inductively, Morrill et al. (2000) then attempt to explain why action tales were much more common than were the more adult-oriented normative, rational, or emotionally expressive tales. One possibility is Carol Gilligan's (1988) theory of moral development, which suggests that younger students are likely to limit themselves to the simpler action tales that "concentrate on taken-for-granted assumptions of their peer and wider cultures, rather than on more self-consciously reflective interpretation and evaluation" (Morrill et al. 2000). More generally, Morrill et al. (2000) argue, "We can begin to think of the building blocks of cultures as different narrative styles in which various aspects of reality are accentuated, constituted, or challenged, just as others are deemphasized or silenced" (p. 556).

Theorizing inductively in this way, Morrill et al.'s (2000) narrative analysis allowed an understanding of youth conflict to emerge from the youths' own stories while informing our understanding of broader social theories and processes.

Grounded theory: Systematic theory developed inductively, based on observations that are summarized into conceptual categories, reevaluated in the research setting, and gradually refined and linked to other conceptual categories.

Grounded Theory

Theory development occurs continually in qualitative data analysis (Coffey and Atkinson 1996), but the goal of many qualitative researchers is to create **grounded theory**—that is, to build up inductively a systematic theory that is "grounded" in, or based on, the observations. The observations are summarized into conceptual

| Exhibit 14.4 | Summary Comparison of Youth Narratives* | | | |

Representation of	Action Tales (N = 144)	Moral Tales (N = 51)	Expressive Tales (N = 35)	Rational Tales (N = 24)
Bases of everyday conflict	Disruption of everyday routines and expectations	Normative violation	Emotional provocation	Goal obstruction
Decision making	Intuitive	Principled stand	Sensual	Calculative choice
Conflict handling	Confrontational	Ritualistic	Cathartic	Deliberative
Physical violence†	In 44% (N = 67)	In 27% (N = 16)	In 49% (N = 20)	In 29% (N = 7)
Adults in youth conflict control	Invisible or background	Sources of rules	Agents of repression	Institutions of social control

Source: Morrill et al. "Telling Tales in School: Youth Culture and Conflict Narratives." *Law and Society Review* 2000:553, Table 1. Copyright 2000. Reprinted with permission of Blackwell Publishing Ltd.

*Total *N* = 254.

†Percentages based on the number of stories in each category.

categories, which are tested directly in the research setting with more observations. Over time, as the conceptual categories are refined and linked, a theory evolves (Glaser and Strauss 1967; Huberman and Miles 1994). Exhibit 14.5 illustrates this process.

As observation, interviewing, and reflection continue, researchers refine their definitions of problems and concepts and select indicators. They can then check the frequency and distribution of phenomena: How many people made a particular type of comment? How often did social interaction lead to arguments? Social system models may then be developed, which specify the relationships among different phenomena. These models are modified as researchers gain experience in the setting. For the final analysis, the researchers check their models carefully against their notes and make a concerted attempt to discover negative evidence that might suggest the model is incorrect.

Heidi Levitt, Rebecca Todd Swanger, and Jenny Butler (2008) used a systematic grounded method of analysis to understand the perspective of male perpetrators of violence on female victims. Research participants were recruited from programs the courts used in Memphis to assess and treat perpetrators who admitted to having physically abused a female intimate partner. The researchers began the analysis of their interview transcripts by dividing them into "meaning units"—"segments of texts that each contain one main idea"—and labeling these units with terms like those used by participants (2008, 437–38). They then compared these labels and combined them into larger descriptive categories. This process continued until they had combined all the meaning units into seven different clusters. Exhibit 14.6 gives an example of two of their clusters and the four categories of meaning units combined within each (Levitt et al. 2008, 439).

Here is how Levitt and her colleagues (2008) discuss the comments that were classified in Cluster 2, Category 3:

Accordingly, when conflicts accumulated that could not be easily resolved, many of the men (5 of 12) thought that ending the relationship was the only way to stop violence from recurring. (p. 440)

"I don't deal with anybody so I don't have any conflicts. . . . It makes me feel bad because I be lonely sometime, but at the same time, it's the best thing going for me right now. I'm trying to rebuild me. I'm trying to put me on a foundation to where I can be a total leader. Like I teach my sons, 'Be leaders instead of followers.'" (p. 440)

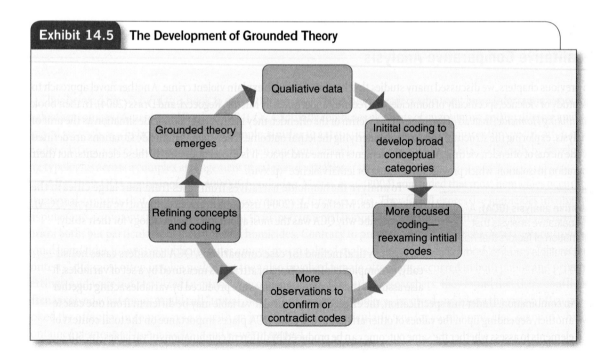

Exhibit 14.5 **The Development of Grounded Theory**

- Qualiative data
- Initital coding to develop broad conceptual categories
- More focused coding—reexaming intitial codes
- More observations to confirm or contradict codes
- Refining concepts and coding
- Grounded theory emerges

as a unique contribution to that literature. In most cases, this hurdle is extraordinarily hard to jump: Most leading journals have a rejection rate of over 90%. Of course, there is also a certain luck of the draw in peer review. One set of two or three reviewers may be inclined to reject an article that another set of reviewers would accept (see the next case study). But in general, the anonymous peer review process results in higher-quality research reports because articles are revised prior to publication in response to the suggestions and criticisms of the experts.

Criminological and criminal justice research is published in a myriad of journals within several disciplines, including criminology, law, sociology, psychology, and economics. As a result, there is no one formatting style that all criminological literature abides by. If, for example, you are submitting your paper to a psychology-related journal, you must abide by the formatting style dictated by the *Publication Manual of the American Psychological Association* (2009). The easiest way to determine how to format a paper for a particular journal is to examine recent volumes of the journal and format your paper accordingly. To give you a general idea of what a journal article looks like, an article in its entirety has been reprinted in Appendix B, along with an illustration of how to read a journal article. There are also numerous articles available on the Student Study Site for this text.

Despite the slight variations in style across journals, there are typically seven standard sections within a journal article in addition to the title page (see Exhibit 15.1).

Exhibit 15.1 **General Sections of a Journal Article**

1. Abstract	This should be a concise and nonevaluative summary of your research paper (no more than 120 words) that describes the research problem, the sample, the method, and the findings.
2. Introduction	The body of a paper should open with an introduction that presents the specific problem under study and describes the research strategy. Before writing this section, you should consider the following questions: What is the point of the study? How do the hypotheses and the research design relate to the problem? What are the theoretical implications of the study, and how does the study relate to previous work in the area? What are the theoretical propositions tested, and how were they derived? A good introduction answers these questions in a few paragraphs by summarizing the relevant argument and the data, giving the reader a sense of what was done and why.
3. Literature Review	Discuss the relevant literature in a way that relates each previous study cited to your research, not in an exhaustive historical review. Citation of and specific credit to relevant earlier works is part of the researchers' scientific and scholarly responsibility. It is essential for the growth of cumulative science. This section should demonstrate the logical continuity between previous research and the research at hand. At the end of this section, you are ready to conceptually define your variables and formally state your hypotheses.
4. Method	Describe in detail how the study was conducted. Such a description enables the reader to evaluate the appropriateness of your methods and the reliability and validity of your results. It also permits experienced investigators to replicate the study if they so desire. In this section, you can include subsections that describe the sample, the independent and dependent variables, and the analytical or statistical procedure you will use to analyze the data.
5. Results	Summarize the results of the statistical or qualitative analyses performed on the data. This can include tables and figures that summarize findings. If statistical analyses are performed, tests of significance should also be highlighted.
6. Discussion	Take the opportunity to evaluate and interpret your results, particularly with respect to your original hypotheses and previous research. Here, you are free to examine and interpret your results as well as draw inferences from them. In general, this section should answer the following questions: What have I contributed to the literature here? How has my study helped resolve the original problem? What conclusions and theoretical implications can I draw from my study? What are the limitations of my study? What are the implications for future research?
7. References	All citations in the manuscript must appear in the reference list, and all references must be cited in the text.

Applied Reports

Unlike journal articles, applied reports are usually commissioned by a particular government agency, corporation, or nonprofit organization. For this reason, the most important problem that applied researchers confront is the need to produce a final report that meets the funding organization's expectations. This is called the hired-gun problem. Of course, the extent to which being a hired gun is a problem varies greatly with the research orientation of the funding organization and with the nature of the research problem posed. The ideal situation is to have few constraints on the nature of the final report, but sometimes research reports are suppressed or distorted because the researcher comes to conclusions that the funding organization does not like.

Applied reports that are written in a less highly charged environment can face another problem—even when they are favorably received by the funding organization, their conclusions are often ignored. This problem can be more a matter of the organization not really knowing how to use research findings than a matter of not wanting to use them. And this is not just a problem of the funding organization; many researchers are prepared only to present their findings, without giving any thought to how research findings can be translated into organizational policies or programs.

An Advisory Committee

An advisory committee can help the applied researcher avoid the problems of incompatible expectations for the final report and insufficient understanding of how to use the research results, without adopting the more engaged strategy of Whyte's (1991) participatory action research or Guba and Lincoln's (1989) constructivist inquiry. An advisory committee should be formed before the start of the project to represent the various organizational segments with stakes in the outcomes of the research. The researcher can use the committee as a source of intelligence about how particular findings may be received and as a sounding board for ideas about how the organization or agency can use research findings. Perhaps most important, an advisory committee can help the researcher work out many problems in research design, implementation, and data collection. Because an advisory committee is meant to comprise all stakeholders, it is inevitable that conflicts will arise among advisory group members. In our experience, however, these conflicts almost invariably can be used to strategize more effectively about the research design and the final product.

Advisory committees are particularly necessary for research investigating controversial issues. For example, after a study conducted in 1999 found that several death row inmates had been wrongly convicted of their crimes, the governor of Illinois placed a moratorium on all death sentences in the state. Other results of the study suggested that the death penalty was handed down unfairly; it found proportionally more minority and poor offenders were sentenced to death than whites and those who could afford hired legal counsel. This caused a great deal of media attention and calls for other states that practice the death penalty to institute similar moratoriums. As a consequence of this attention, other states have begun to examine their implementation of the death penalty as well. Maryland is one such state. In 2001, the state legislature in Maryland commissioned Raymond Paternoster (Paternoster et al. 2004) at the University of Maryland to conduct a study of its practice of the death penalty. The primary goal of the study was to determine whether the administration of the death penalty in the state was affected by the race of the defendant or victim.

As you can imagine, when the study was released, it was controversial. To make sure all interests were represented, Paternoster et al. (2004) set up an advisory committee before undertaking the study. The advisory committee consisted of a group of prosecutors and defense counsel who had experience in capital cases. They advised Professor Paternoster on several critical issues, including the years that the study should cover, the sources where information could be found, and the particularly important variables related to sentencing outcomes. Not only did the advisory committee provide substantive input into the research, but by having a broad spectrum of the legal community "on board," it also provided credibility to the study's findings.

Exhibit 15.3	Compressed Display of the Distribution of Violent Victimization by Victim-Offender Relationship and Age Group, NCVS, 2003–2013

Victim–Offender Relationship	Total	12–24	25–49	50–64	65 or Older
Total	100%	41.2%	44.1%	12.7%	2.1%
Known	100%	44.0	41.7	12.4	1.9
Domestic	100%	32.1	54.5	12.0	1.4
Intimate partner[a]	100%	28.4	62.3	8.5	0.9
Immediate family	100%	40.4	36.0	21.3	2.2
Other relative	100%	39.8	40.7	16.2	3.2
Well-known/casual acquaintance	100%	51.8	33.4	12.6	2.2
Stranger	100%	36.7	47.7	13.2	2.4
Unknown[b]	100%	43.1	42.8	12.2	1.9

Source: Morgan and Mason 2014, 8.

Note: Detail may not sum to total due to rounding. See appendix table 14 for standard errors.
[a] Includes current or former spouses, boyfriends, and girlfriends.
[b] Includes unknown victim–offender relationships and unknown number of offenders.

Exhibit 15.4	Rate of Nonfatal Serious Violence Against Students Ages 12–18 per 1,000 Students, 1992–2012

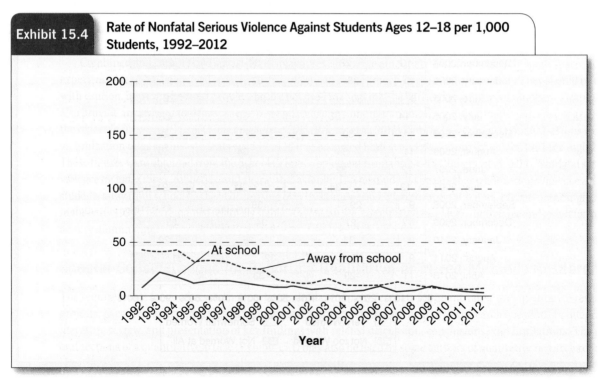

Source: Robers et al. 2014, 11.

Plagiarisı

It may seem depressii
plagiarism, but it woul
a course syllabus detai
specifying the penaltie:
that kind of warning. Y
is revoltingly widespre
million websites on Jun
honesty is widespread. '
connects to the larger is
the way it affects researc

You learned in Ch;
and results—is the foui
honest and open mean
persons for academic e'

An increasing body
his colleagues (Stephens
that one-quarter acknov
ing a complete paper (.3'
such as copying homew
almost all students parti
phrases, paragraphs, tab
without using quotatioi
reported that they had "c

So the plagiarism ț
(Broskoske 2005); plagi

Reports based on qualitative research should be enriched in each section with elements that reflect the more holistic and reflexive approach of qualitative projects. The introduction should include background about the development of the researcher's interest in the topic, whereas the literature review should include some attention to the types of particular qualitative methods used in prior research. The methodology section should describe how the researcher gained access to the setting or individuals studied and the approach used to managing relations with research participants. The presentation of findings in qualitative studies may be organized into sections reflecting different themes identified in interviews or observational sessions. Quotes from participants or from observational notes should be selected to illustrate these themes, although qualitative research reports differ in the extent to which the researcher presents findings in summary form or uses direct quotes to identify key issues. The findings sections in a qualitative report may alternate between presentations of quotes or observations about the research participants, the researcher's interpretations of this material, and some commentary on how the researcher reacted in the setting, although some qualitative researchers will limit their discussion of their reactions to the discussion section.

Reports on mixed-methods projects should include subsections in the methods section that introduce each method, and then distinguish findings from qualitative and quantitative analyses in the findings section. Some mixed-methods research reports may present analyses that use both qualitative and quantitative data in yet another subsection, but others may just discuss implications of analyses of each type for the overall conclusions in the discussions and conclusions sections (Dahlberg, Wittink, and Gallo 2010). When findings based on each method are presented, it is important to consider explicitly the ways in which the specific methods influenced findings obtained with those methods, and to discuss the implications of findings obtained using both methods for the overall study conclusions.

Ethics, Politics, and Reporting Research

It is at the time of reporting research results that the researcher's ethical duty to be honest becomes paramount. Here are some guidelines:

- *Provide an honest accounting of how the research was carried out and where the initial research design had to be changed.* Readers do not have to know about every change you made in your plans and each new idea you had, but they should be informed about major changes in hypotheses or research design. If important hypotheses were not supported, acknowledge this, rather than conveniently forgetting to mention them (Brown and Hedges 2009). If a different approach to collecting or analyzing the data could have led to different conclusions, this should be acknowledged in the limitations section (Bergman 2008).

- *Evaluate honestly the strengths and weaknesses of your research design.* Systematic evaluations suggest that the stronger the research design from the standpoint of establishing internal (causal) validity, the weaker the empirical support that is likely to be found for hypothesized effects (compare Weisburd, Lum, and Petrosino 2001). Finding support for a hypothesis tested with a randomized experimental design is stronger evidence than support based on correlations among variables measured in a cross-sectional survey.

- *Refer to prior research and interpret your findings within the body of literature resulting from that prior research.* Your results are likely to be only the latest research conducted to investigate a research question that others have studied. It borders on unethical practice to present your findings as if they are the only empirical information with which to answer your research question, yet many researchers commit this fundamental mistake (Bergman 2008). For example, a systematic evaluation of citation frequency in articles reporting clinical trial results in medical journals found that, on average, just 21% of the available prior research was cited (for trials with at least three prior articles that could have been cited) (Robinson and Goodman 2011). The result of such omission is that readers may have no idea whether your own research supports a larger body of evidence or differs from it—and so should be subject to even greater scrutiny.

- *Main*
  be on
  dowr
  Tests

- *Avoi*
  picki
  are ea
  alterr
  to yie
  a maj
  or do
  unde

- *Ackn*
  spon
  a spo
  to co
  base
  relev

- *Thar*
  socia

- Be su
  prin

Ethical
and avoid lo
the concept
seem to adn
research rep
research pro
the most pro

Commun

Even followi
sensitive issu
their work? I
of sociologic
policy make
    The soc
media:

1. Focu

2. Dev

3. Pres
   vari

Ultimat

of self-control and their impact on deviance among Chinese university students. *International Journal of Criminal Justice Sciences*, 5, 220–238.

Cretacci, M. A., Rivera, C. J., & Ding, F. (2009). Self-control and Chinese deviance: A look behind the bamboo curtain. *International Journal of Criminal Justice Sciences*, 4, 131–143.

De Li, S. (2004). The impacts of self-control and social bonds on juvenile delinquency in a national sample of midadolescents. *Deviant Behavior*, 25, 351–373.

Evans, T. D., Cullen, F. T., Burton, V. S. Jr., Dunaway, R. G., & Benson, M. L. (1997). The social consequences of self-control: Testing the general theory of crime. *Criminology*, 35, 475–501.

Gibbs, J. J., Giever, D., & Martin, J. (1998). Parental-management and self-control: An empirical test of Gottfredson and Hirschi's general theory. *Journal of Research in Crime and Delinquency*, 35, 42–72.

Gibson, C. L., Wright, J. P., & Tibbetts, S. G. (2000). An empirical assessment of the generality of the general theory of crime: The effects of low self-control on social development. *Journal of Crime and Justice*, 23, 109–134.

Gottfredson, M. R. (2006). The empirical status of control theory in criminology. In F. T. Cullen, J. P. Wright & K. R. Blevins (Eds.), *Taking stock: The status of criminological theory* (pp. 77–100). New Brunswick, NJ: Transaction.

Gottfredson, M. R., & Hirschi, T. (1990). *A general theory of crime*. Stanford, CA: Stanford University Press.

Grasmick, H. G., Tittle, C. R., Bursik, R. J. Jr., & Arneklev, B. J. (1993). Testing the core empirical implications of Gottfredson and Hirschi's general theory of crime. *Journal of Research in Crime and Delinquency*, 30, 5–29.

Greenberger, E., Chen, C., Beam, M., Whang, S., & Dong, Q. (2000). The perceived social contexts of adolescents' misconduct: A comparative study of youths in three cultures. *Journal of Research on Adolescence*, 10, 365–388.

Hirschi, T. (1969). *Causes of delinquency*. Berkeley: University of California Press.

Hirschi, T. (2004). Self-control and crime. In R. F. Baumeister & K. D. Vohs (Eds.), *Handbook of self-Regulation: Research, theory, and applications* (pp. 537–552). New York, NY: Guilford Press.

Hwang, S., & Akers, R. L. (2003). Substance use and Korean adolescents: A cross-cultural test of social learning, social bonding, and self-control theories. In R. L. Akers & G. F. Jensen (Eds.), *Social learning theory and the explanation of crime* (pp. 39–63). New Brunswick, NJ: Transaction.

Jessor, R., Turbin, M. S., Costa, F. M., Dong, Q., Zhang, H., & Wang, C. (2003). Adolescent problem behavior in China and the United States: A cross-national study of psychosocial protective factors. *Journal of Research on Adolescence*, 13, 329–360.

Junger, M., West, R., & Timman, R. (2001). Crime and risky behavior in traffic: An example of cross-situational consistency. *Journal of Research in Crime and Delinquency*, 38, 439–459.

Junger-Tas, J., Enzmann, D., Steketee, M., & Marshall, I. Haen (2012). Concluding observations: The big picture. In J. Junger-Tas, I. Haen Marshall, D. Enzmann, M. Killias, M. Steketeee & B. Gruszczynska, *The many faces of youth crime. Contrasting theoretical perspectives on juvenile delinquency across countries and cultures* (pp.329–353). New York, NY: Springer.

Keane, C., Maxim, P. S., & Teevan, J. J. (1993). Drinking and driving, self-control, and gender: Testing a general theory of crime. *Journal of Research in Crime and Delinquency*, 30, 30–46.

LaGrange, T., & Silverman, R. A. (1999). Low self-control and opportunity: Testing the general theory of crime as an explanation for gender differences in delinquency. *Criminology*, 37, 41–72.

Li, X., Fang, X., & Stanton, B. (1999). Cigarette smoking among schoolboys in Beijing, China. *Journal of Adolescence*, 22, 621–625.

Li, X., Fang, X., Stanton, B., Feigelman, S., & Dong, Q. (1996). The rate and pattern of alcohol consumption among Chinese adolescents. *Journal of Adolescent Health*, 19, 353–361.

Lilly, J. R., Cullen, F. T., & Ball, R. A. (2007). *Criminological theory: Context and consequences* (4th ed.).Thousand Oaks, CA: SAGE.

Longshore, D., Chang, E., & Messina, N. (2005). Self-control and social bonds: A combined control perspective on juvenile offending. *Journal of Quantitative Criminology*, 21, 419–437.

Longshore, D., Turner, S., & Stein, J. (1996). Self-control in a criminal sample: An examination of construct validity. *Criminology*, 3, 209–228.

Mason, W. A., & Windle, M. (2002). Gender, self-control, and informal social control in adolescence: A test of three models of the continuity of delinquent behavior. *Youth and Society*, 33, 497–514.

Marshall, I. H., & Enzmann, D. (2012). The generalizability of self-control theory. In J. Junger-Tas, I. H. Marshall, D. Enzmann, M. Killias, M. Steketee, & B. Gruszczynska, *The many faces of youth crime: Contrasting theoretical perspectives on juvenile delinquency across countries and cultures* (pp. 285–326). New York, NY: Springer.

Marshall, I. H., & Webb, V. J. (1990). *Omaha IRSD Pilot Study*. Paper presented at the meeting of International Self-report Delinquency Project, The Hague, The Netherlands.

Marshall, I. H., & Webb, V. J. (1994). Self-reported delinquency in a midwestern American city. In J. Junger-Tas, G. Terlouw & M. W. Klein (Eds.), *Delinquent behavior among young people in the Western world: First results of the International Self-report Delinquency Study* (pp. 319–342). Amsterdam, The Netherlands: Kugler Publications.

Piquero, A. R., MacIntosh, R., & Hickman, M. (2000). Does self-control affect survey response? Applying exploratory, confirmatory, and item response theory analysis to Grasmick et al.'s self-control scale. *Criminology, 38*, 897–929.

Piquero, A. R., & Rosay, A. B. (1998). The reliability and validity of Grasmick et al.'s self-control scale: A comment on Longshore et al. *Criminology, 36*, 157–173.

Polakowski, M. (1994). Linking self- and social control with deviance: Illuminating the structure underlying a general theory of crime and its relation to deviant activity. *Journal of Quantitative Criminology, 10*, 41–78.

Pratt, T. C., & Cullen, F. T. (2000). The empirical status of Gottfredson and Hirschi's general theory of crime: A meta-analysis. *Criminology, 38*, 931–964.

Romero, E., Gomez-Fraguela, A. J., Luengo, M. A., & Sobral, J. (2003). The self-control construct in the general theory of crime: An investigation in terms of personality psychology. *Psychology Crime & Law, 9*, 61–86.

Teasdale, B., & Silver, E. (2009). Neighborhoods and self-control: Toward an expanded view of socialization. *Social Problems, 56*, 205–222.

Tittle, C. R., & Botchkovar, E. V. (2005). Self-control, criminal motivation and deterrence: An investigation using Russian respondents. *Criminology, 43*, 307–353.

Unger, J. B., Yan, L., Chen, X., Jiang, X., Azen, S., Qian, G., & Johnson, A. (2001). Adolescent smoking in Wuhan, China, Baseline data from the Wuhan smoking prevention trial. *American Journal of Preventive Medicine, 21*, 162–169.

Vazsonyi, A. T., Clifford Wittekind, J. E., Belliston, L. M., & Van Loh, T. D. (2004). Extending the general theory of crime to "The East:" Low self-control in Japanese late adolescents. *Journal of Quantitative Criminology, 20*, 189–216.

Vazsonyi, A. T., & Huang, L. (2010). Where self-control comes from: On the development of self-control and its relationship to deviance over time. *Developmental Psychology, 46*, 245–257.

Vazsonyi, A. T., Pickering, L. E., Junger, M., & Hessing, D. (2001). An empirical test of a general theory of crime: A four-nation comparative study of self-control and the prediction of deviance. *Journal of Research in Crime and Delinquency, 38*, 91–131.

Wang, D. (2006). The study of juvenile delinquency and juvenile protection in the People's Republic of China. *Crime and Justice International, 22*, 4–14.

Wang, G. T., Qiao, H., Hong, S., & Zhang, J. (2002). Adolescent social bond, self-control, and deviant behavior in China. *International Journal of Contemporary Sociology, 39*, 52–68.

Wei, Z., Homel, R., Prichard, J., & Xu, J. (2004). Patterns of juvenile offending in Shanghai and Brisbane. *Australian and New Zealand Journal of Criminology, 37*, 32–51.

Wood, P. B., Pfefferbaum, B., & Arneklev, B. J. (1993). Risk-taking and self-control: Psychological correlates of delinquency. *Journal of Criminal Justice, 16*, 111–130.

Wright, B. R. E., Caspi, A., Moffitt, T. E., & Silva, P. A. (1999). Low self-control, social bonds, and crime: Social causation, social selection, or both? *Criminology, 37*, 479–514.

Yang, K. S. (1995). Chinese social orientation: An integrative analysis. In T. Y. Lin, W. S. Tseng & E. K. Yeh (Eds.), *Chinese societies and mental health* (pp. 19–39). Hong Kong, Oxford University Press.

Zhang, S., Benson, T., & Deng, X. (2000). A test-retest reliability assessment of the International Self-report Delinquency Instrument. *Journal of Criminal Justice, 28*, 283–295.

Author Biographies

Yi-Fen Lu is a doctoral student in the College of Criminal Justice at Sam Houston State University. She earned her MA in Criminal Justice from Sam Houston State University in 2010. Her research interests include public perceptions of crime and criminal justice, biosocial criminology, gene-environmental interactions, and quantitative methodology.

Yi-Chun Yu is a doctoral student in the College of Criminal Justice at Sam Houston State University. She earned her MA in Criminal Justice from Sam Houston State University in 2010. Her areas of research interests are criminological theory, crime mapping, policing, and quantitative methodology.

Ling Ren is an associate professor in the College of Criminal Justice at Sam Houston State University. She earned her PhD from University of Nebraska at Omaha in 2006. Her research interests include policing, cross-national research on crime and delinquency, and the applications of quantitative methodology.

Ineke Haen Marshall is a professor at the School of Criminology and Criminal Justice and the Department of Sociology and Anthropology at Northeastern University. Her research interests are comparative criminology, self-report survey research, criminal careers, and comparative penal policy.

Glossary

Academy of Criminal Justice Sciences (ACJS) Code of Ethics: The Code of Ethics of ACJS sets forth (1) General Principles and (2) Ethical Standards that underlie academy members' professional responsibilities and conduct, along with (3) the Policies and Procedures for enforcing those principles and standards. Membership in the Academy of Criminal Justice Sciences commits individual members to adhere to the ACJS Code of Ethics in determining ethical behavior in the context of their everyday professional activities.

Alternate-forms reliability: A procedure for testing the reliability of responses to survey questions in which subjects' answers are compared after the subjects have been asked slightly different versions of the questions or when randomly selected halves of the sample have been administered slightly different versions of the questions.

Analytic comparative research: Research that seeks to understand how national systems work and the factors related to their operations.

Anchors: Key dates of important events like birthdays that help trigger recall for respondents.

Anomalous findings (serendipitous findings): Unexpected patterns in data, which stimulate new ideas or theoretical approaches.

Anonymity: Provided by research in which no identifying information is recorded that could be used to link respondents to their responses.

Applied research: Research that has an impact on policy and can be immediately utilized and applied.

Arrestee Drug Abuse Monitoring (ADAM): A U.S. monitoring program that uses standardized drug-testing methodologies and predictive models to measure the consequences of drug abuse within each state and across state boundaries.

Association: A criterion for establishing a causal relationship between two variables: variation in one variable is related to variation in another variable as a condition to determine causality.

Authenticity: When the understanding of a social process or social setting is one that reflects fairly the various perspectives of participants in that setting.

Availability sampling: Sampling in which elements are selected on the basis of convenience.

Bar chart: A graphic for qualitative variables in which the variable's distribution is displayed with solid bars separated by spaces.

Base N: The total number of cases in a distribution.

Basic science: In contrast to applied research, the main motivation of basic science is to advance general knowledge and/or to test theoretical propositions.

Before-and-after designs: A quasi-experimental design consisting of before-and-after comparisons involving the same variables but different groups.

Belmont Report: A 1979 National Commission for the Protection of Human Subjects of Biomedical and Behavioral Research report that established three basic ethical principles for the protection of human subjects, including respect for persons, beneficence, and justice.

Beneficence: Minimizing possible harms and maximizing benefits.

Big data: A very large dataset (e.g., contains thousands of cases), accessible in computer-readable form, that is used to reveal patterns, trends, and associations between variables with new computer technology.

Bimodal distribution: A distribution that has two nonadjacent categories with about the same number of cases, and these categories have more cases than any other categories.

Black box evaluation: This type of evaluation occurs when an evaluation ignores, and does not identify, the process by which the program produced the effect.

Campbell Collaboration: Group producing systematic reviews of programs and policies in many areas, including criminal justice, social work, and education.

Case report: A report that helps the reader realize (in the sense of making real) not only the states of affairs that are believed by constructors [research respondents] to exist but also of the underlying motives, feelings, and rationales leading to those beliefs

Case-oriented understanding: An understanding of social processes in a group, formal organization, community, or other collectivity that reflects accurately the standpoint of participants.

Causal effect (nomothetic perspective): When variation in one phenomenon, an independent variable, leads to or results, on average, in variation in another phenomenon, the dependent variable.

Causal effect (idiographic perspective): When a series of concrete events, thoughts, or actions result in a particular event or individual outcome.

Causal effect: The finding that change in one variable leads to change in another variable, *ceteris paribus* (other things being equal).

Causal validity (internal validity): The type of validity that is achieved when a conclusion that one phenomenon leads to or results in another phenomenon—or doesn't lead to or result in another—is correct.

Census: Research in which information is obtained through the responses that all available members of an entire population give to questions.

Certificate of Confidentiality: NIH document that protects researchers from being legally required to disclose confidential information.

Ceteris paribus: Latin term meaning "all other things being equal."

Chi-square: An inferential statistic used to test hypotheses about relationships between two or more variables in a cross-tabulation.

Closed-ended (fixed-choice) questions: A question format in which respondents are provided with explicit responses from which to select.

Cluster: A naturally occurring, mixed aggregate of elements of the population.

Cognitive interview: A technique for evaluating questions in which researchers ask people test questions, and then probe with follow-up questions to learn how they understood the questions and what their answers mean.

Cohort: Individuals or groups with a common starting point. Examples of cohorts include the college class of 1997, people who graduated from high school in the 1980s, General Motors employees who started work between 1990 and 2000, and people who were born in the late 1940s or the 1950s (the baby boom generation).

Combined frequency display: A table that presents together the distributions for a set of conceptually similar variables having the same response categories; common headings are used for the responses.

Comparative research: Research comparing data from more than one time period and/or more than one nation.

Compensatory rivalry (John Henry effect): A type of contamination in experimental and quasi-experimental designs that occurs when control group members are aware that they are being denied some advantage and increase their efforts by way of compensation. This problem has also been referred to as the John Henry effect.

Complete observation: A role in participant observation in which the researcher does not participate in group activities and is publicly defined as a researcher.

Compressed frequency display: A table that presents cross-classification data efficiently by eliminating unnecessary percentages, such as the percentage corresponding to the second value of a dichotomous variable.

Computer-assisted personal interview (CAPI): An interview in which the interviewer carries a laptop computer programmed to display the interview questions and to process the responses that the interviewer types in, as well as to check that these responses fall within the allowed ranges.

Computer-assisted qualitative data analysis: Uses special computer software to assist qualitative analyses through creating, applying, and refining categories; tracing linkages between concepts; and making comparisons among cases and events.

Computer-assisted self-interview (CASI): A system within which respondents interact with a computer-administered questionnaire by using a mouse and following audio instructions delivered via headphones.

Computer-assisted telephone interview (CATI): A telephone interview in which a questionnaire is programmed into a computer, along with relevant skip patterns that must be followed. It essentially combines the tasks of interviewing, data entry, and some data cleaning.

Computer Interactive Voice Response (IVR): Software that uses a touch-tone telephone to interact with people in order to acquire information or enter data into a database.

Concept: A mental image that summarizes a set of similar observations, feelings, or ideas.

Conceptualization: The process of specifying what we mean by a term. In deductive research, conceptualization helps to translate portions of an abstract theory into testable hypotheses involving specific variables. In inductive research, conceptualization is an important part of the process used to make sense of related observations.

Confidence interval: The range defined by the confidence limits for a sample statistic.

Confidence limits: The upper and lower bounds around an estimate of a population parameter based on a sample statistic. The confidence limits show how much confidence can be placed in the estimate.

Constant: A number that has a fixed value in a given situation; a characteristic or value that does not change.

Construct validity: The type of validity that is established by showing that a measure is related to other measures as specified in a theory.

Constructivist paradigm: Methodology based on rejection of belief in an external reality; it emphasizes the importance of exploring the way in which different stakeholders in a social setting construct their beliefs.

Contamination: A source of causal invalidity that occurs when the experimental and/or the comparison group is aware of the other group and is influenced in the posttest as a result.

Content analysis: A research method for systematically analyzing and making inferences from text.

Content validity: The type of validity that establishes a measure covers the full range of the concept's meaning.

Context: A focus of causal explanation; a particular outcome is understood as part of a larger set of interrelated circumstances.

Context effects: Occur in a survey when one or more questions influence how subsequent questions are interpreted.

Contextual effects: Relationships between variables that vary between geographic units or other contexts.

Contingent questions: Questions that are asked of only a subset of survey respondents.

Continuous measure: A measure with numbers indicating the values of variables as points on a continuum.

Control or comparison group: The group of subjects who are either exposed to a different treatment than the experimental group or who receive no treatment at all.

Convergent parallel design: In mixed-methods research, a design in which quantitative and qualitative methods are implemented at the same time. The findings are integrated and interpreted together.

Conversation analysis: Developed from ethnomethodology, this qualitative method focuses on the sequence and details of conversational interaction and on how reality is constructed.

Correlation analysis: A standardized statistical technique that summarizes the strength of a relationship between two quantitative variables in terms of its adherence to a linear pattern.

Correlation coefficient (r): A summary statistic that varies from 0 to 1 or −1, with 0 indicating the absence of a linear relationship between two quantitative variables and 1 or −1 indicating that the relationship is completely described by the line representing the regression of the dependent variable on the independent variable.

Cost-benefit analysis: A type of evaluation research that compares program costs to the economic value of program benefits.

Cost-effectiveness analysis: A type of evaluation research that compares program costs to actual program outcomes.

Counterfactual: The outcome that would have occurred if the subjects who were exposed to the treatment actually were not exposed but otherwise had had identical experiences to those they underwent during the experiment.

Cover letter: The letter sent with a mailed questionnaire. It explains the survey's purpose and auspices and encourages the respondent to participate.

Covert (complete) participation: A role in field research in which the researcher does not reveal his or her identity as a researcher to those who are observed. The covert participant has adopted the role of a "complete participant."

Crime mapping: Geographical mapping strategies used to visualize a number of things, including location, distance, and patterns of crime and their correlates.

Criminological research question: A question about some aspect of crime or criminals, the answer to which is sought through collection and analysis of the firsthand, verifiable, empirical data.

Criterion validity: The type of validity that is established by comparing the scores obtained on the measure being validated to those obtained with a more direct or already validated measure of the same phenomenon (the criterion).

Cronbach's alpha: A statistic that measures the reliability of items in an index or scale.

Cross-population generalizability (external validity): Exists when findings about one group, population, or setting hold true for other groups, populations, or settings.

Cross-sectional research design: A study in which data are collected at only one point in time.

Cross-tabulation (cross-tab): A bivariate (two-variable) distribution showing the distribution of one variable for each category of another variable.

Data cleaning: The process of checking data for errors after the data have been entered in a computer file.

Debriefing: A researcher's informing subjects after an experiment about the experiment's purposes and methods and evaluating subjects' personal reactions to the experiment.

Deception: Used in social experiments to create more "realistic" treatments in which the true purpose of the research is not disclosed to participants, often within the confines of a laboratory.

Deductive reasoning: The type of reasoning that moves from the general to the specific.

Deductive research: The type of research in which a specific expectation is deduced from a general premise and is then tested.

Demoralization: A type of contamination in experimental designs that occurs when control group members are aware they were denied some treatment they believe is valuable, and as a result, they feel demoralized and perform worse than expected.

Dependent variable: A variable that is hypothesized to change or vary depending on the variation in another variable.

Descriptive comparative research: Research that seeks to understand the structure, nature, or scope of a nation's or nations' criminal justice systems or rates of crime.

Descriptive research: Research in which social phenomena are defined and described.

Descriptive statistics: Statistics used to describe the distribution of and relationship among variables.

Deterministic causal approach: An approach in which there is a relationship between an independent and a dependent variable; the independent variable has an effect on the dependent variable in every case under consideration.

Dichotomy: A variable having only two values.

Differential attrition: A problem that occurs in experiments when comparison groups become different because subjects are more likely to drop out of one of the groups than the other, for various reasons.

Direction of association: A pattern in a cross-tabulation; the values of variables tend to change consistently in relation to change in the other variable. Direction of association can be either positive or negative.

Discrete measure: A measure that classifies cases in distinct categories.

Discriminant validity: An approach to construct validation; scores on the measure to be validated are compared to scores on another measure of the same variable and to scores on variables that measure different but related concepts. Discriminant validity is achieved if the measure to be validated is related most strongly to its comparison measure and less so to the measures of other concepts.

Disproportionate stratified sampling: Sampling in which elements are selected from strata in different proportions from those that appear in the population.

Documentation: A list and/or copy of all contacts, interviews, and written documents that preserves a record of the project.

Double-barreled question: A single survey question that actually asks two questions but allows only one answer.

Double-blind procedure: An experimental method in which neither subjects nor the staff delivering experimental treatments know which subjects are getting the treatment and which are receiving a placebo.

Double-negative question: A question or statement that contains two negatives, which can muddy the meaning.

Ecological fallacy: An error in reasoning in which incorrect conclusions about individual-level processes are drawn from group-level data.

Ecometrics: The process of evaluating the reliability and validity of measures about organizations, neighborhoods, or other collective units.

Effect size: A standardized measure of association—often the difference between the mean of the experimental group and the mean of the control group on the dependent variable, adjusted for the average variability in the two groups.

Efficiency analysis: A type of evaluation research that compares program costs to program effects. It can be either a cost-benefit analysis or a cost-effectiveness analysis.

Elaboration analysis: The process of introducing a third variable into an analysis in order to better understand—to elaborate—the bivariate (two-variable) relationship under consideration; additional control variables also can be introduced.

Electronic survey (web-based survey): A survey that is sent and answered by computer, either through e-mail or on the web.

Elements: The individual members of the population whose characteristics are to be measured.

Embedded design: In mixed-methods research, a design in which the primary method is qualitative or quantitative, but the researcher adds the other component to gain additional insight.

Empirical generalizations: Statements that describe patterns found in data.

Endogenous change: A source of causal invalidity that occurs when natural developments or changes in the subjects (independent of the experimental treatment itself) account for some or all of the observed change from the pretest to the posttest.

Enumeration units: Units that contain one or more elements and that are listed in a sampling frame.

Epistemology: A branch of philosophy that studies how knowledge is gained or acquired.

Ethnography: The study of a culture or cultures that some group of people shares, using participant observation over an extended period of time.

Ethnomethodology: A qualitative research method focused on the way that participants in a social setting create and sustain a sense of reality.

Evaluability assessment: A type of evaluation research conducted to determine whether it is feasible to evaluate a program's effects within the available time and resources.

Evaluation research: Research about social programs or interventions.

Event-based design (cohort study): A type of longitudinal study in which data are collected at two or more points in time from individuals in a cohort.

Evidence-based policy: A policy that has been evaluated with a methodologically rigorous design and has been proven to be effective.

Ex post facto control group design: Nonexperimental design in which comparison groups are selected after the treatment, program, or other variation in the independent variable has occurred.

Exhaustive attributes: A variable's attributes or values in which every case can be classified as having one attribute.

Exhaustive responses: A variable's attributes or values in which every case can be classified as having one attribute.

Expectancies of the experimental staff (self-fulfilling prophecy): A source of treatment misidentification in experiments and quasi-experiments that occurs when change among experimental subjects is due to the positive expectancies of the staff who are delivering the treatment, rather than to the treatment itself; also called a *self-fulfilling prophecy*.

Experience sampling method (ESM): A technique for drawing a representative sample of everyday activities, thoughts, and experiences; participants carry a pager and are beeped at random times over several days or weeks; upon hearing the beep, participants complete a report designed by the researcher

Experimental approach: An approach in which the researcher assigns individuals to two or more groups in a way that equates the characteristics of individuals in the groups (with a certain chance of error), except for variation in the groups' exposure to the independent variable.

Experimental group: In an experiment, the group of subjects that receives the treatment or experimental manipulation.

Explanatory research: Research that seeks to identify causes and/or effects of social phenomena.

Explanatory sequential design: In mixed-methods research, a design in which the quantitative method is implemented first and the qualitative method next.

Exploratory research: Research in which social phenomena are investigated without a priori expectations, in order to develop explanations of them.

Exploratory sequential design: In mixed-methods research, a design in which the qualitative method is implemented first and the quantitative method next.

External events (history effect): A source of causal invalidity that occurs when something other than the treatment influences outcome scores; also called an effect of external events.

External validity (cross-population generalizability): Exists when findings about one group, population, or setting hold true for other groups, populations, or settings.

Extraneous variable: A variable that influences both the independent and dependent variables so as to create a spurious association between them that disappears when the extraneous variable is controlled.

Face validity: The type of validity that exists when an inspection of the items used to measure a concept suggests that they are appropriate "on their face."

Factorial survey: A survey in which randomly selected subsets of respondents are asked different questions, or are asked to respond to different vignettes, in order to determine the causal effect of the variables represented by these differences.

Falsifiable: When a theory can be tested and falsified or otherwise not supported by empirical evidence.

Federal Policy for the Protection of Human Subjects: Federal regulations established in 1991 that are based on the principles of the Belmont Report.

Feedback: Information about service delivery system outputs, outcomes, or operations that is available to any program inputs.

Feminist research: Research with a focus on women's lives that often includes an orientation to personal experience, subjective orientations, the researcher's standpoint, and emotions.

Fence-sitters: Survey respondents who see themselves as being neutral on an issue and choose a middle (neutral) response that is offered.

Field experiment: An experimental study conducted in a real-world setting.

Field notes: Notes that describe what has been observed, heard, or otherwise experienced in a participant observation study; these notes usually are written after analysis of data from the observational session.

Field research: Research in which natural social processes are studied as they happen and left relatively undisturbed.

Filter question: A survey question used to identify a subset of respondents who then are asked other questions.

Fixed-choice questions (closed-ended questions): A question format in which respondents are provided with explicit responses from which to select.

Fixed-sample panel design (panel study): A type of longitudinal study in which data are collected from the same individuals—the panel—at two or more points in time. In another type of panel design, panel members who leave are replaced with new members.

Floaters: Survey respondents who provide an opinion on a topic in response to a closed-ended question that does not include a "don't know" option, but will choose "don't know" if it is available.

Focus groups: Unstructured group interviews in which the focus group leader actively encourages discussion among participants on the topics of interest.

Formative evaluation: Process evaluation that is used to shape and refine program operations.

Freedom of Information Act (FOIA): This federal law stipulates that all persons have a right to access all federal agency records unless the records are specifically exempted.

Frequency distributions: Numerical display showing the number of cases, and usually the percentage of cases (the relative frequencies), corresponding to each value or group of values of a variable.

Gamma: A measure of association sometimes used in cross-tabular analyses.

Generalizability: The type of validity that is achieved when a conclusion holds true for the population, group, or groups that we say it does, given the conditions that we specify.

Geographic information system (GIS): The software tool that has made crime mapping increasingly available to researchers since the 1990s.

Grounded theory: Systematic theory developed inductively, based on observations that are summarized into conceptual categories, reevaluated in the research setting, and gradually refined and linked to other conceptual categories.

Group-administered survey: A survey that is completed by individual respondents who are assembled in a group.

Grouped frequency distribution: A frequency distribution in which the data are organized into categories, either because there are more values than can be easily displayed or because the distribution of the variable will be clearer or more meaningful.

Hawthorne effect: A type of contamination in experimental and quasi-experimental designs that occurs when members of the treatment group change in terms of the dependent variable because their participation in the study makes them feel special.

Hermeneutic circle: Represents the dialectical process in which the researcher obtains information from multiple stakeholders in a setting, refines his or her understanding of the setting, and then tests that understanding with successive respondents.

Histogram: A graphic for quantitative variables in which the variable's distribution is displayed with adjacent bars.

Historical events research: Research in which social events of only one time period in the past are studied.

History effect (external events): A source of causal invalidity that occurs when something other than the treatment influences outcome scores; also called an effect of external events.

Hypothesis: A tentative statement about empirical reality involving the relationship between two or more variables.

Idiographic causal explanation: An explanation that identifies the concrete, individual sequence of events, thoughts, or actions that resulted in a particular outcome for a particular individual or that led to a particular event; may be termed an individualist or historicist explanation.

Idiosyncratic variation: Variation in responses to questions that is caused by individuals' reactions to particular words or ideas in the question instead of by variation in the concept that the question is intended to measure.

Illogical reasoning: Prematurely jumping to conclusions and arguing on the basis of invalid assumptions.

Impact evaluation (impact analysis): Analysis of the extent to which a treatment or other service has the intended effect.

Inaccurate observation: Observations based on faulty perceptions of empirical reality.

Independent variable: The variable that is hypothesized to cause, or lead to, variation in another variable.

Index: The sum or average of responses to a set of questions about a concept.

Indicator: The question or other operation used to indicate the value of cases on a variable.

Inductive reasoning: The type of reasoning that moves from the specific to the general.

Inductive research: The type of research in which specific data are used to develop (induce) a general explanation.

Inferential statistics: Mathematical tools for estimating how likely it is that a statistical result based on data from a random sample is representative of the population from which the sample is assumed to have been selected.

In-person interview: A survey in which an interviewer questions respondents and records their answers.

Inputs: Resources, raw materials, clients, and staff that go into a program.

Institutional review board (IRB): Committee in all research organizations, including universities, that reviews research proposals to ensure the protection of human subjects.

Integrative approaches: An orientation to evaluation research that expects researchers to respond to concerns of people involved with stakeholders as well as to the standards and goals of the social scientific community.

Intensive interviewing: Open-ended, relatively unstructured questioning in which the interviewer seeks in-depth information on the interviewee's feelings, experiences, and/or perceptions.

Intercoder reliability: When the same codes are entered by different coders who are recording the same data.

Interitem reliability: An approach that calculates reliability based on the correlation among multiple items used to measure a single concept.

Internal validity (causal validity): The type of validity that is achieved when a conclusion that one phenomenon leads to or results in another phenomenon—or doesn't lead to or result in another—is correct.

Interobserver reliability: When similar measurements are obtained by different observers rating the same persons, events, or places.

Interpretive questions: Questions included in a questionnaire or interview schedule to help explain answers to other important questions.

Interpretivism (interpretivist philosophy): The belief that reality is socially constructed and that the goal of social scientists is to understand what meanings people give to that reality.

Interquartile range: The range in a distribution between the end of the first quartile and the beginning of the third quartile.

Intersubjective agreement: Agreement between scientists about the nature of reality; often upheld as a more reasonable goal for science than certainty about an objective reality.

Interval level of measurement: A measurement of a variable in which the numbers indicating a variable's values represent fixed measurement units, but have no absolute, or fixed, zero point.

Interval–ratio level of measurement: A measurement of a variable in which the numbers indicating the variable's values represent fixed measurement units but there may be no absolute, or fixed, zero point.

Intervening variables: Variables that are influenced by an independent variable and in turn influence variation in a dependent variable, thus helping to explain the relationship between the independent and dependent variables.

Interview schedule: The survey instrument containing the questions asked by the interviewer for an in-person or phone survey.

Intraobserver reliability (intrarater reliability): Consistency of ratings by an observer of an unchanging phenomenon at two or more points in time.

John Henry effect: See *compensatory rivalry.*

Jottings: Brief notes that are jotted down quickly during the observation period that will be expanded into more extensive field notes.

Justice (in research): Distributing benefits and risks of research fairly.

Level of measurement: The complexity of the mathematical means that can be used to express the relationship between a variable's values. The nominal level of measurement, which is qualitative, has no mathematical interpretation; the quantitative levels of measurement (ordinal, interval, and ratio) are progressively more complex mathematically.

Life calendar: An instrument that helps respondents recall events in their past by displaying each month of a given year along with key dates noted within the calendar, such as birthdays, arrests, holidays, anniversaries, et cetera.

Likert-type responses: Survey responses in which respondents indicate the extent to which they agree or disagree with statements.

Longitudinal research design: A study in which data are collected that can be ordered in time; also defined as research in which data are collected at two or more points in time.

Mailed (self-administered) survey: A survey involving a mailed questionnaire to be completed by the respondent.

Marginal distributions: The summary distributions in the margins of a cross-tabulation that correspond to the frequency distribution of the row variable and of the column variable.

Matching: A procedure for equating the characteristics of individuals in different comparison groups in an experiment. Matching can be done on either an individual or an aggregate basis. For individual matching, individuals who are similar in terms of key characteristics are paired prior to assignment, and then one member of each pair is assigned to the two groups. For aggregate matching, groups are chosen for comparisons that are similar in terms of the distribution of key characteristics.

Matrix: A form that systematically records particular features of multiple cases or instances and how they are related.

Mean: The arithmetic, or weighted, average, computed by adding up the value of all the cases and dividing by the total number of cases.

Measure of association: A type of descriptive statistic that summarizes the strength of an association.

Measurement validity: The type of validity that is achieved when a measure measures what it is presumed to measure.

Mechanism: A discernible process that creates a causal connection between two variables.

Median: The position average, or the point that divides a distribution in half (the 50th percentile).

Meta-analysis: The quantitative analysis of findings from multiple studies.

Meta-synthesis: The qualitative analysis of findings from multiple qualitative studies.

Method of agreement: A method proposed by John Stuart Mill for establishing a causal relation, in which the values of cases that agree on an outcome variable also agree on the value of the variable hypothesized to have a causal effect, whereas they differ in terms of other variables.

Mixed-methods research: Research that combines qualitative and quantitative methods in an investigation of the same or related research question(s).

Mixed-mode survey: Surveys that are conducted by more than one method, allowing the strengths of one survey design to compensate for the weaknesses of another and maximizing the likelihood of securing data from different types of respondents; for example, nonrespondents in a mailed survey may be interviewed in person or over the phone.

Mode: The most frequent value in a distribution, also termed the probability average.

Monotonic relationship: A pattern of association in which the value of cases on one variable increases or decreases fairly regularly across the categories of another variable.

Multiphase design: In mixed-methods research, this design involves a series of quantitative and qualitative designs; each design and the findings inform the next phase.

Multiple-group before-and-after design: A quasi-experimental design consisting of several before-and-after comparisons involving the same variables but different groups.

Multistage cluster sampling: Sampling in which elements are selected in two or more stages, with the first stage being the random selection of naturally occurring clusters and the last stage being the random selection of multilevel elements within clusters.

Mutually exclusive attributes: A variable's attributes or values are mutually exclusive if every case can have only one attribute.

Mutually exclusive responses: Response choices on a survey that do not overlap.

Narrative analysis: A form of qualitative analysis in which the analyst focuses on how respondents impose order on the flow of experience in their lives and so make sense of events and actions in which they have participated.

Needs assessment: A type of evaluation research that attempts to determine the needs of some population that might be met with a social program.

Negative relationship: The independent and dependent variables move in opposite directions; as one increases the other decreases.

Negatively skewed: A distribution in which cases cluster to the right side and the left tail of the distribution is longer than the right.

Netnography: The use of ethnographic methods to study online communities; also termed *cyberethnography* and *virtual ethnography*.

Ngrams: Frequency graphs, produced by Google's database, of all words printed in more than one third of the world's books over time (with coverage still expanding).

Nominal level of measurement: Variables whose values have no mathematical interpretation; they vary in kind or quality but not in amount.

Nomothetic causal explanation: A type of causal explanation involving the belief that variation in an independent variable will be followed by variation in the dependent variable, when all other things are equal.

Nonequivalent control group design: A quasi-experimental design in which there are experimental and comparison groups that are designated before the treatment occurs but are not created by random assignment.

Nonprobability sampling methods: Sampling methods in which the probability of selection of population elements is unknown.

Nonresponse: People or other entities who do not participate in a study although they are selected for the sample.

Nonspuriousness: A relationship that exists between two variables that is not due to variation in a third variable.

Normal distribution: A symmetric distribution shaped like a bell and centered around the population mean, with the number of cases tapering off in a predictable pattern on both sides of the mean.

Nuremberg War Crimes Trials: The international military tribunal held by the victorious Allies after World War II in Nuremberg, Germany, that exposed horrific medical experiments conducted by Nazi doctors and others in the name of "science."

Office for Protection From Research Risks in the National Institutes of Health: The organization within the federal government that monitors all IRBs, ensuring federal standards are followed.

Omnibus survey: A survey that covers a range of topics of interest to different social scientists.

One-shot design: A research design that measures the dependent variable after the treatment has been delivered for only those who receive the treatment.

Open-ended questions: Survey questions to which the respondent replies in his or her own words, either by writing or by talking.

Operation: The procedure for actually measuring the concepts we intend to measure, identifying the value of a variable for each case.

Operationalization: The process of specifying the operations that will indicate the value of a variable for each case.

Ordinal level of measurement: A measurement of a variable in which the numbers indicating a variable's values specify only the order of the cases, permitting "greater than" and "less than" distinctions.

Outcomes: The impact of a program process on the cases processed.

Outlier: An exceptionally high or low value in a distribution.

Outputs: The services delivered or new products produced by a program process.

Overgeneralization: An error in reasoning that occurs when we conclude that what we have observed or know to be true for a subset of cases holds true for the entire set.

Participant observation: A type of field research in which a researcher develops a sustained and intensive relationship with people while they go about their normal activities.

Participatory action research: A type of research in which the researcher involves some organizational members as active participants throughout the process of studying an organization; the goal is making changes in the organization.

Peer review: A process in which a journal editor sends a submitted article to two or three experts who judge whether the paper should be accepted, revised and resubmitted, or rejected; the experts also provide comments to explain their decision and guide any revisions.

Percentage: Relative frequencies, computed by dividing the frequency of cases in a particular category by the total number of cases, and multiplying by 100.

Periodicity: A sequence of elements (in a list to be sampled) that varies in some regular, periodic pattern.

Philip Zimbardo's Stanford Prison Experiment: A two-week experiment that simulated the prison life of both prisoners and guards that was ended in just six days because of what the simulation was doing to college students who participated.

Phone survey: A survey in which interviewers question respondents over the phone and then record their answers.

Phrenology: A now defunct field of study, once considered a science in the 19th century, that held that bumps and fissures of the skull determined the character and personality of a person.

Placebo effect: A source of treatment misidentification that can occur when subjects receive a treatment that they consider likely to be beneficial, and improve because of that expectation rather than because of the treatment itself.

Plagiarism: Presenting as one's own the ideas or words of another person or persons for academic evaluation without proper acknowledgment.

Policy research: A process in which research results are used to provide policy actors with recommendations for action that are based on empirical evidence and careful reasoning.

Population: The entire set of elements (e.g., individuals, cities, states, countries, prisons, schools) in which we are interested.

Population parameter: The value of a statistic, such as a mean, computed using the data for the entire population;

a sample statistic is an estimate of a population parameter.

Positive relationship: The independent and dependent variables move in the same direction; as one increases the other increases.

Positively skewed: Describes a distribution in which the cases cluster to the left, and the right tail of the distribution is longer than the left.

Positivism: The belief, shared by most scientists, that there is a reality that exists quite apart from our own perception of it, although our knowledge of this reality may never be complete.

Postpositivism: The belief that there is an empirical reality but that our understanding of it is limited by its complexity and by the biases and other limitations of researchers.

Posttest: Measurement of an outcome (dependent) variable after an experimental intervention or after a presumed independent variable has changed for some other reason.

Pragmatism: A philosophy developed by John Dewey and others that emphasized the importance of taking action and learning from the outcomes to generate knowledge.

Pretest: Measurement of an outcome (dependent) variable prior to an experimental intervention or change in a presumed independent variable for some other reason. The pretest is exactly the same "test" as the posttest, but it is administered at a different time.

Pretested: When a questionnaire is taken by a small subsample of respondents to uncover any problems with the questions or response categories.

Privacy Certificate: Document that protects researchers from being legally required to disclose confidential information.

Probability of selection: The likelihood that an element will be selected from the population for inclusion in the sample. In

a census of all the elements of a population, the probability that any particular element will be selected is 1.0, because everyone will be selected. If half the elements in the population are sampled on the basis of chance (say, by tossing a coin), the probability of selection for each element is one-half, or .5. When the size of the sample as a proportion of the population decreases, so does the probability of selection.

Probability sampling method: Sampling methods that rely on a random, or chance, selection method so that the probability of selection of population elements is known.

Process analysis: A research design in which periodic measures are taken to determine whether a treatment is being delivered as planned, usually in a field experiment.

Process evaluation (program monitoring): Evaluation research that investigates the process of service delivery.

Program process: The complete treatment or service delivered by a program.

Program theory: A descriptive or prescriptive model of how a program operates and produces effects.

Progressive focusing: The process in which a qualitative analyst interacts with the data and gradually refines his or her focus.

Proportionate stratified sampling: Sampling methods in which elements are selected from strata in exact proportion to their representation in the population.

Pseudoscience: Dubious but fascinating claims that are touted as "scientifically proven" and bolstered by fervent, public testimonials of believers who have experienced firsthand or have claimed to have witnessed the phenomenon; however, such evidence is not based on the principles of the scientific method.

Psychometrics: The process of evaluating the reliability and validity of measures about individuals.

Purposive sampling: A nonprobability sampling method in which elements are selected for a purpose, usually because of their unique position. Sometimes referred to as *judgment sampling*.

Qualitative comparative analysis (QCA): A systematic type of qualitative analysis that identifies the combination of factors that had to be present across multiple cases to produce a particular outcome.

Qualitative data analysis: Techniques used to search and code textual, visual, or other content and to explore relationships among the resulting categories.

Qualitative methods: These methods typically involve exploratory research questions, inductive reasoning, an orientation to social context and human subjectivity, and the meanings attached by participants to events and to their lives. Qualitative data are mostly written or spoken words or observations that do not have a direct numerical interpretation.

Quantitative methods: Methods such as surveys and experiments that record variation in social life in terms of categories that vary in amount. Data that are treated as quantitative are either numbers or attributes that can be ordered in terms of magnitude.

Quartiles: The points in a distribution corresponding to the first 25% of the cases, the first 50% of the cases, and the top 25% of the cases.

Quasi-experimental design: A research design in which there is a comparison group that is comparable to the experimental group in critical ways, but subjects are not randomly assigned to the comparison and experimental groups.

Questionnaire: The instrument containing the questions on a self-administered survey.

Quota sampling: A nonprobability sampling method in which elements are selected to ensure that the sample represents certain characteristics in proportion to their prevalence in the population.

Random assignment: A procedure by which each experimental and control group subject is placed in a group randomly.

Random digit dialing (RDD): The random dialing by a machine of numbers within designated phone prefixes, which creates a random sample for phone surveys.

Random number table: A table containing lists of numbers that are ordered solely on the basis of chance; it is used for drawing a random sample.

Random sampling error (chance sampling error): Differences between the population and the sample that are due only to chance factors (random error), not to systematic sampling error. Random sampling error may or may not result in an unrepresentative sample. The magnitude of sampling error from chance factors can be estimated statistically.

Random selection: The fundamental element of probability samples; the essential characteristic of random selection is that every element of the population has a known and independent chance of being selected into the sample.

Range: The true upper limit in a distribution minus the true lower limit (or the highest rounded value minus the lowest rounded value, plus one).

Ratio level of measurement: A measurement of a variable in which the numbers indicating a variable's values represent fixed measuring units, and there is an absolute zero point.

Reactive effect: The changes in individual or group behavior that are due to being observed or otherwise studied.

Reductionist fallacy (reductionism): An error in reasoning that occurs when incorrect conclusions about group-level processes are based on individual-level data.

Refereed journals: Journals that select research papers for publication based on the peer reviews of other social scientists.

Reference period: A time frame in which a survey question asks respondents to place a particular behavior (e.g., in the last six months).

Reflexivity: An accounting by a qualitative researcher that describes the natural history of the development of evidence; this enables others to more adequately evaluate the findings.

Regression analysis: A statistical technique for characterizing the pattern of a relationship between two quantitative variables in terms of a linear equation and for summarizing the strength of this relationship.

Regression effect: A source of causal invalidity that occurs when subjects who are chosen for a study because of their extreme scores on the dependent variable become less extreme on the posttest due to natural cyclical or episodic change in the variable.

Reliability: A measure is reliable when it yields consistent scores or observations of a given phenomenon on different occasions. Reliability is a prerequisite for measurement validity.

Reliability measures: Special statistics that help researchers decide whether responses are consistent.

Repeated cross-sectional design (trend study): A type of longitudinal study in which data are collected at two or more points in time from different samples of the same population.

Repeated measures panel design (time series design): A quasi-experimental design consisting of several pretest and posttest observations of the same group.

Replacement sampling: A method of sampling in which sample elements are returned to the sampling frame after being selected, so they may be sampled again. Random samples may be selected with or without replacement.

Replication: The ability of an entire study or experiment to be duplicated.

Representative sample: A sample that looks like the population from which it was selected in all respects that are potentially relevant to the study. The distribution of characteristics among the elements of a representative sample is the same as the distribution of those characteristics among the total population. In an unrepresentative sample, some characteristics are over-represented or underrepresented, and sampling error emerges.

Research circle: A diagram of the elements of the research process, including theories, hypotheses, data collection, and data analysis.

Resistance to change: Reluctance to change ideas in light of new information, due to ego-based commitments, excessive devotion to tradition, or uncritical agreement with authorities.

Respect for persons: Treating persons as autonomous agents and protecting those with diminished autonomy.

Reverse outlining: Outlining the sections in an already written draft of a paper or report to improve its organization in the next draft.

Risk-terrain modeling (RTM): Modeling that uses data from several sources to predict the probability of crime occurring in the future, using the underlying factors of the environment that are associated with illegal behavior.

Sample: A subset of elements from the larger population.

Sample generalizability: Exists when a conclusion based on a sample, or subset, of a larger population holds true for that population.

Sample statistic: The value of a statistic, such as a mean, computed from sample data.

Sampling distribution: A theoretical distribution of the value of a statistic (i.e. mean) from an infinite number of same-size samples.

Sampling error: Any difference between the characteristics of a sample and the characteristics of a population. The larger the sampling error, the less representative the sample is of the population.

Sampling frame: A list of the elements of a population from which a sample actually is selected.

Sampling interval: The number of cases between one sampled case and the next in a systematic random sample.

Sampling units: The units actually selected in each stage of sampling.

Saturation point: The point at which subject selection is ended in intensive interviewing, when new interviews seem to yield little additional information.

Scale: A composite measure of one concept created from a series of two or more questions.

Science: A set of logical, systematic, documented methods with which to investigate nature and natural processes; the knowledge produced by these investigations.

Secondary data analysis: Analysis of data collected by someone other than the researcher or the researcher's assistant.

Selection bias: A source of internal (causal) invalidity that occurs when characteristics of experimental and comparison group subjects differ in any way that influences the outcome.

Selective distribution of benefits: An ethical issue about how much researchers can influence the benefits subjects receive as part of the treatment being studied in a field experiment.

Selective observation: Observations chosen because they are in accord with preferences or beliefs of the observer.

Self-fulfilling prophecy: See *expectancies of the experimental staff*.

Serendipitous findings (anomalous findings): Unexpected patterns in data, which stimulate new ideas or theoretical approaches.

Simple random sampling: A method of sampling in which every sample element is selected only on the basis of chance, through a random process.

Skewness: A feature of a variable's distribution; refers to the extent to which cases are clustered more at one or the other end of the distribution rather than around the middle.

Skip patterns: The unique combination of questions created in a survey by filter questions and contingent questions.

Snowball sampling: A method of sampling in which sample elements are selected as they are identified by successive informants or interviewees.

Social science: The use of scientific methods to investigate individuals, societies, and social processes, including questions related to criminology and criminal justice; the knowledge produced by these investigations.

Social science approaches: An orientation to evaluation research that expects researchers to emphasize the importance of researcher expertise and maintenance of autonomy from program stakeholders.

Solomon four-group design: An experimental design in which there are four groups. Two of the groups represent a classic experimental design in which there is an experimental and a control group that each receive a pretest. The final two groups represent an experimental and a control group, but neither receives a pretest. This design helps to identify the interaction of testing and treatment.

Specification: A type of relationship involving three or more variables in which the association between the independent and dependent variables varies across the categories of one or more other control variables.

Split-ballot design: Unique questions or other modifications in a survey administered to randomly selected subsets of the total survey sample, so that more questions can be included in the entire survey or so that responses to different question versions can be compared.

Split-halves reliability: Reliability achieved when responses to the same questions by two randomly selected halves of a sample are about the same.

Spurious relationship: A relationship between two variables that is due to variation in a third variable.

Stakeholder approaches (responsive evaluation): An orientation to evaluation research that expects researchers to be responsive primarily to the people involved with the program.

Stakeholders: Individuals and groups who have some basis of concern with a program.

Standard deviation: The square root of the average squared deviation of each case from the mean.

Stanley Milgram's experiments on obedience to authority: Experiments by Stanley Milgram that sought to identify the conditions under which ordinary citizens would be obedient to authority figures' instructions to inflict pain on others.

Statistical control: A technique used in nonexperimental research to reduce the risk of spuriousness. One variable is held constant so the relationship between two or more other variables can be assessed without the influence of variation in the control variable.

Statistical significance: An association that is not likely to be due to chance, judged by a criterion set by the analyst (often that the probability is less than 5 out of 100, or $p < .05$).

Stratified random sampling: A method of sampling in which sample elements are selected separately from population strata that are identified in advance by the researcher.

Subject fatigue: Problems caused by panel members growing weary of repeated interviews and dropping out of

a study or becoming so used to answering the standard questions in the survey that they start giving stock or thoughtless answers.

Subtables: Tables describing the relationship between two variables within the discrete categories of one or more other control variables.

Survey research: Research in which information is obtained from a sample of individuals through their responses to questions about themselves or others.

Surveys: Popular and versatile research instruments using a question format. Surveys can either be self-administered or read by an interviewer.

Systematic bias: Overrepresentation or underrepresentation of some population characteristics in a sample resulting from the method used to select the sample; a sample shaped by systematic sampling error is a biased sample.

Systematic observation: A strategy that increases the reliability of observational data by using explicit rules that standardize coding practices across observers.

Systematic random sampling: A method of sampling in which sample elements are selected from a list or from sequential files, with every nth element being selected after the first element is selected randomly within the first interval.

Systematic review: Summary review about the impact of a program wherein the analyst attempts to account for differences across research designs and samples, often using statistical techniques such as a meta-analysis.

Systemic social observation (SSO): A careful method of observing phenomena.

Tacit knowledge: In field research, a credible sense of understanding of social processes that reflects the researcher's awareness of participants' actions as well as their words, and of what they fail to state, feel deeply, and take for granted.

Target population: A set of elements larger than or different from the population sampled and to which the researcher would like to generalize study findings.

Test-retest reliability: A measurement showing that measures of a phenomenon at two points in time are highly correlated, if the phenomenon has not changed, or have changed only as much as the phenomenon itself.

Theoretical constructs: Parts of a theory that describe what is important to look at to understand, explain, predict, and "do something about" the subject.

Theoretical sampling method: A sampling method recommended for field researchers by Glaser and Strauss (1967). A theoretical sample is drawn in a sequential fashion, with settings or individuals selected for study as earlier observations or interviews indicate that these settings or individuals are influential.

Theory: A logically interrelated set of propositions about empirical reality. Examples of criminological theories are social learning, routine activities, labeling, general strain, and social disorganization theory.

Theory-driven evaluation: A program evaluation that is guided by a theory that specifies the process by which the program has an effect.

Time order: A criterion for establishing a causal relation between two variables; the variation in the independent variable must come before variation in the dependent variable.

Time series design (repeated measures panel design): A quasi-experimental design consisting of many pretest and posttest observations of the same group.

Transformative design: In mixed-methods research, this design uses a social justice focus to improve the well-being of vulnerable populations.

20
0/20
30/40
15/20
80/100
200

190

20
16
18
20
17
18
14
16
20
20
120

210

80

SAGE was founded in 1965 by Sara Miller McCune to support the dissemination of usable knowledge by publishing innovative and high-quality research and teaching content. Today, we publish over 900 journals, including those of more than 400 learned societies, more than 800 new books per year, and a growing range of library products including archives, data, case studies, reports, and video. SAGE remains majority-owned by our founder, and after Sara's lifetime will become owned by a charitable trust that secures our continued independence.

Los Angeles | London | New Delhi | Singapore | Washington DC